SIX SCANDINAVIAN NOVELISTS

LIE · JACOBSEN · HEIDENSTAM
SELMA LAGERLÖF · HAMSUN · SIGRID UNDSET

by Alrik Gustafson

PUBLISHED FOR THE AMERICAN-SCANDINAVIAN FOUNDATION
BY THE UNIVERSITY OF MINNESOTA PRESS, MINNEAPOLIS

Printed in the United States of America at the
North Central Publishing Co., St. Paul

Library of Congress Catalog Card Number: 40-27695

Six Scandinavian Novelists was originally published
by Princeton University Press for the American-
Scandinavian Foundation

126546

PUBLISHED IN GREAT BRITAIN, INDIA, AND PAKISTAN BY THE OXFORD
UNIVERSITY PRESS, LONDON, BOMBAY, AND KARACHI, AND IN CANADA
BY THE COPP CLARK PUBLISHING CO. LIMITED, TORONTO

To Cleyonne

ACKNOWLEDGMENTS

. . . . to three American publishers—The American-Scandinavian Foundation, Coward-McCann, Inc., and Alfred A. Knopf, Inc.—who have very kindly permitted me to quote liberally from their copyrights of translated editions of the Scandinavian novelists.

. . . . to my good friend Professor Einar Haugen, of the University of Wisconsin, who has read two of my chapters in manuscript and has offered some valuable criticism.

. . . . to my colleague Professor Martin B. Ruud, of the University of Minnesota, who has assisted me in innumerable ways, particularly in matters of detail.

. . . . and finally, to Miss Hanna Astrup Larsen, editor of publications for The American-Scandinavian Foundation, whose intelligent and discriminating editorial vigilance in seeing this book through the press has been of invaluable assistance to me.

NOTES ON THE PRESENT PRINTING

WHEN as in the present case a book which appeared a quarter of a century ago is singled out for a reprinting, its author, though flattered, feels nevertheless uneasy. He has some qualms about releasing it for publication again without subjecting it to a rather rigorous revision. Not a few changes in matters of detail would seem called for, while in the case of a couple of essays, those on Heidenstam and Selma Lagerlöf, a more radical revision might be desirable in the light of my present reading of these novelists. But if I allowed my qualms to take over, the result might be a new book, a project which neither my present publishers nor I am at the moment prepared to undertake. I must in consequence limit myself to providing brief additions to two of the essays and hope that my present-day readers will under the circumstances be inclined to be indulgent.

Perhaps—who knows?—it is best to leave the book substantially as it was when it first appeared. In any case I must take the risk.

Should some readers by chance be interested in my latter-day interpretation of the two Swedish novelists dealt with in this book they may turn to *A History of Swedish Literature* (1961), in which Selma Lagerlöf and Heidenstam are subjected by me to a partly new approach.

A. G.

May 1966

CONTENTS

Six Scandinavian Novelists

BY WAY OF INTRODUCTION

TO one who proposes to write at some length on the modern Scandinavian novel it is something of a relief to know that he need not preface his introductory observations with an apology for his subject or a detailed explanation of its significance in present-day literary activity. It is a matter of common knowledge that the Scandinavians, like the Russians, have come to occupy a place of very real importance in the literary history of Europe during the late nineteenth and the early twentieth centuries—a place, indeed, out of all proportion to the relative political and economic importance of the Scandinavian countries in the modern world. Such names as Ibsen and Strindberg, Selma Lagerlöf, Sigrid Undset, and Knut Hamsun are as familiar to the average person of culture in Europe and America today as are the names of Hardy and Galsworthy, or Thomas Mann and Marcel Proust. Whatever one may think of the desirability of the Scandinavian contribution to modern literature (the question has been raised by people of some authority), the *fact* of this contribution is undeniable. It may be said without exaggeration, I think, that the Scandinavian drama and novel, together with Russian fiction, is probably the single most important general influence in certain of the most characteristic developments in modern literature, particularly in the modern drama and the modern novel. German, French, and English writers of fiction—each in their turn—have found much to admire and to follow in Russian and Scandinavian fiction in the years since Tolstoy and Dostoievski, Knut Hamsun and Selma Lagerlöf and Sigrid Undset forced their way into the literary consciousness of Europe.

To analyze the precise nature of the influence which Scandinavian fiction has exercised upon European literature in general is no part of the purpose of the present book. I would here merely point to the existence of such an influence, and offer, in passing, a bit of incidental verification of it. Evidences of such an influence are to be found on every hand. I can choose but two typical instances—each of them in the form of a testimony from an eminent contemporary novelist. Galsworthy, it is interesting to note, ranks the Scandinavian influence with those of France and Russia as one of the three chief foreign influences upon the imaginative literature of England during the last half century.

On our English imaginative literature only three foreign schools or currents of fiction and drama have had influence during the last half century—the French, the Russian, and the Scandinavian. A single writer from other countries here and there, such as d'Annunzio, Hauptmann, Sienkiewicz, Jókai, Maartens, has been read, but has had no deflecting power. How much, on the other hand, we have owed these last thirty years to the French fictionists— Dumas, Flaubert, de Maupassant, Anatole France; to the Russian —Turgenev, Tolstoy, Dostoievski, and Chekhov; to the Scandinavian—Ibsen, Bjørnson, Hamsun, and Strindberg, it would be impossible to unravel and discover.

To this general testimony of Galsworthy's can be added the evidence of a perhaps more than incidental Scandinavian influence upon Thomas Mann. In the Introduction to his *Stories of Three Decades,* Mann admits that his first important novel, *Buddenbrooks,* was originally "planned with Kielland as a model for a novel of merchant life. . . ." Students of Scandinavian literature will remember Alexander Kielland as the brilliant contemporary of Ibsen and Bjørnson. It was Kielland, together with Jonas Lie (the latter coming on the literary scene a bit earlier than Kielland), who created an artistic and intellectual standard in the Norwegian novel of the late nineteenth century which gives to this novel a significance only second to that of the Norwegian drama of the same period.

It has been by means of translations for the most part, of course, that Scandinavian fiction has reached a large non-Scandinavian reading public. These translations appeared in fairly large numbers as early as the late nineteenth century; though it was not until the present century, and particularly since the War, that translations of the Scandinavian novelists began to multiply with an amazing rapidity, until today almost everything that Selma Lagerlöf or Knut Hamsun or Sigrid

Undset writes (not to mention the production of a number of
lesser writers of Scandinavian fiction) finds its way immediately
into foreign translations. The extensive publication of these
translations, especially in Germany, France, Russia, England,
and America, has of course resulted in a considerable amount
of critical preoccupation with the Scandinavian novel, though
most of this criticism is to be found in ephemeral (and oftentimes very misleading) newspaper reviews and in more or less
incidental references to Scandinavian fiction in general criticism
of the contemporary novel. Most of the critics and reviewers—
as well as the general reading public—have responded to the
Scandinavian novel with what might seem to be more than
sufficient enthusiasm. The general judgment seems to be that
the influx of fiction from the North of Europe, together with
that from the semi-oriental Russian East, has been on the whole
remarkably salutary. It is usually held that this new body of
fiction has brought to the older, more sophisticated literatures
of Europe a fresh and invigorating sense of new literary possibilities—new themes, new ways of treating old themes, and,
perhaps most important, a fresh vein of stylistic and narrative
experiments of far-reaching literary significance. But the praise
of this literature, though general, is not always unmixed. And
occasionally there is even to be found a note of sweeping general
condemnation.

In American criticism such negative judgments emanate
largely, as might be expected, from the so-called "new humanists," or from critics of kindred tastes. Such critics are apt to
find themselves seriously alarmed at the tendency of Scandinavian and Russian fiction to all but dominate the literary production of the modern world. These critics frequently find in
the Scandinavian and Russian literature which has flooded the
Western world since the last decades of the nineteenth century
a new form of brutally destructive barbarian invasion, inundat-
ing precious time-honored cultural values in western Europe
(and that part of American culture which takes its origins in
a classical European tradition) as violently and completely as
did the insensitive hordes of Goths and Huns who more than

a millennium earlier momentarily crushed the tradition of classical culture in a semi-decadent Roman Empire.

The attitude of the new humanism toward Russian and Scandinavian literature in general may be said to find characteristic expression in an essay entitled "Decadent Wit" by Paul Elmer More, most sensitive and urbane of the new humanists. The occasion of the essay was the publication of Holbrook Jackson's study in English decadence entitled *The Eighteen Nineties*. In sketching the sources of *fin de siècle* decadence in England, More points first to late eighteenth century German horror literature (early manifested in Heinse's *Ardinghello*) and to German Romanticism in general—to Wackenroder, Novalis, and Schleiermacher, and to what is termed "the morbid obscenities of Friedrich Schlegel's *Lucinde*." Having sketched these remoter origins of modern decadence, More goes on—

But the more immediate literary source of this perversion in the Nineties was rather French than German. Today it is to be found in the group of powerful Russian writers, with their congeners in Scandinavia and the other northern countries [*sic!*], whose works for some time past have been flooding the world in French and English translations. How deeply this literature is tainted could be shown by innumerable examples; one must suffice. If there is any book thoroughly typical of the Russian and Scandinavian ideal it is *Crime and Punishment,* and if there is a single passage in which the moral of that book is typified it is the scene selected by its latest editor in English, Mr. Laurence Irving, as the epitome of "the animating spirit of Dostoievski":

His eyes gleamed, his lips trembled, and, resting his two hands on her shoulders, he cast an angry look on this face bathed in tears. In a moment, he bent downwards, kissing the girl's feet. She started back frightened, as she would have done from a madman. For Rashkolnikoff's face at this moment was that of one.

"What are you doing? And to me?" stammered Sonia, growing pale with sorrow-smitten heart.

Upon this he rose. "I did not bow down to you, personally, but to suffering humanity in your person."

More finally informs us that he had "not long since" had dinner "with a philosopher and two professors of French and English

literature, respectively," on which occasion he passed the casual
observation that his

summer had been darkened by dwelling in the nightmare of *Crime
and Punishment* and other books of its class. At this my friends,
better read in this literature than I, no doubt, admitted the nightmare, but clamorously rebuked me for not feeling uplifted by its
spiritual implications. There it is. Somehow we are to be lifted up
by sympathizing with a madman worshipping humanity in the
person of a girl of the street. Filth, disease, morbid dreams,
bestiality, insanity, sodden crime, these are the natural pathway to
the emancipation of the spirit; these in some mysterious way are
spirituality. And the same lesson runs through Tolstoy and Strindberg and a dozen other moralists who are, as it were, the Prophets
of our young. . . .

The picture as More paints it is a sufficiently disturbing one,
with certain touches that are apparently meant to be almost
terrifying. English literature of the '90's—and to some extent
since (the example of Galsworthy's *The Dark Flower* is cited
later in More's essay)—has become overwhelmed, even contaminated by a foreign literary invasion which is often brutally
barbaric in its outward form and which is inwardly characterized by a succession of psychological abnormalities of a most
dangerous order. And if the picture is a true one for English
literature of the last generation or two, it is equally true of
French and German, even perhaps of American literature during these same years. Dostoievski and Strindberg—and even
Tolstoy, and what our critic refers to vaguely as "a dozen other
moralists"—are the Prophets of modern youth . . . false
prophets, really—wolves, who do not have the ordinary decency
to avail themselves of the traditional sheep's clothing. A sad
picture, certainly—if true. . . .

It would seem, however, that Paul Elmer More's judgment,
at least insofar as Scandinavian literature is concerned, is that
of a hasty alarmist rather than one of a sober critic. He is partially correct, of course, in tracing modern decadence back to
Dostoievski and Strindberg. His inclusion of Tolstoy, however,
as an important direct source of decadence is questionable, especially when it is left in the form of a largely undefined general-

ization. And his assumption that *Crime and Punishment* is "thoroughly typical of the . . . Scandinavian ideal" is one of the most amazing generalizations that have come from the pen of any critic of consequence in the last generation. Such a generalization reveals an ignorance of characteristic developments in Scandinavian literature during the last fifty years which is scarcely pardonable in one who would presume to pass broad and inclusive judgments upon it. It would seem, indeed, that such an ignorant negative generalization is as reprehensible in its way as is the indiscriminate enthusiasm which is more often typical of present-day "criticism" of Scandinavian literature. Neither has any place in the proper evaluation of literary tendencies and influences, be that evaluation historical or otherwise.

Even if the critic were to restrict himself to translations from the Scandinavian, any candid examination of the Scandinavian literature of first importance which has appeared in the last half century would reveal very clearly that the morality (or, as some would have it, the immorality) of *Crime and Punishment* is certainly not "thoroughly typical" of Scandinavian literature. It might be expecting too much of the critics of a "new humanism," intently concerned, as they are, with the supposed sanctity of a classical tradition in literature and ethics, to look with favor upon most of those developments in modern Scandinavian literature which *really are* characteristic of that literature; but one can at least take occasion to protest vigorously the indiscriminate linking of Dostoievski and "the half-mad Strindberg" (it is to be remembered that he was not always half-mad) with those Scandinavian authors who are most representative of modern Scandinavian literature.

It would be interesting to have Paul Elmer More's really careful and defined reaction to the six representative Scandinavian novelists upon whom I propose to concentrate primarily in the chapters which follow in the present volume. An open-minded reading of these authors would certainly have led him to qualify very strongly the hasty incidental judgment which he has passed upon Scandinavian literature in the essay on "Decadent Wit." That More would have been disturbed by Jens Peter Jacobsen's severely objective study of decadent psychol-

ogy in *Niels Lyhne* goes without saying; and that he would
have found little to his taste in Knut Hamsun's "vagabond
heroes" and in the later primitivism of *Growth of the Soil*
seems almost as apparent. My guess is, however, that he would
have found much to delight in among Selma Lagerlöf's tales
and novels, that he would have responded with considerable
enthusiasm to Jonas Lie and Verner von Heidenstam, and that
he would have been deeply impressed by Sigrid Undset's profound studies in religious psychology medieval and modern. He
would have discovered—doubtless to his surprise—that Jonas
Lie was almost as different from "the half-mad Strindberg" as
was More himself; that Heidenstam, after an early friendship
with Strindberg, became the chief critical and creative exponent of that current in modern Swedish literature most opposed
to much that Strindberg stood for; and that Selma Lagerlöf
represents a form of sanely balanced optimistic idealism which is
as innocent of Strindbergian aberrations as is Wordsworth's
Lucy Gray. One might hypothesize—a bit slyly—that were our
critic to yield unconsciously for a moment to the intricate subtle-
ties of Freudian literary analysis he might discover suspicious
evidences of an incipient, though unconscious, sadism in Sigrid
Undset's intently brooding preoccupation with the problem of
evil and the consciousness of sin; but one suspects that the
severe moral dogma of *Kristin Lavransdatter* and *The Master
of Hestviken,* as well as that of the later Undset novels, would
impress a typical critic of the "new humanism" sufficiently to
blind him to possible sadistic implications in the solemn narrative
progression of Sigrid Undset's genius.

I do not mean to suggest, of course, that the modern Scandinavian novel is to be conceived largely as in opposition to those
tendencies in modern literature that are represented so strikingly
in such figures as Strindberg and Dostoievski, though the
thesis might be maintained without a too violent stretching of
the truth. I wish at the present moment merely to insist that the
modern Scandinavian novel is *emphatically not* a direct literary
development from such works as *The Father, Miss Julie,* and
Crime and Punishment. The modern Scandinavian novel has
something of both the great Swede and the great Russian in it;

but for the most part it develops either in opposition to, or quite independent of, what Strindberg and Dostoievski are usually thought to stand for in the development of modern literature. In fact there is only one novel in the total production of the six novelists dealt with in the following chapters that can be said to remind one strongly of Dostoievski. The novel I refer to is Hamsun's *Hunger*—and this novel, it is worthy of note, was composed before Hamsun had read anything of Dostoievski's! It is interesting to observe also in passing that had we occasion to offer a chapter on Strindberg *as a novelist,* we should find his most significant fictional achievement to be *The People of Hemsö,* a remarkably healthy and sane treatment of Swedish archipelago peasant-folk, full of a pleasantly bracing vigor which never approaches violence, and conceived in the spirit of a robustly warm and sympathetic humor. It is, incidentally, one of those strange little ironies in literary history that the simple, healthy sanity of *The People of Hemsö* should appear in 1887, the year that also saw the appearance of Strindberg's brutally naturalistic play *The Father,* and a year before the publication of *Miss Julie* and *Creditors,* two dramas which in their ways match the aching violence of *The Father.* It is dangerous to generalize—even about Strindberg himself.

THE PRESENT BOOK does not pretend to be a history of the modern Scandinavian novel, nor is it an effort to analyze and evaluate broad tendencies in the development of Scandinavian fiction in terms of any particular point of view or according to any special canon of critical dogma. The material is too rich and diversified in both form and content to yield readily to either historical or critical generalizations. Besides, we are at the present time too close to "the great tradition" in the Scandinavian novel to be in a position to judge it with an adequate historical perspective. It seems to me, therefore, that what the general non-Scandinavian reading public needs at present in its effort to understand (and in a sense, if need be, to evaluate) the modern Scandinavian novel is something far less pretentious than historical generalizations and something more honestly *revealing* than critical judgments distorted either by ignorance or by narrow critical dogma or by both. Instead of a general history of the modern Scandinavian novel, our most immediate need is a careful and honest detailed analysis of the important works of a certain few representative Scandinavian novelists of the last half century. This is what I propose in the following essays.

In my choice of novelists (and novels) for particular treatment I have been guided by a few relatively simple considerations: first I have concentrated in each chapter upon a novelist of first importance; secondly, I have chosen novelists who are broadly representative of certain characteristic tendencies in the Scandinavian novel of the last half century; and thirdly, I have tried to keep constantly in mind that I am writing primarily for a general, cultured English-speaking reading public. These considerations have determined both my general critical procedures and the exclusion or inclusion of certain biographical and historical details. The first of these considerations has ruled out of these pages any attention to such figures as Johan Bojer and Trygve Gulbranssen, obviously inferior novelists who by some accident of human taste have attracted very considerable reading publics in England and America as well as in their native Norway. Both the first and the second of these considerations, on the other hand, have come to determine very largely my decision to include in this book a chapter on Verner von Heidenstam, despite the deplorable fact that his *The Tree of the Folkungs* has had little sale in England and America even though the advertising blurbs which accompanied its translation made much of Heidenstam as a winner of the Nobel Prize in Literature. The third of these considerations— that the present book is written primarily for an English and American reading public—accounts to a considerable extent for the fullness of the biographical and historical details which I have felt it necessary to provide in each of the six chapters of this book. This accounts also for my decision to include at least some treatment of those novels by the authors upon whom I concentrate which have not appeared in English translations. A knowledge of such novels—seldom available to the non-Scandinavian reader—is oftentimes as important as is biographical and historical information in the proper understanding and possible evaluation of a given author's work.

It will be noted that I have limited the number of novelists treated in detail to six, even though this has resulted in certain perhaps unfortunate omissions. Considerations of space have made this inevitable. I am convinced that it is far more important at the present moment to provide relatively thorough and complete critical studies of a few of the most representative of the Scandinavian novelists than a rapid, sketchy survey of a larger number; and the confines of one volume hardly allow a detailed treatment of more than a half dozen novelists. Had space permitted I should very much desire to include, in addition to the six novelists I have chosen, chapters on Alexander Kielland, Arne Garborg, Henrik Pontoppidan, Johannes V. Jensen, Martin Andersen Nexö, Olav Duun, and possibly the Norwegian-American novelist O. E. Rølvaag. Kielland, besides ranking with Jonas Lie as one of the two creators of the modern Norwegian novel, has produced in *Skipper Worse* (1882) what is one of the richest veins of humor in any Scandinavian novel. Garborg stands perhaps next to Sigrid Undset as a Norwegian novelist of broodingly penetrating creative intelligence. His sardonically probing analysis of decadence in *Trætte Mænd* ("Weary Men," 1891), not to mention his other later novels and his poetry, marks him as one of the most original and powerful literary figures in modern Norway. Pontoppidan has written, among other things in fictional form, some of the most incisive studies in characteristic trends of modern Danish culture—his *Lykke Per* ("Lucky Per," 1898-1904) providing us with a marvellously understanding and inclusive analysis of the whole cultural history of Denmark at the turn of the century. Jensen's most imposing work, *The Long Journey* (1909-22), is in some senses a failure as a novel, probably primarily because its canvas is too large; but there are portions of it which in lyric intensity and imaginative sweep are among the rare wonders of Danish literature. Nexö's *Pelle the Conqueror* (1906-10) is the classic Scandinavian proletariat novel. Duun's *The People of Juvik* (1918-23) ranks with Thomas Mann's *Buddenbrooks* and Galsworthy's *Forsyte Saga* as one of the most

satisfactory genealogical novels of the twentieth century. And
in Rølvaag's *Giants in the Earth* (1924-25) the Scandinavian-
American immigrant novel has attained its most perfect expression. Important, however, as these novels are, judged by any
standard, and representative of Scandinavian fiction as each of
them is in its way, space forbids a detailed treatment of them
in the present book, though I shall have incidental occasion to
refer to some of them in the chapters which follow.

I HAVE TRIED in this book to avoid the pitfalls of easy generalization, not only because such generalizations are invariably
precarious in themselves, but also because I feel that they are
apt to be peculiarly dangerous when offered to the average
non-Scandinavian reader who is seldom in position properly to
understand and adequately to qualify such generalizations in
the light of a fairly broad first-hand knowledge of the literatures
in question. I have therefore rigidly eschewed facile generalizations about what is sometimes called "the Scandinavian temperament" or "characteristic qualities of Scandinavian art,"
despite the fascination which such nebulous semi-exotic concepts
very naturally exercise over the average non-Scandinavian
mind in its concern with Scandinavian literature and art. No
less rigorously have I insisted upon excluding from these pages
certain popular concepts about things Scandinavian caught up
in such meaningless phrases as "the elemental vigor of Scandinavian genius" and "the profound natural mysticism of the
Scandinavian spirit"—phrases which occur with fatal frequency
in endlessly varied forms in current reviews of Scandinavian
novels. Such phrases—if they are not positively misleading—
get one exactly nowhere in a critical understanding of the Scandinavian literatures.

I feel, however, that it will be of service to those who may
wish to have some idea of the relation between the Scandinavian novel of the last half century and the general literary
conditions out of which that novel grew to offer in the present
Introduction a few *purely historical* generalizations about Scandinavian literature in the late nineteenth century. Such a sketch
of the Scandinavian literatures in the last decades of the nine-

teenth century might serve as a kind of broad point of historical
departure for those who for one reason or another may be concerned with the *development* of the Scandinavian novel, even
though the chapters which follow in the present volume do not
in themselves propose to comprise, strictly speaking, a history
of the modern Scandinavian novel. It is to be emphasized that
each of the chapters in this book is conceived primarily as an
independent critical essay in itself, and may be read quite independent of the other chapters or of the present Introduction.
And yet in a very loose sense of the word "history" these
chapters may be considered as providing the broad general basis
for an historical study of the Scandinavian novel. Each chapter
deals with a representative figure, and seeks among other things
to trace his relationship to the literary conditions of his day;
and the succession of chapters has been arranged to suggest
broadly a sense of historical development in the modern Scandinavian novel. One need not, however, read these chapters
from this point of view; and I would suggest that those readers
who would prefer not to be burdened with even broad historical
considerations simply ignore the immediately succeeding paragraphs and proceed directly to whichever chapter in the body
of this book may for one reason or another most directly
concern them.

Any historical understanding of the origins of the modern
Scandinavian novel presupposes some knowledge of the work
of such representative literary figures in the North as Georg
Brandes, Ibsen, Bjørnson, and Strindberg, though neither
Brandes nor Ibsen wrote prose fiction, while Bjørnson and
Strindberg produced only occasionally in the genre of the novel.
These four men, however, were chiefly instrumental in creating
what has sometimes been called "The New Awakening" in
modern Scandinavian literature, and it was during this "New
Awakening" that the modern Scandinavian novel came into
existence. I cannot, at the moment, pause to review in any
detail the work of each of these men and the relation of each
to the development of the Scandinavian novel. It will perhaps
be sufficient for our immediate purposes to focus our attention
for the moment on Georg Brandes, the brilliant critical apologist

for "The New Awakening," suggesting incidentally, as we proceed, the relation of Ibsen and Bjørnson and Strindberg to Brandes in particular and to the movement as such in general, and indicating briefly the way in which each of the novelists whom I am to treat is related to the whole.

It was in the summer of 1871 that Georg Brandes accepted what might be called his Apostolic blessing as the chief critical exponent of "The New Awakening." This blessing was received at the hands of none other than Henrik Ibsen, who had already taken on some of the pontifical manners of his middle career, and who was just about to embark on a series of social reform plays aimed at what he called, somewhat cryptically, and not without a touch of bombast, a general "revolt of the soul of man." The meeting between Ibsen and Brandes took place in Dresden, where Ibsen was in residence at the time; and it was a natural result of a correspondence which had taken place between the two men for some months before. Brandes was on his way to Copenhagen, after a fairly extensive residence abroad, in Paris and Rome particularly, and for a short period in London. He was fully determined upon his return to Copenhagen to break lances with the champions of what he considered to be a defunct literary tradition; and so the meeting with Ibsen in Dresden merely served to add a kind of immediate official blessing to his proposed program. The last words that Ibsen had shouted to Brandes as the train pulled out of the railway station were: "Provoke the Danes, and I will provoke the Norwegians!" Both of these men did just this in the years that followed—Ibsen with his plays, Brandes as lecturer, critic, and journalist.

Georg Brandes, though young, was sufficiently mature for his task when he returned to Copenhagen. The year which he had spent abroad had been of tremendous significance in his intellectual development, for it had provided the immediate inspiration of personal contacts (with Taine, Comte, and John Stuart Mill among others) and an opportunity to observe at first hand how the larger world outside of Denmark lived and thought. All of this gave to him the solid immediate materials upon which to build a critical point of view which he had already arrived at theoretically before departing from Copenhagen in the early summer of 1870. His brilliant academic career in Denmark during the preceding decade had been marked by a rapid, rather revolutionary intellectual development in which he had come to reject an early enthusiasm for the prevailing abstract and absolute Hegelian aesthetics, concerned primarily with the form of literature, for an empirical and relative critical point of view, which was interested primarily in the contents of literature. For the metaphysical aesthetics of Hegel the young Danish critic wished to substitute a living aesthetic, in which literature was directly and immediately related to all of the pulsing forces of life. His masters were Taine and Sainte-Beuve in literary criticism, Comte and John Stuart Mill in social and political theory; and his constantly reiterated watchword upon his return to Copenhagen after the European travels was that "literature should bring up problems for debate." What he meant by this—it is clear from his introductory lecture to the series of studies which later became his famous *Main Currents in Nineteenth Century European Literature* (1872-90)—was that literature should contain *ideas,* living, vital ideas, and that it should be one of the means whereby a liberal program of reform in all phases of human life might be realized. Great literature, in short, was to be conceived as liberal propaganda.

Brandes's *Main Currents* was not sound literary history, of course, chiefly because its interpretation of literature was too obviously motivated by a particular social and political point of view; but it was excellent propaganda, brilliantly conceived and vigorously executed, and as such it fulfilled its immediate purpose—to introduce liberal ideas into the rather stagnant intellectual life of Denmark. Brandes's immediate critical purpose in these lectures was to prove that the European Romanticism of the late eighteenth and early nineteenth centuries was fundamentally reactionary in its social and political tendencies, and that only in some of its later phases, as manifested in Shelley and Byron in England, Hugo in France, and Heine and Börne and *Das junge Deutschland* in Germany, did it reveal any vital evidences of a significant constructive relationship to modern life. Though Brandes was concerned ostensibly in the *Main*

Currents with the literatures of France and England and Germany, the implied application of his moral to immediate conditions in Denmark in particular and to the other Scandinavian countries in general was unmistakable.

The effect of Brandes's lectures in his native Denmark was startling, and in Norway and Sweden the influence of his critical doctrines soon came to operate hand-in-hand with the conscious *Tendenz* which animated the new social reform drama of Ibsen and Bjørnson and the miscellaneous literary activities of Strindberg in the '70's. In Denmark Brandes became "the man of the hour" almost overnight, where previously he had been known only in the academic circles in which he had moved. Danish conservatives, driven to fury by the hard-hitting young critic, attacked Brandes bitterly. But all of the country's liberal elements, which had been more or less quiescent in want of a rallying point, a vigorous and forceful leader, found in the young Brandes what seemed to amount to a heaven sent power. Particularly did youth flock to Brandes, fascinated by his brilliant oratorical powers and by his bold condemnation of the conservative status quo; and in the field of practical politics Brandes's liberalism appealed strongly to the group which had been attempting, hitherto rather feebly, to agitate democratic reforms against the conservative bureaucracy which had dominated Danish life for decades.

In Denmark the conservative opposition seemed at first to triumph. Brandes's effort to gain a recently vacated professorship in aesthetics at the University ended in failure; the liberal journal—*Det 19. Aarhundrede*—which he had been the leading spirit in founding in 1874 ceased publication in 1877; and Brandes forsook Copenhagen for Berlin. In Germany, however, he continued his critical production, in much the same spirit as he had begun it in Copenhagen; and it soon became evident that the victory of Danish conservatism over the new liberalism was but momentary. Upon the return of Brandes to Denmark in 1882 he found that the newly aroused spirit of liberalism had found immediate practical expression in the organization of a political party of the Left; and two years later he was to witness the establishment of a powerful organ of liberal public opinion in the newspaper *Politiken*.

The new political party had naturally counted upon the direct support of Brandes. In this, however, they were disappointed. Brandes was not by nature a practical politician; and—more important—during his residence in Germany he had gradually come to see that in reality he had no real and profound sympathies with fundamental democratic ideals. It was therefore that he found it necessary in 1884, upon an occasion when he was being honored by a democratic group in Denmark, to deny frankly that he was a democrat in his political faith. "Democracy was a means—" he insisted at this time—"the end was the introduction into Danish intellectual and social life of certain great, new, and rich cultural values." What was to take the place of democracy in Danish cultural development Brandes did not at the time seem to have clearly defined even to himself. It is clear to us now, however, that he was leaning at this time in the direction of some form of cultural aristocracy. In 1886 he discovered Nietzsche, and in the German philosopher's conception of the superman he found the final end of cultural values. Brandes carried on a lively correspondence with Nietzsche in the immediately succeeding years (until Nietzsche's attack of insanity in 1889); and in 1888 the Danish critic introduced the ideas of Nietzsche to the North in a series of much publicized lectures. In 1889 these lectures were incorporated into a book published under the title *Aristocratic Radicalism*, a book which is at one and the same time an interpretation of Nietzsche and a confession of Brandes's own final faith. At the close of this book Brandes rejects categorically most of the ideas characteristic of his earlier criticism, referring to them in a vein of not too subtle irony as "certain theories of heredity, with a little Darwinism, a little emancipation of women, a little morality of happiness, a little free thought, a little cult of the people, etc. . . ." It is in the great personality, the superman, that Brandes finally came to find the source and end of human culture; and his criticism therefore became increasingly preoccupied with the great personality (Shakespeare, Goethe, Voltaire, Caesar, Michelangelo, each of whom he takes up in a full-length biography) which rises above the conditions of his time and creates cultural values largely independent of what is considered to be characteristic thought trends of the period in which he lives. Nietzsche had thus completely triumphed over Taine and John Stuart Mill in the critical thinking of Georg Brandes.

Recent Danish scholarship, particularly that of Professor Rubow, has demonstrated rather conclusively that Brandes never had been a democrat in spirit, and that his flirtation with democratic tendencies in the '70's is therefore to be considered merely a tentative aspect of his development, resulting naturally from his early preoccupation with Taine and Mill. This does not mean, however, that the contemporaries of Brandes sensed in the '70's or the early '80's any fundamental anti-democratic strain in his nature; and certain it is that Brandes's chief significance in the development of modern Scandinavian literature lies in his early criticism—a criticism which had identified itself largely with realism and naturalism as art forms and with the essentially democratic social and political ideas of positivism and utilitarianism.

Brandes's critical doctrines of the early 1870's certainly had a determining part in the tendency of the Scandinavian literatures of the '70's and '80's to "bring up problems for debate"—particularly social and political problems. Ibsen, indeed, had already in the late '60's put out feelers in the direction of a new social reform drama; but *The League of Youth* (1869) was tentative and experimental on the whole, and it was not until well along in the '70's, after the weight of Brandes's lectures had tipped the scale in favor of a "literature of ideas," that Ibsen began producing in earnest that great series of social dramas which gave practical expression to what he had called "the revolt of the soul of man" in his famous letter to Brandes in December of 1870. Kielland's novels from the early '80's are to be considered as an even more direct and immediate result of Brandes's critical doctrines, as is also a great deal of the work of the so-called *Unga Sverige,* including, besides the young Strindberg, Gustaf af Geijerstam, Tor Hedberg, Axel Lundegård, and, in the '80's, Ola Hansson. Even Bjørnson, who could not endure Brandes as a personality (perhaps chiefly because Brandes could not endure him!), owes much to the Danish critic's championing of the cause of Continental ideas in the North.

In fact it might be argued without much exaggeration, I think, that Bjørnson was in many respects the most consistent literary product of that movement which Brandes's critical doctrines had so much to do with originating in the '70's. Where men like Ibsen and Strindberg go on to other things in their later careers, and develop rather independently of the ideas of the '70's, Bjørnson tends to become as time goes on the rapt apostle of nearly all of the characteristic ideas of the '70's—and this despite his quarrel with Brandes and the so-called "Christiania bohême" on the subject of morals. Bjørnson might be called the pedagogue *par excellence* of Scandinavian literature, and certainly any literature which proposes to "bring up problems for debate" must be basically a pedagogic literature. Bjørnson's plays and novels, his short stories and essays, and even many of his lyric poems, are taken up largely with an exposition of contemporary ideas—an exposition which usually in his case amounts either to undisguised propaganda or to something closely resembling it. "Very seldom does one of his [Bjørnson's] characters speak in his own voice," writes a recent Norwegian critic. "Seldom are they permitted to live their own lives. Bjørnson takes charge, teaching and leading. There is always something which Bjørnson has just read, recently heard about, or just thought of that finally must be forced upon us." This *is* literature which "brings up problems for debate"!

Though the literature concerned with ideas and with social reform seems to have triumphed all along the line in the '70's and the early '80's, signs of a reaction begin to appear at least as early as the middle '80's, and by 1890 defections seem to be occurring on every hand. Incidental signs of a reaction against Brandes's early naturalistic and utilitarian conception of literature appear perhaps earliest in Denmark, where both Holger Drachmann and Karl Gjellerup, early members of the Brandes circle, broke deliberately with "the Master." Their break, however, was of little immediate consequence, for Drachmann's volatile genius underwent so many changes in his mercurial career that his original adherence to Brandes seems to have been more or less accidental, and Gjellerup's turning in the middle of the '80's to the classicism of Goethe and Schiller hardly had a sufficient positive appeal to his immediate contemporaries to make any significant contribution to new literary developments. In the early '90's, however, French symbolism had a strong momentary influence upon lyric poetry in Denmark, particularly on that of Johannes Jørgensen; and in Sweden and Norway the reaction against realism and naturalism took on certain fruitful positive forms which came soon to have a very vital significance for the whole future of the Scandinavian literatures. The success of the reaction in Sweden and Norway is to be attributed partly to the fresh and forceful intelligence of the new criticism, though perhaps more to the rich flood of creative literature which followed directly upon the theoretical attack on naturalism and which demonstrated unmistakably the fertility and vigor of the new aesthetics that was being formulated in these years. Verner von Heidenstam and Oscar Levertin in Sweden and Arne Garborg and Knut Hamsun in Norway gave the most forceful critical expression to the new aesthetics; and these authors, together with a host of other literary figures of first importance, including Selma Lagerlöf, Gustaf Fröding, Erik Axel Karlfeldt, and Sigbjørn Obstfelder, proved the rich positive vitality of the new aesthetics in terms of a lyric and a prose narrative production of vast proportions and of marvelously diversified beauty and power. Even Strindberg added his fresh and powerful contribution to the new literature around the turn of the century in a rich efflorescence of late dramatic work—his experiments in the expressionistic religious play and his vigorous historical dramas.

In the chapters which follow in the present book I have reviewed in some detail how each of the novelists treated is related to these new literary developments on the one hand and to the utilitarian aesthetics of the early Georg Brandes on the other. It will be seen that only one of the six novelists treated in these chapters—Jens Peter Jacobsen—considered himself a direct and consistent disciple of Brandes; and even in his case the kinship to Brandes's early aesthetics is not really as close as is often supposed. Otherwise all of these novelists are in one way or another in more or less conscious reaction against the naturalistic and utilitarian aesthetics for which Georg Brandes stood in the '70's. Jonas Lie was on friendly personal terms with Brandes; but we shall see that this did not prevent him from judging "much of that culture which blows over to us from Denmark (Brandes, etc., etc.)" to be "just as sterile and enervating for our Norwegian circumstances as a sirocco from the Sahara." It was not until the early '90's, however, that the reaction in fiction gained sufficient strength to challenge seriously the ideal of literature characteristic of the preceding two decades. In the field of fiction the new developments are represented by Hamsun in Norway, Selma Lagerlöf and Heidenstam in Sweden. Hamsun followed up the publication of *Hunger* in 1890 with a series of public lectures in Norway in which he vigorously attacked Ibsen, Bjørnson, Kielland, and Lie, the chief representatives of what he referred to in the sardonically ironic phrase "the world famous Norwegian literature"; and the basic reason for Hamsun's condemnation of these authors at this time was that they all insisted upon making literature, directly or indirectly, a medium for social or economic or political or religious reform. Though Selma Lagerlöf did not indulge in a militant critical attack on the spirit of the '80's, she found very soon that she could not write her famous *Saga* in the sober realistic prose characteristic of the fiction of the day; and only when she deliberately defied this tradition in fiction was she able to complete *Gösta Berling's Saga* in 1891. This novel, it is not too much to say, utterly flabbergasted most of Selma Lagerlöf's Swedish contemporaries with its fantastically free action, its unbelievable episodes, its unblushing play with the reader's emotions, and its lyrically intoxicated style—all so violently at cross purposes with the serious "problem literature" of the '80's. Sigrid Undset, the last of the novelists with whom I shall deal, did not come upon the literary scene until after the turn of the century; but her autobiographical fragment entitled *The Longest Years* (1934) provides plenty of evidence that even as a young school girl during the '90's she felt an instinctive, though quite undefined, distaste for the strenuous pedagogical strain of the literature of the preceding decade. She—the young Sigrid—found that "it had altogether too strong a smack of books and pedagogy, and it roused a spirit of opposition in her more than anything else"!

It is, however, in Verner von Heidenstam, among the six novelists with whom we shall be concerned primarily in the present book, that we find developed the most consciously formulated and detailed constructive aesthetics in opposition to the naturalism of the '70's and '80's and all that this naturalism tended to stand for in terms of the prevailing ideas of the period. Heidenstam's new literary program was contained in two critical essays, "Renascence" (1889) and "Pepita's Wedding" (1890), the latter composed jointly with Oscar Levertin. I have subjected the former of these essays, the more important of the two, to a fairly detailed analysis in my chapter on Heidenstam (see especially pp. 133-135). It is in one of the final paragraphs in the essay that Heidenstam suggests *renässans* (renascence) as the word which might perhaps best describe the new literary movement which he proposes for Sweden. And then he goes on—

. . . It should justify such a name in part because of the peculiarities in our own national temper that should then come to be honored, in part because of its readoption of the methods of the older schools, in part also because of its own inner nature, its favoring of the subjective, of personal independence, its uniting of the imagination, the sense of the beautiful, and bold, racy realism.

Though Heidenstam's essay is written directly for a Swedish public, one is certainly not taking too great a liberty with the word "renascence" (in the inclusive sense in which it is defined by Heidenstam), if one looks upon it more broadly as suggesting the main lines of development of all three of the Scandinavian literatures since 1890. Heidenstam's essay, it is to be remembered, had a direct, as well as a broadly pervasive, influence on the literatures of Denmark and Norway; and the literary movement which came into existence in Sweden in the 1890's has had a parallel development in Norway and Denmark. In each country, of course, this development took on somewhat different forms, depending upon variations in national temperament and the accidental vagaries of individual literary genius. These various national literary developments are one, however, in their common general negation of the type of "problem literature" characteristic of the '70's and '80's; and even in many of their positive manifestations they reveal striking general similarities without sacrificing vigorously diversified individual traits.

In fact, what one is most struck by in surveying this modern Scandinavian renascence as it finds expression in prose fiction is the rich diversity of narrative gifts represented in the Scandinavian literatures since 1890, together with the abounding vitality of this prose fiction in a modern world that seems so full of brilliant but often relatively sterile performances in literary art. The Scandinavian novel since 1890 ranges boldly across the whole scale of human experience and human emotions, from the vigorous and exuberant vitality of Hamsun and Selma Lagerlöf to the nobly strong spirit of mature resignation in the later Heidenstam and the heavily brooding tragic note of Sigrid Undset. Perhaps the best evidence of the abiding *vitality* of the modern Scandinavian novel is that even when it is pitched in the distinctly minor key of Sigrid Undset, we listen to notes that are neither apathetic nor weakly negative. In her work there is to be heard neither the thin melodies of a late-born Romanticism nor the drear, world-weary tonal combinations of a *fin de siècle* decadence. Sigrid Undset broods, it is true, but she broods *strongly*; and out of the massively troubled brooding of her genius is created at the last something which we come to recognize as tragedy in its highest form. One should not fear for the vitality of Scandinavian fiction when it can create in an uncertain and fear-burdened modern age a literary form which to the virile mind of the ancient Greek was the most bracing and ennobling of all literary forms.

IMPRESSIONISTIC REALISM

JONAS LIE

OF the literary generation in Norway that produced Ibsen and Bjørnson only one author, besides these two masters, was able to attract international attention. Jonas Lie, the first really important Scandinavian novelist, has this distinction. It must be admitted immediately, of course, that Lie's Continental vogue was by no means as extensive as was that of Ibsen; and it probably even fell considerably short of that of Bjørnson. Lie was sufficiently well known in Paris, in the 1890's, however, to attract the attention of a correspondent of the *Figaro,* though the interview which was arranged in consequence, instead of being reported in the *Figaro,* ultimately became assimiliated into a series of essays on modern Scandinavian literary figures under the general title "Les révoltés scandinaves" and published in 1894 in the *Revue des deux Mondes.* In England, at about the same time, Edmund Gosse found occasion to speak words of rather high praise on Lie in an introduction to an English translation of the Norwegian novelist's *The Commodore's Daughters.* But even this English critic, whose pronouncements are not always without a certain uncritical enthusiasm, especially in matters Scandinavian, is cautious in predicting for Lie any such international reputation as that of either Ibsen or Bjørnson. Gosse recollects in his Introduction a meeting with the publisher Hegel in Copenhagen, on which occasion the elegant Danish publisher presented him with the first copy of a new novel.

"You shall take this with you, if you will," said Mr. Hegel, "and make acquaintance with Jonas Lie." "And who is Jonas Lie?" I asked. "He is a Norwegian," he answered, "like our friends Bjørnson and Ibsen, and, though comparatively few people know his name to-day, I predict that in ten years' time he will have more readers than any other Scandinavian writer." The prophecy has come true, at all events so far as Scandinavia is concerned. At this moment Jonas Lie is locally the most popular of the Scandinavian novelists.

Gosse is perhaps right in claiming for Lie such preeminent Scandinavian popularity in the '90's; for it is fairly apparent that by this time even Norwegians were beginning to tire a bit of the strenuous artistic and ethical creeds of Ibsen and Bjørnson, and found themselves considerably more at ease in the unassuming impressionistic manner that they had come to know as the peculiar mark of Jonas Lie. Ibsen and Bjørnson had with the years gradually come to take on the stature of literary giants among their contemporaries; and in consequence they had aroused both tremendous enthusiasms and bitterly uncompromising antipathies among Scandinavian readers during the three decades previous to 1890. Lie's less aggressive personality and more quiet artistry had, on the other hand, by the '90's captured the abiding sympathy of nearly all Norwegian readers, the discriminating as well as the popular; and since that time he has become by common consent one with Ibsen and Bjørnson—the three comprising "the great triumvirate" of late nineteenth century Norwegian authors.

The reasons for Lie's popularity in the Scandinavian countries, particularly in his own Norway, are not difficult to discover. In the first place, as a literary artist devoted almost exclusively to the novel he came upon the scene first. Except for Bjørnson's early experiments in the short idyllic peasant novel and Camilla Collett's one significant novel *The Governor's Daughters* (1855), Norwegian literary genius had occupied itself very largely during the last half of the nineteenth century either with the drama of social reform or with political pamphleteering in various scantly disguised literary forms. It was not until Lie had rather firmly established himself as a novelist that his countrymen Kielland and Garborg came upon the scene to challenge his preeminence in the novel; and significant as each of these men was in his way, neither quite attained the solid distinction in the novel that Lie had come to establish for himself by the end of the century.

And neither Denmark nor Sweden produced novelists of consistent distinction during the last half of the nineteenth century, though individual novels of real importance appeared at this time in these countries. In Denmark, J. P. Jacobsen, with his

Marie Grubbe (1876) and *Niels Lyhne* (1880), and Herman Bang, with his *Haabløse Slægter* ("Generations without Hope," 1880), produced novels of lasting significance; but Jacobsen died before his literary production could become anything but an unforgettably brilliant episode in Danish literary history, and Bang, it is now clear, had shot his bolt in his one important novel. In Sweden the novel during these years was scarcely more important than in Denmark. Between Viktor Rydberg's historical novel *The Last Athenian* (1859) and Selma Lagerlöf's *Gösta Berling's Saga* (1891) there were few novels of any real distinction produced in Sweden. Strindberg might well have been Sweden's great novelist during these years had he so chosen, for his *The Red Room* (1879) was brilliantly ruthless impressionistic satire in fictional form, and *The People of Hemsö* (1887) is certainly to be ranked among the best modern peasant novels; but Strindberg's genius was too restless to submit to any particular literary form over any considerable period of time, and besides, the drama seemed to be his favorite form insofar as any genre could consistently attract his unquiet, volatile spirit.

Jonas Lie, steadily productive, quietly persistent in his solid, careful literary workmanship, had thus no serious competitor, with the possible exception of the brilliant Kielland of the '80's, during the two decades following upon the publication of his first story, *Den Fremsynte* ("The Visionary"), in 1870. He had time, therefore, to become thoroughly established with a wide Scandinavian reading public well before the rocketlike rise in the '90's of such significant novelists as Selma Lagerlöf in Sweden and Knut Hamsun in Norway.

At least two other factors, however, contributed to Lie's constantly increasing popularity with the Scandinavian reading public: first, he took a middle way in the intense controversial activities that set the tone in the literature of the Scandinavian countries during the last half of the nineteenth century; and secondly, Lie's novels were so genuinely Norwegian in every detail that his countrymen were delighted to find in his pages a constant source of quiet, genial, understanding interpretation of that which was most immediately characteristic of their daily lives. Lie's "middle way," we shall attempt to demonstrate later, was not the easy compromise of the weak sentimentalist or the soft seeker after popular acclaim. It was rather the *via media* of a vigorous, independent intelligence that consistently refused to become the mouthpiece of any particular party or movement, simply because Lie's native intelligence was profound enough to recognize that truth is too complex to be resolved readily into any facile credo, literary or ethical. Lie, in consequence, maintained throughout the often bitter controversies in the Scandinavian countries during the late nineteenth century that independent critical "disinterestedness of spirit" which Matthew Arnold during these very years was postulating as *the* criterion of the true critical spirit.

It may well be that the chief reason for Lie's critical balance during these years was simply that he was so deeply and soundly rooted in the essential soil of his homeland that he could not so easily become a prey to the numerous Continental and English -isms which lay back of so much of the work of Ibsen and Bjørnson, Strindberg and Brandes. Despite the fact that Lie spent nearly his entire productive career outside of Norway (first in Rome, then in southern Germany, and finally, the longest period, in Paris), it seems to be the general consensus of opinion in Norway that no Norwegian novelist has written more close to the pulsing soul of Norway than has Jonas Lie. He could do so, of course, only because he had a rare facility at preserving his artistic and intellectual balance in the midst of a thousand foreign impressions. This Ibsen could seldom do; nor could Bjørnson even, for the most part. Ibsen in consequence became, by degrees, but inevitably, an "international" author: his "problems" came with the years to be almost mechanically "universal" ones, and in his dramas they were often fitted rather loosely into an only apparently Norwegian milieu. And Bjørnson—vociferously Norwegian as he tried to be, and *is* in many respects—fought most of his life, paradoxically enough, to import into his native Norway a multitude of only half-assimilated European ideas.

It must be admitted in passing, however, that the peculiarly Norwegian quality of Lie's genius is not without its drawbacks.

There is to be found in his work, for example, an occasional
cropping out of a kind of provincialism that is somewhat distasteful to the non-Norwegian reader. Particularly is this apparent—to take a couple of instances almost at random—in the
strongly unfavorable contrast between Norwegian seafaring
men and those of other nations in *Lodsen og hans Hustru*
("The Pilot and His Wife," 1874), or in the equally smug
contrast between the Norwegian girl Katharina Linstow and
a Miss Wilkins, with her English ways, in *Thomas Ross*
(1878). In Lie's more mature novels, however, such as *The
Family at Gilje* (1883) and *The Commodore's Daughters*
(1886), he has outgrown such crude provincially motivated
methods of contrast. These later novels treat purely Norwegian
characters in purely Norwegian milieus, with no naïve admix-
ture of popular, provincially motivated contrasts.

I

Jonas Lauritz Idemil Lie was born on the 6th day of November 1833 at Hougsund, in Eker, not far from Oslo. His
father had descended from substantial, hard-working Norwegian peasant stock, though three generations back the family
had broken away from the soil and established itself in civil
and judicial positions in various parts of Norway. The mother
of Jonas seems to have had marked traces of Finnish, possibly
Gipsy, blood in her veins. "I remember very well—" writes
Boyesen of this interesting woman in his *Essays on Scandinavian Literature*—"this black-eyed, eccentric little lady, with
her queer ways, extraordinary costumes, and still more extraordinary conversation. It is from her Jonas Lie has inherited the
fantastic strain in his blood, the strange, superstitious terrors,
and the luxuriant wealth of color which he lavished upon his
poems and his first novel, *The Visionary*." It is not clear as to
just how far present-day criticism can go in accepting Boyesen's
ready application of late nineteenth century theories of heredity
to the literary genius of Jonas Lie; and yet it is perhaps reasonable enough to assume that the chaotic, wayward imaginative-
ness of the young Lie is to be explained largely by the fact that
he was the son of this energetic, fascinatingly exotic little lady

who had brought new, somewhat disturbing blood into the solid, steady peasant stock of the purely Norwegian Lie family.

At the time of the birth of Jonas, the father was practising law in Eker, though five years later he moved with his family to Tromsø, a city in the far north of Norway beyond the Polar Circle; and here the Lies were to live until Jonas was twelve years of age. Here a weirdly fantastic physical environment was to combine with hereditary characteristics to emphasize the eccentric strain in the impressionable young boy. The strange contrasts of the Far North, its kaleidoscopic shifting of landscape effects, its lurid intensities of light and darkness, its eternal night of winter and continuous day of summer, its fantastic world of darksome superstitions—these things impressed themselves with an almost fateful fascination upon one side of the young boy's consciousness.

It must not be assumed, however, that Jonas Lie as a boy was a prodigy of brooding introspection, concerned alone during his early boyhood in the Far North with moody tales of Arctic nixies and sea-bogies which were supposed to haunt the coastal regions of the North with long, blood-curdling howls and wild, heart-rending cries. It was perhaps merely the fantastic which chiefly interested him as a boy in these stories, though later in life he became profoundly conscious of the sinister supernaturalism of it all. In any case, he seems never to have permitted such material to occupy his boyhood consciousness to the exclusion of more normal, healthy boyish pursuits. The fact is that in most regards Jonas was a quite normal child. As a school-boy he was apparently the traditional young barbarian, truant when he could be, and apt to neglect his studies, though intelligent enough in those things that really interested him. Delightfully fresh are Lie's recollections of these school-days in the Far North. Here is a specimen—

I can still feel how she [the maidservant in the Lie family] pulled us, cowering and reluctant, out of our warm beds, where we lay snug, like birds in their nests, between the reindeer skin and the sheepskin covering. I remember how I stood asleep and tottering on the floor, until I got a shower of cold water from the bathing-sponge over my back and became wide awake. Then to jump into

our clothes! And now for the lessons! It was a problem how to
get a peep at them during the scant quarter hour, while the breakfast was being devoured down in the dining-room with mother,
who sat and poured out tea before the big astral lamp, while darkness and snowdrift lay black upon the window-panes. Then up
and away! . . .

A bit later, in the schoolroom—

There I sat and perspired in the sultry heat of the stove, and
with a studiously unconcerned face watched with strained anxiety
every expression and gesture of the teacher. Was he in good
humor today? Would that I might escape reciting! He began at
the top. . . . That was a perfect millstone lifted from my breast,
though, as yet, nothing could be sure. Now for a surreptitious
peep at the end of the lesson.

The characteristic school-boy waywardness reflected in these
paragraphs did not seem to present any serious problem to his
family in those early Nordland days. This trait of character
became more disturbing to the boy's parents, however, upon its
continued manifestation, even intensification, during his youthful teens, when, on the family's return to more southerly regions
of Norway, Jonas was to prepare himself to enter one of the
learned professions.

The father, by this time a prominent judicial official, naturally wanted the boy to enter one of the learned professions.
Books, however, seemed to be most distasteful to the young
Jonas; and the learned professions were to be approached only
through books. The boy himself (like Jørgen in Lie's novel
The Family at Gilje) wanted to be a gunsmith, among other
things. The father finally compromised between the learned professions and the sphere of a craftsman by sending Jonas to the
naval academy at Fredriksværn, for the boy was fascinated
by the sea. At Fredriksværn he plugged along not too successfully for a year, upon which he was dismissed, chiefly, we are
told, because his extreme near-sightedness disqualified him from
a future as a naval officer. The only possibility left for Jonas,
unless he was to disappoint his family by sinking beneath his
class, was to prepare for entrance to the University as the key
to one of the learned professions—which of them it was not

decided for the time being. At the cathedral school in Bergen and at Heltberg's famous "student factory" in Christiania, he managed to encompass sufficient learning in the humanities to pass successfully the University entrance examinations. At both Bergen and Christiania he lived normally enough among his school-fellows, although he did strike them as "a bit queer," especially because of his reputation as a brilliant school-boy raconteur, a fascinating teller-of-tall-tales, in which the line of demarcation between fact and fiction was not always scrupulously regarded. So fascinating were these tales to his youthful contemporaries, that he was gleefully encouraged by his school-mates to develop his stories with ever increasing imaginative additions.

More worthily motivated, however, than this general school-boy approbation of Lie's narrative talents was the genuine, understanding encouragement that the young Lie received during these years at the hands of Bjørnstjerne Bjørnson, whom Jonas found enrolled at Heltberg's together with the young Henrik Ibsen and a number of other young Norwegians of definite literary promise. Bjørnson—in these years a handsome, strapping youth, bursting with the promise of genius—took a deep interest in his awkward, near-sighted school-mate, the young Lie; and he seems to have been largely responsible for the saner, more realistic, less fantastic tone that came into Lie's life during his university years. Generously frank is Lie's own admission on this point in a letter to Bjørnson many years later—

I was going about there in Christiania as a young student, undeveloped, dim, and unclear—a kind of poetic visionary, a Nordland twilight nature—which after a fashion espied what was abroad in the age, but indistinctly in the dusk, as through a water telescope —when I met a young, clear, full-born force, pregnant with the nation's new day, the blue steel-flash of determination in his eyes and the happily found national form—pugnacious to the very point of his pen. I gazed and stared, fascinated, and took this new thing aboard along the whole gun-wale. Here, I felt, were definite forms, no mere dusk and fantastic haze—something to fashion into poetry. . . . From the first hour you knew how to look straight into this strange twilight of mine, and you espied flashes of the aurora there when no one else did, like the true and faithful friend you are. You helped and guided and found grains of gold, where others saw mostly nonsense, and perhaps half a screw loose. While I was straying in search of the spiritual tinsel, with which the *esprits forts* of the age were glittering, you taught me, and impressed upon me, again and again, that I had to seek in myself for whatever I might possess of sentiment and simplicity—and that it was out of this I would have to build my fiction.

This realistic direction which Bjørnson gave to the young Lie's energies was not, however, to find immediate effect in literary activity; for Lie first sought the practice of law rather than the writing of fiction as the primary outlet for his vigorous youthful energies.

His university training thus came to be directed into the field of law, though for a very short time he thought of specializing in theology; and by 1858 he had taken his degree and entered the legal profession, at first as a copyist in a government bureau in Christiania. Two years later a chance came to establish himself as a practising attorney at Kongsvinger, a "boom town" at this time near the Swedish border north and east of Christiania. Lie rose rapidly to a position of eminence in this flourishing little town, so that by the middle of the '60's, when the boom in lumber came to Kongsvinger, he was known as a wealthy, successful young lawyer, who had influential connections in Christiania and had begun to dabble in politics. In 1868, however, the boom in lumber collapsed, and Lie found himself a ruined man. With characteristic honesty, he sold everything he had, turned over to his creditors all of the proceeds, and returned to the capital, determined to recoup his fortunes in some way and ultimately pay everything he still owed to his creditors. It was not, indeed, until years after the Kongsvinger crash that he was dissuaded by friends to cease sending the hopelessly small trickle of payments to his creditors that he was able to save from his modest royalties as an author.

During the Kongsvinger years Lie had not lost the interest in literature which had been aroused during his university years, though his time was so much occupied by the many business

and social duties of a successful young lawyer that only a few
occasional poems and a scattering of newspaper articles issued
from his pen during these years. Now, however, he decided to
turn to his pen for a living, and renounce law forever. The
struggle at first was very hard. He managed to attract some
attention as a keen observer of the European political scene in
a series of articles which appeared in a leading newspaper of
the capital; but journalism was an ill-paid profession, and Lie
and his family barely managed to keep the wolf from the door.
During these crucial years, however, there were two persons—
Thomasine Lie, the author's wife, and Bjørnstjerne Bjørnson,
his friend from university days—whose constant loyalty and
cheerful encouragement combined to keep up Lie's spirits.

Bjørnson, by this time a successful author and one of Norway's "coming men," was largely responsible for the acceptance
by Hegel of the manuscript of Lie's first story, *The Visionary*,
in 1870; and it was the immediate popular success of this book
that led to Lie's becoming the recipient of a government stipend
for the purpose of study and travel in Nordland with a view
toward gathering more literary material from these Arctic
regions of Norway. The friendship between Bjørnson and Lie,
which continued with unabated intimacy for years, is one of
those pleasant chapters in the personal side of Norwegian literature which is seldom more than mentioned in the pages of
formal literary history. The many letters which passed back
and forth between these two men bear witness to the rich
generosity with which each of them recognized the genius of
the other; and yet these letters were much more than the exchange of mere literary felicitations. They contain a very frank
critical vein, particularly on the part of Lie, who felt keenly
that Bjørnson's activity in the practical politics of Norway
in the '70's and the '80's was a very unfortunate matter. Time
and again in his letters to Bjørnson in the '70's he pleads with
his friend to devote his energies exclusively to literature and to
eschew "the market-place of politics" as unworthy of the literary
genius of Bjørnson. It may well be that Lie's candor in his
reaction against some of Bjørnson's more extreme political
activities in the early '80's had something to do with the break

between the two friends that came later, though this would be difficult to demonstrate with any exactness. The actual break between the two friends did come, we know, as an immediate consequence of the diametrically opposed attitudes of Bjørnson and Lie toward the trial of Hans Jæger, one of their contemporaries who, by publishing a flagrantly decadent novel entitled *Fra Kristiania-Bohêmen* ("From the Christiania Bohême") in 1885, precipitated an *affaire scandaleuse* which had repercussions of an even more violent character in the Norwegian capital of the '80's than did the trial of Oscar Wilde under somewhat similar circumstances in London about a decade later. It was Lie's liberal attitude toward Jæger's book that deeply offended Bjørnson and was the occasion for the break in friendship between the two men. Not until the last year of Lie's life was the old friendship reestablished.

Thomasine Lie was the perfect wife, as Bjørnson was the valued friend, through all of Jonas Lie's early struggles as an author. In fact all down through her husband's literary career she was of invaluable assistance to him. She faced cheerfully the trying days of near poverty in Christiania which followed upon the Kongsvinger crash; and as the years passed, and Lie devoted himself with growing intensity to his art, she became quite indispensable to her husband. It can be said, I think, that seldom in the history of literary genius has a man been as well mated as was Jonas Lie. Thomasine was much more than a mere "inspiration" to him: she was an excellent manager in days when the household was existing on the most precarious economic basis; she saw to it that her husband enjoyed the most perfect of possible circumstances for work, by jealously guarding him against unnecessary interruptions when he was at work on a manuscript; and finally, and perhaps most important, she was her husband's most penetrating and intelligent critic. Thomasine's criticism of her husband's manuscripts, in fact, was of such importance to Lie that whenever any final copy was sent off to the publisher it amounted in a sense to a work of collaboration between husband and wife. "If I have written anything that is good," wrote Lie on one occasion, and probably with little exaggeration, "then my wife deserves as much credit for it as myself. . . . Without her nothing would have come of it except nonsense."

No less a person than Henrik Ibsen bears witness to Fru Thomasine's ability to create a domestic atmosphere of perfect rest and quiet undisturbed by the insistent babble of undesired "callers." In the summer of 1881 both he and the Lies happened to have settled down in the beautiful Bavarian mountain village of Berchtesgaden, the dramatist at the Hotel Salzburgerhof and the novelist with his family in somewhat more private apartments nearby. Ibsen was in the habit of visiting with the Lies quite frequently in the evenings; and though he was not seldom on these occasions the stiff, unyielding Ibsen whom we know from tradition in the resounding discussions into which the two authors entered as the evening hours drifted by, he could on occasion become quite mellow under the peaceful influence of the household over which Thomasine reigned—so much so on one occasion, at least, that he felt called upon, with a rare show of gallantry, to compliment Thomasine on her skill at insuring her husband the quiet necessary for serious creative work. Ibsen's words are recorded by Erik Lie in his *Erindringer fra ett Dikterhjem* ("Reminiscences from an Author's Home," 1928).

Ibsen finished his glass and began to brew a new toddy.

"Here it is so good and peaceful, Fru Lie," he burst out suddenly. "How do you manage to insure quiet for your husband to work? At home in Munich I have had to transform my residence into a fortress in order to defend myself against the attack of strangers. And I have had to transform myself into a thorn-bush, which must attack and defend itself at all points. I cannot even sit in peace and read my newspapers. The door-bell rings incessantly, and it is either one of my 'dear countrymen,' who insists upon greeting me, or a journalist or a critic. The critics are the worst, for they always have found or divined in my work mysterious profundities which I for my part have never had in my head. What should I answer? I decide to remain cryptic, and this they always find marvelously interesting. Yes, it is a comedy!"

Ibsen laughed and enjoyed the thought.

It was late at night, and Ibsen's face beamed with kindliness. There were many toddies that were imbibed, and then when my mother came in with some tidbits and I was sent up to Gasthaus Neuhaus to fetch fresh ale, he was in his element. . . .

Poor papa Ibsen!—even he deserved a better fate at the hands of insistent journalists and critics . . . happy for him, in contrast, were the hours of undisturbed domestic *Gemütlichkeit* which he found in the Lie ménage in Berchtesgaden those long, peaceful summer evenings in the early 1880's.

II

Two years after the summer from which this Berchtesgaden anecdote dates, Jonas Lie was to publish his most important novel, *The Family at Gilje.* The thirteen years which elapsed between the appearance of the great Gilje novel and the publication of Lie's first tale, *The Visionary,* in 1870, were years of strenuous creative application on Lie's part. His production in the field of fiction during these years was almost as regular as was that of Ibsen in the drama—seven full-length novels coming from his pen in the bit more than a decade before the appearance of *The Family at Gilje.* He also tried his hand at the drama, but hardly with encouraging results.

His novels, though built invariably with a solid, evenly artistic workmanship, were not always equally successful with critics and public. *The Visionary,* Lie's earliest effort at fiction, was an unqualified popular success with the general Norwegian public, chiefly perhaps because of the sentimentally melancholy love story which provides a kind of structural unity to the otherwise rather diverse mass of Nordland reminiscence and folklore which is more apt to impress the discerning reader. Norwegian critics hailed *The Visionary* as a début work which revealed great promise despite its idealizing sentimentalities and its crudely contrived narrative pattern. They found Lie's description of the Far North unmatched in Norwegian literature up to this time, and they were deeply impressed by the inclusion of bits of Nordland legend and superstition in this first novel. The public and critical acclaim of *The Visionary* brought to Lie government recognition in the form of a stipend to be used for travel in Nordland, in order that he might gather materials for more tales from the Far North.

Lie did not, however, upon his return from Nordland continue to develop the rich vein of Arctic legend and superstition that he had worked so successfully in certain parts of *The Visionary*. Some of his novels that follow in the next couple of decades have touches of this material, but only casually and by the way. Not until 1891, in the first volume of *Trolls,* did Lie return to these fascinatingly primitive northern materials. Meantime he goes another way, choosing his subjects almost exclusively from contemporary life or from a period only a generation or two earlier than his own day.

Lie's second novel, *Tremasteren "Fremtiden"* ("The Barque 'Future' "), published in 1872, shortly after his return from Nordland, was an improvement on *The Visionary* in some respects, particularly in that it was more robust in tone, avoiding most of the mere sentimentalities of Lie's first novel. And yet *The Barque "Future"* is certainly not a great novel: its treatment of character is superficial and uncertain, and the story itself is based upon a wire-drawn plot that reminds one too much of the traditional mystery story. Before the publication of *The Barque "Future,"* however, Lie had become the recipient of another stipend from the government—this second stipend permitting residence abroad. He removed immediately with his family to Rome, where he remained for three years, working very hard on a new novel, *Lodsen og hans Hustru* ("The Pilot and His Wife"), which came out in 1874. This novel seemed to justify in most regards the faith which public and critics alike had shown in his genius after the early literary promise suggested by *The Visionary*.

In *The Pilot and His Wife* Lie combined a story of domestic life with the romance of the sea, the former element predominating, the latter being used largely as effective background. In careful and penetrating analysis of character this novel is a great advance over Lie's previous stories. He had learned by his earlier partial artistic failures to be more selective in his technique, to centre his attention upon character rather than upon background, and to create freely rather than lose himself in the mere photographic reproduction of outward detail. "The trip

to Nordland," he writes to Bjørnson in the midst of his work
on the manuscript of *The Pilot and His Wife*, "was not of
much benefit because it drowned me in a multitude of details
and of already-told stories, all of which I afterward discarded
because they only burdened my free creation. I have now
learned this (perhaps somewhat dearly): that I myself must
create if the material is to form itself naturally; for all of these
'curious' realities are not at all poetically natural and can be
jotted down by any travelling newspaper reporter."

Despite this growth of a sound self-critical intelligence in
Lie, and its happy result in *The Pilot and His Wife*, the two
novels which followed from Lie's pen in the late '70's—*Thomas
Ross* (1878) and *Adam Schrader* (1879)—reveal a tentative
falling off in quality. Somehow they do not seem to move and
live as had his earlier novels on sailor folk and the sea, chiefly
perhaps because Lie was trying a bit too hard in an entirely new
manner and subject matter—soberly realistic fictional treatment
of a comparatively diversified urban life. Lie himself believed,
however, that these two novels were better than his critics and
the public were prepared to admit. He was, in fact, rather irritated at the insistence of his critics that he return to stories of
sea-faring life. "The critics would have me at sea," he wrote in
1881 to a friend. "What they will do with me when I do not
obey orders I do not know." That he was willing to capitulate
partly to his critics, however, is evidenced by the fact that he
did return temporarily "to the sea" in the early '80's in two
vividly conceived sea tales, *Rutland*, appearing in 1880, and
two years later the greatest of his sea novels *Gaa paa!* ("Go
Ahead!"). Something of the intensity with which Lie threw
himself into the creation of *Go Ahead!*—a creative intensity
which largely accounts for its success—is suggested in the
closing paragraph of a letter to Bjørnson dated the 18th of
September 1881. "I am now engaged with a sea story," he
writes, "and I bore down into my material like a mole, or rather
a porpoise—at times I lie all night as in a heavy sea—if only I
do not break up also!"

III

Lie had finished with the sea, however, in the virile characterization and the vividly gripping scenes of *Go Ahead!* Effective
as he had become at writing this kind of tale, he felt that it had
certain inherent limitations as a type of fiction and that his own
future development as a novelist depended upon his "return to
land." With sound artistic instinct he sensed the dangers of a
cheaply popular, largely exotic "Romanticism" so potential in
stories of the sea. Besides—on the positive side of his critical
thinking—he was becoming during these years increasingly
conscious of the necessity of fundamentally realistic material
as the foundation of any enduring modern art. "The times
refuse, as you know, my dear Lady"—he writes in a letter from
the fall of 1881—"to be stirred by the Romantic,—on the
respectable grounds that it wishes to be stirred *more deeply*."
The italics are Lie's.

The statement is to be found, it is significant to note, in a
long letter concerned chiefly with the first germinating ideas
which were soon to become the story contained in *The Family
at Gilje*. Later letters reveal how seriously Lie worked on the
manuscript for this novel, especially in seeking first-hand knowledge of characteristic background for his story and in defining
clearly to himself the central problem of the novel. Two years
after the first reference to the novel in his letters, the great
Gilje story was given to the public; and in this novel it is clear
that Lie had finally found the type of story best suited to his
genius. In it he escapes entirely from the rather broad, loose
canvases of most of his early work—both from the exotic
romanticism of his sea tales and from the awkwardly uncertain
realism of the novels dealing with contemporary urban life. In
his new novel Lie limits himself rigidly in both plot and scene.
The story is concerned almost exclusively with the narrow circumstances and the humdrum existence of Norwegian provincial officialdom in the '40's of the nineteenth century. The scene
is as restricted as is the narrative groundwork of the story.
Gilje is neither a small town nor a sprawling provincial village;
it is but the isolated official residence, located "nine days by

sleigh from Christiania," of a Norwegian army officer of the mid-nineteenth century. No subject would seem to hold less promise for an interesting tale: even an American Main Street might seem to offer the romance of diversity by comparison. And yet Lie makes Gilje *live*—vividly, intimately, from the first page to the last. Out of the unpromising daily commonplaces of an isolated provincial official's residence of the '40's, Lie manages somehow to spin an intimate domestic tale which is rapid in its movement, penetrating in its character portrayal, rich in a warmly scintillating humor, and instinct with a profoundly real human problem. Lie had finally found in *The Family at Gilje* a genre peculiarly fitted to his genius. He came to find with the years that it is with interiors that he succeeds best—intimately realistic fictional studies in the life of the home, studies which may be said to have a certain broad kinship to Jane Austen's novels from the early nineteenth century in England. Lie's strength as a novelist lies in depth of imaginative insight rather than in bold breadth of coloring. His real triumphs (with the single exception of *Trolls*) occur in those novels in which he concentrates on character, using a carefully selected detail realism of scene merely to invest his characters with a sense of immediate reality. In *The Family at Gilje,* his first effort in this rigidly limited type of fiction, we find his greatest triumph as a novelist, though in *The Commodore's Daughters* (1886) he is almost equally successful.

Lie manages to attain a vivid unity of effect in *The Family at Gilje* by limiting all the directly narrated action of the story to the Gilje farm or to the immediately contiguous countryside. We do not, however, feel particularly oppressed by such a rigid limitation of scene, because Lie constantly keeps us aware of a larger world outside by various skillfully handled indirect methods of narration. We catch numerous glimpses of Christiania life, and even of a larger world than this at times, through vivid letters from the capital—chiefly those of Inger-Johanna, the eldest daughter of the Gilje family and the character about whom the action of the story in one sense centres. It is a part also of Lie's deft narrative technique in this novel that the larger outer world is constantly viewed through Gilje eyes; for Inger-

Johanna, though momentarily impressed by the *beaux monde* into which she is suddenly thrown in Christiania, never quite succumbs to this world—she sees fundamentally with Gilje eyes in the end, and to Gilje she therefore ultimately returns.

Vivid as is the reader's impression of the Gilje farm and the surrounding countryside as he moves through the pages of *The Family at Gilje,* it is not easy to define precisely Lie's general method in attaining this effect. The vaguely descriptive phrase, "these uncompromising specimens of modern realism," in Boyesen's general description of Lie's method as a novelist, gets one nowhere; in fact, insofar as the phrase suggests anything at all definite, it is misleading. Certainly Lie's technique is not to be identified with naturalism, as the words "uncompromising realism" might suggest. Though Lie did in certain respects admire Zola, the great master of naturalism on the Continent, he was never willing to accept the basic doctrine of naturalism: that literature was merely an objective photograph of actual life. We have already seen how in the earliest years of Lie's literary career he reacted scornfully against the notion that a mere photographic reproduction of reality is the essence of literary art. Such a "literary art," he had insisted, could be produced by "any travelling newspaper reporter." Even stronger is Lie's later reaction against a rigidly documentary naturalism. Very revealing in this connection is a letter written in 1886 to Arne Garborg, in which Lie protests strongly against Garborg's statement that he only wished he could swear to the *actual truth* of every detail in his severely naturalistic novel *Mannfolk* ("Men," 1886)—

. . . You say that you wish that you could swear to the actual truth of every detail in your story;—but the important thing is that one should write so that *the reader* is ready to vouch that it is real;—what the devil does it matter if the author stands and swears on a fragment of accidental reality; that which is essential is to force the spirit in the reader's breast to testify that *this is reality*;—to write and suggest as you, for example, have with regard to Helene. Whether any such person as Helene has ever actually lived or not is of no consequence if we have had the feeling, the inner assurance, that there are a thousand such. . . .

The distinction Lie makes here between that which *has happened* and that which *the reader would readily admit "is real"* is fundamental in any understanding of the particular quality of Lie's own realism.

Lie is essentially an impressionist in his realistic technique, i.e. he insists upon using the materials of actual life as the basis of his novels; but he is equally insistent that the author, instead of being tied down to any particular body of "accidental reality," should be free to select those aspects of reality which most adequately fulfill the demands of his own creative insight in any given case. Such an impressionistic realism is very closely related to that form of realism defined by Guy de Maupassant in the famous Preface to his *Pierre et Jean*: "Each of us makes for himself an illusion of the world—an illusion poetic, sentimental, joyous, melancholy, degraded or gloomy, according to his own nature. And the writer has no other mission than to reproduce faithfully this illusion with all the methods of art at his disposal." Jonas Lie, as Guy de Maupassant, belongs essentially among those artists, in painting and in literature, who in the late nineteenth century called themselves "impressionists"—artists who did not wish to deny the aesthetic validity of actuality (as the symbolists tended to do), but wished to subject the materials of actuality to the selective processes of individual artistic creation.

The principle of selection is central in the impressionist's art. His aim is not to present an accidental, largely miscellaneous "cross section of life"; it is rather to present reality in such a way as his own individual creative insight sees life at any given point. The impressionist eschews the chaotic disorganization inherent in naturalism as an art form; he insists, in fact, that naturalism in the last analysis is not an art form at all. Instead of *copying* life in all of its casual disorganization, the impressionistic realist seeks to reproduce *his impression* of life in some one of its many actual and conceivable forms. And inasmuch as an impression has in its essence a certain *unity* that is usually lacking in the miscellaneous detail of any outward, purely objective reality, the picture of life that the impressionist gives to us is apt to have an essential unity often lacking in a more purely naturalistic art. In order to effect such a unity in his art form, the impressionist must be highly selective in his inclusion of detail; or, conversely, he must be rigidly severe in his exclusion of all unnecessary detail—detail that might disturb the general unity of effect sought in his particular work of art. The true impressionist in fiction handles all the detail of his art—scene, episode, characterization, and even "the problem," if there is one—with an absolute reverence for the central artistic principle of selection. *The Family at Gilje* is perhaps the most remarkable example in Norwegian literature of scrupulous fidelity to this principle.

Lie's novel, we have said, limits its scene rigidly to the isolated Gilje residence of Captain Jæger and to the immediately adjacent countryside. It is therefore with a rural scene in the strictest sense of the term that we have to deal. With the subtle instinct of the born impressionist, Lie sees the necessity in a domestic tale such as *The Family at Gilje* of concentrating primarily upon the interior of the Jæger home. Yet he does not neglect the possibility of increasing the effectiveness of his realism by including on occasion snatches of the less confined phases of the rural scene: the farm itself, its busy barnyard, its broad stretches of field and meadow; and beyond these the rich sweep of natural landscape stretching on to the point where fjeld meets sky in the magnificent irregularities of mountain horizon to be seen from the Gilje lands.

The reader feels that he knows every physical detail of the Jæger household—all that this home presents to the eye, the ear, the nose, and to the tactual and gustatory sensations. And yet in Lie's art there is almost an irreducible minimum of mere "description"—such long inventories of household detail as would inevitably be indulged in under similar circumstances by a Balzac or a Zola. Lie never pauses merely "to describe"; his primary concern is at every point his story, and descriptive detail is offered, in consequence, only in deft, vivid bits, in striking fragments—by the way as it were. A few short passages, taken almost at random, should suffice to illustrate Lie's method. Note, for example, how in the following passage bits of domestic interior are deftly introduced between phases of vivid narration dealing immediately with the progress of a card game between Captain Jæger and two guests, former army comrades who are on a visit to Gilje—

Soon the three gentlemen sat comfortably at their cards, each one smoking his pipe and with a glass of hot arrack punch by his side. Two moulded tallow candles in tall brass candlesticks stood on the card-table and two on the folding-table; they illuminated just enough so that you could see the almanac, which hung down by a piece of twine from a nail under the looking-glass, and a part of the lady's tall form and countenance, while she sat knitting in her frilled cap. In the darkness of the room the chairs farthest off by the stove could hardly be distinguished from the kitchen door— from which now and then came the hissing of the roasting meat.

"Three tricks, as true as I live—three tricks, and by those cards!" exclaimed Captain Rønnow, eager in the game. . . .

Less direct, and perhaps therefore even more essentially impressionistic, is the unforgettable impression of this scene that the reader enjoys as he stands a bit later with the curious, shivering children in "the great, cold, dark hall" above and catches up broken fragments of the scene below—

. . . There they all three stood, leaning over the balustrade, and gazing down on the fur coats and mufflers, which hung on the timber wall, and on the whip and the two sabre sheaths and the case of bottles, which were dimly lighted by the stable lantern on the hall table.

They smelt the odor of the roast as it came up, warm and appetizing, and saw when the guests, each with his punch-glass in his hand and with flickering candle, went across the hall into the large room. They heard the folding-table moved out and set, and later caught the sound of the clinking glasses, laughter, and loud voices.

Every sound from below was given a meaning, every fragment of speech was converted into a romance for their thirsty fancy.

They stood there in the cold till their teeth chattered and their limbs shook against the wood-work, so that they were obliged to get into bed again to thaw out.

They heard how the chairs made a noise when the guests arose from the table, and they went out in the hall again, Thinka and Inger-Johanna,—Thea was asleep. It helped a little when they put their feet upon the lowest rail of the balustrade, or hung over it with their legs bent double under them.

Thinka held out because Inger-Johanna held out; but finally she was compelled to give up, she could not feel her legs any more. And now Inger-Johanna alone hung down over the balustrade.

A sort of close odor of punch and tobacco smoke frozen together rose up through the stairs in the cold, and every time the door was opened and showed the heavy, smoky, blue gleam of light in the great room, she could hear officers' names, fragments of laughter, of violent positive assertions, with profane imprecations by all possible and impossible powers of the heavens above and the earth beneath, and between them her father's gay voice,—all chopped off in mince-meat every time the door was shut.

It is the ear and the nose, rather than the eye, which operate to register our impression of scene here; and yet how vividly do we seem to "see" the strangely confused and chaotic scene below in "the great-room." Equally deft, though handled differently, is Lie's impressionism in his treatment of the larger background of his story, the immediate phenomena of the farmyard and the vaguely sensed regions beyond on a typical day in midsummer—

It was midsummer. The mountain region was hazy in the heat; all the distance was as if enveloped in smoke. The girls on the farm went about barefooted, in waists and short petticoats. It was a scorching heat, so that the pitch ran in sticky white lines down from the fat knots in the timber of the newly built pigsty, where Marit was giving swill to the hogs. Some sand-scoured wooden milk-pans stood on edge by the well, drying, while one or two sparrows and wagtails hopped about or perched nodding on the well-curb, and the blows of the axe resounded from the wood-shed in the quiet of the afternoon. Pasop lay panting in the shade behind the outer door, which stood open.

The Captain had finished his afternoon nap, and stood by the field looking at Great-Ola and the horses ploughing up an old grassland which was to be laid down again.

In each of these passages we catch vivid, living glimpses of the Gilje scene. None of them is extended in its enumeration of detail, and each of them fits incidentally—as casually as such material usually does in our actual experience of life—into the rapid onward movement of episode and story.

How differently Zola would have treated the barnyard scene should be apparent to anyone who has braved the detailed and pugnacious realism of *La Terre*. Still, it must be noted, Lie does not for a moment evade the essential realistic detail of his scene: he does not hesitate to mention the pigsty and the swilling hogs, though he does not see it as the end of a realistic art to wallow at inordinate length in a pigsty simply because his domestic tale had led him to the Norwegian countryside. Lie, it must be emphasized, could never tolerate that false fastidiousness which recoils from calling a thing by its real name. His attitude toward over-delicacy in these matters is given incidental expression by Inger-Johanna, when she reacts in a letter to her parents against the hyper-refinements of the urban upper classes as reflected in the conversational indirections of the affected *beaux monde* of the capital: "I really begin to suspect that several of our gentlemen have never seen a live pig, or a duck, or a colt (which is the prettiest thing I know). They become so stupid as soon as I merely name something from the country; it might be understood if I said it in French—*un canard, un cheval, un cochon, une vache.*"

The point is pushed home with even broader implications in the paragraph which follows in the same letter: "Student Grip contends that of those who have been born in the city not one in ten has ever seen a cow milked. He also provokes aunt by saying that everything which happens in French is so much finer, and thinks that we like to read and cry over two lovers who jump into the water from *Pont Neuf*; but only let the same thing happen here at home, from Vaterland's bridge, then it is vulgar. . . ."

It is by a subtle accumulation of incidental bits of realistic detail rather than by labored composition of long descriptive passages that Lie makes us so vividly conscious of the scene in *The Family at Gilje*. Usually he gives to such incidental bits of realistic detail only a short paragraph, sometimes even less— a sentence, a telling phrase, even a single provocative word— before he again plunges into the rapid onward movement of the story itself.

In his handling of episode he is equally selective in his use of detail, similarly impressionistic in his general method. Despite the dull daily commonplaces often associated with such rural isolation as one comes upon in *The Family at Gilje*, Lie manages to select and develop his episodes in such a way as to gain the impression of a constantly moving, vividly rapid action. The discriminating reader is struck, first of all, by the care which Lie has exercised in choosing episodes central to the purposes of his story. From the opening episode, in which we are introduced to nearly all of the central elements in the story which is to follow, down to the final episode, which sketches with deft, telling strokes the final tragedy of Student Grip and the high resolve of Inger-Johanna, the story moves rapidly, with no let-down of interest on the part of the reader. Each episode is necessary to the conduct of the story as a whole; no episode is irrelevant.

It is in the development of each episode within itself, however, that Lie's impressionistic technique attains its most characteristic quality—a certain vivid, full-bodied, tensely animated movement. The opening episode of the novel, for example, is a masterpiece of the story teller's art. The narrative movement of the episode is swift—it never flags; and yet Lie manages to pack into the episode very much more than merely the beginning of a purely narrative thread which he proposes to unravel as the materials of the Gilje story. In it we are introduced intimately to the Gilje scene. In it nearly all of the major characters in the novel are introduced, and definitely characterized— Captain Jæger, full-blooded, violent, bellicose of exterior, yet genial and kindly in his own way withal. . . . Ma, with "her meagre yellowish face," her "somewhat thoughtful, anxious expression," her many cares and her many plans. . . . Captain Rønnow, with his immaculately vain exterior and his man-of-the-world taste for feminine beauty. . . . And so on. In this episode also the core of the Gilje "problem"—the future of the children, so precarious because of the family's straitened financial circumstances—is brought into due prominence by means of deft narrative devices.

Other episodes in the novel are handled with equal skill, perhaps none more beautifully impressionistic in its manner than the one which relates the story of Captain Jæger's death. It must be quoted entire—

The autumn was already far advanced. The snow had come and gone twice, and had now been swept off by the wind from the slippery, hard-frozen road.

The slopes and mountains were white, with red and yellow tones of the frost-touched leaves of the leafy forest still showing in many places, and the lake down below was shining coldly blue, ready to freeze over.

There was a thundering over the country road hard with frost, so it waked the echoes in the quiet October day; one crow was standing, and another started up from the hedge-post at the sound.

It was the wheels of a cariole, and in it was sitting, with a long whip hanging down behind his back, in cloak and large overshoes, the Captain of Gilje.

He had been ten miles down and had his yearly settlement with Bardon Kleven.

It is true, the bailiff had not been willing to let him go out of the house without compelling him to taste a little brandy in a small tumbler, with a little ale in addition, and a little something to eat. But he had been prudent. It was almost the only trip he had made away from home for a long time, except his visit to the sheriff.

Old Svarten ran over the long, flat stretches in the heavy, strong trot to which he was accustomed; the road showed that he was sharp shod with full caulks. He knew that he was not to stop till he had done the three miles to the foot of the steep ascent up the Gilje hills.

It was probably because he was newly shod, and the lumps of mud were so large and were frozen hard; but now he stumbled.

It was the first time it had happened. Perhaps he felt it himself, for he kept on at a brisker trot—but then slackened up by degrees. He felt that the reins were loose and slack; their folds fell longer and longer down over his shoulders.

The whip-lash hung down as before over the Captain's back, only still more slantingly.

He had begun to feel such cold shivers, just as if he had suddenly got cold all over—and now he had become so sleepy—had such a longing for a nap.

He saw the reins, the ears, and the hanging mane over the neck of Svarten nodding up and down before him, and the ground beneath him flying away—

It was just as if a crow flew up and made it dark right over his face; but he could not get his arm up to catch it—so let it be.

And there stood the grain-poles, like crooked old witches, crouched down—they wanted to avenge themselves—with straw forelocks they resisted him more and more like goblins and would forbid him to get his arms up to take the reins and drive to Gilje. They were swarming between heaven and earth, as it were, swimming, dancing—were bright and dark. Then there was something like a shout or a crash from somewhere. There was Inger-Johanna coming—

Svarten had got the reins quite down over his forelegs: a little more and he would be stepping on them.

From the gentle trot, into which he had at last fallen, he began to walk.

Then he turned his head round—and remained standing in the middle of the road.

The whip-lash hung down as before. The Captain sat there immovable with his head a little tipped back—

They were still on the level, and Svarten stood patiently looking toward the Gilje hill, which lay a bit farther on, until he turned his head round again two or three times and looked into the cariole.

Now he began to paw on the ground with one forefoot, harder and harder—so that the lumps flew about.

Then he neighed.

A good hour later, in the twilight, there was a conversation in an undertone out in the yard, and the sound of cariole wheels which moved slowly.

Great-Ola was called down to the gate by the man down yonder at the Sørgaard; he had met the cariole with the Captain down in the road.

"What is it?" Ma's voice was heard to say through the darkness from the porch.

Thus the curtain is quietly drawn upon the life-span of the Captain at Gilje. An old man in a quaint old cariole . . . his favorite horse drawing him rapidly across the hills toward Gilje farm . . . a sudden blurred sensation, "and now he had become sleepy—had such a longing for a nap. . . ." And then the end, a strong life quickly snuffed out . . . an end witnessed directly by no one—not even Old Svarten, who only felt, dumbly, that it was somewhat strange that the reins had slackened across his shoulders. Quiet in tone, simply laconic in phrasing, serenely dignified in every detail is this death scene. Even more appropriately laconic is the description of the Captain's funeral—

At the entrance of the churchyard, a week later, Old Svarten and Young Svarten stood before an empty sleigh.

A salute before and after the lowering into the ground informed the parish that here lay Captain Peter Wennechen Jæger.

Though Lie attains his illusion of reality in the development of episode largely by means of a highly selective impressionistic technique, the whole secret of his success in the handling of episode is not to be found in a mere selection of effective narrative detail. A careful examination of his method will reveal that he skillfully combines with his technique of selective detail at least two more particular technical devices: first, he exercises great care in the way in which he opens his episodes; and secondly, he tends to use throughout his development of any particular episode the most strongly *active* kinds of words—especially verbs. And in addition to these two particular techniques, he employs quite frequently a delicately genial play of humor, which, among other effects tends to give further animation and sense of movement to Lie's handling of narrative episode.

Lie usually opens his episode in the midst of an action, oftentimes with a precipitate, almost explosive force, which goes far to insure the reader's rapt attention throughout the development of the episode that is to follow. Such a method lends itself with unique aptness, of course, to depicting the precipitate, outwardly bellicose manner of Captain Jæger. One of the typical episodes in *The Family at Gilje* bursts in upon the reader in almost cyclonic fashion—

There was a roaring in the stove on one of the following forenoons while the Captain sat in his office chair, and wrote so that his quill pen sputtered.

Only less forceful in manner, and yet potentially even more charged with possibilities of action, are the paragraphs which serve to introduce another episode—

The Captain was in a dreadful humor; the doors were banging the whole forenoon.

At dinner time there was a sultry breathing spell, during which Jørgen and Thea sat with their eyes on their plates, extremely cautious not to give any occasion for an explosion.

The fruit of Jørgen's best exertions to keep himself unnoticed was nevertheless as usual, less happy. During the soup he accidentally made a loud noise in eating with his spoon which led to a thundering, "Don't slobber like a hog, boy."

After dinner the Captain all at once felt the necessity of completing certain computations on a chart and surveying matter that had been left since last autumn.

And now it was not advisable to come too near the office! He had an almost Indian quickness of hearing for the least noise, and was absolutely wild when he was disturbed.

It became quiet, a dead calm over the whole house. The spinning-wheel alone could be heard humming in the sitting-room, and they went gently through the doors below, in genuine terror when in spite of all they creaked or someone happened to let the trap-door into the cellar fall or make the porch door rattle.

How could that foolish Torbjørg hit upon scouring the stairs now? When she hurriedly retreated with her sand pail, her open mouth and staring eyes showed plainly that she did not comprehend the peculiar inward connection between her scouring and the Captain who was sitting safely up there in his office; it was enough that he would fall at once like a tempest down from the upper story.

It should be noted, incidentally, that these paragraphs are surcharged with the characteristically genial humor of Lie and that they illustrate Lie's use of strenuous verb forms for purposes of heightening the effect of the action.

Though Lie, unlike his French contemporaries Flaubert and Guy de Maupassant, never developed in theory a carefully defined doctrine of *le mot juste*, in practice he seems to have taken almost the same care with his word choice as did these two representatives of a precisely disciplined French realism. Lie's style is marked by a marvelous economy of words; every word strikes home. Particularly does Lie's style suggest that he sensed the unique value of the verb as a means toward a forceful, animated immediacy of expression. Everywhere in the pages of *The Family at Gilje* does one come upon examples of the effective use of the verb.

"He *blew out* like a whale," we are told on one famous occasion when the good Captain was trying vainly to hide a sentimental embarrassment. On another disturbing occasion for the Captain—

He went quickly, so that his spurs rattled, and his sabre flapped under his coat, down to his horse without looking to the right or left or speaking to anyone. He pressed his shako more firmly down on his forehead before he got into the cariole.

Later, in a moment of triumph, when the Captain read to Ma the letter of proposal for Thinka's hand sent to the Captain by the widowed Sheriff—

He stood leaning against the desk, and went through its three pages, period by period, with great moderation, till he came to the point, then he hurled it out so that it buzzed in the air, and hugged Ma wildly.

But it is not alone in his treatment of the Captain that Lie shows a marked preference for the forceful verb or verbal constructions. Note this description of an auction room at a sale—

There sat Bardon in the crowded, steaming room, calling over and over again, with his well-known, strong, husky voice, threatening with the hammer, giving utterance to a joke, finally threatening for the last, last time, until with the law's blows he nailed the bid firmly forever down on top of the table. They made way for the Captain as he came.

Or this paragraph, boisterously active with all the growing, surging natural forces of early spring-time in the mountains—

Time flew with tearing haste towards St. John's Day. Spring was brewing in the air and over the lakes. The meadow stood moist and damp, hillock on hillock, like the luxuriant forelocks of horses. The swollen brooks sighed and roared with freshly shining banks. They boiled over, as it were, with the power of the same generating life and sap that made the buds burst in alder, willow, and birch almost audibly, and shows its nature in the bouncing, vigorous movements of the mountain boy, in his rapid speech, his lively shining eyes, and his elastic walk.

Besides verb forms strictly speaking, these passages lean heavily upon adverbs, and upon adjectives of a clearly verbal character. Nouns, and even more particularly pure adjectival forms, are of definitely secondary importance. Much of the sense of *movement* so peculiar to Lie's development of scene and episode is to be explained in terms of the prominence in Lie's style of verbs and other words deriving directly from verb forms. The original Norwegian is even more characterized by such forms than is the translation; in the Norwegian the sum total aliveness of stylistic effect is intensified by the flavor of racy colloquial turns of speech which defy the most careful art of the translator.

Skillful, however, as Lie is in his handling of every detail in the development of scene and episode in *The Family at Gilje*, it is perhaps in the revelation of character that his art is most completely satisfying in this novel. We have the evidence of Lie's letters to prove that he felt the careful and honest depiction of character to be the central artistic problem of the novelist. He wrote to Bjørnson as early as 1873 with reference to his own early tales: "I have included too much of nature and of peasant life and customs in order really to have the space in which to become absorbed in the *development* [the italics are Lie's] of my characters, with the exception of *The Visionary* and bits of *Fanfulla.*" This early recognition of a fundamental weakness in his early tales was to have its effect on Lie's later novels. After 1873 his novels reveal a growing preoccupation with character, until we find in *The Family at Gilje*, appearing ten years after the letter to Bjørnson was written, the most mature and satisfactory creative result of Lie's concentration upon character as the central artistic problem of modern fiction. In this novel the reader inevitably becomes engrossed in the author's central preoccupation with his characters—with the Captain, with Ma, with Inger-Johanna and the other Gilje children, with Student Grip, and with numerous less important figures. So engrossed, in fact, do we become in this living, very human world of characters that the larger implications of the novel, its moral significance as a vivid social document, are for the moment forced into the background of our consciousness. Only after we have completed our reading of the novel do we become conscious of the fact that the fortunes of these characters are really inextricably bound up with a very real human "problem" —a problem, indeed, which stretches far beyond the narrow confines of the isolated mountain residence at Gilje into the whole scheme of Norwegian social and political organization in the middle of the nineteenth century. The novel is really in the last analysis an indictment—nonetheless significant for being indirect—of Norway's system of provincial officialdom in the nineteenth century.

Very subtle is Lie's art here—an art which implies rather than obtrusively states this larger problem of a bureaucratic national organism which finds in Lie's novel its homely, immediate manifestation within the narrow domestic phenomena of Gilje life. So subtle was it, indeed, that Lie's contemporaries, delighted with the story as such, did not always see the implied "message" which the novel really contained. Alexander Kielland, for example, in a letter written in December 1883 to Georg Brandes, finds *The Family at Gilje* "unspeakably insignificant" because it does not directly satirize the conditions which it seeks to depict: "Jonas Lie's [book—*The Family at Gilje,* it is clear] is good, but unspeakably insignificant; if only he had had the courage to expose his gluttonous, guzzling officials as the fathers of the present ones, then it would have been a book—now it is a charming novel about nothing." It is not without significance that these words were addressed to Georg Brandes, the brilliant critical exponent of a literature "which should bring up problems for debate," and that they were written by Alexander Kielland, an equally brilliant creative exponent of Brandes's early utilitarian literary program. Though Kielland's scintillating narrative performance *Skipper Worse* (1882) proves that he could on occasion write a novel with not too obvious propagandist purposes, most of Kielland's work—particularly such things as *Arbeidsfolk* ("Working People") and *Else,* both published in

1881, and *Sne* ("Snow"), appearing in 1886—reveal a novelist who was primarily concerned with literature as a means of direct, all but violent social criticism. It is easy to see, therefore, why Kielland found *The Family at Gilje* to be "a charming novel about nothing." Lie's social satire was not sufficiently direct to satisfy such a militant social reformer in fiction as was Kielland.

It is clear to us now, however, that Lie really never evaded the immediate social issues of his time. He simply refused to be swept off his feet by the popular catch-words of his generation; and most important of all to discerning readers of a later generation than his own, he insisted on retaining at all costs a rigid intellectual and artistic independence. Lie was on the whole friendly with nearly all of his famous contemporaries in the Scandinavian countries, carrying on an extensive correspondence with Bjørnson and a fairly frequent exchange of letters with Kielland, Garborg, and Brandes among others; and yet he never permitted himself to become a part of any contemporary "movement," political, social, or literary. As early as 1872 Lie judged "much of that culture which blows over to us from Denmark (Brandes, etc., etc.)" to be "just as sterile and enervating for our Norwegian circumstances as a sirocco from the Saharas"; and though throughout his literary career Lie revealed distinctly liberal tendencies in his thinking, he never gave himself over completely to any of the popular ideologies of the hour. He felt, indeed, that literature should deal with the problems of our daily life, but that it should do so indirectly rather than by the obtrusive methods of the aggressive literary propagandist. Politics and art, he insisted, should never be identified with each other. The way of politics is the direct, active way— the way of propaganda, and too often the way of prejudice. Art, on the other hand, attains the same end as politics by more indirect means—it *insinuates itself* into the moral consciousness of man, and by a process of very subtle, but profoundly effective indirection tends to remake the conditions of life under which man lives. It was on the basis of such reasoning that Lie reacted very strongly against Bjørnson's political activities, lamenting the fact that his friend insisted upon confusing art and politics—

to the detriment perhaps of both. He felt that Bjørnson's genius should devote itself to pure literature only, and he never hesitated in urging his friend to depart from his methods of active journalistic reform and propaganda. "To my mind"—he wrote on one occasion to Bjørnson, who had become engaged in attempting to arouse a Norwegian national consciousness by means of active propaganda—"a Norwegian national consciousness can a thousand times more easily be insinuated into the people than it can be pounded into them; the intangible influences of a work of creative art are more powerful than the external, more tangible kind in politics,—of this I am certain." Lie never seriously swerved from this central conviction during the whole course of his creative career.

It is this conviction which more than anything else gives an almost unique quality to Lie's unobtrusive but telling criticism of life in the midst of so much of the Scandinavian literature from his generation which has "had its day and ceased to be." Ibsen's *An Enemy of the People* (1882) and Bjørnson's *The King* (1877)—to mention only two direct "problem dramas" among the dozens from Lie's generation—are on occasion produced even today, but as "revivals," not as significant living documents for a twentieth century civilization. For all practical purposes they are now *dead*. Likewise the early democratic critical pronunciamentos of Georg Brandes are now for the most part so many curious "documents"—not at all the provocative utterances, the "calls to battle" that they were in the '70's of the last century. We have already begun to "date" these things; they are essentially literature of a particular day—a day that is no longer ours.

Such literary performances as *The Family at Gilje,* however, continue to delight, and even to influence, a constantly increasing number of readers—and this primarily because the "problem" that Lie presents in it is so finely subordinated to his primary artistic concern with certain fundamental laws of human nature as revealed in his vividly sketched characters.

The "problem" of Gilje centres most obviously upon the age-old question of the relation between parents and children; but in a larger sense the novel contains an indirect criticism of the whole social and political structure of mid-nineteenth century Norway which made the immediate domestic problem of Gilje inevitable. In their efforts to get Inger-Johanna and Thinka married to the best advantage, and Jørgen well situated in life, the Captain at Gilje and his wife (always referred to by the author in a tone of genial irony as "Ma") tended to do violence to the usual modern conception of the relation between parents and children. And yet the parents at Gilje are unfair to their children through no inherent viciousness on their part. They themselves are, in fact, no less the victims of a set of circumstances than are their children; and it is this set of circumstances which, in the last analysis, determines the procedure which they adopt with regard to their children.

The core of the Gilje problem is really a financial one; the Captain has to exist, and raise a family, on a salary so small that in the course of the years he has been transformed from what must have been at one time a large, amiable, sanguine spirit, essentially good at heart, into a man whose domestic activities, distorted by provincial isolation and straitened financial circumstances, are often petty, blustering, and dictatorial. And Ma, a more practical nature from the outset perhaps, is even more pathetically a victim of narrow provincial isolation and immediate economic stress. Her constant concern for the household, and especially for "the children," has reduced her in the course of the years almost to the status of a domestic automaton.

Though it is around Inger-Johanna's fate that the plot of the Gilje story tends to centre, the most convincingly drawn characters in the novel are undoubtedly those of Inger-Johanna's parents—the Captain, with "his plethoric, vociferous, somewhat confused nature," and Ma, the Captain's self-effacing, hardworking, externally cautious wife, under whose severely plain exterior lurked both a vigorous practical intelligence and a sensitive woman's soul. It is in Ma, in fact, that we find Lie's greatest attainment in the art of characterization in *The Family at Gilje*. The Captain *seems* merely to loom larger in the story because of his domineering manner and his vociferous methods of procedure. It is really Ma, with her quiet, self-effacing man-

ner, who always finally determines family policies after the
heavy artillery of the Captain has spent itself in violently explosive inconsequences. In episode after episode, deftly, and
usually by scarcely perceptible indirections, Lie makes us conscious of Ma's real power at Gilje. In her unassuming manner
she comes by degrees to command our admiration and respect,
and to appeal to our deepest sympathies; while the Captain, in his
blustering way, too often invites the reader to a reaction scarcely
so serious and dignified. It is only toward the end of the novel,
when the Captain, a sick and worn-out hulk of a man, becomes
finally resigned to Inger-Johanna's decision not to marry into
"high society," that we come upon any real mark of essential
nobility in Captain Jæger's character. And by this time, perhaps,
we are not so much impressed by the Captain's tragedy; for a
weakly pathetic, half-resigned spirit in a sick, completely broken
body is not usually taken to be the human symbol of high tragedy. Lie might conceivably be accused of resorting to the appeal
of sentimentality in creating such a pathetic dénouement for the
Captain, though if so he is not without the company of great
genius, among them Shakespeare himself.

Perhaps the most remarkable feature of Lie's creation of
the character of Ma is that he avoids all false pathos in it,
retaining toward her throughout his novel an attitude of sympathetic understanding which is remarkably objective in its
quality. Lie strikes a happy medium here, avoiding both the
cold, scientific objectivity of a Flaubert on the one hand and
the excessively sentimental subjectivity of a Dickens on the
other. Lie's subject for characterization—a mother whose spirit
has been all but crushed by narrow, petty circumstances—is surcharged with sentimental potentialities; and yet Lie never yields
to the temptation which a lesser, or a careless author would
inevitably fall into here. Though his attitude toward Ma is
sympathetic, it is neither excessively nor obtrusively so. Lie's
sympathy for this character is insinuated into the text in his
best impressionistic manner—by skillful indirection, yet with
the delicate persistence of constantly recurring, cumulative
detail. Already in the opening chapter of the novel—so filled,
otherwise, with rapid, boisterous action—appear a number of

quiet, short unobtrusive paragraphs which give us the key to Ma's character. How fittingly does Lie introduce her—plain, lean, stiff of figure, anxiously engaged in patching Jørgen's trousers!

In the common room below, between the sofa and the stove, the Captain's wife, in an old brown linsey-woolsey dress, sat sewing. She had a tall, stiff figure, and a strong, but gaunt, dried-up face, and had the appearance of being anxiously occupied at present by an intricate problem—the possibility of again being able to put a new durable patch on the seat of Jørgen's trousers; they were always bottomless—almost to desperation.

We note a bit later her "somewhat anxious, thoughtful expression" when she ponders the immediate practical problem as to whether the veal roast, "which she had reserved for the Dean," or the pig should be served to her husband's unexpected visitors, Captain Rønnow and Lieutenant Mein. Then her introduction by Captain Jæger to the visiting officers—

"— If you please, gentlemen. Captain Rønnow and Lieutenant Mein, Ma," he said as he opened the door.

The mistress of the house rose from her place at the table, where she was now sitting with fine white knitting-work. She greeted Captain Rønnow as heartily as her stiff figure would allow, and the Lieutenant somewhat critically. It was the Governor's sister to whom the salaam was made, as Captain Rønnow afterwards expressed it—an old, great family.

Later, in the opening episode, we note a touch of bitterness in Ma's character when Captain Rønnow suggests incidentally that he might recommend Inger-Johanna's acceptance into the Christiania residence of Ma's brother, the highly respected Governor.

The Captain's wife answered slowly and with some stress; something of a suppressed bitterness rose up in her. "That would be an entirely unexpected piece of good fortune; but more than we out-of-the-way country folk can expect of our grand, distinguished sister-in-law. Small circumstances make small folk, more's the pity; large ones ought to make them otherwise.—My brother has made her a happy wife."

And the day after the boisterous party of the three military officers—

Ma went about the house as usual with her bunch of keys; she had hardly slept at all that night.

She had become old before her time, like so many other "mas," in the household affairs of that period—old by bearing petty annoyances, by toil and trouble, by never having money enough, by bending and bowing, by continually looking like nothing and being everything—the one on whom the whole anxious care of the house weighed.

But—"One lives for the children."

That was Ma's pet sigh of consolation. And the new time had not yet come to the "mas" with the question whether they were not also bound to realize their own personal lives.

These paragraphs reveal how clearly Lie saw the personal and social problem resulting from the isolation and the economic conditions at Gilje, conditions characteristic of many a provincial official's residence throughout Norway in the nineteenth century. Never again in the novel does Lie pose this problem in such definite terms as he does here, and yet the whole action of the novel is by implication an intimate development of the theme here propounded. Ma is simply *one* of the victims of a system which made pettiness well-nigh inevitable and a large spirited attitude toward life almost impossible. Lie's ironic reference in the last of these paragraphs to "the new time" suggests that he is also aware of the point to which some of his contemporaries, such as Ibsen in *A Doll's House* (1879), had carried the conception of the "independence of women"; though by a sly thrust of innuendo he suggests that the championing of so-called "women's rights" has implications far beyond the immediate "personal rights" of the individual woman herself.

In the light of the passages that we have quoted from the opening chapter of *The Family at Gilje* it should be apparent that Kielland was quite unfair in judging the novel as "good, but unspeakably insignificant . . . a charming novel about nothing." Lie was as deeply interested in social and political reform as was either Kielland or Bjørnson, both of whom electrified so many Norwegian readers with frankly propagandist literature; but Lie looked upon the artist as a more disengaged spirit than the politician, and he felt that in the long run the

social influence of a novel like *The Family at Gilje* would be more
salutary and profound than would political pamphlets scantly
disguised as fiction. Nothing is more revealing on this point than
a letter, generous in its appreciation, yet frank in its condemnation, which Lie wrote to Kielland on the occasion of his reading
of Kielland's *Arbeidsfolk* ("Working People," 1881), a violent
attack upon contemporary Norwegian bureaucracy.

Well, now I have read *Working People*! It has moved me and
it has irritated me. . . . Njædel, Kristine, and the Doctor have
gripped me deeply, and the exposé is magnificently brilliant. . . .
But you have attacked personalities in a one-sided and malicious
manner. With the exception of Delphin . . . they are black as
ink! But now my father was also incidentally a juridical official,
one of the country's best, and he would get up in his night-shirt
on a winter night, distressed when he thought that a cottager had
suffered a wrong, and remitted by express many miles away, turning back some years as much in fees as he now has as a pension.
. . . It is therefore, you see, that your attack is uninformed,
and where it is this it is weak in its effect. It is created with the
poetry of hate!—My joy in your book is in its *Art*—your sharp
sense of reality when you sketch; and you will doubtless usher
many influential books out into the world. And new times will
come—with or without a Death's Head in the sails. With many
good wishes for your creative work!

Lie would propose, in contrast to the frankly propagandist
method of Kielland, a middle way in fiction: a realistic novel
dealing with an actual problem, but not one in which the heat
of propagandist purpose misleads the artist into distorting the
truth of an actuality which may exist about us.

IV

Lie lived for a quarter of a century after the publication of
The Family at Gilje in 1883; and these years found his pen at
least as busy as it had been during the first dozen years of his
authorship. The novels and tales which he wrote after *The Family
at Gilje*, however, reveal a partial shift in both his point of
view and his technique, though he continues—with one remarkable exception—to centre his attention on domestic interiors.

In the matter of technique Lie's later novels seem gradually to take on a sharper, more stylized impressionistic manner, characterized chiefly by an even more scrupulously conscious word choice and by a new emphasis on the basic importance of individual episode. In point of view Lie's later novels seem to lose some of the easy and familiar geniality of his earlier work. Only with increasing difficulty is Lie able in his later novels to view human existence with his former happy vigor and basic amiability. It was perhaps his growing concern with the intricacies of human psychology, and the actions often determined by this psychology, that led his honest, searching mind to a more sober view of the problems of human existence, a view which had little commerce with the relatively facile optimism of some of his early work.

The Family at Gilje itself has its "problems," as we have seen, and it is not lacking in certain tragic elements. Yet this novel on the whole exudes a vital warmth of feeling, a rich human sympathy, and a spirit of happy good will that is almost contagious. Even Georg Brandes, who might have been expected to be somewhat critical of some of the idealizing tendencies in this novel, wrote in a letter from 1884: *"The Family at Gilje* is an entirely excellent work." And it was no doubt this work in particular that Brandes had in mind when he spoke of Lie as Norway's "most amiable author." Though tragic elements are present in the pages of *The Family at Gilje,* we are apt to remember the novel primarily for its genially human qualities.

In the same year, however, which saw the publication of *The Family at Gilje,* Lie published another novel, *Livsslaven* ("The Life Convict"), which contains little trace of the ingratiating geniality of his great Gilje novel. *The Life Convict* is in substance a sombrely realistic study in the development of a criminal type; and though its manner of handling the material is relatively objective throughout, it does not seem to have been written without a certain definitely implied *Tendenz.* It at least raises the question—if it does not actually point an accusing finger—of society's responsibility in the creation of the criminal type. *The Life Convict* is not in itself among Lie's great works; but it is of definite importance in any study of Lie's development as a novelist, for it serves to point the way toward a new phase in his development. It should be emphasized, more than previous critics have been willing to do, that in no work after *The Family at Gilje* does Lie reveal with any steady consistency that quietly pervasive geniality of spirit which is so centrally characteristic of his great Gilje novel. Rather do his novels after 1883 reveal a Lie who is becoming slowly enveloped in shadows. Not that his essential amiability of temper ever departs completely from him, nor that he finally develops into a basically tragic author. In his late novels he still retains something of the Lie that we learn to know so intimately in the pages of *The Family at Gilje*; but this Lie has become by degrees more deeply aware of life's darker undercurrents, of those evil powers, lurking seductively on every hand, which distort character and destroy ideal human values—and he does not hesitate to pose as central themes in his later novels some of the characteristic forms which these powers of disintegration take in the life of man.

Many of the titles of his late novels—*En Malstrøm* ("A Maelstrom," 1884), *Onde Magter* ("Evil Powers," 1890), *Trold,* I, II ("Trolls," 1891, 1892), *Niobe* (1893), and *Naar Sol gaar ned* ("When the Sun Goes Down," 1895)—give their sinister hints of the gathering shadows. And other novels from these years—such as *The Commodore's Daughters* (1886), *Et Samliv* ("A Wedded Life," 1887), and *Maisa Jons* (1888)— contain tales of sufficiently sombre and tragic implications, even though the titles in themselves do not betray stories of a heavy, darkening import. Some of these tales preserve not a little of the Lie of the earlier novels; but most of them are concerned so frankly and realistically with those "evil powers" which are said to people the substrata of life that the reader soon becomes convinced that Lie is now moving farther and farther away from the near-idyll which we find so frequently in his earlier tales of the sea and his early domestic interiors. *A Maelstrom,* for instance, is a sombrely realistic study in the decay of an old, respected business house—an early Scandinavian example of the *Buddenbrooks* problem. *A Wedded Life* is a melancholy tale about marriage, which ends, indeed, on an idyllic note, but which impresses one otherwise throughout with the disillusioning forthrightness of its realism in the treatment of a common domestic problem. *When the Sun Goes Down* contains the morbid tale of a faithless demoniac wife, whose life must finally be snuffed out in order to save the rest of the family from corruption. *Niobe*—perhaps the most hopeless in tone of all of Lie's novels—is a ghastly study in the dangers of aestheticism and decadence.

Though none of these are great novels, each of them provides its own burden of evidence that Lie is becoming increasingly preoccupied in the last two decades of his life with problems that permit little of the warmly genial spirit of his early work to be operative in his fiction. Lie's two important works from this period—*The Commodore's Daughters* and the two volumes of *Trolls*—provide further evidence of the same kind. The former of these is a contemporary domestic interior, which concentrates on the double tragedy of two vivacious, promising young ladies, each of whose lives is made a sacrifice to narrow parental conceptions of proper social procedures. *Trolls*—perhaps the most remarkable work that Lie has ever written—is a marvelously diversified medley of ancient legends and superstitions, some of them told in the straightforward, unadorned narrative manner of the original folk tale, others conceived in the profoundly lyric vein of the best of romantic nature mysticism, and still others written with an obvious and immediate moral purpose.

The two volumes of *Trolls* are, in a word, different. Not only do they differ from anything Lie had previously written (with the exception of parts of *The Visionary,* and a few other fragments), but they are in a sense unique in the whole of Scandinavian literature in the nineteenth century. This uniqueness is to be found in the fact that Lie handles his folk materials in a way peculiar to himself—in general conception and in composition *they bear the Lie stamp*. As the outward framework, or form, of his two volumes of *Trolls*, Lie uses essentially the same kind of folk materials as did Asbjørnsen and Moe in their famous *Norske Folkeeventyr* ("Norwegian Fairy Tales," which began to appear as early as 1842); and in many of the individual stories, he reproduces the old folk tale with the same happy truth to the originals as had his two predecessors in the genre of the Norwegian folk tale. But Lie's *Trolls* differs from Asbjørnsen and Moe's *Norwegian Fairy Tales* in at least two important respects: first, Lie restricts his choice of tales almost entirely to Finnmarken, those dreary, magnificently primitive regions in the far north of Norway; and secondly—and most important—he uses these materials in such a vigorously original variety of ways that the two volumes of *Trolls* become something far more than merely another "collection of folk legends."

It was, of course, quite natural for Lie to limit his choice of tales to the Far North. These were the tales that he had listened to with such intense absorption during his boyhood days at Tromsø. He could not forget them . . . could no more shake them off than he could forget any of his other childhood experiences: "it is as if they had been preserved deep down in a cellar," Lie himself tells us, "where nothing has been able to get at them." Lie had *lived* these stories in his vivid childhood imagination long before he had become conscious of any possible line of demarcation between legend and reality; and the years of maturity which had taught Lie something of that distinction which man tries to draw between fiction and fact had never *quite* convinced him that there was not more than a little truth in the old world of legend and superstition. It was therefore, no doubt, that Lie could preserve the old legends in his memory with so little loss of the original flavor and spirit of these legends; and it was therefore that he could also on occasion apply the materials of these old tales to problems of so-called "modern import" in a way that marks the two volumes of *Trolls* as one of the most original books ever to come out of Norway.

Much well-deserved praise has been showered by Norwegian critics upon those tales in *Trolls* which preserve the true spirit and manner of the originals—a spirit and manner objective and unadorned, scrupulously avoiding such "modern additions" as a romantic lyric vein or a tendency to "point a moral." Unquestionably the tales which attain this fresh, primitive narrative ideal are artistically the most satisfactory ones in Lie—the ones that rank Lie together with Selma Lagerlöf just below the great master Hans Christian Andersen in the modern literary creation of the Scandinavian fairy tale. And yet it must be remembered—

at least by the literary historian—that such happily conceived tales are in the minority in *Trolls*. Moreover, it must not be forgotten that even those tales which have no apparent "purpose," aside from the mere desire to tell a tale, were included in a work to which an Introduction was written that definitely points a broad but profound parallel (which amounts, in a sense, to an identification) between the "evil powers" of an ancient world of folk legend and those "evil powers" which some hold still live on in a so-called "civilized modern life."

That there are Trolls in human beings everyone knows who has an eye for that kind of thing. They lie within the personality and bind it like the immovable part of a mountain, like a capricious sea and uncontrollable weather—evil broods big and little—from the giant mountain or ocean Troll, which by its own will can enter into the general stream of life, to the Water-sprite, the Elf, the Goblin, and the Nixie, which storm about and enter into folk with their capricious whims, their pranks, and their capers.

One time when I drove with a sleigh through a forest my horse bolted at a large, awesome stone-block, which lay and peered forth in the moonlight from under a birch shaped like the forelock of a Troll.

I have since met it again in an old judicial official—a strikingly tired face, the eyes like two wearily veiled precious stones, a marvelously sure power of judgment, impossible to be moved or led astray by impressions. Circumstances blew off him like weather and wind; his understanding so infinitely stone-sure—nothing could bind him. He was only a pointer. Trolldom lives at this stage inside mankind as temperament, natural will, explosive power.

It is essentially a step farther and above this when it exists as penitence, fear of darkness and fear of spirits. Penitence is mankind's first step in his desire to separate himself from and lift himself above the elemental powers, and is followed by all kinds of magic and mediatory means to force the elemental powers down.

And, how far this stage of Trolldom follows mankind even into civilized life might be a very useful and instructive demonstration—perhaps also somewhat astonishing. The fear of existence, the great unknown about us, which is also the foundation of our religious feeling, constantly shifts its form and name according to the various levels of enlightenment. It lives in the mystical experimentalist as table-turning, spirit-rapping, and such, in the learned under high-sounding scientific conditions such as the "fourth dimension," which in the past has in a sense been the lumber-closet into which man puts all of that which he cannot explain to himself.

It is clear from these opening paragraphs in the Introduction to *Trolls* that Lie is prepared in the tales included in these volumes to use the word "Trolls" in a far more inclusive sense than the usual historical one. He conceives of "Trolls" as not only existing in the minds of the uncultured peasant and fisherfolk of an ancient pagan North, but also as having a kind of very real existence in the life of a modern world. In consequence he uses the word "Trolls" as broadly symbolizing those mysterious, often tragic undercurrents of human life which a modern psychology knows under the names of "the unconscious" or "the irrational." The fact that his tales are restricted in time and place to the world of Norwegian medieval superstition should in no way, Lie feels, limit their possible application to a more civilized time; for the irrational, the demoniac is always with us, lurking in the sinister substrata of human consciousness and emerging at crucial moments in human life to determine human action—oftentimes a blindly tragic human action.

One cannot mistake the parallel between Lie's theory of the irrational expressed in the Introduction to *Trolls* and the sinister psychological moods that determine the actions of many of the chief characters in Lie's late novels dealing with contemporary life. Modern life has its "Trolls," though they have taken on different forms than the Draug and the Nixies and the Elves of ancient northern superstition. And it may be that these "modern Trolls" are even more sinister in their actions—more sinister because they are less natural, more frequently an expression of a general spiritual *malaise* working upon a whole human culture. In *Niobe* we find that three of the five children in the Borvig family have in the years of their early manhood and womanhood succumbed, in one way or another, to such a general cultural *malaise*. The father, a robust country doctor, broods wearily over the matter as he moves across the countryside in his cariole one day on a professional errand.

One has a feeling of something abnormally misty over everything. It must be a general softening of the brain in our time—
which breaks out in all sorts of nervous diseases. . . . Should have
liked to be young again and go into the matter, have it properly laid
before the world. The result no doubt of the overwhelming number
of important inventions and discoveries which have been made in
our generation; the brain has not been able to receive and digest
them all. . . . The consequences of each one, being so far reaching,
change the possibilities and conceptions to such an extent that only
the next generation or perhaps the one after that, born under the
new state of things, will be able fully to understand and live up
to it. . . . If we suddenly got into daily postal communication with
Mars, we should not feel surprised at it for more than a half hour,
and in a week we should be quite accustomed to it. We have no
time to think out the results of the new impressions on the brain.
. . . Quite a new epoch in human culture which will fall like an
avalanche upon the race.

Niobe is Lie's sober contribution to the literature of decadence.
It takes its place alongside of such Scandinavian novels as
Jens Peter Jacobsen's *Niels Lyhne,* Herman Bang's *Generations without Hope,* Hans Jæger's *From the Kristiania-Bo-
hême,* and Garborg's *Weary Men.* As a literary work it has its
faults—its character portrayal is somewhat wooden and its
handling of episode is often highly melodramatic. But as a
study in the psychology of decadence it has its very real critical
distinction—a distinction perhaps largely to be accounted for
by the application in this novel on modern life of the theory
of the irrational which had found theoretical expression in the
opening paragraphs of *Trolls.*

The brilliant originality of *Trolls,* both in conception and
execution, suggests that Lie had large reserves of narrative
power which might rank him even higher than he is now placed
among Norwegian novelists had these unique reserves been
more freely drawn upon. They flash out uncertainly, yet with
intriguing promise, in Lie's first novel, *The Visionary;* and they
burn with a marvelously varied and intense glow in the two
volumes of *Trolls* very late in Lie's career. Otherwise we can but
guess at their existence in the far reaches of Lie's consciousness

during those years of his life when he chose to concentrate largely upon robustly bracing sea tales and on soberly realistic portrayals of the contemporary scene. He stands unexcelled even today, thirty years after his death, as the Norwegian master of sea tale and the domestic interior; but each of these genres is a definitely limited one, in which happy detailed craftsmanship carries one almost as far as striking imaginative powers. That Lie insisted upon restricting himself largely to these two genres, particularly to the latter, is therefore perhaps to be regretted.

And yet his mastery of the novel of contemporary scene was no mean attainment in itself, and the significance which this attainment has had in the general development of the Norwegian novel since Lie's day is incalculable. It might be said that Lie really created the Norwegian novel, as Ibsen created the Norwegian drama. And Lie's creation—solid and honest at every point—served to give a much needed firmness of form and substance to Norwegian fiction at the very beginning of its development.

As a personality and as an artist Lie does not perhaps immediately impress one among his famous contemporaries in Norway. He had none of the pugnacious aggressiveness of a Bjørnson or a Kielland, nor did he have any of that enigmatic impressiveness which we have come to associate with the sphinx-like Ibsen. Lie's genius was more unassuming, his work less pretentious than the work of any of these men; and yet in some ways Lie's work is more permanently satisfactory than that of either Ibsen or Bjørnson or Kielland. He differs perhaps most markedly from these three Norwegians—and from the Dane Georg Brandes, whose critical pronouncements had such importance for these Norwegians—in the quietly persistent independence of his genius, in his ability to retain an artistic and intellectual balance in an age when Scandinavian literature was swept by so many winds of doctrine, literary and otherwise, from the Continent. Lie, it is to be stressed, always remained *himself,* and he remained *Norwegian,* in a Scandinavian generation so prone to be impressed by the various ideologies which swept over the North from England and from France. Lie believed in reform, but he did not believe that literature should conceive its primary purpose to be the active agent of reform. He believed in progress, but he remained skeptical of most of the catchwords of his generation which were presumed to spell progress. He was unmoved by the words "democracy" and "superman," realizing that they too often represented merely abstract conceptions which had little validity outside the lecture room and the propagandist platform.

It is therefore that Lie condemned many of the popular efforts toward "reform" that characterized the Norwegian life of his time. He felt that his own generation in Norway was making a profound mistake in championing a program of reform based for the most part on popularly appealing foreign catchwords. His generation, he felt, tended to ignore the deeplying roots of a basically Norwegian culture in its feverish desire to renovate the tree and its branches. Norway, he always insisted, had a culture of its own, which should be permitted to evolve in terms of its own past, its own national temper—*not* in terms of Continental and English ideas. "Brandes"—the Danish publisher Hegel had once said—"represents Europe's multiplicity—Lie Norway's simplicity." The characterization is as apt as an epigram can be; and the epigram has a certain application also to the fundamental distinction between the work of Ibsen, Bjørnson, and Kielland on the one hand and Lie on the other in Norway. Much as Lie admired the creative gifts of his great contemporaries, he felt that their literary activities were too often—especially, as we have noted, in the cases of Bjørnson and Kielland—unhappily dominated by the spirit of direct propaganda. And he felt also—with a finely balanced intuitive judgment—that the rich creative gifts of his generation in Norway needed constantly to be tempered by the culture of the past if a great Norwegian culture of the present were to be attained. The Norway of the late nineteenth century, he held, represented essentially a young, promising culture, with plenty of power, plenty of fresh creative energies, which should be fused with older cultural strains in order that its apparent immediate fertility be not a final sterility. "I do not find art anywhere"—Lie wrote in a letter from 1892—"in *merely* primitive racial groups." Nor, it might be added, did he find it

in a modern rhetorical bombast which ignored deep-lying racial
and cultural considerations.

We can today, perhaps, appreciate the soundness of Lie's
position better than could many of his contemporaries, who, in
the smoke of the conflict which raged in late nineteenth century
Norway around the general concept of "a greater Norway,"
not infrequently felt that Lie's persistent refusal to "take sides"
implied an essential weakness on his part. It is refreshing to
remember, in this connection, that no less a person than Georg
Brandes is prepared, in 1887, to pass a more favorable general
judgment on Lie than on several of Lie's famous Norwegian
contemporaries. I quote from a letter by Brandes to Lie, written from Copenhagen.

How happy I would be to meet you some time. How gladly would
I hear your opinions about many things. We two men, who live
for spiritual things and have thoughts to exchange, should (as did
the best French authors twenty years ago) dine together twice
a month and break lances with each other, so that the splinters
flew. Many authors (like Ibsen), because they isolate themselves,
become almost incapable of offering anything in a conversation;
others (like Bjørnson) are so set in their ideas and so conceited
that they cannot tolerate in their presence the expression of another's conviction; and all suffer from the absence of contacts with
their equals. I seldom know, literally, where I should go here in the
city when I go out of my door. I live only when I travel. . . .

The beautiful thing about you as a man is that—while all of the
other Norwegian authors become superior and self-important as
soon as they have experienced success—you are as human as if you
had never had good fortune with a book. I believe, or rather know,
that the very greatest masters have been similarly simple. I know
that there has been no one more simple than Shakespeare. Turgenev
likewise. Stuart Mill likewise.

It might be suspected that these paragraphs, written to Lie,
were dictated by the motive of mere flattery; but there is no
reason to believe that Brandes did not mean what he wrote
here—and certainly his words are in keeping with the general
impression which we have today of Lie's person and his art.
A sound and healthy natural simplicity is the distinguishing
mark of the man and the artist which is Jonas Lie.

TOWARD DECADENCE
JENS PETER JACOBSEN

ONE evening in the spring of 1872 a group of liberal spirits, all deeply interested in the future of Danish literature, and having certain rather revolutionary opinions as to just what direction Denmark's literary future should take, met informally, as was their custom, at D'Angleterre, a quiet little restaurant in Copenhagen, in order to consider together some of the problems which lay nearest their hearts. The group—including among others Georg Brandes and Holger Drachmann, Vilhelm Møller and Jens Peter Jacobsen—had been only recently organized under the name "Litteraturselskabet." Its members, with the exception of Brandes, were little known at the time outside this literary circle, though at least two of them, Jacobsen and Drachmann, were soon to become famous as the chief Danish creative exponents of those new conceptions of the nature and purpose of literature which the brilliant critical gift of Brandes was introducing into his quietly conservative little land after an extended visit to Continental centres of culture.

On the particular evening in question it was Jens Peter Jacobsen's turn to deliver an informal address, which in the course of the evening was to be discussed by the others. Jacobsen— young, just turned twenty-five—had already shown some promise in two widely disparate fields: as a student of botany he had attracted the attention of the scientific staff at the University, and as the author of a strikingly original short story, entitled "Mogens," he had been recognized by his colleagues in "Litteraturselskabet" as one of the first genuine creative gifts to the new movement in literature which they were trying to get under way. Besides, he had combined science and belles-lettres in a series of articles on Darwin in a liberal Danish periodical; and this series of articles had aroused sufficient general public interest to provoke an eminent Danish bishop to a spirited reply in the pages of the same journal. It was therefore with a reasonably pardonable pride in their youthful speaker that "Litteraturselskabet" met together on an evening in the spring of 1872 to listen to an informal address by Jens Peter Jacobsen.

But the "address" proved to be a fiasco. The brilliant young scientist and budding littérateur began his talk timidly, continued with a desperately increasing incoherence, and finished in a maze of unintelligible indirections. Jens Peter Jacobsen, all but an angel with the pen, was found on this occasion to be pretty much of a fool with the tongue. Painful as it must have been for Jacobsen's friends to endure his floundering talk on Darwin, it seems that they chose rather to remember, even on the evening of the fiasco, that their young colleague had written the marvelous prose of "Mogens" and a series of brilliant essays on Darwin for their new liberal journal. After all—they may have consoled themselves—many a great writer had been a poor speaker. And Jacobsen, though not yet numbered among the great, was ultimately to justify the literary promise of his early work despite the sad part he played in the little episode which was modestly to introduce him for the first time as a public speaker.

I

The twenty-five years which had passed between the birth of Jens Peter Jacobsen and the unfortunate evening in Copenhagen when he was to deliver his ill-fated talk on Darwin were very full years for the future novelist. His boyhood was an unusually happy one, the years fleeting rapidly by in a constantly varied round of play and school-work and darkened neither by harshly domineering parents nor by economic distress of any kind. Thisted, a little harbor town in northwestern Jutland, was the place of his birth, on the 7th of April 1847; and here it was that he spent all of the years of his boyhood and earliest youth. His father, Chresten Jacobsen, had married a schoolmaster's daughter, Benthe Marie Hundahl, from the neighboring village of Hunstrup. Chresten Jacobsen was a shrewd, hardworking merchant, and in the course of his life he had developed a thriving business from an exceedingly modest beginning. Four children were born to Benthe and Chresten Jacobsen—two daughters, one of whom died very early, and two sons, Jens Peter and William.

Peter, as Jens Peter was called at home, was the eldest of the children. His parents, early recognizing in him a boy of unusual parts, sent him to school at the age of four, and encouraged him in every possible way in his early education. And yet they did not force him. His early years were spent equally at play and at his studies; and oftentimes play and study were happily joined into one by the natural ingenuities of Jens Peter and his play-mates. In the early pages of *Niels Lyhne,* one of Jacobsen's two great novels, we come upon a literary game (recollected from Jacobsen's own boyhood) which seems to have sprung up quite spontaneously between Niels and his playmate Fritiof—

Niels was quite a lad now, twelve years old, nearing thirteen, and he no longer needed to hack thistles and burdocks in order to feed his knightly fancies, any more than he had to launch his explorer's dreams in a mussel-shell. A book and a corner of the sofa were enough for him now, and if the book refused to bear him to the coast of his desires, he would hunt up Fritiof and tell him the tale which the book would not yield. Arm in arm, they would saunter down the road, one telling, both listening; but when they wanted to revel to the full and really give their imagination free play, they would hide in the fragrant dimness of the hayloft. After a while, these stories, which always ended just when you had really entered into them, grew into a single long story that never ended, but lived and died with one generation after the other; for when the hero had grown old, or you had been careless enough to let him die, you could always give him a son, who would inherit everything from the father, and whom, in addition, you could dower with any other virtues that you happened to value particularly just at the moment.

The game here described reminds one somewhat of the juvenilia of the precocious Brontë children. The starting point of the game of Jens Peter and his playmates we know now to be Ingemann's romantic tale *De underjordiske* ("Those of the Netherworld").

If the reading of romantic literature led to one kind of play for Jens Peter and his playmates, elementary studies in the sciences led inevitably to others. Though Jens Peter was an ordinary enough student in most of his school subjects, he was fascinated as a boy by scientific studies—chemistry and physics, and particularly botany. At the time he began with chemistry and physics in school, he was so enthusiastic about these subjects that he insisted on establishing a private "laboratory," where he and his playmates might carry on their "experiments" undisturbed by a possibly reproving parental eye. The boys finally hit upon the idea of using for their purposes an empty loft in one of the buildings included in the Chresten Jacobsen property; and here they performed their simple experiments with all the breathless mysteriousness of a medieval alchemist. But Jens Peter also used his rudimentary chemical knowledge for other than supposedly serious "scientific purposes." On at least one occasion science joined hands with boyish impishness to provide the materials for a bit of practical joking. We come upon him one day in the kitchen. He is dressed in a curious makeshift laboratory apron, busily engaged in mixing snow and salt in a bowl; and from the sly twinkle in his pert, boyish eyes we can divine that he is "experimenting" for other than purely scientific reasons. We discover soon that he is preparing the mixture in order to perpetrate a practical joke. He wishes to frighten the simple-minded maidservant by freezing a bowl fast to a place on the table on which a bit of water had been spilled!

Thus do play and school studies and the irrepressible boyish spirit of practical joking weave naturally in and out through the happy fabric of the free, natural existence which is Jens Peter's boyhood. The most serious of his intellectual concerns already during these early years comes to be his study of botany. Almost daily in his late boyhood and early youth he was occupied during his spare time in collecting and identifying all the variety of flora in the immediate neighborhood of his home; and on the holidays that the week-ends provided he was constantly venturing farther and farther afield in search of botanical specimens, especially to Silstrup Banks about three miles out from Thisted on the shores of Limfjorden. These Banks were a paradise for a young botanist: the landscape here was varied in contour and in soil texture, and all kinds of wild flowers grew profusely on the Banks. It was here that Jens Peter for the first time buried himself in the glories of what was to be even in maturity his favorite science. It is perhaps not too much to say that here at Silstrup Banks he first became conscious of that larger enthusiasm for scientific study which was the guiding motive in all of his later intellectual life. And it is probable also that during these same days the artist in him became more than half-conscious of all the nuances of form and of color that played so subtly over the Silstrup Banks. Plant growth—it is important to keep in mind—was never *merely* an object of scientific analysis to Jacobsen. He handled plants as if they were human—delicately as the mother handles the child. Years after the Silstrup days, when Jacobsen's professor in botany at the University wished to pay his favorite student the highest possible compliment, he was in the habit of saying: "No, there is no one who takes up a flower as he can. As he can!—so softly, so tenderly, and so that the whole root comes with it!" This habit of the mature scientist had been learned by the boy scientist during the joyous hours that he spent on the Silstrup Banks.

But the happy days at Thisted had to end. The small provincial school which Jens Peter attended here was not sufficiently advanced in its curriculum to prepare the boy finally for his entrance examinations to the University; and so his parents decided to send him to Copenhagen to complete his studies. In the spring of 1863 he was prepared for confirmation—the last bit of official training that Thisted was to afford before Jens Peter departed for Copenhagen in the autumn. Sensitive as the boy was to all impressions, he entered into the religious spirit of the confirmation period with a kind of youthful fanatical zeal. During the weeks of preparation previous to the final act of confirmation he would kneel before his bed each evening in long and fervent boyish prayer. His brother William, who seemed less impressionable to religious matters, asked him on one occasion while he was thus kneeling in prayer: "Why do you kneel there on your bare knees?" And without waiting for a reply, William offered to his elder brother a practical suggestion—"you can wait with your prayer until you get in bed." To which bit of adolescent irreverence Jens Peter replied firmly, "No, there is no reverence in such prayer." The answer was characteristic. Jens Peter was deeply affected by anything about him, or he wasn't affected at all. He tended, both

as a child and in his later life, to be a bit of a fanatic in anything
that he undertook. He was prone to be an extremist—in his
negations as well as his affirmations. When later in life, for
example, he began to feel religious doubts, and ultimately lost
his childhood faith, his break with the earlier dogmas was
absolute: he became a frank and uncompromising atheist. To
him there could be no halfway measures in matters of faith; he
thoroughly despised the easy compromises so characteristic of
many weakly evasive modern minds. The mature Jacobsen's
veiled contempt for one kind of modern religious compromise is
given characteristic expression in the fine irony of the passage
in *Niels Lyhne* in which he concludes his critical analysis of
the facile doctrinal juggling of the tutor, Herr Bigum: "He
was, in fact, religious in the slightly artistic, superior manner
such talented people affect, not afraid of a little harmonizing,
easily enticed into half unconscious rearrangements and adapta-
tions, because, whatever they do, they must assert their own
personality and, in whatever spheres they fly, must hear the
whirring of their own wings."

In the fall of 1863, at the age of sixteen, Jens Peter left his
home and the quiet little provincial village in northwestern
Jutland for Copenhagen, the city which he came ultimately to
love above almost anything else on earth. His immediate object
in moving to Copenhagen—to prepare himself for the university
entrance examinations—was not attained particularly rapidly,
chiefly because he expended so much energy in his pursuit of
belles-lettres and botany that he had little time left for the general exercises which had to be completed before the University
would open its doors to him.

Though his numerous activities in Copenhagen during these
early years kept him very busy, he found time, at least during
the first year, to maintain a lively correspondence with those
whom he had left behind in Thisted, particularly with one of
his former schoolmates, Nikolaj Nielsen, who had been his
comrade in the early scientific expeditions in and about Thisted.
Botany had been their mutual passion when Jens Peter was at
home; and now they came to exchange letters—which oftentimes swelled almost into the proportions of an academic dis-

sertation—on their favorite subject. These letters drip with learned botanical phrases and glow with the ideal enthusiasms of these serious young searchers after scientific truth. Vast were their plans. They dreamed of writing a book on "Thylands Flora"—actually began planning such a book. And to emphasize the nature of the tie which bound these two young enthusiasts to one another, they addressed each other in such delightfully pretentious phrases as "Dear friend and brother in Flora" or "To amicus naturae J. P. Jacobsen"!

The evidence is plentiful that literature also claimed much of the young Jacobsen's attention during his first years in Copenhagen. Already at this time he had confided to at least one person, Anna, daughter of a doctor's widow who lived near the Jacobsens in Thisted, that he intended to become "a poet." Ingratiatingly naïve is one of Anna's letters to Jens Peter in Copenhagen in which she refers to her former playmate's literary ambitions: "It was naturally a great fault in me to write to you *The Poet (Digteren)*, for how will the after-world judge me if it be found in my letters. It is therefore my prayer that you burn them, and particularly this one"! Jens Peter meanwhile was not only dreaming of poetry in these years; he was *writing* it—and by the year 1869 he had accumulated a sufficient number of poems to constitute a volume (entitled *Hervert Sperling*), which he unfortunately submitted to Georg Brandes under certain unfortunate circumstances that resulted in anything but an encouraging reception. These poems, with few exceptions, remained in manuscript form until after Jacobsen's death, when a selection from them was made by Edvard Brandes and published in a little volume entitled *Digte og Udkast* ("Poems and Sketches," 1886).

In the years immediately preceding the cool reception of his poems at the hands of Georg Brandes, Jacobsen had passed his examinations for entrance to the University, though hardly in a distinguished fashion. His first effort, indeed, ended in failure. "Your son's *abilities*"—wrote the professor in charge of the examination to Jens Peter's parents—"led us to expect good results in the examination; but in spite of repeated warnings and reminders, in spite of insistent admonitions against occupying himself with a study (botany) irrelevant to the final examinations, we have not had the pleasure to find that he has shown industry and regularity in keeping with his abilities." This letter was dated July 17, 1866. The following summer, when the young Jacobsen was twenty years of age, he finally passed the examinations, though in a mediocre manner. He might have consoled himself that Bjørnson and Ibsen, not much more than a decade earlier, had managed to squeeze equally ingloriously through similar examinations in Christiania.

His entrance into the University, freeing him as it did from the dreary grind of general "required subjects," permitted Jacobsen to concentrate more exclusively on his beloved botanical studies. Brandes's cold reception of his manuscript poems tended further to force him into serious scientific studies, though he by no means gave up literature entirely during these years. During his earliest days in Copenhagen he had settled on algae as his special field of interest, and his friends from these days tell us that all his spare moments were spent "fishing" for specimens at the seaside and in all of the streams and lagoons and ponds in the neighborhood of the capital. Early in 1870, a few months after the disappointment connected with Brandes's cold reception of his poems, he became involved with almost feverish intensity in his study of algae. His immediate practical need was a microscope. "I must have a microscope, even if it must fall down from Heaven," he wrote to his parents at this time. His good bourgeois father, somewhat cautious in money matters, and not entirely able to appreciate "scientific values," was very slow in sending money for such a mysterious scientific luxury as a microscope; and Heaven seemed just as heartless as a commercial-minded father. Toward the end of the year, however, the father, who was essentially human, relented, apparently under gentle but persistent pressure from his wife and daughter, to whom Jens Peter had meantime appealed as intermediaries. In December, the month in which he received money to purchase the longed-for microscope, the University authorities announced as the subject of a prize competition in botany the *desmidiaceae*, which happened to be the young Jacobsen's special field of interest. He therefore felt it his duty to enter the competition; worked very intensively on the subject for a couple of years; finished the study—which he entitled *Aperçu systematique et critique sur les desmidiasées du Danemark*—in the fall of 1872; and received the gold medal award for his work in the spring of 1873. The study created a sensation in the botanical faculty of the University and seemed to promise a brilliant future for the young botanist in his chosen field.

Meantime, however, Jacobsen had also been occupied with some other matters—chiefly literary. Even before he began his study of the *desmidiaceae,* he had come upon the work of Darwin as an immediate consequence of his predilection at this time for books written in English. Darwin's *On the Origin of Species by Means of Natural Selection* (1859) naturally fascinated the young Danish scientist; and soon he became the first important Darwin enthusiast in Denmark. He came to feel it to be his peculiar calling to make Darwin widely known in Denmark; and it was not long before the opportunity came for him to realize this calling in an immediately significant way. It happened just at this time that Vilhelm Møller, an enthusiastic young critic and a warm friend of Jacobsen's, was contemplating the founding of a new liberal journal in Denmark; and he enlisted Jacobsen among his contributors. In October 1870 the first number of Møller's *Nyt dansk Maanedsskrift* appeared, and in it was included an article by Jacobsen entitled "Om Bevægelsen i Planteriget" ("On Evolution in the World of Plants"). In January and February of 1871 Jacobsen published a long article in the same journal entitled "Darwins Theori" ("Darwin's Theory"), in which for the first time he proceeds to champion vigorously the English scientist's theories as found in both the *Origin of Species* and *Animals and Plants under Domestication.* This article, it is important to note, seeks both to explain Darwin's scientific theories as they relate themselves to pure science and to suggest those larger implications for human thought in general which seem implicit in these scientific theories. The article begins, in a tone of some naïveté, with an enthusiastic apostrophe to the wonders of the natural

world and to Darwin as the unique guide through this wondrous
world of nature—

Nature is like a wonderfully great palace with thousands of large
salons and smaller rooms, with shadowy secret passages that lead
out into the light of day, and with open galleries that lead back
into gloom and darkness. There are entrance halls with open colon-
nades where one likewise can enter, and rooms that are accessible
when one pulls firmly at the doors; but there are also many doors
that may be opened only after decades of effort and care, and there
are doors that will not open despite all our exertions and all our
care. For a long time the palace was deserted; many stood afar
off and were gladdened by its beauty and its majesty; a few were
occupied in the forecourts, and fewer yet took hold of the closed
doors. But now it is bustling with life; door after door is forced
open, and one man after another comes out of the palace and tells
of the wonderful things he has seen there. About a half score
years ago an old man came out of the palace. He had wandered
around therein about twenty, perhaps thirty years among the many
small rooms, through many winding passages, until he came to the
Great Hall with the marvelous vaulted dome, with great depths
and large, wide perspectives. And he told of what he had seen in
the rooms and the halls. And some thought that he had penetrated
to the heart of the palace, but others insisted that he had dreamed
only in the forecourts. The man was Charles Darwin, and what
he talked about was how all that which grows on the earth was as
a great robe which has woven itself, in which any single thread's
form and color conditioned the others, and that all, as time passed,
became woven more richly and beautifully. We shall now follow
him on his wanderings and learn to know what he saw first in the
small rooms and then in the Great Hall.

After this glowing preliminary paean to Nature, and to Darwin,
Nature's Master Guide, Jacobsen proceeds in more sober, tempered language to explain with exemplary clarity and discerning
critical intelligence the substance of Darwin's scientific teachings. And he closes his study with the general theoretical observation that, though in the light of Darwin's scientific theories
"the poetry of miracles" must cease to be, there is really another
poetry to be found in these teachings of Darwin—the poetry
of personal emotions humbly yielding to satisfy the severely
beautiful law of higher spiritual necessities.

This concluding generalization in Jacobsen's first article on Darwin gives expression to a point of view that becomes of primary importance to the positive side of Jacobsen's thinking in the years to come. The substance of it appears again and again in a variety of forms in the immediately succeeding articles from Jacobsen's pen in the *Nyt dansk Maanedsskrift*; and it recurs with such steady persistence in his fiction, particularly in "Mogens" and *Niels Lyhne*, that no observant reader of Jacobsen can fail to recognize its central importance in nearly all of his work. Though Darwin's ideas interested Jacobsen profoundly as a scientist, it might be said that he was interested even more in the broader implications of Darwin's ideas—the way in which a theory such as that of organic evolution might become the basis upon which to build a positive general philosophy of life, an ethics, even a religion. Jacobsen, it should be remembered, came to read Darwin at a particularly crucial moment in his development, just after he had felt forced, on intellectual grounds, to give up the religion of his childhood and youth. A void had been left in Jacobsen's spiritual life which Darwin now came to fill.

Jacobsen found in Darwin's scientific teaching a completely satisfactory basis for a new religion: a natural religion as opposed to a supernatural one, a religion which to his mind at least was far more dignified and infinitely more beautiful because it was more universally acceptable and intelligent than traditional religions basing their authority on supernatural revelation in one form or another. One of Jacobsen's early articles on the subject of the origins of man—an article in which he points out that man is the highest development in an organic world which has slowly developed from lower forms of life— concludes with the following characteristic words:

. . . If now this point of view at first glance seems to be the most crass materialism, a profoundly inconsiderate outrage on man's sense of his own dignity, does it not yet upon closer examination reveal itself to be healthier, sounder, and more honest than vague dreams about Adam and Eve in the never discovered Garden of Eden? And certainly, profoundly viewed, it is far more ideal, in that it points toward perfectibility and promises a constant growth in human intelligence.

Such ideas as these did not, of course, go unchallenged in the conservative Denmark of the early '70's; but space forbids us to trace even the general outlines of the controversy which they aroused—a controversy which among other things provided incidentally a Danish parallel to the famous Oxford joust between Huxley and Bishop Wilberforce in the England of the preceding decade. Most important for our immediate purposes is it merely to stress the point that it is in some such "poetry of science" as we have outlined above that Jacobsen finally found a kind of spiritual harmony. The new biology seemed to provide a sufficient basis for his "new faith."

Interested as Jacobsen had become in science during the early '70's, it is into creative literature that he came to pour his chief energies in the years that are to come. His first venture in the genre of fiction, the short story "Mogens," appeared in the *Nyt dansk Maanedsskrift* during the very months in which he was agitating so strenuously in this same journal the general intellectual and religious significance of Darwin's theories. We are not therefore surprised upon reading "Mogens" to find that its intellectual and religious ideas are of a piece with the articles on Darwin. This little story, in fact, finds its chief *raison d'être* —aside from its being an amazing bit of stylistic virtuosity— in its presentation of what was purported to be a new, more objective attitude toward nature, together with the religious implications so closely bound up in Jacobsen's mind with such a view of nature. The central idea in "Mogens" is that nature *in itself* is sufficient unto the spiritual wants of man, that no romantic "additions" to it are necessary or desirable. Jacobsen here rigidly rejects, as intellectually dishonest and spiritually superfluous, the supernatural existences with which Romantic poets had invested their nature; and yet he rejoices in nature nonetheless *for what it is*—a steady, organic, meaningful flow of ceaselessly aspiring life. It is thus the optimistic implications of Darwin's theory of evolution that find expression in "Mogens"; for Jacobsen was still in these years very young, and as yet he had experienced little of the heavy night-side of life. The shadows which ultimately cast their sombre gloom over him begin to appear only in Jacobsen's later, more mature work—to some extent in *Marie Grubbe* (1876), more ominously in *Niels Lyhne* (1880).

Jacobsen had since early youth, as we have seen, dreamed of being an author; and he had never really lost faith in himself despite at least one early literary disappointment. Edvard Brandes relates, in a volume of Jacobsen's letters that he has edited, a characteristic story which reveals how deeply Jacobsen was convinced of his own literary powers. It happened on one occasion that Edvard Brandes had casually dropped into Jacobsen's modest quarters in Copenhagen. Brandes had thrown himself wearily on a convenient sofa while Jacobsen searched about for some manuscript. Upon finding what he wanted, Jacobsen began reading aloud one of his poems—at first poorly, with a certain hesitating timidity, but soon with growing sureness and a quietly persuasive eloquence. Upon the completion of the reading, Brandes, who had forgotten his previous weariness and had become all attention, burst out in astonishment: "Why, man, you are a poet!" Whereupon Jacobsen replied quietly: "Yes, that do I know well enough, and I have always known it." On another, more merry occasion, Jacobsen expressed the same conviction with an equal note of confidence. He had been invited, together with some other Danes, to a men's dinner at a little restaurant in the Swedish city of Malmö, which lies just opposite Copenhagen across the body of water known as Öresund. The party was happy, as such Swedish parties are apt to be; and in the midst of the general gaiety, as the guests were sipping their *svensk punsch*, Jacobsen, who was normally self-conscious in public to the point of the ridiculous, suddenly sprang up on a convenient piece of furniture and delivered an eloquent impromptu address, which he brought to a resounding close with the surprisingly bald announcement: "I am a poet!—the devil take me I am a poet!" The announcement was received with appropriately tumultuous applause by the none-too-sober Swedes who were present. Many a person momentarily befuddled by things less elevating than Swedish punch have been guilty of such semi-public outbreaks as this without ever attaining in later years any genuine literary fame; and therefore the story would be merely amusing had it happened to the average man. But in Jacobsen's case the words represented a conviction lying far deeper in his consciousness than might be intimated in the casual surface effusions of a befuddled state of elevation. He meant profoundly what he said on this occasion, albeit the occasion was somewhat riotous. And he was soon to prove conclusively that his words were more than the empty gesture of an expansive, semi-drunken state of mind.

It was the success of "Mogens," together with the encouragement which contact with Georg Brandes and the other members of "Litteraturselskabet" brought to Jacobsen in the early 1870's, that was decisive in directing practically all of his best energies from these years on into the field of creative literature. In fact the only serious activity, besides the writing of fiction, which Jacobsen indulged in from this time until his death was the translation into Danish of two of Darwin's most significant works, the *Origin of Species* (under the Danish title *Arternes Oprindelse*, 1872) and the *Descent of Man* (*Menneskets Afstamning*, 1874). These translations are to be regarded, of course, simply as the last phase of the work that Jacobsen had begun in his articles championing Darwin's ideas in the pages of the *Nyt dansk Maanedsskrift*.

Already while he was engaged on these translations he had begun work on *Marie Grubbe*, the first in appearance of the two novels for which his name is now famous. *Marie Grubbe* is an historical novel dealing with Danish life in the late seventeenth century. Jacobsen manages in this novel to build up what is on the whole a brilliantly convincing background for his central action; and yet this background—minute, detailed, strikingly realistic—is never permitted to engage the reader's entire interest at the expense of the central character. Marie Grubbe was a Danish noblewoman, who had early been married into high places, and yet who ultimately spurned the artificial life of court intrigue and came to find what joy there might be "in our essentially tragic human life" by becoming first the mistress and later

the wife of a simple peasant workman. The story of this interesting Danish woman of a couple of centuries before had been
kept alive in Holberg's *Epistler* (the Danish dramatist had met
and conversed with Marie Grubbe in her last years) and in
Hans Christian Andersen's tales entitled *Hønse-Grethe for-
tæller*; and it is in these two sources that Jacobsen seems first
to have come upon the story which was to form the basis of his
novel. In March 1873 he was busily occupied at the Royal
Library in Copenhagen making source studies for his novel. He
worked among the sources with the severe conscientiousness
of the historical scholar; and composition proceeded therefore
very, very slowly.

His research in the archives was interrupted temporarily, in
late June of the same year, when he set out on a trip across the
Continent: first going to Berlin; later to Dresden, Prague, and
Vienna; then to Munich and Innsbrück; and finally to Italy—
Venice, Bologna, Ravenna, Florence. He seems to have enjoyed
these travels immensely; and the host of new impressions that
clamored in upon his consciousness had a bracing effect upon
his mind and imagination. But at Florence he and his companions were subjected to an unexpected shock: Jacobsen, who
had not been feeling his best, spat up some blood. Outwardly,
among his companions, Jacobsen tried to make light of the
episode; but it is clear that at this time he suddenly lost all
interest in travel and wished to return to Denmark, especially
to Thisted and the quiet of his home there. In October 1873 he
did hasten home—a man marked by death, though the real
seriousness of his case was not as yet apparent.

The family doctor at Thisted, however, saw the truth, and
his investigation of Jacobsen's condition led him to very grave
conclusions. After observing the symptoms of his patient for a
month, he wrote among other things the following statement
on Jacobsen's condition: "When Herr Jacobsen in the autumn
came back to Thisted after his foreign travel his condition was
to a high degree disquieting. He was extremely underweight,
breathed with difficulty, coughed, suffered constantly from night
sweating; his voice was markedly hoarse, and upon stethoscopic
examination there was observed a congestion in the tip of the

right lung, plus a cavern." The doctor gave Jacobsen, who was then only twenty-six, about two years to live.

Two years to live—and he had only begun a literary career which held so much of promise. One thinks inevitably of Keats. The judgment of the physician was hard; but Jacobsen did not lose spirit. By exercising extreme care he was able to stretch the two years into some months more than eleven years; and during these eleven years, by means of persistent, courageous effort, periodically interrupted for months at a time by recurrent lapses into severely distressing tubercular attacks, he brought forth that small body of exquisitely finished work which will remain as long as a Danish literary tradition remains as one of the most worthy chapters in the history of Danish fiction.

Marie Grubbe, whose first two chapters Jacobsen had permitted to appear in the journal edited by the Brandes brothers *Det nittende Aarhundrede* in 1874, was later taken over by the publisher Hegel and appeared finally in full-length form for the Christmas book trade of 1876. The novel was received by public and critics alike almost without exception with tremendous enthusiasm. A second edition had to be published in February 1877; and very soon afterward the novel appeared in both Swedish and German translations. Readers of *Marie Grubbe* were particularly impressed by Jacobsen's brilliant handling of historical episode and historical background, and by the amazing stylistic virtuosity of the novelist. Danish literature had never known prose like this. The opening passage of the novel, with its unforgettably caressing movement, its soft, haunting melodies, and its brilliantly suggestive coloring, had an overwhelming fascination for Jacobsen's Danish readers; and other passages in the novel were equally effective in their way.

Only one serious protest seems to have been raised, and this by a critic in the Swedish *Göteborgs Handels Tidning*. The Swedish critic found both the moral implications of the novel and the brilliant sensuousness of its style distinctly dangerous literary phenomena. The attack, from one point of view, was not without a certain foundation. Jacobsen had in *Marie Grubbe* touched upon certain phases of morality and sex in a manner to which a relatively conservative North had not as yet become accustomed. Ibsen's *Ghosts* was not to appear for another five years, and *Hedda Gabler* came nine years after *Ghosts*; while Strindberg's brutally frank naturalistic studies in sex and the family did not come until well along in the '80's—the two volumes of *Married* in 1884 and 1885, *The Father* in 1887, and *Miss Julia* in 1888. Possibly it was the form in which Jacobsen wrote—the historical novel—which exposed him less immediately to the attack of the moralists who later were to be so sensitive to *Ghosts* and *Miss Julia* and other aggressively frank treatments of the problem of sex. In any case it is a matter of record that at least one Swedish critic did see some of the "dangerous" ethical implications of Jacobsen's *Marie Grubbe*, and minced no words in pointing them out. Danish critics apparently took little cognizance of this matter, until it reappeared in more obvious form in the pages of *Niels Lyhne* in 1880; but then some of the more "moral" among them did take up the hue and cry—and this time with a vengeance.

II

Unlike *Marie Grubbe*, Jacobsen's second novel *Niels Lyhne* deals with contemporary Danish life—not with the '70's and '80's, Jacobsen's own generation strictly speaking, but with the transitional period which led immediately up to these two decades and which reflected many of the essential problems of these decades. *Niels Lyhne* is primarily a study in decadent psychology. Niels, the hero of the novel, goes through all of the successive phases of a progressive disillusionment, a disillusionment which finally brings him to "the death—the difficult death." An incurable romantic dreamer by temperament, and yet harboring a skeptical hereditary strain in direct opposition to his romantic dream world, Niels came to find that the realities of life serve but to shatter his inner dream world at every point. And so he finally dies—bravely? . . . yes, so we are told. Yet how sadly hopeless his last days were, days without form or direction, a poignantly meaningless succession of hours: "He had lost faith in himself, lost his belief in the power of human beings to bear the life they had to live. Existence had sprung a leak, and its contents were seeping out through all the cracks without plan or purpose." The reader of the novel may be permitted to judge for himself with what degree of buoyancy or vigor Niels at last came to formulate the final solitary postulate in his ultimate strangely decadent stoic profession of faith: "To bear life as it is! to bear life as it is and allow life to shape itself according to its own laws."

If *Niels Lyhne* is, in the first place, a study in the decadent psychology of a particular individual, whose every mood is dissected and whose final tragic destiny is pursued relentlessly to its hopeless end, the novel is also to be looked upon more broadly as symptomatic of a generation. Niels is the transition type of the mid-nineteenth century—a youth nurtured early in an unreal world of Romantic literature, but a youth who comes by degrees face to face with the sterner materials of an actual world. He comes thus, in the last analysis, to represent the tragic merging in a single personality of romanticism and realism—

> wandering between two worlds,
> The one dead, the other powerless to be born.

The novel in this sense becomes a penetrating analysis in fictional form of certain developmental phases in nineteenth century European culture, particularly as they find expression in the artistic and intellectual life of Scandinavia in the middle and late nineteenth century. The two worlds which make their impacts upon Niels, the world of romance and the world of reality, are illustrated in the pages of the novel in a great variety of ways. Most significant, perhaps, in the impressionable, formative period of Niels's childhood and early youth, were the extreme romantic tastes of his mother, who was constantly dreaming about

> . . . snowy Alpine peaks above blue-black mountain lakes, and sparkling rivers between vine-clad banks, and long lines of mountains with ruins peeping out of the woods, and then lofty halls with marble gods. . . .

and who found so much sustenance for such dreams in

. . . the poems! They teemed with new ideas and profound truths about life in the great outside world, where grief was black, and joy was red; they glowed with images, foamed and sparkled with rhythm and rhyme. They were all about young girls, and the girls were noble and beautiful—how noble and beautiful they never knew themselves. Their hearts and their love meant more than the wealth of all the earth; men bore them up in their hands, lifted them high in the sunshine of joy, honored and worshipped them, and were delighted to share with them their thoughts and plans, their triumphs and renown. They would even say that these same fortunate girls had inspired all the plans and achieved all the triumphs.

Why might not she herself be such a girl? They were thus and so—and they never knew it themselves. How was she to know what she really was? And the poets all said very plainly that this was life, and that it was not life to sit and sew, work about the house, and make stupid calls.

The almost too obvious irony of these last lines is resolved into a crushing *reductio ad absurdum* in the paragraph that immediately follows—

When all this was sifted down, it meant little beyond a slightly morbid desire to realize herself, a longing to find herself, which she had in common with many other young girls with talents a little above the ordinary. It was only a pity that there was not in her circle a single individual of sufficient distinction to give her the measure of her own powers. There was not even a kindred nature. So she came to look upon herself as something wonderful, unique, a sort of exotic plant that had grown in these ungentle climes and had barely strength enough to unfold its leaves; though in more genial warmth, under a more powerful sun, it might have shot up, straight and tall, with a gloriously rich and brilliant bloom. Such was the image of her real self that she carried about in her mind. She dreamed a thousand dreams of those sunlit regions and was consumed with longing for this other and richer self, forgetting— what is so easily forgotten—that even the fairest dreams and the deepest longings do not add an inch to the stature of the human soul.

Though these paragraphs describe Niels's mother before her marriage, she was no different after marriage, even when her first child came; and Niels, in consequence, as we shall see in some detail later, was brought up as a boy on an increasingly hectic diet of unbelievable romantic tales and dangerously egotistical romantic poetry.

But this dream world of Romanticism, into which Niels had been introduced by his mother was already crumbling under the weight of its own extravagant superstructure long before the middle of the nineteenth century. And what remained of the crumbling edifice was shattered almost beyond recognition by the new spirit of science and the frontal attack of the empirical sister philosophies of utilitarianism and positivism. Men had come to see that there is a tremendous disparity between the fairest dreams of romance and the cold facts of reality; and many of them went on to conclude, as Jacobsen puts it, "that even the fairest dreams and the deepest longings do not add an inch to the stature of the human soul." And so they turned their backs on romanticism and hailed a new order of realism.

Those who were strong could make such a shift with impunity, and suffer no ill effects. Not so with the more sensitive, those who were more emotionally impressionable; and among these was Niels Lyhne. Gladly as Niels ultimately welcomed, on the theoretical side, the new intellectual freedom afforded by a world of reality, his emotional roots, and all that these implied in terms of his unconscious and subconscious character, were too deeply implanted in the world of romance to be summarily torn up with no attendant strain upon the delicately balanced fibres of his spiritual organism. And so he became—not consciously it must be stressed (for a conscious artistic "program" of decadence had not as yet been formulated), and yet very really—an inevitable victim of that kind of spiritual *malaise* which came by the end of the century to be called decadence. If one objects, on purely literary historical grounds, to calling Niels a decadent, he is in any case a transition figure of the mid-nineteenth century which was being swept rapidly toward decadence in the more strictly historical *fin de siècle* sense of the term.

The composition of *Niels Lyhne* proceeded even more slowly than had *Marie Grubbe*, if that is possible. Jacobsen had chosen his subject and had already considered certain aspects of his approach to the problem long before the completion of *Marie Grubbe*; but he did not undertake any part of the actual composition of *Niels Lyhne* (except for a fragment which he had written long before he had planned his novel and with no intention at the time of incorporating it in his novel) until *Marie Grubbe* had been completed. Then, however, he set resolutely about the composition of his new novel; but the attacks of his illness recurred now with increasing frequency and intensity, and his work in consequence suffered severely from constant forced interruptions.

He insisted always, however, upon the same scrupulous standard of workmanship which he had maintained in the composition of *Marie Grubbe*; and yet conscientious care in matters of detail could hardly save *Niels Lyhne* from a certain hectic artificiality of manner—a manner perhaps inevitable in the creative product of a man who stood hourly in the shadow of death. Those who have read both *Marie Grubbe* and *Niels Lyhne* in the original will feel a distinct difference in stylistic tone; and this difference will be felt even more sharply by those readers who have also gone through the pages of "Mogens," the short story which was composed before Jacobsen first became stricken by disease. There is a certain youthful effusiveness, a kind of hearty exuberance just short of vigor in the description of nature in both "Mogens" and *Marie Grubbe* that is almost totally lacking in *Niels Lyhne*. Marvelously beautiful as are some of the descriptive passages in *Niels Lyhne*, theirs is the beauty of decay: a note of nervous artificiality infuses them. One might dip into the pages of *Niels Lyhne* and find almost anywhere such passages as these:

. . . The sitting-room was flooded with sunshine, and a blossoming oleander made the air heavy with its sweet fragrance. There was no sound except a muffled splash from the flower-stand whenever the goldfish moved in their glass dish. . . .

One evening she [Niels's mother] was sitting alone in the summer parlor, gazing out through the wide-open doors. The trees of the garden hid the gold and crimson of the sunset, but in one spot the trunks parted to reveal a bit of fiery sky, from which a sunburst of long, deep golden rays shot out, waking green tints and bronze-brown reflections in the dark leafy masses.

High above the restless tree-tops, the clouds drifted dark against a smoke-red sky, and as they hurried on, they left behind them little loosened tufts, tiny little strips of cloud which the sunlight steeped in a wine-colored glow.

It is clear from such passages that the subtly beautiful disintegration of decadence is at work on Jacobsen's style, a style which in earlier years, despite its disturbing involutions, its artificial mannerisms, and its laboured precision of word choice, managed somehow to retain a certain spontaneity, a certain undeniable vigor of its own—a vigor as of the fine breath of springtime, pulsing though never violent, strong and yet not muscular. The style of *Niels Lyhne*, on the other hand, is a style fitted to late summer and early autumn moods—a style enervatingly heavy in both its movement and its imagery, a style thoroughly in keeping with the weary ennui which Niels always came to feel after some tentative excursion into the world of action and passion outside his own brooding inner self. It must have been particularly *Niels Lyhne* that the Swedish poet and critic Ola Hansson had in mind when he spoke of Jacobsen's style as reminding one of a "hot-house or a garden of roses."

In November 1878 Jacobsen, who because of the precarious condition of his health had fled temporarily to Montreux in the south of France, penned a long letter to Georg Brandes in which he indicates what he is trying to do in *Niels Lyhne*. This letter reveals clearly that Jacobsen's central purpose in *Niels Lyhne* was to make a careful, objective study in a transitional decadent generation—a generation of youth which sought various ways out of a common dilemma, with no single individual of this generation finding a wholly satisfactory solution of his immediate personal problem. The novel itself reveals how carefully Jacobsen had analyzed the various types representative of this generation of youth and the way in which each attempted to work his way out of the hopelessly entangled web of mood and idea and circumstance which surrounded him. Those who—according to Jacobsen's letter to Brandes—"struck out against the old but did not respect the new which they themselves accepted" are represented in the novel by Dr. Hjerrild, a young medical man, completely disillusioned, a thoroughgoing skeptic, who scoffed freely in one of the important passages in the novel at Niels's idealistic atheism. Those who—as described in the letter—finally succumbed to "the siren voices of tradition and childhood memories on the one hand and the thundering condemnation of society on the other" are to be found represented in the novel in such a character as Fru Boye, who talked with a certain daring charm of the necessity of freedom in art and poetry, and even for that matter in love, but who finally found established society too strong for her.

Fru Boye and Dr. Hjerrild are but two of the typical representatives of a generation of transition which *Niels Lyhne* concerns itself with. Others are also sketched by Jacobsen in these pages, some in greater, some in less detail. It is, of course, in Niels himself that we find by far the most exhaustive and penetrating analysis of a representative of this generation of transition. Idealistic in intent, yet often weak in character, Niels goes through his short experience of life a constant victim of his own ineptness and his own illusions. Both heredity and an early environment had dealt unkindly with him; and ultimately, in young manhood, he comes to succumb to an inevitable, almost sordid fate—without, however, either yielding, as had Fru Boye, to a society which he despised, or giving himself up to the kind of worldly cynicism represented in Dr. Hjerrild. For the former of these he was too sensitive, for the latter he was perhaps too weak.

In some regards Jacobsen's study in the gradual decay of the character of Niels reminds one of Flaubert's analysis of the disintegration of character in *Madame Bovary*. Both authors maintain throughout their novels a relatively severe objective attitude toward their central characters; and in each case sentimental romantic illusions, nurtured by the early reading of romantic literature, are to a considerable extent responsible for the final tragedy. And yet in many respects the character of Niels differs very markedly from that of Emma Bovary, particularly in his essentially intellectual cast of mind, and his broad though rather futile theoretical concern with the larger problems of humanity and human culture—a concern which Emma Bovary, in her paltry romantic neuroticism, was incapable of even remotely conceiving.

At various times in his short, tragic experience of life Niels becomes deeply preoccupied with religious considerations. Sincere as Jacobsen doubtless was in his effort to present the religious theme in his novel, it must, I think, be the judgment of posterity that the specifically religious element in *Niels Lyhne* is hardly convincing. There is something forced and wooden for the most part in the way in which the religious material is introduced, so forced and wooden that even the sympathetic reader who preserves any vestige of critical balance tends to be disturbed, if not definitely skeptical for a moment, both as to Jacobsen's knowledge of human psychology and his ability to motivate with intelligence and critical taste certain of the narrative episodes in his novel. We are expected, for example, to accept without protest the assumption that Niels as a boy of twelve, because of a single experience in which his prayer had not been answered, arrives at the theoretical conclusion that there is no God. Hardy's grotesquely pathetic little Father Time goes even farther, we remember, not without a shudder; but Father Time is one of those melancholy prodigies in the English novelist which even Hardy enthusiasts would rather pass over in silence. About the only thing we can be thankful for is that Hardy *did kill* his gruesome little creation at a tender age. What he should have done with Father Time had the child continued to drag out an unbearable existence is beyond at least the average human imagination.

The boyhood atheism in Jacobsen's Niels seems questionable enough in itself; but we might feel, at least, that it was fitted less artificially into the general narrative pattern of the novel were we kept even occasionally aware of Niels's religious position in the years which immediately follow. But not so. We do not come upon the religious theme again until quite late in the novel, when Niels has reached the estate of manhood—and then in an episode which seems rather forcibly foisted upon the reader for purposes expository rather than narrative. It is in this passage that Niels defines his position as an idealistic atheist to his friend Dr. Hjerrild, whose practical-minded skepticism cannot but smile in not entirely gentle irony at the adolescent vehemence with which Niels insists upon his melancholy paradox: "There is no God, and man is his prophet." Near the very end of the novel, it is true, the religious element seems more convincingly motivated than it had been before; but perhaps our impression is more favorable at this point largely because we sense in the later developments of the novel the close autobiographical parallel in Jacobsen's treatment of the religious theme. We know that Jacobsen himself was soon to face "the death—the difficult death"; and we know that he was steeling himself to face death, as Niels did finally, without the comforting solace of a traditional religion. Though our consciousness of this parallel may tend to soften the severity of our judgment of Jacobsen's treatment of the religious theme in the last chapters of *Niels Lyhne*, we can hardly count Jacobsen among the novelists who deal adequately with the religious theme. Jacobsen's *Niels Lyhne* lacks almost entirely the profundity of religious analysis which we come upon in Sigrid Undset's *Kristin Lavransdatter*; and even Selma Lagerlöf's *Jerusalem* goes far beyond *Niels Lyhne* in its understanding of religious psychology. It may be that Jacobsen's characters hardly lend themselves to convincing religious portraiture . . . it may be that Jacobsen himself was temperamentally incapable of creating a convincing religious problem in fiction . . . it may be—and this seems most reasonable—that Jacobsen, a scientist, was too close to the essentially materialistic science of his century. . . . Whatever the reason, it would seem apparent that Jacobsen is superficial in his religious analysis in *Niels Lyhne*—superficial at least in comparison with the maturity of his art and critical judgment as reflected in almost any other important aspect of his novel.

It should perhaps be pointed out in passing, simply as a refreshing curiosity in the history of decadent literature, that Jacobsen does not make of Niels the usual type of decadent (appearing both in fiction and in life late in the century), who finds ultimate "solace" in some vague form of "mysticism" strangely compounded of a weary sensuousness and a false humility which was so often but another form of egotism. Confused as Niels was in most of his experiences of life, he never sought a weak solace in that form of "religious mysticism" which often hovered like a paradoxically macabre spirit at the end of a path of satiated sensuousness. Niels maintained, with only one momentary relapse, a clear-headed materialistic idealism to the end—even though he found this to be the hard way.

If Jacobsen's touch is uncertain in his handling of the religious problem in *Niels Lyhne*, he is by contrast firm and convincing in his treatment of those other phases of Niels's inner development which affected his character and gradually combined to result in an attitude of disillusioned hopelessness which finally led him to a form of exit from this world just short of suicide. It is in Jacobsen's penetrating analysis of the double influence on Niels's character of heredity and environment, and the way in which these two influences ultimately come to affect the will, that the novel achieves its real intellectual distinction and its permanent critical significance.

As a scientist Jacobsen was by training highly conscious of the determining influence of heredity upon human character. It is therefore natural for him to sketch in the opening chapters of *Niels Lyhne* the family history of Niels's parents, though he does not go to the length of providing the reader with such an elaborate genealogical machinery as is to be found in Zola's Rougon-Macquart novels. Especially important are the detailed references to heredity which Jacobsen introduces so skillfully in the two opening chapters of *Niels Lyhne*. The first chapter is given over almost entirely to an analysis of the temperament and character of the parents of Niels as they had been determined by the earlier history of their families. The opening paragraphs strike the note which is maintained throughout the chapter—

She [Niels's mother] had the black, luminous eyes of the Blid family with delicate, straight eyebrows; she had their boldly shaped nose, their strong chin, and full lips. The curious line of mingled pain and sensuousness about the corners of her mouth was likewise an inheritance from them, and so were the restless movements of her head; but her cheek was pale; her hair was soft as silk, and was wound smoothly around her head.

Not so the Blids; their coloring was of roses and bronze. Their hair was rough and curly, heavy as a mane, and their full, deep, resonant voices bore out the tales told of their forefathers, whose noisy hunting-parties, solemn morning prayers, and thousand and one amorous adventures were matters of family tradition.

The Blids had lived solidly, at times even lustily; but "beauty never stirred any raptures in them, and they were never visited by vague longings or day-dreams." But Bartholine, daughter of the Blids and future mother of Niels, differed markedly from the usual Blid formula—"She had no interest in the affairs of the fields and the stables, no taste for the dairy and the kitchen—none whatever." Poetry, in consequence, became her passion—romantic poetry, we recall, in which "grief was black, and joy was red," and in which fantastically heroic men found inspiration for triumphantly heroic labors in passionately devoted women.

And as Bartholine read such poetry she dreamed—dreamed, and prayed, that *she* might one day meet and be loved by a prince among men. A suitor did finally come to her—almost, it seemed, as in her beloved poems.

Young Lyhne of Lønborggaard was the man, and he was the last male scion of a family whose members had for three generations been among the most distinguished people in the county. As burgomasters, revenue-collectors, or royal commissioners, often rewarded with the title of councillor of justice, the Lyhnes in their maturer years had served king and country with diligence and honor. In their younger days they had travelled in France and Germany, and these trips, carefully planned and carried out with great thoroughness, had enriched their receptive minds with all the scenes of beauty and the knowledge of life that foreign lands had to offer. Nor were these years of travel pushed into the background, after their return, as mere reminiscences, like the memory of a feast after the last candle has burned down and the last note of music has died away. No, life in their homes was built on these years; the tastes awakened in this manner were not allowed to languish, but were nourished and developed by every means at their command. Rare copper plates, costly bronzes, German poetry, French juridical works, and French philosophy were everyday matters and common topics in the Lyhne households.

Their bearing had an old-fashioned ease, a courtly graciousness, which contrasted oddly with the heavy majesty and awkward pomposity of the other county families. Their speech was well rounded, delicately precise, a little marred, perhaps, by rhetorical affectation, yet it somehow went well with those large, broad figures with their domelike foreheads, their bushy hair growing far back on their temples, their calm, smiling eyes, and slightly aquiline noses. The lower part of the face was too heavy, however, the mouth too wide, and the lips much too full.

Bartholine's suitor, the young Lyhne, was, it is to be noted, "the *last* scion" of what had once been a strong, vigorous family; but the family had just about exhausted its early vigor after "three generations . . . among the most distinguished people in the county." We are told further that in the young Lyhne's person, was to be observed all of the physical traits of his family—

but more faintly, and, in the same manner, the family intelligence seemed to have grown weary in him. None of the mental problems or finer artistic enjoyments that he encountered stirred him to any zeal or desire whatsoever. He had simply striven with them in a painstaking effort which was never brightened by joy in feeling his own powers unfold or pride in finding them adequate. Mere satisfaction in a task accomplished was the only reward that came to him.

During his courtship with Bartholine, however, the young Lyhne managed somehow, and not without a certain sincerity of feeling, to overcome the natural lethargy which he normally had toward the world of beauty which was supposed to be found in nature and in books. And Bartholine was entranced, beyond herself with joy—here, in the flesh, *was* her hero of romance!

Bartholine was happy; for her love enabled her to dissolve the twenty-four hours into a string of romantic episodes. It was romance when she went down the road to meet him; their meeting was romance, and so was their parting. It was romance when she stood on the hilltop in the light of the setting sun and waved him one last farewell before going up to her quiet little chamber, wistfully happy to give herself up to thoughts of him; and when she included his name in her evening prayer, that was romance, too.

The period of courtship was short, full, intense: for Bartholine it was breath-takingly perfect; and for young Lyhne of Lønborggaard it provided a genuine, though momentary, glow of young, romantic enthusiasm. And the first year of married life continued in the same exaggerated lyric vein,—

But when their wedded life had lost its newness, Lyhne could no longer conceal from himself that he wearied of always seeking new expressions for his love. He was tired of donning the plumage of romance and eternally spreading his wings to fly through all the heavens of sentiment and all the abysses of thought. He longed to settle peacefully on his own quiet perch and drowse, with his tired head under the soft, feathery shelter of a wing. He had never conceived of love as an ever-wakeful, restless flame, casting its strong, flickering light into every nook and corner of existence, making everything seem fantastically large and strange. Love to him was more like the quiet glow of embers on their bed of ashes, spreading a gentle warmth, while the faint dusk wraps all distant things in forgetfulness and makes the near seem nearer and more intimate.

He was tired, worn out. He could not stand all this romance. He longed for the firm support of the commonplace under his feet, as a fish suffocating in hot air languishes for the clear, fresh coolness of the waves. It must end sometime, when it had run its course. Bartholine was no longer inexperienced either in life or books. She knew them as well as he. He had given her all he had—and now he was expected to go on giving. . . .

Bartholine, indeed, gradually came to feel some half-formed misgivings that her "hero" was not all that she had dreamed him to be; but her own romantic yearnings were insatiable, and so her husband's apparently growing indifference to an artificial world of romance "only made her pursue romance the more ardently, and she tried to bring back the old state of things by lavishing on him a still greater wealth of sentiment and a still greater rapture, but she met so little response that she almost felt as if she were stilted and unnatural." When she finally came to see clearly that her husband could not maintain the almost tropical romantic luxuriance with which her own dream-world had invested him, she became bitterly disappointed in him and withdrew into herself to grieve over her disillusionment.

And the opening chapter of *Niels Lyhne* is brought to a conclusion with a short paragraph containing the single laconic announcement: "Such was the state of things between man and wife when Bartholine brought forth her first child. It was a boy, and they called him Niels."

The second chapter continues, and with even greater emphasis, to develop the implications of hereditary influence upon character—now upon Niels, the delicately sensitive child of such a strangely assorted mating as was that of Bartholine and young Lyhne of Lønborggaard. And in addition to the emphasis which this chapter places upon the influence of heredity, we find preliminary evidences in these pages of that other influence—environment—which is to play a profoundly tragic part in the formation of the character of Niels. The child, we find, combines in his temperament both his mother's dangerously romantic ecstasy, and his father's curious compound of practicality and "strange, vegetative trance." At first the child drew mother and father together again, but only momentarily—only over his cradle; for as Niels began to grow the parents again drew apart, inevitably, struggling "unconsciously for mastery over his young soul from the moment the first gleam of intelligence in him gave them something to work on."

Bartholine, of course, tried to influence her child through his imagination. She never tired of telling Niels stories of high romance, tales in which magnificent heroes, often sorely tried, managed always somehow to extricate themselves from what seemed to be inextricable predicaments. Niels, as a child of Bartholine's, was not lacking in imaginative sensibility; and so he would often follow his mother's words with an emotional abandon which went far to alleviate the bitterness which Bartholine had felt earlier on the occasion of the gradual defection of her husband from these same worlds of romance. But her joy in Niels was not unmixed. Intensely as the boy would enter into the stories of his mother's romantic dream-world, he would oftentimes, in the very midst of some impossibly heroic narrative, feel half-consciously that this world of story was a conjured one—not one that really existed, or even could exist.

. . . Often his mother would tell him stories and describe the woeful plight of the hero, until Niels could not see any way out of all this trouble, and could not understand how the misery closing like an impenetrable wall tighter and tighter around him and the hero could be overcome. Then it happened more than eleven times that he would suddenly press his cheek against his mother's and whisper, with eyes full of tears and lips trembling, "But it isn't *really* true?" And when he had received the comforting answer he wanted, he would heave a deep sigh of relief and settle down contentedly to listen to the end.

His mother did not quite like this defection.

It is clear from this passage, and from the paragraphs in the novel which immediately follow, that the boy's half-formed consciousness of the discrepancy between the actual world and the world of romance was not primarily a sign of a saner, healthier, more balanced view of existence which might later in life enable him to break the subtly decadent appeal that romance exercised over his boyhood imagination. Niels's boyhood skepticism—it is important to note—was motivated more by fear than by insight. The romances terrified the boy, even while they fascinated him. But life, as he viewed it afar off, terrified him even more. He half suspected, with the vague premonitory clairvoyance of the child, that life itself might be evil—and that, unlike the heroes of his mother's romantic tales, who always somehow triumphed over insuperable odds, he might not have the power to cope successfully with life.

This consciousness roused in him a craving to enjoy his childhood to the full, to suck it up through every sense, not to spill a drop, not a single one. Therefore his play had an intensity, sometimes lashed into a passion, under the pressure of an uneasy sense that time was flowing away from him before he could gather from its treasureladen waters all they brought, as one wave broke upon another. He would sometimes throw himself down on the ground and sob in despair when a holiday hung heavy on his hands for the lack of one thing or another—playmates, inventiveness, or fair weather—and he hated to go to bed, because sleep was empty of events and devoid of sensation.

This was the mother in Niels—the ecstatic yearning to escape from reality into a world of exaggerated sensations and of dreams. But at times he could not maintain the ecstasy. "It would sometimes happen," we are told, "that he grew weary, and his imagination ran out of colors." On such occasions he would feel dispirited, wretched, dimly conscious that he was not living up to the magnificent ideals of his mother's romantic heroes. Wretched as he felt, however, he could not summon sufficient strength to lift himself back into the magniloquently facile world of his mother's tales.

On such days he would shun his mother, and, with a sense of following an ignoble instinct, would seek his father, turning a willing ear and a receptive mind to the latter's earth-bound thoughts and matter-of-fact explanations. He felt at home with his father and rejoiced in the likeness between them, well-nigh forgetting that it was the same father whom he was wont to look down upon with pity from the pinnacles of his dream-castle. Of course this was not present in his childish mind with the clearness and definiteness given it by the spoken word, but it was all there, though unformed, unborn, in a vague and intangible embryo form. It was like the curious vegetation at the bottom of the sea when seen through layers of ice. Break the ice, or draw that which lives in the dimness out into the full light of speech—what happens is the same: that which is now seen and now grasped is not, in its clearness, the shadowy thing that was.

Thus it was that a curiously defective mixed heredity and a hopelessly dual and contradictory childhood training combined to make a pathetically confused battlefield of the delicately sensitive mind and soul of the young Niels. The dangerous ecstasy of his mother's temperament gave battle in Niels's very blood to the vegetative earthiness of his father's essentially heavy, placid nature; and neither could attain the mastery, for neither contained sufficient vigor to give any substantial centrality to Niels's boyhood character. And this struggle in the blood was intensified, as the boy grew up, by two modes of training diametrically opposed, each appealing to the boy by turns, and the two in combination certainly portending final disaster for Niels.

As the novel proceeds, less specific attention is given to the
element of family inheritance; but the emphasis already placed
upon heredity in the first two chapters lingers on in the reader's
memory—tending to explain by a kind of echo-like implication
much that follows in Niels's life, and lending a deeply rooted,
organic inevitability to the final tragedy of Niels.

It is with the problem of the will that Jacobsen becomes
primarily concerned in his analysis of the character of Niels
in the remainder of the novel. Jacobsen saw—as did his French
contemporary Paul Bourget in the *Essais de psychologie con-
temporaine* (1883)—that the central, or at least the ultimate,
problem in the psychology of decadence is the problem of the
will. The genuine decadent is a completely disillusioned man, a
man, therefore, in whom will, as an instrument of morality,
tends to become increasingly less active—until, theoretically at
least, it ceases to exist at all as a stabilizing influence in life or
art. In the character of Niels, Jacobsen analyzes this process of
individual decadence, the gradual disintegration of a human
will. Not that Niels becomes a deliberate doctrinaire decadent,
such as Huysmans has created in the character of des Esseintes
in *A Rebours* (1884). Niels retains some of his early idealisms
even to the end; but by nature and by his early childhood training he is fundamentally unstable in character, and this instability became more pronounced in his youth and early manhood,
ultimately culminating in a series of personal disasters that
destroy almost every vestige of any power of will that he may
have had earlier in life.

Despite Niels's tentative childhood skepticisms over against
the world of romance to which his mother introduced him, a
skepticism that grew even more pronounced in his youth, he
never could quite shake off, even when he had grown to manhood, the early fascination that this world of romance had held
for him. It is not difficult to see that the emotional abandon with
which Niels threw himself into certain experiences of his later
life, particularly his series of distinctly dubious *affaires du
coeur*, found their psychological, if not physiological, origins
largely in the sensuous emotional chaos growing out of his

early interest in literary romances. In later life he merely trans-
fers his romantic sensibilities to a new object—women in the
flesh. The half-hesitant hysterical intensity of his emotional
responses to at least two of these women, Fru Boye and Fennimore, is of a piece with his childhood passion for romantic
tales. He was fascinated by these women, and yet half-fearful
of plunging boldly into the full warm stream of passion. He
"was afraid in his inmost heart," we are told in connection with
the Fru Boye affair, "of this mighty thing called passion." Fru
Boye he never actually possessed, except in the spasmodic mor-
bidities of an imagined world. Fennimore he did possess, though
only after she had become another man's wife. In both cases,
however, ultimate frustration was his fate; and in both cases
frustration led to disillusionment, disillusionment to a brooding
melancholy, and brooding melancholy to mental and emotional
lassitude—a slow but steady disintegration of the will.

It might be said that Niels's will, like Hamlet's, was "sicklied
o'er with the pale cast of thought." He lived timidly, always in
a world of reflection, and shrank instinctively from deliberate
vigorous action.

There was in Niels Lyhne's nature a lame reflectiveness, child
of an instinctive shrinking from decisive action, grandchild of a
subconscious sense that he lacked personality. He was always
struggling against this reflectiveness, sometimes goading himself by
calling it vile names, then again decking it out as a virtue that was
a part of his inmost self and was bound up with all his possibilities
and powers. But whatever he made of it, and however he looked
upon it, he hated it as a secret infirmity, which he might perhaps
hide from the world, but never from himself; it was always there
to humiliate him whenever he was alone with himself. How he
envied the audacity that rushes confidently into words, never heed-
ing that words bring actions, and actions bring consequences—
until those consequences are at its heels. People who possessed it
always seemed to him like centaurs—man and horse cast in a single
mould. With them impulse and leap were one, whereas he was
divided into rider and horse—impulse one thing, leap something
very different.

It is in such a weak, hesitant state of mind that Niels often found himself in the days of his maturity—especially in his relations with women and in his abortive efforts to become a poet. He found himself in such a condition in the very midst of his strange bit of love-making with Fru Boye, whom he might easily have possessed had he been a man of action. Instead, with characteristic indecision, he merely surrounded her in his imagination with a passionately sentimental halo; and when finally she announced to Niels her decision to capitulate to a critical society by "marrying into respectability," Niels could but brood and reflect—and with what characteristic inability to pass any vigorous judgment!

. . . But it was hard for him to throw stones, for had he not himself felt the magnetic attraction of honest bourgeoisie? If it had not been for that last meeting! If that really was what he accused her of, if it had been intended for a madcap farewell to the old life, one last wanton prank before she withdrew behind "the quintessence of propriety"—could it be possible? Such boundless self-scorn, such a cynical mockery of herself and him and all that they had shared of memories and hopes, of enthusiasm and sacred ideals! It made him blush and rage by turns.—But was he fair to her? After all, what had she done but tell him frankly and honestly: such and such things draw me to the other side and draw me powerfully, but I recognize your right even more fully than you ask, and here I am. If you can take me, I am yours; if not, I go where the power is greatest.—And if it were so, had she not been entirely within her rights? He had not been able to take her. The final decision *might* depend on such a little thing, on the shadow of a thought, the vibration of a mood.

The tone of these melancholy, indecisive reflections on a frustrated love is but the basic tone of Niels's love in itself: both his love and his after judgment of Fru Boye and himself as her lover are characterized by a fundamental timidity, a weak spirit of indecision which had its roots deep down in that "lame reflectiveness" which formed the ground-work of Niels's character. His later infatuation with Fennimore was less platonic than the affair with Fru Boye, probably because Fennimore was less discreetly sentimental than was Fru Boye. But here again Niels met with ultimate frustration; and the disillusionment which followed led him to a condition of absolute hopelessness, a mood in which even his powers of analysis—always sharp enough in the Fru Boye affair—were practically destroyed. "Whither could he flee to escape these attempts that always ended in the ditch?" he asked himself, nervously weak and sick at heart, when his affair with Fennimore had crashed beyond repair. And he goes on to reflect, wearily: "All his life had been nothing else, and it would never be anything else in the future; he knew that and felt it with such certainty that he sickened at the thought of all this futile endeavor, and he wished with his soul that he could run away and escape this meaningless fate."

Niels's feeble efforts to become a poet—no more happy than his adventures with women—serve further to illustrate that "lame reflectiveness" in his character. In fact here, even more than in his *affaires du coeur,* do we come upon evidences of a weak indecision—an indecision which proved to be completely fatal to any successful creative efforts. From the days of his childhood Niels had dreamed of one day becoming a poet. Characteristically, however, in those later days of youth and early manhood when the creative urge tends to be most vigorous, Niels revealed a temperamental indecision which made impossible on his part any vigorous creative activity as a poet. He was intelligent enough in these years to recognize the faults of the older Romantic poetry, its bombast, its love of facile paradox, its superficial primitivism; but he was not strong enough to create anything more significant, more virile—he could not bring himself to break fresh ground in other directions.

. . . What did they [the Romantics] write when they gave the call to battle? Pessimistic verses in which they declared that dogs were often more faithful than men and jailbirds more honest than those who walked freely about, eloquent odes to the effect that green woods and brown heath were preferable to dusty cities, stories of peasant virtue and rich men's vice, of red-blooded nature and anemic civilization, the narrowness of age and the divine right of youth. What modest demands they made when they wrote! They were at least bolder when they talked within four safe walls.

No, when his time came, he would give them music—a clarion call!

But Niels's proud "clarion call" never materialized in any strong and sustained creative efforts; it remained but an enthusiastic dream of his youth—a dream that became more nebulous and unreal the longer he lived, until at last it also "dies the death," a quiet, uncomplaining victim of disillusionment and indecision.

Niels's creative instinct, it is interesting to note, was most active during the emotional upsurge in the first stages of his strange love affair with Fru Boye. After that—except for a weak, wholly tentative rekindling of his poetic enthusiasms which happened to be associated with his mother's death days— Niels's creative energies steadily diminished, until they finally ceased to exist at all long before Niels himself found some kind of peace in physical death. The scrupulously exacting ideal of art which he had talked of to his mother as she lay dying was obviously beyond his power of execution, though he insisted on this occasion, with characteristic emotional accompaniments, upon making eternal vows to realize it. "Dearest, dearest!" he cries out to his dying mother, in a flood of hysterically heroic sentiment,

I *shall* be one of those who fight for the greatest, and I promise you that I shall not fail, that I shall always be faithful to myself and my gift. Nothing but the best shall be good enough. No compromise, Mother! When I weigh what I have done and feel that it isn't sterling, or when I hear that it has a crack or a flaw—into the oven it goes! Every single work must be my best! . . .

Such a rigid ideal of a perfected art requires the severest discipline of will to realize—the very quality of character most obviously lacking in Niels. He had poetic sensitivity, imaginative insight, and a rare gift of language; but he was timid in moments of actual creative activity, too critical of his own work—and so in the end everything went "into the oven." His poetic flights were fragmentary, incomplete, infused so deeply with the disintegrating breath of decadence that they had not sufficient vitality to take the final, perfect form of which he dreamed. To Niels had not been given the rare creative gift of a Baudelaire, who alone among decadent poets seemed able to express pro-

foundly decadent themes in a strong and perfectly moulded
classical art form.

Niels's mother died soon after her son's vows had been given.
Immediately thereafter Fru Boye broke with Niels. Meantime he
read much, and wrote a little—nothing, however, that satisfied
his own fastidious spirit. It was Fennimore's engagement, and
subsequent marriage, to Niels's friend Erik that became the last,
and fatal, blow to Niels's waning desire to become a poet. He
could not even at this time, however, totally forget his early
dreams of a poetic career. They haunted him oftentimes, like
subtly leering, strangely reproachful spirits; but they could not
lash him into action. They merely served to feed his already
"lame reflectiveness" with more materials productive of self-
irritation, self-disgust, and an ever more enervating weariness.

That unexpected engagement had been a hard blow to Niels. It
had a benumbing effect on him. He grew more bitter and less con-
fiding, and had no longer so much enthusiasm to pit against Hjerrild's pessimism. Though he still pursued his studies, their plan
was less and less definite, while his purpose of some time completing them and beginning his real life-work flickered uncertainly.
He lived much among people, but very little with them. They interested him, but he did not in the least care to have them be interested
in him; for he felt the force that should have driven him to do his
part with the others or against them slowly ebbing out of him. He
could wait, he told himself, even if he had to wait till it was too
late. Whoever has faith is in no hurry—that was his excuse to
himself. For he believed that, when he came down to the bed-rock
of his own nature, he did have faith strong enough to move mountains—the trouble was that he never managed to set his shoulder
to them. Once in a while, the impulse to create welled up in him,
and he longed to see a part of himself freed in work that should
be his very own. For days he would be excited with the happy,
titanic effort of carting the clay for his Adam, but he never formed
it in his own image. The will power necessary to persistent self-
concentration was not in him. Weeks would pass before he could
make up his mind to abandon the work, but he did abandon it,
asking himself, in a fit of irritation, why he should continue. What
more had he to gain? He had tasted the rapture of conception;
there remained the toil of rearing, cherishing, nourishing, carrying
to perfection—Why? For whom? He was no pelican, he told

himself. But argue as he might, he was dissatisfied with himself
and felt that he had not fulfilled his own expectations; nor did
it avail him to carp at these expectations and ask whether they
were well founded. He had reached the point where he had to
choose, for when first youth is past—early or late in accordance
with each person's individuality—then, early or late, dawns the
day when Resignation comes to us as a temptress, luring us to
forego the impossible and be content. And Resignation has much
in her favor; for how often have not the idealistic aspirations of
youth been beaten back, its enthusiasms been shamed, its hopes
laid waste!—The ideals, the fair and beautiful, have lost nothing
of their radiance, but they no longer walk here among us as in the
early days of our youth. The broad, firmly planted stairway of
worldly wisdom has conveyed them back, step by step, to that
heaven whence our simpler faith once brought them down; and
there they sit, radiant but distant, smiling but weary, in divine
quiescence, while the incense of a slothful adoration rises, puff on
puff, in festive convolutions.

Niels Lyhne was tired. These repeated runnings to a leap that
was never leaped had wearied him. Everything seemed to him
hollow and worthless, distorted and confused, and, oh, so petty! He
preferred to stop his ears and stop his mouth and to immerse himself in studies that had nothing to do with the busy everyday
world, but were like an ocean apart, where he could wander peacefully in silent forests of seaweed among curious animals.

He was tired, and the root of his weariness sprang from his
baffled hope of love; thence it had spread, quickly and surely,
through his whole being, to all his faculties and all his thoughts. . . .

Thus with a kind of infinitely oppressive weariness, brought on
by personal disillusionment and indecision, and intensified by
the vacillation and enervating spirit of his generation, Niels
Lyhne finally resigns himself to the emptily quiet waters of
poetic sterility.

Niels was but one of the weak, indecisive, over-reflective
children of an uncertain, weakly groping period of transition
moving on vaguely toward what seemed to be a more vigorous
modern world. He had little strength of his own, and only had
he been carried on the sturdy shoulders of a literary movement
which had something of the outward strength and confidence
of a *fait accompli* might he actually have opened his creative

vein. He rejects the methods and themes of Romantic poetry
as outworn, inadequate, unreal, and therefore not worthy of
his own talents; but he has not sufficient strength of will to shape
the products of a new, living, and vigorous literary realism. He
remains, in consequence, unproductive, sterile—a poet not
meanly endowed by nature, but one who never brought the
creative process to fruition. Heredity had given to him poetic
sensibilities, together with a character that was essentially
weak; and the environment of his youth—falling in an unstable
period of intellectual and aesthetic transition—had provided
that further element of instability in his life which made the
final fate of Niels, as artist and as man, inevitable. The skillful
manner in which Jacobsen traces this intricate interplay of forces
that work upon Niels's will and finally effect the complete decay
of his creative powers remains one of the few permanent
achievements in the analysis of decadent literary psychology. If
Niels Lyhne had no other qualities as a novel, it would remain
a classic on the strength of this distinction alone.

We have seen, however, that Jacobsen's novel can claim distinctions other than that which concerns itself narrowly with the
particular psychological problem of the disintegration of the
individual will. *Niels Lyhne* is a memorable novel because of a
remarkably subtle and beautifully modulated style . . . because
of its penetrating analysis of certain general cultural phases of
mid-nineteenth century life . . . because of its incisive study
of particular influences, hereditary and environmental, upon the
developing taste and intelligence of Niels. To these another—
finally—must be added. *Niels Lyhne* is the first Scandinavian
novel which gives an adequate treatment to those treacherous
subconscious and unconscious levels of human consciousness
which have come so to preoccupy many a novelist of our later
day. To the present-day reader, who has been exposed to a
James Joyce and Marcel Proust, a Dorothy Richardson and a
Virginia Woolf, Jacobsen's occasional ventures in the pages
of *Niels Lyhne* into the field of the subconscious and the unconscious may seem so incidental and fragmentary as to be of
no real importance. The impression, however, is hardly a fair

one; for, in the first place, it must be remembered that Jacobsen was something of a pioneer in the fictional emphasis upon the unconscious and subconscious phases of human psychology, and, in the second place, his actual accomplishments in the portrayal of such psychological phenomena are certainly neither mean nor accidental.

It is too much, of course, to expect to find in *Niels Lyhne* a thoroughgoing stream-of-consciousness novel in the manner of *Ulysses* or *Remembrance of Things Past*, or even *The Waves*. Niels is not being subjected more or less constantly by the author to any either elaborate or simple psychoanalytic treatment in which a host of more or less wayward impulses are noted or explained. Having been composed in the late 1870's, *Niels Lyhne* illustrates in substance most of the traditional practices in the technique of the novel as it was written during these years in Denmark and on the Continent. The discerning reader of Jacobsen's novel, however, will take note of some passages, not so infrequent, which strike a new note—if not in the broad processes of narrative technique, at least in the immediate manner of conceiving human character under the stress of particular circumstances. Space will permit me to deal with only one of these passages in any detail, though such passages might readily be multiplied. The passage in question—of central importance in the conduct of the novel because it deals penetratingly with the psychology of one of Niels's loves—should be quoted in some detail:

They [Fennimore and Niels] scoured the forest from end to end, eager to find all its treasures and marvels. They had divided it between them as children do; the part on one side of the road was Fennimore's property, and that on the other side was Niels's, and they would compare their realms and quarrel about which was the more glorious. Everything there had names—clefts and hillocks, paths and stiles, ditches and pools; and when they found a particularly magnificent tree, they gave that too a name. In this way they took complete possession and created a little world of their own which no one else knew and no one else was at home in, and yet they had no secret which all the world might not have heard.

As yet they had not.

But love was in their hearts, and was not there, as the crystals are present in a saturated solution, and yet are not present, not until a splinter or the merest particle of the right matter is thrown into the solution, releasing the slumbering atoms as if by magic, and they rush to meet one another, joining and riveting themselves together according to unsearchable laws, and in the same instant there is crystal—crystal.

So it was a trifle that made them feel they loved.

There is nothing to tell. It was a day like all other days, when they were alone together in the sitting-room, as they had been a hundred times before; their conversation was about things of no moment, and that which happened was outwardly as common and as every-day-like as possible. It was nothing except that Niels stood looking out of the window, and Fennimore came over to him and looked out too. That was all, but it was enough, for in a flash like lightning, the past and present and future were transformed for Niels Lyhne by the consciousness that he loved the woman standing by his side, not as anything bright and sweet and happy and beautiful that would lift him to ecstasy or rapture—such was not the nature of his love—but he loved her as something he could no more do without than the breath of life itself, and he reached out, as a drowning man clutches, and pressed her hand to his heart.

She understood him. With almost a scream, in a voice full of terror and agony, she cried out to him an answer and confession: "Oh, *yes,* Niels!" and snatched away her hand in the same instant. A moment she stood, pale and shrinking, then sank down with one knee in an upholstered chair, hiding her face against the harsh velvet of the back, and sobbed aloud.

That latter-day form of the stream-of-consciousness technique —which drops all exposition and allows the odd fragments of consciousness to take more or less exact form in equally odd fragments of words, phrases, or sentences—is not here attained; nor for that matter is it attempted. But the passage—in its emphasis upon the dramatic, unconscious *precipitation* of emotional experience into forms beyond our control, and yet forms of a most significant kind—reflects a conception of human psychology which, when more universally grasped and more consistently applied by later novelists, was to issue into that literary technique in fiction which we now refer to as the **stream-of-consciousness** technique.

At least two things would seem to be of particular interest in the passage quoted: first, the novelist's explicit recognition of the supreme importance of accidental, quite unconscious, even unidentifiable detail, physical or psychic, or both, which precipitated the instantaneous emotional recognition on the part of Fennimore and Niels; and secondly, the completeness of that recognition—a completeness which suggests the fundamentally organic nature of the psychic experience and the relation which the whole has to certain deep-seated laws of nature, primarily psychic in kind, and yet inextricably intertwined with and dependent upon the laws which govern physical phenomena. It is such a passage as this that gives significant content to a slightly cryptic statement by Jacobsen in his letter to Georg Brandes on the origins and composition of *Niels Lyhne*: "The emphasis throughout is placed particularly upon the psychological and also upon the physiological." As a scientist Jacobsen felt profoundly the intimate relation between the mind and the body, the mental and the material; and everywhere in his novels does he keep this relationship in mind. The paragraphs from *Niels Lyhne* which I have quoted should sufficiently demonstrate Jacobsen's consciousness of the intimate relation existing between the physical and the mental. If more evidence is needed, I refer the reader to the pages immediately following the quoted passage, pages in which the physical phases of the love of Fennimore and Niels are given what for Jacobsen is almost brutally sensual expression.

Upon reading these pages we can understand perhaps even today why it was that they—conceived with a severely naturalistic objectivity, and containing no expression of either praise or blame for the actions described—stirred up a fury of criticism among such critics in Denmark as felt it their duty to guard "the moral contents of literature." The novel was roundly condemned for its immoral tendencies by a critic in *Fædrelandet;* and many smaller organs of opinion took up the hue and cry from this very influential journal. The liberal Danish critics, such as Georg Brandes, were not of course disturbed by the moral questions involved. They praised the novel as a matter of course, though there seems to be some evidence to prove that they were not entirely satisfied with it—at least not as satisfied as they had been with *Marie Grubbe* four years earlier. It is interesting to note, incidentally, that the most enthusiastic contemporary praise for *Niels Lyhne* came from two famous Norwegians, Henrik Ibsen and Alexander Kielland. Ibsen, who seems to have been tremendously impressed by the novel, is reported to have said: *"Niels Lyhne* is the best book in our century."* And Kielland had written to Hegel: "That book, it seems to me, is the greatest that has appeared in my time. There is an infinity of things one can learn from it and admire in it."

It was natural that the novel should arouse both shocked condemnation and extreme praise at the time of its appearance. Its daring treatment of certain phases of the psychology of sex and its apparently sympathetic attitude toward literary and aesthetic decadence (a sympathy which Jacobsen himself denied vigorously) would hardly fail to invite indignant attacks upon the novel; and attacks on the part of the shocked "moral guardians" of society would naturally arouse the liberal critics of the day to a spirited defense. *Niels Lyhne,* however, is not to be finally evaluated in terms either of contemporary condemnation or contemporary praise. Today it neither shocks us as it did one class of an earlier generation, nor does it strike us as being the best book in the century. Present day criticism is ready to admit, however, that *Niels Lyhne* is a notable novel—perhaps the greatest among the group of novels written in the last two decades of the nineteenth century which occupy themselves with the problem of decadence. *Dorian Gray* is by comparison merely clever, *A Rebours* by comparison but a kind of fictional *tour de force,* and Herman Bang's *Generations without Hope* a decadent novel too heavily burdened with a massive weight of naturalistic detail. Garborg's *Trætte Mænd* ("Weary Men"), with its grim Carlylean irony, is in some senses a more powerful decadent novel than *Niels Lyhne*; but it does not hold together with the finely balanced unity of tone and theme that is attained by Jacobsen in his profoundly subtle characterization of a decadent spirit.

III
Jacobsen had only four and a half years left to live after the publication of *Niels Lyhne* in December of 1880. Three of these years—from May 1881 to July 1884—he resided in Copenhagen; the last year he awaited death at his parental home in Thisted. These were years of a hopelessly steady decline in his health. We know from his letters that he had definite plans for new literary work when he went up to Copenhagen in the spring of 1881; but his strength was hardly equal to the severe labor that literary creation always demanded of him. He managed, however, to maintain some kind of contact in the capital with his former circle of friends, and made a few new ones, notably with Alexander Kielland, who was resident with his family in Copenhagen in 1881-82. Jacobsen had dinner with the Kiellands almost every Sunday during these months; and regularly on these days, as the darkening hours of evening settled quietly down upon the home, he would gather the Kielland children about him and in his soft, gentle voice tell them tales from the *Arabian Nights*. Contact with these innocently lovely children seemed to bring him great pleasure during these days when his strength was slowly ebbing. Children—and flowers. The latter —his earliest and perhaps deepest love in life—brought him the greatest pleasure in his declining days. His friends were in the habit of sending flowers of all kinds in great abundance up to his darkly bare and melancholy quarters in Copenhagen; and Jacobsen would spend hour upon hour observing the delicately varied beauty of form and color and breathing in the marvelous fragrance of these flowers. "How he needed these flowers, how he understood them!" writes Georg Brandes in his admirable critical essay on Jacobsen. "Certainly no one in Denmark has loved and understood and sung of flowers as he."

Except for a few fragments of prose and poetry, Jacobsen was able to write only two short stories during these years: "Pesten i Bergamo" ("The Pestilence in Bergamo," 1881), a strangely gripping tale from the Italian Renaissance, and "Fru Fønss," which he finished in May of 1882. The latter was written as Jacobsen's literary farewell—first to his intimate circle of friends, and then to all the Danish people. The story itself is merely a narrative vehicle into which the author fits the letter which brings the story to a close. The letter is represented in the story as the farewell message of Fru Fønss to her children, composed upon her deathbed. The parallel with Jacobsen himself is apparent. Two thoughts in particular from this letter are those of Jacobsen himself as he prepares to leave the world: first, the love which he felt for the beautiful things of this world, and then the prayer that he might perchance be remembered by those who have held him dear in life.

. . . The one who must die, dear children, is so very poor. I am so poor now, for the whole beautiful world that has been my rich and blessed home these many years is to be taken away from me; my chair will be empty; the door will be locked on me; and I shall never put my foot into the world again. I therefore look at the world with the prayer in my eyes that it be fond of me; and therefore I come to you, praying that you will love me with all the love you once bestowed on me; for bear this in mind: to be remembered is the only morsel in the world of man that from now on will be mine. Only to be remembered, that and nothing else.

The words fall with such gently poignant simplicity that one is moved to forget, as one reads, some of the sentimentalities of the story into which the letter is fitted. Criticism has ever in the past been gentle with "Fru Fønss," and it is no desire of mine at the moment to destroy the delicate illusion of beauty which these final epistolary paragraphs of the tale seem always to cast upon the reader.

Jacobsen was living with death as he wrote "Fru Fønss." The signs of physical decay increased almost daily in the months that followed upon the completion of his last tale. Seldom, however, does Jacobsen mention the wasting away of his physical powers in the letters from these days; and when he does so he does not complain—rather does he pass off his troubles with some half-grim witticism, some airy bit of evasion. His friends in Copenhagen, however, were sufficiently aware of his plight: they looked upon the horrible evidences of extreme physical decline with the hopeless compassion of those who would but could not help. Georg Brandes, who saw Jacobsen frequently during these months, describes the condition of his friend's health at this time in these words: "His health deteriorated steadily. He was broken down slowly, as one breaks down a house, piece by piece, stone by stone. At times it was terrible to hear his coughing. One did not know what one should do with one's eyes in order that he should not catch the note of compassion in one's look." In the spring of 1884 Jacobsen is aware that his disease is approaching its last, fatal stage. And so he plans to leave his beloved Copenhagen—go home to Thisted to meet his death. And here in the snug little harbor village on Limfjorden where he had first looked upon life Jacobsen finally died—on the 30th of April 1885. Death came to Jens Peter Jacobsen, as his Danish biographer puts it, "not on 'An autumn night, wild and gloomy,' as he had written in the days of his youth, but on an April day while a mild spring-time rain slowly fell outside."

When Jacobsen died he had just passed his thirty-eighth birthday. Only two full-length novels had come from his pen, together with a few short stories, and a sheaf of exquisite poems. This production seems small, yet under the circumstances such a limited production was inevitable. The precarious condition of his health on the one hand and his scrupulous care as an artist on the other determined the limited amount of his production. Like Flaubert he filed his finely modulated sentences and searched for *le mot juste* with an infinitely sensitive critical care; and like Zola he always sought to document his work as conscientiously as possible. Jacobsen's art, however, can scarcely be said to resemble that of either Flaubert or Zola, except possibly some of his short stories, which are not unlike certain of the tales of Flaubert. If one were to compare Jacobsen's prose in general with that of any of his contemporaries, one thinks inevitably of Walter Pater. Jacobsen's prose resembles Pater's in the exquisite sensitivity of its feeling, in the marvelously delicate lyric quality of its phrasing, and in its subtly probing power of analysis. The broad philosophical sweep of Pater's mind is scarcely characteristic of Jacobsen's genius; but the

fundamental *cast* of Jacobsen's mind resembles that of Pater—
intently searching, ever serious, and at times gently ironic, the
irony being tempered almost invariably by a serene, all-inclusive
tolerance. It is in Jacobsen's tolerance—his constant, sympathetic
effort to understand, never harshly to judge—that we find the
chief difference between him and most of his important Scandinavian contemporaries. Only with Jonas Lie—among these
contemporaries—does Jacobsen have this tolerance in common.
How it was that Kielland, under the circumstances, could not
endure his countryman Lie and yet could become almost ful-
somely enthusiastic about the work of Jacobsen remains one of
the mysterious critical reactions in late nineteenth century Scandinavian literary history.

A complete solution of this mystery is perhaps impossible, for
it probably has most of its roots in a world of half-formed,
largely subconscious prejudices of which Kielland himself may
have been only partially aware. It would seem, however, that
at least a part of the explanation is to be found in the curiously
mixed nature of Jacobsen's own mind and work. Jacobsen, like
his hero Niels Lyhne, combined in his artistic temperament
certain logically irreconcilable elements. He was both a poet and
a scientist; and—what is more important—he was both poet and
scientist in their most definitive forms. His highly figurative,
richly colorful lyric prose style was that of romantic poetry.
Likewise his delicately intuitive imaginative response to natural
phenomena. Yet Jacobsen was deeply impressed by the pseudo-
scientific method of literary "documentation" affected by Zola
and his followers; and his training as a scientist drove him to
atheism and to a new kind of "religion of science" based directly
upon an objective study of natural phenomena. Thus Jacobsen's
genius is torn between two largely antipathetic methods of
responding to life. This strange combination of gifts accounts
largely, no doubt, for his unique ability to analyze the tragic
transitional type of character that we find in Niels Lyhne; but
the combination—in its less satisfactory, and perhaps more
characteristic manifestations—was probably also partially responsible for the lack of freedom and rapidity in Jacobsen's

creative processes. Jacobsen, in short, was not without some taint of that "lame reflectiveness" which made Niels Lyhne's literary efforts so hopelessly abortive.

What Jacobsen did produce tended to be fastidiously finished, an art with scarcely a flaw in matters of detail. And yet, his art, in the last analysis, lacks *strength*—the vigorous, animated strength of a genius confident of its own powers. This difficulty is to be explained, at least in part, in Jacobsen's remarkable sensitivity to *all* of the intellectual and literary currents of his day—and to many earlier currents. He read widely and intensely, and according to his own testimony he was influenced by a wide diversity of sources. In 1877, for instance, he writes to Georg Brandes apropos of *Marie Grubbe,* in which the critics had "discovered" so many evidences of a great variety of literary influences—

It is a pitiful childishness and a horrible imposture to hear an author attempt to deny that he has learned anything from others and boast that everything he has done is his own—and I certainly have no such desire. I confess that I have learned from all (yet not from Zola or Daudet, whom I first came to know after my book came out); but I would say that I have learned more from Beyle and Shakespeare than from Mérimée, more from Sainte-Beuve than from Taine, and that my style is much more closely related to Hans Christian Andersen's tales than to Bjørnson. . . .

One is tempted to hypothesize, upon reading such a confession, that Jacobsen might have written even more significantly than he did had he read less and communed more intimately and independently with himself. There was in him, one feels, the stuff of an essentially original genius, which should have been allowed to develop more freely, as independent as possible of the diversely conflicting currents of thought and art that the late nineteenth century had to offer to a sensitive, entirely open-minded spirit such as Jacobsen's. Eclecticism in thought has its obvious dangers—in art it is often fatal. In Jacobsen it cannot be said to have been fatal, for his work in the novel remains among the best that the late nineteenth century in the Scandinavian countries produced; and yet that it left a somewhat unhappy mark upon an otherwise exquisite literary gift is the sad suspicion that tends to persist in the mind of the discriminating reader the farther he gets away from the marvelously seductive fascination of immediate contact with the pages of *Marie Grubbe* and *Niels Lyhne*.

NATIONALISM REINTERPRETED
VERNER von HEIDENSTAM

SCHLOSS BRUNEGG, a picturesque medieval castle situated near Othmarsingen, in the canton of Aargau, northern
Switzerland, was in the summer of 1886 the scene of one of the
most interesting episodes in the history of modern Swedish
literature. It was in the grand hall of this old feudal castle that
August Strindberg and Verner von Heidenstam, both in temporary self-imposed exile from Sweden, came together frequently during these summer months to exchange ideas on a
great variety of problems which were of vital interest to both
of them. They had met for the first time more than a year before,
probably in consequence of a letter which Heidenstam had
addressed to Strindberg at the time of the legal prosecution
occasioned by the first volume of Strindberg's *Married* (1884).
Early in 1885—a short time after Strindberg's return to the
Continent from the Stockholm journey necessitated by the legal
prosecution—Strindberg and Heidenstam travelled together to
Rome and Venice; and during the summer of the same year
they met again at Grèz, favorite gathering place at this time
of Scandinavian artists. It seems that it was not until the summer of the following year, however, that these two self-exiled
and restless spirits—the one an author already famous, the other
a young poet still to make his début—came together for serious,
prolonged discussion of the many questions that disturbed both
of them deeply. Neither the exigencies of travel in Italy nor the
variety of social intercourse provided by the art colony at Grèz
had given them sufficient privacy and leisure for an intimate and
thoroughgoing discussion of the problems with which each of
them was grappling at the time. Brunegg, the old castle which
Heidenstam had leased in 1886, offered a perfect retreat. Here
the two men could cross mental swords at their leisure, and
without fear of interruption.

Curious, however, were the incongruities between the scene
on the one hand and the characters and problems they discussed

on the other when Heidenstam played the genial host to Strindberg at Schloss Brunegg during the summer of 1886: *the scene*
—the grand hall of the castle, with its tarnished ancient trap-
pings, its faded feudal memories, its strange isolation from
modernity; *the characters*—two relatively young men, with
their skepticisms, their intense spirit of searching, their distaste
for much of the past, their eyes on the present and the future
. . . the *problems*—modern problems, with their utilitarian
emphasis, their practical social and political implications, their
intense immediacy of appeal. . . . Strange as were these contrasts, perhaps neither Strindberg nor Heidenstam was at the
time especially conscious of them. They were probably too intent upon their immediate intellectual preoccupations to permit
the mere accident of scene to disturb the free and vivid flow
of eager, pulsing ideas. One can readily imagine that Strindberg, especially, would tend to forget completely the immediate
physical surroundings. Certainly the solemn, heroic stature of
two magnificent coats-of-mail standing mute guard over ancient
feudal memories in the grand hall of Schloss Brunegg were in
sufficiently ludicrous incongruity to the picture we gather from
contemporary sources of a half-reclining Strindberg, his lips
with alternate vehemence pouring out billows of cigarette smoke
and a rapid flow of words, his arms gesticulating the while with
a nervous, twitching, intensely animated movement. Here medieval grotesque and the modern spirit met unconsciously to precipitate a new form of the grotesque—one not without subtly
ironic implications to a sensitive present-day mind.

Fascinating as it may be for the fancy to call up the amusing
details of the scene at Brunegg castle in the summer of 1886,
the episode has its more serious significance in the light that it
throws upon the point of development at this time of two of
Sweden's most important literary figures of the last fifty years.
The episode is particularly important in any analysis of the
artistic and intellectual development of Heidenstam, inasmuch
as our sources for a study of the early years of Heidenstam's
development are not as yet especially rich. When we remember
also that Strindberg and Heidenstam later became the leading
representative figures in two antipodal lines of development in

modern Swedish literature, we find the Brunegg episode all the more interesting. Strong were the powers of attraction that momentarily drew Strindberg and Heidenstam together at Schloss Brunegg; and yet not many years were to pass after the summer of 1886 before it was to become apparent that the powers of repulsion were much stronger—stronger because more deeply rooted in the essentially contrasting geniuses of the two men. What was it, then, that drew these two men tentatively together in the middle of the '80's? and why did they draw steadily apart almost immediately after this, until at last they became the most implacable of opponents in the cultural history of modern Sweden?

I

It is improbable that their common condition of exile from the homeland played the dominant rôle in the mutual attraction they had for one another in 1886. Heidenstam, who had been abroad for a full decade, except for an occasional short stay in Sweden, had originally departed from his homeland in the interests of his health. Later, in 1880, after a visit to Sweden, he left the homeland, apparently permanently, when a marriage which he contracted at this time resulted in a violent quarrel with his father. Strindberg, on the other hand, had gone abroad in the autumn of 1883 because of a threatened nervous breakdown occasioned by overwork and by an intense feeling of antipathy toward his countrymen for not sufficiently appreciating his work. Such a difference in the immediate motivations of Heidenstam's and Strindberg's common condition of exile would seem to argue against the assumption that their exile was the central motive in drawing them together in 1886, although some Swedish critics have suggested the possibility. The real reason for their mutual attraction would seem to be more positive.

Heidenstam seems to have been attracted to Strindberg at this time chiefly because he saw in Strindberg a kindred intellectual spirit. For years Heidenstam had been living at various places abroad, at first in the Orient, later on the European Continent, engaged in extensive studies in art, literature, history, and philosophy, and trying his hand creatively in the fields of painting and poetry. It seems that he had not been especially impressed by Strindberg's earliest work, some of which he had read. *The Red Room*, Strindberg's first important public success, appearing in 1879, had found Heidenstam indifferent. The appearance in 1884, however, of the first volume of *Married* interested him definitely; and when, in October 1884, Strindberg was being prosecuted as the author of *Married* for "mockery of God's word and the sacraments," Heidenstam wrote the letter to Strindberg which seems to have been the first step in drawing the two men together. The letter, in turn, resulted in the first of a series of meetings between the two men—the last, and most important, of which were those which took place at Schloss Brunegg in the summer of 1886.

We know from letters and from two autobiographical documents—Strindberg's *The Author* (fourth volume of *A Maid Servant's Son*) and Heidenstam's "Slottet Brunegg" (a chapter in *Från Col di Tenda till Blocksberg*)—that the subject matter of the discussions between Strindberg and Heidenstam was extremely diversified and inclusive. The young Heidenstam whom we meet in Strindberg's *The Author* has a lively interest in all of the immediate questions of the day—in social problems, particularly the class struggle of the '80's; in Zola's *Germinal*, a powerful expression in fictional form of certain aspects of this class struggle; and in "the woman question," which Strindberg had treated with what was for its day such violent originality in *Married, I*. The unprejudiced, skeptical frame of mind in which both men approached these problems is extremely interesting, chiefly perhaps because each of them in his own way represents already in the middle of the '80's a partial departure from the characteristic thought tendencies of this decade in Sweden. Strindberg, who had by 1886 begun to draw away from his Rousseauistic socialism of the early '80's, was, when he met Heidenstam, in the midst of one of those frequent "crises" which swept over his stormy career during the late '80's and the '90's—crises which led him first to Nietzsche and the cult of the superman, and later, in strong reaction, to a nondogmatic form of Christianity. Heidenstam, a disillusioned

young aristocrat, brought to the discussion an equally independent, keenly skeptical mind capable of entering, at least for
the moment, into any conceivable point of view. Though both
men were sympathetic toward some of the governing ideas of
the '80's, neither felt in any way bound by the doctrinaire, programmatic credo into which these ideas were gradually harden-
ing in the hands of the so-called *Unga Sverige*, a group of
young literary champions of the liberal ideas of the '80's. Strindberg and Heidenstam had a common admiration for the political equality which they found in Switzerland, being particularly
fascinated by the *Landesgemeinde*, a form of pure democracy
existing in those days in the tiny canton Appenzell; and in this
admiration for an actual, working democracy they were on
common ground with the democratic ideals of the *Unga Sverige*.
But their lack of sympathy with certain other ruling ideas of
the '80's is perhaps even more apparent than are their points
of agreement. Most revealing is their departure from most of
their Scandinavian contemporaries on the much bruited "woman
question."

Of all the particular "problems" which haunted the Scandinavian mind during the late nineteenth century, perhaps the
"woman question" was the most constantly recurrent and the
one which aroused the most intense forms of reaction in all
classes of society. The woman question was, of course, simply
one phase of that struggle toward social and political democracy characteristic of the '70's and '80's in the Scandinavian
countries; but no other particular phase of this struggle seems
to have so persistently attracted the best Scandinavian pens of
the period. Scores of works appearing during these years—
plays, novels, studies in essay form, occasionally even lyric
poems—took up the defense of woman against what was commonly considered the unfairness of a man-made social order.
This body of "woman literature" up to 1886—the date of publication of Strindberg's *Married, I*—had found its most striking
literary expressions in Ibsen's *A Doll's House* (1879) and
Bjørnson's *A Gauntlet* (1883); but these two works are to be
considered as relatively late-born literary manifestations of a
body of ideas on woman's rights that can be traced much farther

back—at least to Camilla Collett's *The Governor's Daughters* (1855) and to Georg Brandes's translation (1869) of John Stuart Mill's *The Subjection of Women*. It is perhaps not too much to say that a veritable "woman cult" had finally emerged in the Scandinavian literature of the '70's and '80's.

Against this large body of literature defending the rights of women—a literature which often took on extremely chivalric sentimental forms—Strindberg reacted with characteristically brutal violence in his two volumes of short stories entitled *Married* and in his later naturalistic plays, *The Father* (1887), *The Comrades* (1888), and *The Creditors* (1888). In fact as early as 1882 (in *Herr Bengts hustru*) Strindberg had written an attack upon Ibsen's conception of Nora in *A Doll's House*, though the attack at that time had not raised the storm of protest which Strindberg's later works on the woman question did. His later attacks really drew blood, plenty of it; and they became the rallying point both for attack and defense in a new phase of the "woman literature" during the last years of the century. Though Heidenstam's characteristic personal reserve did not permit him to rage brutally against the sentimental cult of the feminine as did Strindberg's easily eruptive temperament, he found himself in the middle of the '80's in essential agreement with Strindberg's heterodoxy on the woman question.

Heidenstam's general point of view during these years toward a number of the central problems of the day is perhaps most clearly revealed in a famous passage in Strindberg's *The Author*. Heidenstam is there reported as saying to Strindberg in one of their discussions at Schloss Brunegg—

. . . You belong to the new nobility of the nerves (*nervadeln*), which is proceeding toward a new House of the Nobility. I belong to the dying nobility of the muscles (*muskeladeln*); for we are dying, we are already half overcome by the bourgeois (*penningadeln*), who are in turn being slowly undermined by the newest nobility, the proletariat. I read *Germinal* recently, and I became frightened, literally frightened. We have in the possession of our family, as you know, an ironworks. The laborers have gone on strike the last few years at the time for delivery, losses have overtaken us from time to time, and ruin is at hand. . . . We are too cultured or too weak to employ the same forms of barbarism as they do; therefore we will go under, and with us culture itself. I have seen the giant corpse of the Orient, which has passed into its last stage of illusion; if we live we shall soon see Europe lying likewise—an ugly corpse.

The passage is especially interesting in its revelation of the young Heidenstam as a disillusioned aristocrat, who looks upon the disintegration of his class as an inevitable social development determined by natural economic laws. It is worthy of note that the attitude which Heidenstam here takes is thoroughly consistent with one of the ideas most characteristic of *fin de siècle* decadence—a decadence born of the scientific implications of fictional naturalism as developed by Zola in the Rougon-Macquart novels and later manifested in such more purely decadent novels as Jacobsen's *Niels Lyhne* (1880), Herman Bang's *Generations without Hope* (1880), Huysman's *A Rebours* (1884), and in Heidenstam's own early autobiographical novel *Hans Alienus* (1892).

And yet though in the middle of the '80's Heidenstam's view of the future of his own class is dark enough, he did not permit this view to lead him ultimately into either of the two characteristic blind alleys of *fin de siècle* decadence—the sordidly fatalistic hopelessness typified by Bang's *Generations without Hope* or the thinly veiled sensuousness parading as religious mysticism which runs through much of Huysman's late work. Heidenstam, as we shall see, came finally to work out a new synthesis of the spirit of the age, a synthesis essentially optimistic in its tone, idealistic in its aims, critically constructive in its manner of procedure. He conceived this new synthesis as largely in opposition to the current naturalism and decadence, though by no means in such complete negation of it as was Brunetière's contemporaneous attack upon these literary developments in France. Heidenstam was no mere dogmatic reactionary, any more than he was an irresponsible aesthete resting sensuously in the slumbrously mystical shades of a resuscitated Romanticism. His reinterpretation of Sweden's national past, first becoming manifest in the more mature portions of *Dikter* ("Poems," 1895), has proved to be one of the most solid, bracing contributions to Swedish literature and to Swedish culture in the last fifty years. In the best of his poetry and prose since 1895—and little of it falls below the best, so critical is his artistic self-judgment—he has given expression to an heroic national ideal with no less dignity and reserve than freshness and vigor. And for this modern Sweden is incomparably the richer.

II

In March 1887 Heidenstam, who was residing at the time in San Remo, hurried northward to the bedside of his father, who lay dying in Stockholm. Upon the death of his father, early in June, he retired to Olshammar, the family estate on the northern shores of Lake Vättern in Östergötland. Sweden was to remain his home now permanently—a Sweden toward which he had often yearned during long years of exile and a Sweden to whose literature he had prepared during those years of exile to make his magnificent contribution. The first volume to come from Heidenstam's pen—*Vallfart och vandringsår* ("Pilgrimage and Wander-Years")—was published in April 1888. Though this first volume was late in coming—the author was twenty-nine at the time—we have seen from Heidenstam's conversations with Strindberg that he had been deeply interested in literature during the immediately preceding years. Some of his letters from the early '80's reveal that even before he met Strindberg he had tried his hand seriously at poetry, though he was too critical of his work to seek publication for his poems at this time. In a letter to Topelius, whose counsel he had sought on these early poems, he confesses how intensely he had labored on his verse; and yet he finds it artificial and imitative in form, superficial and immature in subject matter. According to his own confession, his inability to give adequate expression to his moods and ideas at this time was to be explained primarily by the fact that these years represented a period of uncertainty and revolt which could hardly lend itself readily to coherent poetic creation. "That I have not long before this," he wrote to Topelius at the time of publication of his *Pilgrimage and Wander-Years*, "made my poetic début is because all that I have written during the past years has been of such a kind that it would be received with a shout of (perhaps deserved) derision. I have had my *Sturm und Drang* period. I have been in revolt against everything, against myself, against the Swedish language."

In all probability Heidenstam was wise in postponing his ·poetic début a few years. None of his earliest poetry has survived; but "Organ Chords" (the sentimental title of the collection sent to Topelius) perhaps sufficiently hints the limitations of Heidenstam's earliest ventures in poetic composition. When, in 1888, his first volume of poems did appear, it aroused immediate admiration. Rydberg, Snoilsky, and Levertin, the leading poets of the day in Sweden, all recognized in the author of *Pilgrimage and Wander-Years* a new poet of very real promise; and Fröding—the most important lyric poet of the '90's—has told us that for a time *Pilgrimage and Wander-Years* was his Bible. Some of the acclaim of critics and public was perhaps occasioned by the exotic background of many of the poems in Heidenstam's first volume; but more significant, no doubt, was the vigorous freshness of tone which animated most of these poems. The imagery, brilliantly alive, was boldly conceived and not sparing in broad, vivid splashes of color—a startling contrast to the grays and blacks of the contemporary naturalism and decadence. And in the narrative poems, especially, the metrical technique was marvelously flexible, invariably appropriate to the diverse pattern of the themes. Most of the poems tended to glorify youth and beauty, the pleasures of the moment, the unlimited power of love. Strange themes these—strange, and seductively fascinating—to a literary generation which had been taught to admire rigid utilitarian ideals of social conscience and an art rigorously subordinated to immediate, observable fact.

Much, however, as Heidenstam's poems in this volume seemed to glory in undisciplined, spontaneously youthful responses to all the diverse wealth of life which the poet had experienced, this was not the only note struck in *Pilgrimage and Wander-Years*. Nor, in the light of Heidenstam's later development, was it the most important. The discriminating reader is aware of occasional notes of questioning, of skepticism even, in the zest-

ful abundance of Heidenstam's oriental tales; and that these
notes were neither accidental nor a pale reflection of an earlier
Romantic nostalgia is suggested by the formal inclusion in the
volume of a section of short, confessional lyrics entitled
"Thoughts in Loneliness." Levertin had, indeed, in his review
of the volume, dismissed this section with the phrase "uninter-
esting sentimental lyricism"; but his judgment was obviously
hasty. In these poems we find the first genuine evidences of the
great note that is to come more richly into Heidenstam's poetry
in such mature later volumes as *Dikter* ("Poems," 1895) and
Nya Dikter ("New Poems," 1915).

Each of the poems in the section "Thoughts in Loneliness"
is a highly concentrated, exquisitely beautiful expression of
some mood or idea that had intimately and deeply moved
Heidenstam in these early years: his loneliness in an essentially
unfriendly contemporary world; his yearning for the homeland;
his desire to identify his spirit with something outside itself,
with nature or with the past; his proud rejection of Christianity
in favor of an atheism more consistent with the modern temper
—yet an atheism with its own deep humility, originating in
Heidenstam's consciousness of the solemn human mission of
the poet. The contrast is curious, and very marked, between
the poetic extravaganzas of the oriental poems and the beautifully restrained lyric dignity of the "Thoughts in Loneliness."
The former remind one in their vivid and glowing imagery and
in their spontaneous romantic lyricism of Byron or the young
Hugo, the latter in their epigrammatic concentration of phrase
and their emotional restraint of Runeberg and Rydberg, or of
Goethe in such a lyric as "Über allen Gipfeln." We know,
indeed, from Heidenstam's letters that Runeberg has been of
the greatest importance in his early poetic development; and
it was natural enough that Goethe and Schiller—particularly
the former—should later come to stand next to Runeberg among
those who most strongly influenced his verse. Very revealing in
this connection are some words of Heidenstam from 1890,
occasioned by a letter on "Pepita's Wedding": "Levertin grows
enthusiastic about the dawning 'neo-idealism' of Paris, I for
Rome and Weimar and for plastic ideals of art." This sentence

gives the key to the essential difference between Levertin and Heidenstam, throwing into bold relief the ideal of art—restrained, dignified, classical—which down through the years is to become increasingly important for Heidenstam. The section "Thoughts in Loneliness" included in *Pilgrimage and Wander-Years* hints as early as 1888 the poetic ideal which Heidenstam's genius is to follow in the future. It is not, however, until seven years later—in that remarkable volume entitled with appropriate simplicity *Poems*—that this ideal becomes realized with that steady, even consistency of artistic performance which gives witness of a really distinguished poetic gift.

Before *Poems* appeared in 1895, however, Heidenstam was engaged in a rather prolific literary production, for the most part in prose, and largely conceived in the vividly colorful manner of the oriental tales from *Pilgrimage and Wander-Years.* In these works Heidenstam casts up accounts with his youth and with the Sweden of the '80's in a series of autobiographical fragments (*From Col di Tenda to Blocksberg*, 1888; *Endymion*, 1889; *Hans Alienus*, 1892) and in two very important controversial essays ("Renascence," 1889; and "Pepita's Wedding," together with Levertin, 1890). We find in these works that he is as severely critical with the extravagances of his own youth as he is with the sober, utilitarian spirit of the '80's against which in his youth he had so strongly reacted.

The critical essay "Renascence" and the autobiographical fantasia *Hans Alienus* are the most important of these works. *Hans Alienus* was obviously written as a discipline in thinking, despite the fantastic allegorical framework in which it is cast. In it Heidenstam was taking inventory of his spiritual resources at the close of his period of revolt in preparation for the more constructive period which was to follow. Hans Alienus, at the close of the novel, dies rather sordidly—a kind of aristocratic Wilhelm Meister who found no solution to the riddle of the universe at the close of his chaotic, strangely hopeless "wanderyears." It is not to be so with the Heidenstam who is to come, however. The universe, it is true, always comes to retain for him its deep, inexplicable mystery. But this mystery he finds, ultimately, to be a bracing, invigorating challenge to the free human spirit, to the best instincts of man; and out of the mystery, even in its profoundly tragic aspects, man must inevitably grow in moral stature—dignified, heroic, noble to the very end. The mystery of the universe, Heidenstam's mature thought would suggest, is a deeply *moving* mystery—a mystery that can finally spell unity rather than chaos, a mystery that challenges a noble gathering of one's spiritual resources rather than one that precipitates hopelessness and despair and spiritual decadence.

The essay "Renascence" is to be looked upon as a preliminary statement of general literary aims and ideals rather than a carefully worked out aesthetics. It is a pronunciamento, more interested in sketching future possibilities for literature than in lingering over past accomplishments or failures, though its opening sections do concern themselves with the limitations of the prevailing naturalism. It proposes, in short, to give impetus to a new literary and cultural movement in Sweden; and it did just this. Its most immediate concern was to define with some care the limitations of naturalism as a literary method and to announce that the day of naturalism had passed and that a new aesthetics must be ushered in if Swedish literature was to retain vitality and lasting significance. Heidenstam does not in this essay condemn naturalism and the spirit of the Swedish '80's *sub specie aeternitates*. He looks upon it rather as a passing phase in literary taste, which had in it something of good, though in its extreme manifestations as an art form, it had more of evil; and certainly it had run its course and should give way to a new literary form. He admits that naturalism had exercised an "extraordinarily salutary" influence on prose fiction, though for poetry it had perhaps chiefly a negative significance. He holds naturalism responsible for much of the false note of melancholy to be found in the chill "gray weather" poetry of the '80's. He insists that both this poetry and the contemporary philosophical pessimism, with which such poetry is closely related, must soon give way to other moods and other points of view. "The times thirst for joy," he maintains—though not, of course, for a superficial, hysterical joy. Man needs a deep, abiding joy—a joy that is to be made consistent ultimately with the spirit of resignation. "The literature of Europe," he writes, with reference to certain phases of literary decadence, "has gone so far as to intoxicate itself with a sort of crucifix-coquetry, but how many great things are still left unsaid about resignation. Is there anything more gripping than to see suffering raise itself with proud resignation!" And later, in protest against the neurotic tendencies of the age : "Never shall any permanent joy be founded upon quivering nerves, but on the firm marble of resignation, even though it chills." Particularly desirable, he finally argues, is a departure from naturalism, and its ultimate form, *fin de siècle* decadence, in the literature of Sweden; for the spirit and technique of naturalism are basically foreign to the Swedish national temperament. Sweden needs a new *national* literature, developing naturally out of the healthy, vigorous organism of its own basic racial and national temper.

If my dream should become more than a dream, if a stream actually should burst forth in the direction which has been pointed out, what name should we give to it? Might it not best be characterized by the name "renascence"? It should justify such a name in part because of the peculiarities in our own national temper that should then come to be honored, in part because of its readoption of the methods of older schools, in part also because of its own inner nature, its favoring of the subjective, of personal independence, its uniting of the imagination, the sense of the beautiful, and bold, racy realism.

Heidenstam's dream did come true. Sweden has in the last half century realized a fresh, original, and vigorous national literature; and if any one figure is to be singled out as the one most responsible for this new national literature, that figure is perhaps Heidenstam. It is for this reason that when the Swedish Academy in 1916 honored Heidenstam with the Nobel Prize in literature it did so with the proud national citation : "the advocate of a new epoch in our literature." Just how Heidenstam justifies such a citation, especially as an author of prose fiction, it shall be the business of the remainder of the present essay to define and illustrate.

III

Heidenstam's period of literary maturity began with a volume of poems and reached its crowning achievement in another volume of poems. He is, it should be emphasized, first of all a great lyricist—as are nearly all of Sweden's greatest literary figures: Bellman, Geijer, Tegnér, Rydberg, Runeberg, and Heidenstam's two great contemporaries, Fröding and Karlfeldt. Strindberg's literary greatness, it is true, is to be found largely in his dramas, and Selma Lagerlöf's in prose fiction; but these are perhaps merely the exceptions that are said to prove the rule—and besides it should be noted that Selma Lagerlöf's prose is in substance prose poetry, at its best always lyric in essence even though it foregoes the formalities of metrical form. Though Heidenstam's true greatness must always be sought in the best of his lyric poetry, he wrote much prose, most of it in quality just short of much of his greatest lyric poetry. Practically all of his most significant prose falls within the score of years marked off by his two great volumes of poetry, *Poems* (1895) and *New Poems* (1915). He reveals himself in this prose as an essayist of sparkling epigrammatic power, as a short story writer of marvelous dramatic concentration, and as a novelist of very real distinction. During the years in which this prose was written he had "arrived" as an artist and thinker; the critical ideas which had been given preliminary expression in "Renascence" had by this time matured and deepened into a creative production of marvelous depth and power.

The subject matter of most of Heidenstam's poetry and prose tends to expand and illustrate the ideal of a Swedish national literature which had been proposed in the closing paragraphs of "Renascence." The volume of *Poems* (1895) contained something more than hints of Heidenstam's movement in this direction. Some of the poems in it, to be sure, are closely related to his earlier work, particularly to *Pilgrimage and Wander-Years* and to *Hans Alienus*. Here is to be found the old theme of the poet's loneliness, his inability to identify himself with the immediate realities of contemporary life and thought. Here are poems also with the bold, vivid imagery of *Pilgrimage and Wander-*

Years. Moreover two of the poems in *Hans Alienus* appear again, unchanged, in *Poems* (1895).

And yet how different on the whole are these new *Poems*! The old brooding, the old skepticisms bordering on pessimism are for the most part gone. They give way to a new spirit of optimism, restrained, dignified, characterized by a deep-flowing, quietly vigorous zest for life; and they suggest a new, constructive attitude toward life—an attitude filled with a warm, understanding humanity which finds its deepest roots in a feeling for Sweden's national past. In *Pilgrimage and Wander-Years* he had longed for his homeland—but for its soil, its stones, rather than for its people.

> I've yearned for home now eight long years.
> In my very sleep I have felt the yearning.
> I yearn for home. I yearn where'er I go
> —though not to people! I long for the soil,
> I yearn for the stones where as a child I played.

Now, however, in such poems as "Tiveden," "Songs in the Church Tower," "How easily men's cheeks are hot with wrath," and "Home" Heidenstam strikes a new note, a touchingly intimate human note. Now he loves not only the landscape of the homeland; he feels for its people, its thousand sacred memories, its great national past.

> Oh, say not that our elders,
> whose eyes are closed forever,
> that those we fain would banish
> and from our lives would sever,—
> say not their colors vanish
> like flowers and like grasses,
> that we from hearts efface them
> like dust, when one would clear it
> from ancient window-glasses.
> In power they upraise them,
> a host they of the spirit.
> The whole white earth enshrouding,
> our thoughts too overclouding,
> whate'er our fate or fortune,
> thoughts that, like swallows crowding,

fly home at evening duly.
A home! How firm its base is
by walls securely shielded—
our world—the one thing truly
we in this world have builded.

The poem from which these lines are taken is inspired immediately by Heidenstam's loving reverence for Olshammar, his own family's ancient estate on Lake Vättern. But these lines go far beyond the immediate confines of Olshammar and its memories —memories stretching back at least as far as Saint Birgitta. The lines swell out into a kind of universal harmony, serving to symbolize Heidenstam's love for *the past as such*—all of its marvelous wealth of memory, all of its sober, quietly mellow lessons for mankind. Twenty years after these lines had been published their symbolical implications become more definite in outline, more particularly applied to the Swedish national past in many of the lyrics included in *New Poems*. Meantime, however, Heidenstam went the way of prose to give expression to these ideas.

His first important prose work was the two volumes of *Karolinerna* ("The Charles Men," 1897-98), a noble literary monument raised in honor of Charles XII and the heroes, high ranking or humble, who followed him loyally on those far-flung campaigns that were to be ended with tragic abruptness by the bullet which penetrated the hero-king's skull in the trenches outside Fredrikshald on a cold winter's night in 1718. In casting about for subjects worthy of a great national literature, Heidenstam had been led inevitably to the tragic figure of Charles XII. The very fact that Charles XII was held in almost universal ill-repute in the Sweden to which Heidenstam had returned in 1887 made him all the more acceptable to Heidenstam, who had not been impressed by the utilitarian, bourgeois spirit which he felt dominated Swedish culture at the close of the century. In the tragic-heroic figure of Charles XII Heidenstam came to find at one and the same time a constructive national ideal of the truly heroic and a point of departure for a severe critical analysis of the cultural materialism of Sweden at the turn of the century.

As early as 1892 Heidenstam had published "Fifty Years After," the first to appear of the tales that ultimately went into the pages of *The Charles Men*. In Heidenstam's early treatment of these tales he seems to have been largely fascinated by the romantic, robustly saga-like nature of his material; but the longer his genius occupied itself with the theme the more he became impressed with the sombre, tragic grandeur of the material. Heidenstam's final picture of Charles XII is, in consequence, a picture of heroic sacrifice, of magnificent resignation to a hopeless train of circumstance; and in this picture, characteristically, the humble, undying loyalty of the private soldier comes to serve as a fittingly heroic background for the central portrait of Charles himself—a Charles whom his soldiers worshipped even in the moments of their severest trials.

The Charles Men was in form a series of short stories, each a complete artistic unit within itself, but all of them combining to form a brilliant composite of tales centering about the person of Charles XII. Heidenstam's immediate model was apparently *The Tales of Ensign Stål* (1848-60), Runeberg's famous cycle of heroic poems dealing with the Finnish war of 1808-09. A more remote, and less important, model was possibly Tegnér's *Frithiof's Saga* (1825).

In 1901 Heidenstam published *Heliga Birgittas pilgrimsfärd* ("Saint Birgitta's Pilgrimage"), an historical novel whose aim was to glorify the Swedish national past—this time in terms of Sweden's most famous heroine. The story of Saint Birgitta led Heidenstam back to the fourteenth century, four hundred years earlier than the time of Charles XII. It led him also into religious concerns primarily, rather than into political and military activities; and yet here, as in *The Charles Men,* his chief preoccupation is with the heroic *character* rather than with historical detail in general, and one discerns in his finely imaginative conception of Saint Birgitta many of the same strengths and weaknesses with which he had previously invested Sweden's hero-king of the early eighteenth century. Here are the same heroic proportions, the same fanaticisms, the same gloriously feverish activity, the same ultimate tragedy—except that now all of this is placed over against a religious background.

And yet one notes a difference—a difference not in kind, but in emphasis; and the difference is very important. The great personality, the strong will, is treated with the same sympathy in *Saint Birgitta's Pilgrimage* as it is in *The Charles Men*; but it is to be noted that the domineering will of Saint Birgitta must ultimately undergo a cleansing transformation—its instinctive fanatical brutality must finally be transformed by humility, by resignation, by a profoundly human spiritual experience, before the great deeds of Birgitta can be anything more than a mere mockery of fate. This is a new note in Heidenstam, pointing the way to a new conception of the heroic and the tragic, and hinting a new ethics. It is, however, in *Folkungaträdet* ("The Tree of the Folkungs," 1905-07)—the first part of which (*Folke Filbyter*) follows *Saint Birgitta's Pilgrimage* by only four years—that Heidenstam's mature ethics of heroic resignation is given its most complete and consistent expression.

IV

The Tree of the Folkungs reaches still farther back into Swedish history than had *Saint Birgitta's Pilgrimage*. Its first volume, indeed, pushes us back beyond the pages of sober historical documents into that only half-historical region of the early Scandinavian sagas. Myth and legend, tradition and saga provide only partially complete materials to Heidenstam's historical imagination as he sketches in bold, realistic outlines the character of Folke Filbyter, that legendary peasant founder of a family which a couple of centuries after his death was to occupy the throne of Svea Land and Göta Land. The very tenuousness of the historical material permits Heidenstam the greatest imaginative freedom in his treatment of the origins of the Folkung family; and the result—as in the case of Shakespeare's Lear—becomes a tragedy of profound and moving power.

Solemn, ominous, full of fateful forebodings is the note struck in the opening scene of *The Tree of the Folkungs,* as the modern novelist, like an ancient saga narrator, offers to the listener the heavy moral burden of the story that is to be told—

How the dwarfs lost the horn Månegarm and how a seed was laid in the earth from which a great tree was to grow, is here to be related. Here we shall tell the story of a race which attained to the highest honor and then was swept away and left no trace behind. What thoughts the mighty ones of this kin had of their golden crowns, when their old age lay before them like cold and slippery stairs descending to hell, and how the unhappy ones lamented their fetters, shall also be told. Let those who will hear these things give heed. Nothing shall be kept back. Vast distances separate them from us, but all human destinies are spun by the same weird Sisters.

Then follows a vivid description of the landing made by a Viking ship on a spit of land marked by the huge mound-grave of an ancient Scandinavian shield maiden. Mystery and terror are added to the violent realism of the scene by the presence of a shaggy, wild-eyed Finn dwarf, Jorgrimme, who crouches animal-like upon the ancient burial mound at the approach of the Viking ship, uttering in an unintelligible gibberish incantations and prophecies.

"Mound-dwellers! Do you hear? This night the women weep in the hall of Fyrisvall. Long is the way thither, seven days' journey, but never before did I hear such wailing. Never before did such terror fare over the land."

He searched for a while in the frozen grass and collected some dry herbs; then he stopped again, listening.

"Strike thy shield hard, mound-maiden!" he said. "Rouse thy peers from the sleep of death! Now creak the floor-planks behind the stone of sacrifice in the Sveas' holiest temple. It is Asa Thor's image that is trembling. Mercy, mercy upon all that has life!"

Shortly after the wild, fantastic little dwarf-figure finishes these weird incantations, the Viking ship has landed, two of the men carrying their chieftain on shoulder through the open stretch of water between the ice-clad ship and the towering grave-mound.

. . . With a broad, sure tread he [the chieftain] ascended the mound, without paying much heed to the dwarf, who was still standing there with his face turned inland. From the pouch of his ragged cloak the chief took out a handful of earth and threw it upon the grass. Then he bent forward and addressed the shield maiden in the stone chamber below, as was the wont of returned vikings.

"When I set out," he said, "I took this mould from your mound that it might bring me luck. Generously have you helped me. Poor was I when I sailed, driven from my father's house, where too many sons thronged the bench. Homeless I was as the wailing guillemot under the autumn sky. Since then I have never drained a horn under sooty roof-tree, nor slept in downy bed, but seven strongholds have I burnt in Frankland. Now I am rich enough to buy land for myself, and I am sick and weary of the sea, which my murmuring crew are so unwilling to leave. The servants of the sea are thralls of a fickle master. Thralls, too, are they who writhe in longing for fame or who see in all their dreams a woman. Therefore my men are thralls, but I alone am free, for I have no longing and I love no woman nor anything under the sun. Mound-woman, when did so free a man speak with you? When did so happy a man stand upon your grave? Here I offer to you my tokens of thraldom, my helmet and my sword. The world may go as it will for me. I shall enjoy my years in peace. Early each morning I shall go to my trap to fetch what it has caught that night. Then I shall doze upon my seat of turf in the sunshine and hear the corn growing."

It is Folke Filbyter, crude peasant founder of the future Folkung dynasty, who speaks; and as he finishes his greeting and address to the ancient inhabitant of the grave-mound, he thrusts his sword in the mound and places his chieftain's helmet upon the handle, so that he stands finally bare-headed on this bitter-cold, wintry evening of his return to the homeland.

The Finn dwarf, however, does not permit the returning Viking chieftain to remain long undisturbed in his complacent peasant dream of future wealth and peace.

"And I tell you that you would do better to go back to your ship," answered the dwarf, with a shrill cry. "I tell you, chief, I tell you, franklin, that if it is peace you seek, you must fly. For generations without number no man has beheld such things as are now at hand. The Æsir are now descending upon the land to seek out a seed of vigorous growth, and no man knows where their choice may fall. They will not choose the fairest or the noblest, but that which promises the strongest shoot. From this seed will grow a shady tree with tempests and calm stars in its topmost branches. So high shall the tree rise that it will overshadow all living things, not only men but the steeds in their stalls and the oxen at the plough, nay, even the wild beasts in the woods. For when its boughs drip sunshine or blood, all will feel it. And all will be hurt when the stem is rent and falls. Thus do the high Æsir speak by me to-night."

To this wild, semi-intelligible gibberish Folke Filbyter replied with a sneer, little realizing that it was he who was to be the fateful seed chosen by the Æsir—

"Practice your sorcery upon the dead beneath their mounds, dwarf, and let the living take care of themselves! I believe in no gods, but in my own strength. It is a far cry to the mighty ones at Fyrisvall, and in their field I have no mind to .dig. And now, my men, bring hither the sack and the dice and the balance, and let us divide the booty before it grows darker. The Great Wain and Freya's Spinning-wheel are already kindled in the sky."

As the men carried the heavy booty to land "the sound glittered in the last rays of the evening sun like countless slimy snakes" and the heavy thunder of breakers echoed across the frost-bound landscape. Upon the completion of the division of booty— which consisted simply in the chieftain giving to his men as much gold as each could hold in the open hands—Folke Filbyter covetously tied up the sack again, lifted the heavy burden with some difficulty upon his shoulder, and trudged heavily away "like a beggar with his scrip . . . over the ancient burial grounds." And as the heavy crunch of his boots slowly died away in the dark distance, the mysterious tone of fatalism that has insinu-ated itself into the whole scene which we have witnessed—its action, its characters, its strangely weird prophecies—rings out again, still more ominously than before, in the final words of the Finn dwarf.

"Mound-dwellers!" cried the dwarf, turning again to landward. "I hear the brides of the sacrifice opening the gates of Uppsala temple, and in the court of the king's house servants are running with tapers. I see a white-bearded old man lying in his closed bed with open and motionless eyes. Now dies the last king of Ivar Vidfadme's race."

For two nights Folke Filbyter wanders inland with his heavy burden, lurking in clumps of trees during the daytime in fear of outlaws. On the third day he stumbles upon a cave inhabited by

Finnish dwarfs—Jorgrimme himself, the dwarf-prophet at the mound, and his two wild daughters. Near their hovel he ultimately decides to settle, swearing to make of these strange creatures his thralls. And he names his farm in the wilderness Folketuna.

The remainder of the first volume of *The Tree of the Folkungs* occupies itself with the life of this Folke Filbyter at Folketuna and the fortunes of his three sons and single grandson. The booty that Folke Filbyter had brought back from his expedition of plunder served as the basis for the fortune he was to build up as a peasant landowner. Covetous he was, particularly for land; and his holdings at Folketuna increased manyfold during the years of his life. He was, however, a good enough husbandman to his thralls, providing them liberally with food and clothing and protection against outlawry in return for their vassalage; though he on occasion could treat them with a brutality exceptional even for his day. They might not have grumbled at the brutality, however, had he been a bit more distant in his relations with them and had he established a certain colorful grandeur in his household in keeping with his wealth. Always did he remain simply a peasant among peasants—coarse in manner, superstitious, essentially a thrall himself in spirit. And yet he was a peasant cast in a larger mold than were his vassals.

The lack of any definite consciousness of his personal eminence is seen in the way he took a woman unto himself to bear his sons. She was one of the daughters of Jorgrimme who had fallen into a huge wolf trap on the Folketuna lands. It had amused the coarse peasant humor in Folke Filbyter to keep her after he had rescued her from his thralls, who had begun to bury her alive in the wolf trap into which she had fallen. It was certainly not chivalry that had motivated this action of Folke Filbyter, as is seen by the outwardly insignificant part that the little Finnish woman played in the Folketuna household. She simply became the mother of his sons; else she was treated as the very meanest of the thralls.

Three sons—Ingemund, Hallsten, and Ingevald—were born to this curious union of ancient Scandinavian peasant stock and a mysterious Finnish dwarf race. The two oldest went abroad on a viking expedition as soon as they were old enough to bear arms, coming ultimately to serve in the emperor's guard at Constantinople. The youngest, Ingevald, remained at home, presumably to inherit Folketuna. He died young, however, though not before a son had been born to him by Holmdis, the proud and beautiful daughter of Ulv Ulvsson who had been stolen from her home by Ingevald and the Folketuna thralls because of her insulting refusal to marry him. Ingevald's son by Holmdis, however, is later stolen from Folketuna by a wandering Christian beggar, Jacob, instigated to the deed by Ingevald, who before his death had accepted the Christian faith and who hoped that his son, by escaping from the brutal heathendom of Folketuna, might ultimately atone for the many sins of his family by deeds of Christian heroism. After the child had been stolen, Folke Filbyter, who had come to love his grandson more than anything on earth, spent many of his aging years in wandering about the country in search of his lost grandson.

For years his efforts are fruitless; but at last he did find the long lost grandson—as the powerful Christian Earl of King Inge. Folke Filbyter, however, is a broken old man by this time; and his grandson, together with Hallsten and Ingemund (who had now returned to their homeland and become Christian members of the King's bodyguard), wish to keep their humble Folketuna origin a secret until they had more strongly established their political fortunes in the kingdom. To this arrangement the weary old man must submit.

Alone in the world, though surrounded by scores of his faithful thralls, he drags out his last weary years at Folketuna—a pitiful, and yet a not ignoble figure. Only at the very end do his sons and his grandson, the Earl, make a fleeting visit to Folketuna. On this occasion they eat and drink in all haste with Folke Filbyter; and when their horses are led forward to the door, a signal for departure, the Earl turns to his grandfather—

"You have scarce spoken to us, father," he said, as he emptied the last cup of milk. "It is we who have talked all the time, and now we must go. You have told us nothing of yourself. What can we do for you at this time? How have you passed the long summer days while your people were out in the fields?"

"I have sat picking the moths out of my coat," he said, with his face wrapt to the eyes in the wolf's hair. "The moth frets and devours, but between your fingers it is nothing but a pinch of golden dust. And so it is with a long sorrow. When you crumble it between your fingers you ask yourself : was it this little drop of heart's blood, was it this poor gold dust of false human dreams that consumed you so? In the days when I went to sea I used to try at night to sail a race with the moonbeam, but it always led me by an arm's length. Why did I not learn by this?"

"That is what we ask you, father."

"And I will answer you, Folke. Little by little I have learnt the wisdom of a husbandman, and I have left off complaining. Now I will go with you to the door. The sun shines so fairly to-day that it is hard not to be out. The cuckoo cries in the wood and the goats' bells tinkle in the fields, where my herds are ever growing and increasing. Even here I can listen to the swaying of the corn, everywhere is growth and sprouting, in the meadow, on the roof of the house : even the old logs of the wall are turning green with moss. And I can even feel that my own shrunken body puts out new shoots and leaves. You have grown old and wintry, Frey, and you must die that you may arise in youth and fertility."

"In us you arise, father."

"You have grown so far above me, children, that you can no longer reach down to me. The only thing I asked of you is not in your power to give me. But I rejoice. I am proud, I glory in my offspring, and I wish you success, Folkungs!"

Folke Filbyter still remains the peasant, the instinctive lover of growing things, in the very shadow of death and in his deep sorrow that his children cannot give him that which he most desired—their love. But suffering had finally transformed the coarser elements in his peasant nature into an essential nobility of character that earthly success had long kept from him; and in his final resignation to the inevitable there had come over him a certain tenderness, a gentleness, even spiritual peace of a kind. It was in this spirit that he

. . . stood and watched them depart. Many of his household were gathered about the door, but after a while the women began to place fresh hay under the benches and strewed it with the fairest wild flowers. Then all the thralls, male and female, went out, except one.

He stayed to close the door from within, as was the custom at a house-sacrifice.

On this very day the broken old man had been preparing to open his own veins, in accordance with an old heathen custom, and allow his life to seep slowly away. The arrival of his sons had but postponed for a few hours the house-sacrifice.

The reader, however, is not permitted to witness the act of self-immolation. Instead, he merely follows, with Folke Filbyter's aging eyes, the rapid departure of the young Folkungs from Folketuna farm.

The causeway thundered under the hoofs of the Folkungs' troop and soon they reached the nearest stretch of forest. Hallsten's bride sat in the saddle in front of him and he played with the ring on her finger, holding it up before her in the sunshine. When the three kinsmen came out into the open again, they set spurs to their horses and fixed their eyes on the edge of the next wood. There the unknown awaited them, fresh deeds and new lands to be won. All three rode abreast, talking of gain and worldly success.

What mellow irony lies in the last sentence of this final scene at Folketuna! In the foreground stands the tragic, broken figure of an old man, one who years before had gone out into the world to seek booty, great wealth, and through these presumably to find happiness. He had gained wealth—and with it an achingly empty old age. . . . In the near background—in marvelously ironic contrast—we see this broken old man's descendants, young, optimistic, full of abounding energies, swinging out into the world and "talking of gain and worldly success."

In a later generation—the one we come upon in *The Bjälbo Heritage,* second volume in *The Tree of the Folkungs*—the old man's descendants have gone so far in worldly success as to gain a throne. Yet this throne brings no more peace and happiness to Valdemar and Magnus, late fruit of the Folkung tree, than had the wealth of Folketuna brought happiness to the original Folkung, Folke Filbyter, who had stood silently on a gay spring morning, the day of his death by self-immolation, and watched his sons and grandson disappear at the horizon.

This outline of the story contained in *The Tree of the Folkungs* provides only the faintest suggestion—if it does even that—of the narrative skill with which Heidenstam has developed the tragic theme of the novel. It throws little light on his conception of the tragic as such, and only hints at the ethics upon which this conception of the tragic rests. It touches not at all, moreover, on the more purely aesthetic aspects of Heidenstam's fictional technique: his method of employing historical material; his occasional use of poetic symbolism to give to the novel a unity even beyond that provided by the plot; and his richly varied prose style, a prose style which is vigorous and idyllic by turns, which never draws back from the most bold realistic phrase if the action demands it and yet is always completely controlled, restrained, finely disciplined.

By the time Heidenstam came to write *The Tree of the Folkungs* one of the ideas most frequently recurring in his work is that the only solution of the many problems of his generation was to return to an essentially classical spirit and point of view. Runeberg, his earliest master in heroic narrative poetry, had pointed the way; and Goethe and Schiller, with their so-called "Weimar classicism," had later confirmed Heidenstam's faith in some form of modern humanism as a philosophic and aesthetic necessity for the modern world.

Most of the forms of modern culture, it is clear from Heidenstam's early critical essays, were looked upon by Heidenstam as essentially "barbarian"—a word which he often used in his critical essays as broadly antithetic to classical and humanistic. All excesses in modern life were conceived as so many crude barbaric violations of the classical ideals of serenity and restraint. In consequence, he came to condemn with equal severity such seemingly diverse manifestations of late nineteenth century Swedish culture as the proletariat movement and bourgeois materialism, the evangelical tendencies in religious sectarianism and the hysterical "mysticism" affected by a decadent aesthetics. Particularly incisive is Heidenstam's early critical analysis of *fin de siècle* aestheticism, and of the vogue for the Neo-Gothic which accompanied this aestheticism; and his condemnation of these tendencies, as fundamentally inconsistent with a true modern spirit, is as vigorous as his critical analysis is penetrating.

. . . Perhaps the more decadent strain in the temper of our day, the religious mysticism which has suddenly swept over poetry and art, can in some way tolerate our Neo-Gothic. But this strain is temporary; it is, like the earlier Romanticism, much more a necessary revolt against the altogether too complacent materialism of a preceding age than it is an outbreak of genuine piety. . . .

A modified form of classical paganism is held to be far more consistent with a true modern spirit than is this Neo-Gothic decadence; and it is toward such a paganism, Heidenstam prophesies, that the modern spirit will finally and inevitably tend.

. . . We are moving toward paganism, toward a profounder antiquity, whose healthy nature-mysticism is called the worship of beauty; and even though we are wiser in building for ourselves rather than the future, the pure beauty of the basilica, with its mark of an earlier Christianity and its kinship to paganism, should give a more intimate and truthful architectural portrait of our day than does any Neo-Gothicism.

These words, written in 1894, provide a key to a proper understanding of both the spirit and the form of all of Heidenstam's later work.

It is, for example, Heidenstam's profound reverence for the classical, combined with his conception of the proper method of the historian, that determines the architectonics of his historical fiction, of which *The Tree of the Folkungs* is the most mature expression. History, according to Heidenstam, should be conceived primarily in terms of the revealing anecdote. "The personal," he writes, in the essay from which we have quoted above, "is the most important element in history, and it is most intimately illuminated by the anecdote. . . ." Earlier in the same essay he had written: "The day shall come when Fryxell's history [*Berättelser ur svenska historien, 1823 ff.*], despite its many errors, will be honored as our best, our most clear and living, because he, as the artist, employs the anecdote and creates human beings." The juxtaposition—tantamount to an identification—which Heidenstam suggests here between the historian and the artist is of first importance in a proper understanding

of Heidenstam's historical fiction. The artist who seeks to compose historical novels, according to Heidenstam, must of
necessity concentrate on the historical anecdote as the basis of
his treatment of fictional episode; and the pattern of his general
narrative must consist of a succession of appropriately selected
(on occasion perhaps partially imagined) anecdotes developed
with vividly human dramatic concentration. In such a conception of the historical novel great care must be exercised in the
choice of anecdotes. They should be anecdotes not merely his-
torically well-founded; they must be aesthetically consistent with
the novel conceived as a whole. Everything must be subordinated to the central scheme, to the main impression which the
novelist aims to give; and yet each individual episode must also
have in itself an immediate interest and an essentially independent vitality.

It is illuminating to note in this connection how the narrative
technique in Heidenstam's historical fiction develops from the
publication of *The Charles Men* in the late 1890's to the appearance of *The Tree of the Folkungs* less than ten years later. In
The Charles Men each episode is a complete artistic unit within
itself, closely related to the collection of stories of which it is
in a sense a part, but quite capable of an entirely independent
aesthetic existence. In *Saint Birgitta's Pilgrimage* (1902) the
individual episodes are somewhat more definitely subordinated
to the general composite picture which the novel seeks to give.
In *The Tree of the Folkungs* the novelist's canvas has increased
immensely in size (the action extending over two centuries of
time); and yet the episodes are not loosely related to one
another—each is definitely subordinated to the central historical conception, each becomes organically related to the novel
as a whole. *The Tree of the Folkungs* is, in fact, the only work
of Heidenstam's that can be termed a thoroughly unified,
organically developed *novel*: in it alone among Heidenstam's
fictional performances, anecdote has been carefully selected and
skillfully fitted into a general fictional performance of classical
balance and proportion. *The Charles Men* and *Saint Birgitta's
Pilgrimage* were merely tentative steps in this direction.

Intent as Heidenstam is in *The Tree of the Folkungs* on the development of striking individual episodes carefully subordinated to the narrative conception as a whole, he does not fail to realize also the possibilities of the use of appropriate historical background. True to the essential aesthetic economy of his classical standards, however, he never permits detail of historical scene to submerge the central action.

That scene plays a very important part in *The Tree of the Folkungs* is apparent already in the opening episode; but scene is handled here, as elsewhere in this novel, with an appropriate selective restraint, sparing in its use of detail, and always severely subordinated to the immediate narrative action. Heidenstam felt that the author's historical imagination should always remain reasonably free, that it should never be dominated by the numerous minutiae of mere historical actuality. "When living poetry flees back to the past"—he once wrote, particularly with reference to historical fiction—"in order to there use some event, it is not in order to mimic dead forms or to describe in what way man in a certain century fastened his mantle; but it is in order to reach a freer region for the imagination, which must always remain independent of the accidental, the commonplace, and the insignificant." As a consequence of this attitude toward his historical materials, Heidenstam refused to permit the antiquarian passion to leave its stultifying mark upon his historical fiction. He refused to become concerned primarily, in his handling of historical scene, with the detail of historical costume, with archaic affectations in style, with all the mere historical "machinery" which have left their unhappy mark at times even on the robust pages of Scott and which were largely responsible for Flaubert's magnificent failure in *Salammbô*.

Deeply as Heidenstam was interested in the past, and profound as is his detail knowledge of the Swedish national past, it cannot be too strongly insisted upon that he has never been guilty of narrow antiquarian propensities either in his art or in his criticism. It is the *living past* in which he is interested, i.e. those aspects of the past which can be of vital significance to a *living present*. Modern Sweden, an immediate contemporary Sweden, is Heidenstam's real passion. He goes back into

Sweden's national past for his fictional material in order to interpret, and if possible to *direct,* Sweden's national present and future. He feels that a great modern Sweden must grow directly out of a great Sweden of the past—else it cannot grow at all. But the Sweden of the past that can be great to a Sweden of the present is not the Sweden of an archaic phraseology, of curious costumes, of merely outward and accidental historical detail. It is rather the Sweden that is to be discovered by the sensitive and discriminating artist-historian in its permanent racial characteristics, in its great actions as determined by deep-lying native psychological urges, in permanent achievements of a national spirit contending with all the complex material of its environment down through the long generations of its history. It is because Heidenstam has so deeply sensed these deeper roots of the Swedish national spirit that his art in *The Tree of the Folkungs* impresses the reader as being so profoundly *organic*—as if its handling of scene and character and stylistic detail develop directly and naturally out of the central action, the general narrative pattern of the novel. The action itself (in the outward sense of successive episodes forming a narrative plot) grows naturally, in its turn, out of Heidenstam's conception of nationalism—a concept of nationalism which has found its necessary guide in a mature intellectual discipline and which comes to be realized in an art which is thoroughly consistent at every point with Heidenstam's philosophy of life.

The approach to an adequate understanding of the ultimate greatness of *The Tree of the Folkungs* must in consequence be made primarily through an analysis of the guiding ideas of Heidenstam's mature general thought. Heidenstam's ethics is at the core of this body of thought. He found his way to the ethics of *The Tree of the Folkungs* only by a long and arduous route. We have seen that his earliest volume of poetry, *Pilgrimage and Wander-Years,* reveals little if any concern with social and moral problems. The poems in this volume, with the exception of those contained in the section entitled "Thoughts in Loneliness," are largely concerned with a spontaneous enjoyment of the immediate physical pleasures of life. And even the "Thoughts in Loneliness" are partly epicurean in tone, though it is the epicureanism of Romantic melancholy rather than the robust epicureanism of a glorified youthful sensuousness. Nowhere in *Pilgrimage and Wander-Years* is there any sympathetic response to the large world of humanity beyond the poet's own created world of beauty. The poems in the volume are essentially amoral in their point of view; they concern themselves primarily with the poet's own ego, and when a larger world outside this ego makes itself felt at all, the poet finds this world negative, disturbing, something from which to escape. In *Poems* (1895), a somewhat maturer note is struck: the poet has begun to identify himself with the world about him, and this identification, partial and fragmentary as it is, leads him inevitably to a consideration of broad social values—social values which in such a poem as "Home" take on the form of a nascent nationalism.

In *The Charles Men* (1897-98) Heidenstam's growing concern with the world outside himself takes on a much more definite form. In this novel he centres his attention primarily, as we have seen, on the character of Charles XII and the way in which this character represents in Swedish history an heroic moral ideal. Heidenstam finds the greatness of Charles XII to lie in a stern, self-sacrificing attitude toward his conception of duty. In striving to fulfill his destiny Charles XII found no personal sacrifice too great to make; and he expected the same ideal of sacrifice to actuate his people. The individual may thus be able to realize greatness, but only, in Heidenstam's view, as he identifies himself with the larger strivings of his people.

In *Saint Birgitta's Pilgrimage* (1902), Heidenstam's second venture into historical fiction, the figure of the famous Swedish saint seems at first conceived in precisely the same manner as Charles XII had been. She is on occasion inhuman, demanding of those about her the most undeviating loyalty to a harsh, almost brutal conception of duty; and her inhumanity is intensified by the driving motive of a severe religious fanaticism. And yet Birgitta is a character of a subtly complex, even of a paradoxical, kind. At times she yearns passionately for human sympathy, a sympathy which she had shut out from herself because of the fierce fanaticism that actuated her sense of duty. "If only people knew," she burst out on one occasion, "how much more passionately I yearn to their hearts than they to mine!" Later, in the closing years of her "Pilgrimage," when she has realized the things for which she had striven, and death is nigh at hand, there comes over her a deep humility of spirit, a warm flood of human sympathy, and with this a much more profound knowledge of the nature of good and evil than a narrow fanaticism had earlier been able to teach her.

Nothing, nothing human have I loved more than my husband and my children, and no one have I caused more sorrow . . . and I myself can no longer sorrow. They no longer cry from their graves in order to threaten or complain, but rather to forgive and thank me. Are they not in their devoted goodness worth a thousand times more honor than I? Thou hast answered all of my questions, Eternal Judge, but whenever I have falteringly asked that question it has become dark about me and I have no longer apprehended Thy words. A beggar's two empty hands is all I have to offer Thee. So is it Thy meaning that also they who most intensely burn with desire to serve Thy love and righteousness shall do evil like the evil ones, and bitter tears shall follow them over the earth.

Saint Birgitta was great, her will had triumphed among her kind; but her greatness was not pure, unalloyed—in her devout spirit good and evil were both present, as it is in all of human life. She came to see this finally—this deep mystery which lies at the core of existence. And when she perceives it there sweeps over her a warm, intimately touching humanity, a humble resignation to the great mystery of life—a desire, finally, for peace rather than strife, for humble self-effacing prayer rather than for that vigorous aggressiveness of spirit which performs evil even when it yearns most intensely to do good.

In this closing scene of *Saint Birgitta's Pilgrimage* it is to be noted that Heidenstam's ethics has undergone a subtle, yet basic transformation. The heroic ideal of Charles XII, which was not perhaps without a certain tinge of albeit noble chauvinism, becomes now the humble final heroism of a religious saint, whose spirit of questioning, touched in the hour of death by a sensitive human feeling for those whom she had wronged in the aggressive spirituality of her career, leads her steps at last to those regions where man faces directly the most baffling problem of existence, the problem of the relation between good and evil. And as she broods over this problem—a problem which neither ceaseless prayer nor heroic personal sacrifice seems capable of solving for her—she can but find solace in a deep humility, a profound resignation, recognizing that good and evil exist side by side in life, evil oftentimes *resulting* even from a sincere desire to do good.

The ethical paradox contained in Saint Birgitta's final confession to her God becomes the basis for the ethics of *The Tree of the Folkungs,* though in this novel Heidenstam comes to apply the paradox more boldly and sweepingly to an interpretation of broad national and cultural issues rather than to an immediate personal religious experience. Gunnar Castrén, a recent Swedish critic, sums up the ethics of this novel excellently when he writes that *The Tree of the Folkungs* "is a saga of large proportions about how culture has grown up from good and evil, from both the light and the dark powers in man's spirit. Culture is built upon meanness and greatness, upon egotistical greed and upon the ideal will to create, upon earthly envy and upon a deep yearning for purity. No one who has a purpose in life to realize can go through life blameless and without stain. But life can reconcile and ennoble."

The famous Folkung dynasty which came to govern Sweden upon the death in 1250 of King Erik, the last feeble descendant in the Saint Erik dynasty, had its origins, we have seen, two hundred years earlier within the crude and primitive environs of Folketuna farm; and in the blood of this early Swedish dynasty flowed a strangely unpromising racial combination—the steady, plodding practicality of the Swedish peasant and the mysterious volatility, the stealthy adaptability of a Finnish dwarf race. The early founding of this family, which was to occupy a throne, is to be traced back ultimately, Heidenstam makes clear in *Folke Filbyter,* to the motive of economic greed, a driving passion for physical possession in terms primarily of gold and land. A singular brutality came, in consequence, to dominate the early Folkung strain: even Ingevald, the least brutal of Folke Filbyter's sons, gains his bride against her will by taking her by violence from her family; and the son which is born of this union of violence becomes the first Folkung to gain political power—by an inhuman persecution of those who insisted upon maintaining their heathen beliefs against the infiltration of Christianity into the land. Later, in *The Bjälbo Heritage* (second of the two volumes included in *The Tree of the Folkungs*), Valdemar, the first Folkung to occupy the Swedish throne, is forced from his throne by his brother, Magnus, a curiously complex character: mean and petty and envious, harsh and inhuman, and yet able as law-man, administrator, and king; and all of this, it seems, because of a certain essential nobility of character. Valdemar, on the other hand, though generous and kind, and quite unable to brook ill-feelings even toward his worst enemies, proved to be, *just because* of his lovable personal qualities, quite incapable as the leader of a nation, the constructive builder of a sound national culture. He had lived for love and the pleasures of war and the hunt rather than for the higher glories of serious and constructive public service; and he had fallen, not because he was evil in thought, but because his irresponsible spirit of goodness had in its fruits the seed of national evil, of final cultural decay. For a time after having been dethroned Valdemar tried to regain the throne which his brother had taken from him; but soon he lost all interest in the larger affairs of life, and he died a weak, thoroughly disillusioned man, finding such solace as he could in his last years at the bosom of a mistress whom he had been permitted to retain as a prison companion.

And yet even Valdemar had gained wisdom, of a kind, in the days of his decline. "Noble knights!"—he burst out, with a pathetic mixture of bravado and sore-bought wisdom, to a group of his brother's knights who were forced against their wills to entertain him in the guest-house at Vreta convent just before his final imprisonment—"the way to be happy is to live for one thing alone. And I have lived for love. But if Magnus, who had other things to accomplish in life, had been human enough to think also of love, curses and woe would have followed him into his last hour." Later, on the occasion when he voluntarily gave himself up to his brother, he admits that the freedom he had promised his people was but a will-o'-the-wisp, an unattainable though beautiful ideal. He had failed as king, he admits; . . . and yet his brother?—was Magnus, the successful ruler of a united people, any more happy, having chosen the way of duty?

Valdemar walked to the top of the burial mound.

"Their ribs crackle under my feet like dry twigs," he said; "and fingers and empty brainpans lie strewed all about. Are these the relics of my former friends? Poor sinners, I promised you a realm of liberty which is nowhere to be found, and you followed me. That was your crime. Had I not just sent off my minstrel, he should play to you all the night long. That were indeed the only honour I could show you. I am a poor lonely man and soon shall be vile dust like you. We all belonged to the host of the lost ones, for whom there is no redemption. But I am sickened with my own complaints, they touch no other hearts than mine. I am glad to see you, brother. Are you happy now?"

Magnus was quieting his horse, which stamped and snorted under its cloth and steel headpiece.

"You learned that question in the women's chambers, Valdemar. I lead a life that would wear out a dog. That is my pride. But why do you come to me of your own accord?"

The reason for Magnus's cryptic, half-evasive reply upon being asked by Valdemar whether he was now happy is revealed with dramatic completeness in the last episode of *The Bjälbo Heritage*. Magnus, who was at this time slowly dying of an incurable disease, visits his brother in the prison room at Nyköping. All has gone well for him outwardly—his hold upon the throne is secure, his followers are legion, enthusiastic and loyal to the last man, proud to be his sworn knights. Still, despite all of this, Magnus broods; he is fundamentally an unhappy man as he meets his brother—and this not because of fear of the disease that is eating slowly away at his body. He suggests, when he comes in to his brother, that he might open the prison doors if Valdemar should so desire.

"I go out!" answered Valdemar . . . with an anxious look. "I defended my cause to the utmost—but now! Whither should I go? My former subjects would stone me and tear the clothes off me. No. I am better off here. The walls are thick and there are strong skins across the window. If I may but keep Luitgard. And let me sometimes sit in the common room. It has the sun."

"I shall give orders for it. If only I don't forget; I have so much to think of. . . . And we ought to have many things yet to speak of, you and I. Answer me one question, but answer it fully: When you ponder your life and the days that are past, does not the pain at last grow so sore that you feel it will burst your bosom?"

Valdemar still lay with his neck on Luitgard's lap, looking up at the vaulting.

"You forget one thing," he answered. "I am a man who is at peace with the world."

Magnus had to smile.

"Our saga is written out, Valdemar. Nor you nor I can any more disturb the other's fate. But understand my words. When it is dark . . . when you sit alone . . . do not visions and memories rise about you? Do you never suffer pangs of conscience?"

Valdemar played with the tassel of his belt, dropped it, picked it up again and lay a long while in thought.

"Perhaps I treated people too kindly. I sometimes blush for that."

"And that is all you have to say? You answer for yours and I for mine. Now brother I begin to understand why Satan loses his power when I answer him: Take me!"

There was a gleam in Magnus's eye, and he absently drained the horn.

"A manly word in the face of death," he said, rising, "that is a key to heaven's gate even for two of the lost!"

He picked up his cloak, which had slipped on to the bench, and fastened it.

The bell was already ringing for Mass, and the tramp of hoofs proclaimed that his knights were assembling.

He stepped out into the common room, dazzled by the sunshine. When his eyes recovered, he took his stand at the open window, and his dark-grey mantle fluttered in the draught.

The tone of this closing episode in *The Tree of the Folkungs* seems at first oppressive; the ethical implications of the dialogue seem hopelessly skeptical, cankered by a subtly disintegrating cynicism. Valdemar admits that he feels shame only on occasion, when he thinks that he has perhaps been too friendly to people about him. Otherwise he has no pangs of conscience—this pleasure-loving man, now old, who had loved many women and had done little else. Magnus, outwardly upright, noble, the strong leader of a united people, is the one who broods, whose conscience is restless, seared, incapable of even momentary peace.

Good and evil . . . so hopelessly intertwined in life, in individual men's lives and in the national structures which men try to build before they die. Can any good come out of conditions of existence so confused, so ominously chaotic, so ceaselessly at strife among themselves? Heidenstam does not answer the question definitely. He is too much of the critical philosophic mind to venture a dogmatic assertion; and yet as a poet he has a presentiment that good shall finally triumph, a profound historical intuition that man shall finally succeed, through aching lessons taught by trial and error, in building something approaching an ideal social and political structure which shall ultimately prevail. Heidenstam is too much the artist to give to this faith of his a direct, clear-cut expression . . . it is found to be implicit, however, in the tone which dominates the last paragraph of the novel—a paragraph buoyant, though not to excess, optimistic, yet with restraint, breathing a quiet note of triumph in its dignified progression of phrase and in its firm march of imagery. Magnus stands on a balcony reviewing an assembling of his knighthood in a courtyard below.

There seemed no end to the growing host below. It was the whole knighthood of the country, his sworn body-guard, which he had conjured up from wild bands and filled with noble purpose. There waved the gauntlet, on a hand that would never be raised to harm a woman. There gleamed the ring and the belt, symbols of loyalty. There the black sole under the mailed hose constantly reminded the overweening of the grave's mould. And the arms displayed on every shield had made an end of every treacherous ambush. All the knights were bare-headed and looked before them, full of confidence. They had dropped their reins and held their swords upright in both hands like tapers, and the steel points flashed like flames for the suppression of war and violence. And as the numbers grew, the song of victory from Hofva rose ever louder to the clear autumn sky:

> Jesu, grant Thy servants' boon.
> Children of this world are we,
> Crying to Thee every one:
> Give us rest and peace with Thee.

Man in the North had gone far in the two hundred years that had elapsed since Folke Filbyter had established a severe primitive authority over his crude, brutish thralls at Folketuna farm. Meanness and greed and brutal violence, only occasionally relieved by a gleam of gentleness and nobility, had dominated Folketuna life in those early days. But out of these circumstances—so unpromising ethically considered—was born a later royal dynasty, which, in the person of King Magnus, himself a character of mixed virtues and vices, found at the last its chief glory in deeds of knightly kindness, in a common desire for everlasting peace among men. Good had triumphed over evil, at least for the moment; an ideal national culture was becoming slowly realized in a subtle fusing of the heroic virtues of the early Viking and the ideals of gentleness and chivalry that motivated medieval Christianity at its best. The Folkungs themselves, we know, finally passed away, and evil days were to come again before their dynasty ceased to occupy the ancient throne of the Sveas and the Goths; but a Swedish national culture continued to exist, through evil hours and good, groping instinctively onward toward man's ultimate ideal—"Peace, peace, peace!" This is the burden of Heidenstam's ethical message in *The Tree of the Folkungs.*

Closely related to Heidenstam's ethics is that phase of his aesthetics that concerns itself with his theory of tragedy as illustrated in *The Charles Men,* in *Saint Birgitta's Pilgrimage,* and finally, in a sense most magnificently, in *The Tree of the Folkungs.* It is to be observed in this last novel that the three characters most completely developed—Folke Filbyter, Valdemar, and Magnus—are all conceived as essentially tragic figures. Each of these characters has his day of triumph, such as it is; but all of them bow ultimately to circumstances of existence outside themselves which are too strong for them. Folke Filbyter, we remember, had on one occasion defied Jorgrimme's ominous incantations and prophecies with the words, "I believe in no gods, but rely rather on my own strength"; yet he lived to see the day when his own strength availed him nothing in gaining that which he most desired. Valdemar, first of the Folkung kings, lived well and blithely, and promised his people freedom from oppression; yet he ultimately came to see —when it was too late for *him* to change the current of affairs— that the nonchalant spirit of royal irresponsibility which inspired his sentimental dreams of political freedom for his people was the very *cause* of a political chaos which brought new forms of oppression in its wake. Magnus had indeed succeeded where Valdemar had failed—he had welded a rather truant, barbaric race into a strong, basically peace-loving nation. Still even he found no final happiness in life, for his laudable political aims had been finally attained by means which were often sinuous, low-minded, and petty—specifically by deeds of treachery toward his brother.

It is not difficult to discern the relation between Heidenstam's ethics on the one hand and his conception of tragic fates such as those of Folke Filbyter, Valdemar, and Magnus on the other. A world primarily conditioned by a ceaseless struggle between good and evil would necessarily place man on occasion in moral dilemmas incapable of being solved. That Heidenstam saw the relation between his ethics and his conception of tragedy years before he came to write *The Tree of the Folkungs* is clearly revealed in an essay "Charles XII and the Tragic," a series of notes on the theory of tragedy which he came to jot down during the years in which his interpretation of Charles XII and his fellow campaigners was taking form. Two passages from this essay are particularly to our purposes. Early in the essay he refers in passing to "the apparent or real mixture of good and evil, which is the necessary foundation of a tragic character." And later in the essay he applies this general statement of his theory of tragedy specifically to the case of Charles XII.

A tragic problem consists in a conflict between opposing claims of justice (*rättskrav*), which appear so strong that it is impossible for human righteousness to reject either. Not only the blood-red thread which the logic of misfortune spins through the tragic is impossible to break; but even with regard to the ethical judgment we are unable to reach out farther than to a gloomy, skeptical questioning. This awakens sympathy, or even devoted admiration, for the tragic hero; but it also provides a challenge to our reflection, a search for a possible solution, even though it is not to be found. Man cannot solve the tragic problem; and this explains the general chaos that surrounds efforts to analyze the case of Charles XII— the constant dissension between admiration on the one hand and our feeling of moral responsibility on the other. If a solution were at any time possible this would mean that he would not be really tragic; but we need not fear. What is it that is in the profoundest classical sense tragic if not the conflict between personal and public claims of justice, which are presented to us in life! . . .

These passages, it is clear, are just as applicable to an interpretation of the tragic element in *The Tree of the Folkungs* as they are to *The Charles Men*. In *The Tree of the Folkungs* Heidenstam has but shifted the tragic scene: his tragic heroes in this late novel are merely taken from an earlier and more crude civilization, from a period of transition in Swedish history when man was first emerging from the comparative barbarism of ancient Scandinavian life. Man's tragic dilemma, however, is essentially the same be he an inhabitant of a primitive medieval society or the citizen of an enlightened nation of the early eighteenth century; man's life differs only in externals from one historical period to another. It is therefore that the crude, semi-barbaric figure of Folke Filbyter can be invested by Heidenstam with the same tragic grandeur that distinguishes the gallant heroic figure of Charles XII, though in externals one could hardly conceive a greater contrast between two men of real heroic proportions. It would seem apparent that the primary source of Heidenstam's conception of tragedy is a classical one; and yet in *The Tree of the Folkungs* he reveals himself capable of applying classical tragic theory with a bold, modern creative flexibility which is capable of finding true tragic greatness in even the curious primitive fate of the coarse-grained peasant Folke Filbyter.

The flexibility with which Heidenstam comes ultimately to apply his theory of tragedy to peasant and king alike suggests the possibility of an influence from the Icelandic sagas—perhaps equal to that of classical tragedy—on the conception of tragic action in *The Tree of the Folkungs*. It might be said, indeed, that in his tragic conception of the founder of the Folkung family Heidenstam merges the aristocratic framework of classical tragedy with the more homely, if not democratic, tragedy that we come upon in the Icelandic family sagas. And this is an eminently happy procedure here, for Folke Filbyter is a typical saga hero in all essential respects. Like many a saga hero he bears the stain of outlawry, he lives largely by deeds of violence, and his end is a tragically resigned one. In his final resignation Folke Filbyter had found goodness—but not happiness; for the confusion which dominates existence had woven too strong and intricate a web for him to disentangle. A noble fatalism was the spirit in which he faced the end. One is reminded, as one reads of Folke Filbyter's fate, that through many an Icelandic saga of the heroic age had run a recurring phrase: "There are two choices, and neither of them good." The phrase might well have been chosen as a motto for *The Tree of the Folkungs*, for in the stoic burden of this phrase from the ancient sagas is contained the kernel of Heidenstam's ethics in his historical novel and the key to the theory of tragedy which dominates its action.

Anyone familiar with the Icelandic sagas will be aware also of certain details of narrative method in *The Tree of the Folkungs* akin to the technique of the sagas. We have already noted in the opening scene of Heidenstam's novel the use made of incantation and prophecy to state the general outline of the action and to forbode evil and ultimate tragedy. This is a detail of narrative method frequently used in the sagas. Narrative symbolism, a device of common occurrence in the sagas, is also employed by Heidenstam. In *Folke Filbyter,* the first part of Heidenstam's novel, the horn Månegarm, originally in the possession of Jorgrimme, the Finnish dwarf-sorcerer, becomes the mysterious symbol of good fortune, superstitiously revered by the people as capable of exercising divine powers. In *The Bjälbo Heritage* it is the sword Gråne which is supposed to bring good fortune, though its attributes of divine power are bound up with late medieval Christian superstitions rather than with an older heathen sorcery. In each case, however, Heidenstam uses these symbols to provide a sort of narrative unity and to relate the tragic action of his novel to those unknown, mysterious worlds outside human understanding which man in the past has conceived as ordering his fate and determining his final destiny. As a poet Heidenstam could appreciate profoundly the rich, suggestive possibilities in the skillful use of such narrative symbolism; and he employs it throughout the novel with a happy lyric intuition which never fails to bring to the sensitive reader a deeply moving consciousness of those mysterious powers which medieval superstition conceived as floating in and about and through life—powers marvelously active, sometimes good, sometimes malevolent, but always in some strange way seeming to determine in the end the destiny of man.

Heidenstam's poetic gifts did not leave their mark alone, however, upon this aspect of his fictional technique. His prose style is everywhere in direct debt to his essentially lyric genius. Heidenstam's poetry, especially that of the maturer lyrics in *Poems* (1895), had been marked by economy of phrase, by a vigorously realistic diction, by bold, plastic imagery, and by a reasonably firm classical restraint in its expression of emotion and of thought. All these traits of his best poetry reappear in the clear, sinewy prose of *The Tree of the Folkungs*.

The most striking particular characteristic of Heidenstam's prose style is its terse, clipped epigrammatic form, usually accompanied by a forceful, vigorous, concrete diction entirely consistent with the world in which his characters move. That which gives this epigrammatic prose its chief distinction, however, is the strange lyric power of the figurative language which dominates it and yet which is so subtly woven into the living fabric of the style as not to call undue attention to itself. One might illustrate this stylistic quality with the passage describing the heavy sorrow that came over Folke Filbyter upon his discovery of the loss of his tiny grandson—

. . . Below them there was a hollow in the earthen floor, made by himself when he sat by the cradle. It made him think of a plundered nest, and he burst into wailing. It was not weeping and it had no words. It was a complaint like that the hunter sometimes hears at night from distant lairs in the forest. It rose and sank, and now and again it was stifled and still. He began to walk in a circle about the empty place, heavily swaying like a she-bear whose cubs have been stolen.

Still more characteristic, perhaps, is the laconic description— prefaced by a magnificently moving figure of speech—of Filke Filbyter some years later, when a weary spirit of resignation had settled down upon him in consequence of his failure to find any trace of the stolen child.

. . . If the master himself spoke of olden days, it sounded like a distant voice from the wilds, where the wanderer takes clouds for mountains and meadows for lakes. His riches increased continually and filled more and more chests, which were nailed down when full and never again opened. During the long winter evenings he sat among the cinders with empty hands, saying nothing, and grew old but could not die.

Equally epigrammatic, and weighted with a rare burden of marvelously appropriate imagery, is the language in which Heidenstam sketches the great change, toward goodness, that swept over Folke Filbyter in his final resignation to the inevitable; though the note of harshness is gone now—a more tender, gentle tone suffuses the aching pathos of the theme.

. . . Nothing had ever grown in his heart but weeds and thistles, and now that the fire of misfortune had burnt and cleansed it, it had the untilled fertility of virgin soil. Strange little flowers opened their eyes within him and began to shoot up thicker and thicker, till his once barren heart was like one great flower-bed. It would have puzzled him sorely if he had tried to put a name to these unknown visitors; but he did not tell them over in any feeling of joy, if indeed he noticed their presence. He merely began to wonder that everyone called him wicked, for that moment, when his first grief had passed, he was conscious of no wicked will.

And still later—

His misfortunes in recent years had greatly changed him. His face still had the broad fullness of the peasant, but its more sensitive lines had become sharper and nobler, and his red and wrinkled eyelids seemed worn with weeping. He dozed in the sunshine and his bushy hair spread over his shoulders and back. The kettle hat lay on his knee, and with the hay heaped all about him he looked like a buried warrior who had left his mound to thaw his limbs in the fine winter weather.

Such passages as these show how far Heidenstam had departed from the prose style of naturalism with its fondness for a detailed photographic objectivity, and its frequent attendant note of the sordid and the hopeless. The author of *The Tree of the Folkungs,* unlike many another novelist of his day, was able to find in human tragedy a beauty all its own: a beauty severe, realistic, and stoic in tone; but in addition a beauty as of flowers and quiet winter landscapes . . . and of peace—soft, gentle, all-embracing and all-forgiving peace. It is the poet in Heidenstam that sensed the profound undertones of these tragic values and gave to them a finely nuanced, forcefully lyric expression which pulses with a quiet, unobtrusive strength in the sharp, aggressive externals of action that compose the outward narrative movement of *The Tree of the Folkungs.*

More directly a part of the action itself is the dialogue in the novel; and this dialogue is no less epigrammatic in form, though perhaps less profoundly lyric in some of its essential qualities. Heidenstam's constant emphasis upon striking episodes (the anecdote of history) required various vigorous stylistic devices in the building up of the narrative action; and not the least important of these is the forceful epigram, which is able to suggest in a few terse, strikingly colorful words the essential nature of the conflict at any particular point in the action. Two passages from *Folke Filbyter* will serve to illustrate. The first is a part of the speech of the elder brother of Holmdis, when he strongly opposes the marriage of his sister into the Folkung family—

". . . Ill does it beseem us, who are of ancient Lawman's stock, to ally ourselves with Folketuna. Gold can go far, but not farthest. From Folketuna will never come a son who can be our brother in power and repute, and the shining sword of your old age. From a corrupted seed no tree will grow. Can you conceive Folke Filbyter as the ancestor of a mighty lineage? Folketuna is a despised house, founded by a stranger of whom we know nothing but ill. Let him marry his son among thralls or Finn folk. That is fitting for one who, when he dies, will lie forgotten, with no pillar stone to mark his grave. We believe you meant well, father, when you made this unhappy proposal; but I tell you frankly that in that hour your wonted prudence had forsaken you. The times are overcast and threatening, but my sister is too good for a bantling of Folketuna. We, her brothers, say 'No' and raise our ban, for we purpose to make our race renowned."

The second is the noble impromptu address delivered from the ancient Thing mound at Old Uppsala. The peasant Lawman from Tiundaland speaks, driven by a fury of indignation to utter the strong condemnation of his fellows against King Inge's Earl, the grandson of Folke Filbyter.

"We franklins have not come this long way to hear your learning, Earl, nor to vote upon any trifling decrees. Nor do we ask whether it was the Christian who burned our grove, for what is done in the darkness of night partakes of that darkness and remains dark even in the light of day. Nor do we ask whether it be true that you would forbid us franklins to buy and sell freely at our homes in order that the craftsmen and foreign chapmen of Aros and Sigtuna may make the more profit and wear yet warmer furs. We know that you wish to forbid us to hold Thing and to carry arms, and that you would force us to call the Body-guard lords and to pay tithes to the bishops and the Pope in distant Rome. Hitherto it was we who laid foreign lands under tribute and filled our homes with their treasures. We were a free people of husbandmen and had plenty of cattle and good horses. You lay upon us a foreign yoke, and it is none the less heavy for being graced with many ornaments. A man must be as young as you to dream of so many new things. We have not chosen you. You are a fine white loaf from the King's House. The people bake a coarser bread with bran in it. Who was your father and who was your mother? A parcel of priests you call your parents, because they taught you to read. Many rumours are whispered about you, but it was not for your sake we came here. Open your rolls and read the law of kings. The Sveas have the right to make a king or break a king. We ask you, King Inge, will you lay down the power and the kingdom, or will you now come down among us and sacrifice to the old gods for a good harvest?"

Both of these passages are central in the development of dramatic episode, as will be seen if they are examined in their contexts; and each of them gains its peculiar immediate intensity of effect largely by means of the terse, direct, concretely epigrammatic language in which it is cast. Nearly all of the dialogue in *The Tree of the Folkungs* is cast in a similar mold.

Some Swedish critics have observed, not without some reason, a certain inflexibility, an occasional lack of ease in Heidenstam's narrative prose in *The Tree of the Folkungs* which seems to place it just below real greatness. There is some truth to the charge. Heidenstam's genius, being primarily a lyric one, it is natural that he did not do his very best work in extended prose forms. It is therefore, probably, that despite his very real distinction as a novelist he has attained his most consistently happy purely stylistic success in fiction in the genre of the short heroic tale as represented in *The Charles Men*. A severely hostile critic of Heidenstam might go so far as to brand *The Tree of the Folkungs* as merely an extended fictional *tour de force*, powerful enough in individual scenes, but not attaining a unit narrative impression at once natural in style and smoothly organic in its general narrative movement. This would be to dispose of it unfairly, however. To admit that Heidenstam's chief claim to greatness lies in his lyric poetry, and that his greatest stylistic triumph in prose is *The Charles Men,* is not to deny genuine and great artistic virtue to *The Tree of the Folkungs;* for in this novel he merges purely lyric qualities with a dramatic action of magnificent power and profound ethical implications, and the result is certainly something just short of the historical novel at its very best. Only Sigrid Undset surpasses Heidenstam as a historical novelist in the Scandinavian countries; and as for writers of historical fiction outside of Scandinavia, Heidenstam must be said to rank among the foremost from Sir Walter Scott down to our own day.

V

It would be both pleasant and illuminating to trace in some detail Heidenstam's activities as an essayist and on the lecture platform since the publication of the last part of *The Tree of the Folkungs* in 1905; for it was during these years that he found release from his aristocratic isolation as a poet and came to speak on occasion directly to the Swedish nation on subjects that lay closest to his heart. But this phase of Heidenstam's career is of direct, primary interest only to the Swedish people themselves, and it had best therefore be written by a Swedish scholar or critic for Swedish consumption. One of the most fascinating developments in this phase of Heidenstam's career might, however, be noted in passing. I refer to the bitter controversy with Strindberg in the years just before Strindberg's death, a controversy precipitated by Strindberg's violent polemics in *En blå bok* ("A Blue Book," 1907; several continuations 1908-12) and *Svarta fanor* ("Black Banners," 1907). In the first of the so-called *Blue Books* Heidenstam had been disposed of in the brutally slurring phrase, "Sweden's most unintelligent man"!

Heidenstam's chief contribution to the controversy which raged about Strindberg's stormy personality up to the very edge of the grave was a series of essays entitled *Proletärfilosofiens upplösning och fall* ("The Decline and Fall of the Philosophy of the Proletariat," 1911). These essays are primarily concerned with attacking the Swedish proletariat movement of the late nineteenth and the early twentieth centuries as being essentially "barbaric" in all of its characteristic manifestations and fundamentally foreign to what Heidenstam conceived to be a true Swedish national spirit. Strindberg is pilloried in the third of this series of essays as "the full-blooded barbarian in our literature." The essay is entitled "Strindberg as Seen through a Telescope." The burlesque irony of the title is perhaps a sufficient final commentary on how far apart Heidenstam and Strindberg had swung since those days at Schloss Brunegg when each of these men had such a strong, though momentary attraction for the other. And the tone of the essay reveals how directly Heidenstam could proceed to the attack when he was sufficiently aroused.

Never again, however, does Heidenstam permit himself to be drawn so completely out of his usual dignity and reserve with reference to immediate contemporary affairs. He continued after 1911 to interest himself in everything which concerned Swedish culture and its immediate manifestations in the life about him; but he seldom entered into a direct, public expression of opinion on these subjects, retiring more and more as the years went by into that half-distant aristocratic reserve which is the chief mark of his character both as an artist and as a man.

And yet he was not inarticulate. He chose to speak to his people by the more indirect means of his poetry rather than from the forum or in the market-place. His own personality he learned more and more with the years to keep rigidly in the background.

> Glide on, my life! I love thee not so much
> That I would set thine hours with busy care
> In a shop-window for a common show.

This boast was not an idle one; in it is expressed, simply, and without pose, that quiet dignity of spirit which flows nobly through every line of those poems which are included in Heidenstam's greatest contribution to Swedish literature—the slender volume entitled *New Poems* which appeared in 1915. Twenty years had elapsed since the *Poems* (1895), years in which Heidenstam had produced largely in the form of narrative prose. His lyric vein, however, had not ceased to flow, as anyone might have sensed who had read with a sufficiently attentive ear his marvelous prose during these years. The exquisitely finished lyrics included in *New Poems* had been composed at various times between 1895 and 1915; and they represent, when they finally appear, the most mature and perfect expression of Heidenstam's genius. For them the Swedish people have come to be deeply grateful.

These poems occupy a peculiarly distinguished—if not an actually unique—place in the great flowering of lyric poetry which is the chief glory of Swedish literature since the 1890's. They do not have the lyric *inevitability* of Fröding in his happiest moments, nor are they "popular" in the fine sense which either Fröding's or Karlfeldt's poetry is at its best; and yet Sweden in the past twenty-five years has come to reserve for them a poetic shrine alongside those shrines in which the best poetry of Fröding and Karlfeldt has come to be placed. And the worship which the Swedish people bring to Heidenstam, though perhaps less spontaneous than that which they bring to Fröding and Karlfeldt, is none the less real and profound. In Heidenstam's poems Sweden has come to find, not without a deeply ennobling sense of humility, a profound national discipline—a discipline which she may have needed even more than the perfect music of Fröding or the robustly virile tones of Karlfeldt. For *New Poems* (1915) is essentially *a discipline*: an artistic and ethical discipline for Heidenstam himself, and a discipline of like kind for anyone who may come to linger long enough over these poems to fathom in some measure the deeper meanings which flow with nobly quiet dignity through them. Only the Swedish nation, to whom these poems were dedicated and directed, can hope to sense their finer, ultimate values.

What we find in these poems, fundamentally, is the quiet, meditative note of the "Thoughts in Loneliness" and of *Poems* (1895); except that now this note has taken on a new strength and richness, a new and arresting maturity. Its thought is infinitely more profound; its emotional overtones are more restrained, without losing their basic freshness and vitality; and its form is invariably exquisite, crystal clear, with no ornamental excrescences—in a word severely, nobly classical.

To see the distance that Heidenstam had traversed in excellence of lyric utterance between 1895 and 1915 one has but to compare two such poems as "Home" and "Homeland," each of them representative of the volumes in which they originally appeared. Both of these poems are on the same theme—a glorification of memories, of tradition, of the treasures of the past.

The first, beautiful though it be in its way, is somewhat vague in outline and perhaps verges at times on the merely sentimental; and its theme, insofar as it emerges at all clearly, seems relatively restricted in its application, almost personal—it is *the poet* who speaks of *his own* love of memories. The second of these poems, on the other hand, is a marvel of simple artistic restraint in expression; and its thought is as wide in its possible application as is the collective consciousness of a people.

What old man has not in his mournful keeping
The smallest thing that made his life of worth?
He sees a door, a woman bent and weeping,
As toward a grave the young man journeyed forth.

He recollects each room, though poor and base,
Each window-sill, of myrtle faintly smelling.
How should the heart less fervently embrace
The land that is our home, our earthly dwelling.

They stand there yet by lake or lone morass,
Red cottages and manor-halls majestic.
Behind yon frosted panes our sires would pass,
And Yule-tide candles glowed with joy domestic.

This was their vision, this it was that drove
Their hands to build for us, the coming races.
All that which bound them unto life with love
Lives yet in memories round their vacant places.

By the same hearth, when evening shadows come,
We speak of them, some childish hand caressing.
O thou, our native land, our larger home,
Weave of our lives thy glory and thy blessing!

These lines, properly understood, are not merely the quiet musings of a poet concerned with his own private emotions, his personal memories; they are *the proudly chastened meditation of a nation through a poet*. The values over which they brood quietly are the mature values of an old and noble culture, free of all vanity, of all pomp and circumstance, of all cheap national chauvinism . . . satisfied with its destiny, though in deep humility of spirit, because it has finally come upon *the* values

which all noble men strive for in all generations—unknowingly
perhaps, darkly, yet deeply. We find here that it is the immediate, elemental things of life which Heidenstam comes finally
to admire: the home, with its simple physical pleasures . . .
the nation, conceived as but a larger home, with its memories,
its heritage of culture, its deep human significance for the way
of man on the earth.

Even when in the *New Poems* Heidenstam bares primarily
his own heart rather than that of the Swedish people in the
larger sense, he does so with a noble restraint, a proudly controlled stoic calm only imperfectly approximated in some of his
earlier poems.

> Already I'm upon the bridge that leads
> From earth unto a land beyond my ken,
> And far to me is now what once was near.
> Beneath, as formerly, the race of men
> Praise, blame, and forge their darts for warlike deeds;
> From here I see that true and noble creeds
> Even on foemen's shields are blazoned clear.
> No more does life bewilder with its riot.
> I am as lonely as a man may be;
> Still is the air, austere, and winter-quiet;
> Self is forgot, and I go forward free.
> I loose my shoes and cast aside my stave.
> Softly I go, for I would not defile
> With dust a world so pure, all white as snow.
> Beneath, men soon may carry to the grave
> A wretched shape of human clay, the while
> Mumbling a name—'t was mine once long ago.

There is nothing in this poem of the fine romantic pose, the
youthful lyric sentiment of "Grant that we Die Young," a poem
on a similar theme from *Poems* (1895). The poet has now
reached his spiritual maturity; and as he views the way of man
with man he does so with an Olympian calm, an ability to discern cultural values even in the "foemen," a desire to encompass
that larger universal human faith which knows no distinctions
of race or nation or creed. It is the note of Goethe. Heidenstam
in his maturity neither welcomes death nor fears it; he accepts

it as one of those inevitable conditions which are, probably happily, given to life, and he but asks simply, in the presence of death, that he in life may "not defile with dust a world so pure, all white as snow."

Through the crude medium of translation a foreign reader can but catch a clouded, uncertain glimpse of the lyric power which flashes through Heidenstam's *New Poems*. Perhaps something of the pure poetry of the original manages to shine through the phrases of the translation; but all too much is lost— the most essential lyric qualities remain alone in the original to speak finally alone to the Swede. And this is perhaps as it should be; for Heidenstam writes in these poems—as few poets have written so exclusively—for his people, his nation, and of a culture which he could in the last analysis share with his people alone.

With Goethe Heidenstam shared a faith in human progress; and with Goethe his vision of human possibilities was universal in its inclusiveness—it eschewed narrow nationalistic formulae. With Goethe also, however,—and this is of first importance in an interpretation of Heidenstam's ideas—the Swedish poet felt that a properly conceived nationalism must be the fundamental postulate of all life, of all progress. Civilization does not progress by denying the validity of national institutions; it progresses by *using* them—always, however, with a proper sense of national self-discipline and a broadly human tolerance of other peoples. But such a tolerant nationalism is not to be identified with slavish imitation of other nations. In fact, Heidenstam's chief point of criticism of his countrymen (a criticism that occurs very frequently in both his prose and poetry, though it finds its *locus classici* in the essay entitled "Of Swedish National Temperament".) is that the Swede is too cosmopolitan, too ready to fashion himself after others, too willing to divest himself of his own national character. In one of his addresses, from 1907, Heidenstam refers in passing to his own complete "lack of a sense for foreign patterns of culture." And he goes on, in the closing words of the address, to urge upon his Swedish hearers a profounder sense of their own peculiar national character.

. . . Whatever outward combinations [political or cultural] which in the future may be valid, one fact must certainly remain firm. This is that an obliteration of folk-peculiarities should last of all be considered desirable. Not even a universal speech is worth striving for. . . . On every new day we feel the more strongly that our people is a being in itself, an individual, a giant, if you will, perhaps with a peasant's breadth between the shoulders and somewhat barbaric in his innermost spirit, but with deep-lying eyes and no man's vassal.

We find ourselves here upon a mountain top, surrounded on all sides by stretches of forest and field. This is your sunny and open-faced home province. And if we should continue day after day up toward the forests, we have still the same land about us, *our* land, fair and extensive and lovely or bitter to inhabit, according as we ourselves prepare and arrange it. Warm our hearts, thou new generation of youth, which is beginning to gleam forth as the dawn after a short summer night! Consecrate this gathering of youth into a folk-army, which in a singing mood draws out into life to lift its own fatherland to that place in the North which is the natural and the predestined.

These words may seem uncritically rhetorical to some, an extravagant oratorical vision to others. They were spoken, it must be noted, on the inspiration of a moment to a group of Swedish youth gathered to commemorate the summer solstice, one of the most ancient festival days on the Swedish calendar. But making all allowances for the occasion, and for Swedish love of oratory, these paragraphs in essence contain one of the most fundamental articles in Heidenstam's confession of faith—a faith which had begun to stir gropingly in his early volumes of poetry, a faith which had grown to maturity under the discipline of a prose that included such triumphs in historical fiction as *The Charles Men, Saint Birgitta's Pilgrimage*, and *The Tree of the Folkungs*, and a faith which had found its most exquisite and mature lyric flowering in *New Poems* (1915).

The year after the appearance of *New Poems* its author became the recipient of the Nobel Prize in Literature, with the citation: "The leader of a new era in our literature." The reference to "a new era" was clearly the 1890's, in which Heidenstam was not only its most aggressive and articulate critical champion but one of its major creative talents. But in the years after the appearance of *New Poems*, down to Heidenstam's death nearly a quarter of a century later, his voice was largely silent. During the years of World War One and its aftermath, culminating in another World War, he withdrew into himself while literary developments in Sweden passed him by. New figures appeared on the Swedish literary scene, authors whose work reflected the immediate problems of a rapidly changing Europe. In these contexts Heidenstam was either forgotten or rejected. His more intransigent critics found in him a self-conscious aristocratic poseur and were irritated by his tendency to indulge in merely decorative effects. Though there is more than a little truth in these charges, they focus in part on externals, too often neglecting the core of Heidenstam's works. A more valid charge is that his genius was limited, in the sense that it lacked flexibility, that it had little capacity of growth, that he became in the last analysis a prisoner of the 1890's, the literary program of which he was the first to define and whose rich efflorescence of poetry and prose found in Heidenstam one of its most representative figures.

SAGA AND LEGEND OF A PROVINCE

SELMA LAGERLÖF

Once upon a time there was a saga which wished to be told and led out into the world. This was quite natural, for it knew within itself that it was as good as finished. Many had been instrumental in creating it through remarkable actions; others had added their bits to it by again and again recounting its episodes. What was necessary was that it be carefully composed so that it could travel comfortably about in the whole land. It was still only a strange medley of tales, a formless cloud of adventures, which drifted back and forth like a swarm of stray bees on a summer's day, and did not know where they might find someone who could gather them into a hive.

THE words are those of Selma Lagerlöf. She is writing about the origins and the composition of her most famous novel, *Gösta Berling's Saga.* Very revealing are the words, "Once upon a time there was a saga which wished to be told"; for *Gösta Berling's Saga* is not a novel which Selma Lagerlöf deliberately *decided* to write. The tales of which it is composed simply forced themselves upon her, with a steady, lovingly begging persistence, until she found that to compose these tales for the world was simply an inevitable work of love. Seldom in the history of literature has a novelist been so clearly constrained to tell a given story as was Selma Lagerlöf in the case of *Gösta Berling's Saga.*

How inevitable the composition of this novel was is perhaps best seen if we examine the numerous forces which for years stood in the way of the story ever being told, each of them to be ultimately pushed aside by the steadily persistent voice of that marvelous embryonic staga life which stirred Selma Lagerlöf's youthful imaginative sensibilities constantly and which finally insisted that it be "led out into the world."

I

Those forces which operated to postpone the arrival into the world of *Gösta Berling's Saga* have been outlined for us by the author herself in the fascinating autobiographical fragment, "A Saga about a Saga," from which we have quoted above. It is doubtful that one can depend upon this source in matters of detail, for Selma Lagerlöf is notoriously "free" in her handling of what literary historians are wont to refer to as "fact"; but there is no reason to believe that the general outlines of her sketch of the origins of *Gösta Berling's Saga* in "A Saga about a Saga" are in any essential measure false or misleading. We find, in the first place, from this document that she needed more knowledge of the world in general, and perhaps of literature in particular, before she would be able to give any kind of adequate narrative form to the motley medley of Värmland tales which teemed in her busy young brain.

From her earliest childhood she had been the eager, even greedy recipient of a rich store of local legends—related by her grandmother, by her father and mother, by servants in the home, and by wayside vagrants or provincial originals who never failed to take advantage of the hospitality at Mårbacka, the happy home of little Selma, when they happened to come that way. The child responded with precocious sensibility to these vivid, colorful local tales. And to this diverse assortment of local tales which she heard directly from the lips of the natives of Värmland—tales often fantastic enough in substance, yet retaining somehow that firm, wholesome flavor of reality characteristic of the Swedish folk-tale—she added, as time went on, the more complicated and seductive Romantic world of her early reading. Her parents seem to have allowed her to read as miscellaneously as her own childhood ardour dictated among the rather limited resources of private provincial collections. It is not surprising, therefore, to find her early immersed in Sir Walter Scott, in the Icelandic sagas and the Arabian Nights, in Hans Christian Andersen, Runeberg, and Tegnér.

Interestingly enough, it was this relatively remote world of literary romance, rather than the more immediate world of local Värmland legend and tale, which came to challenge the girl's earliest efforts at literary composition. "Now it was not at all so," Selma Lagerlöf herself relates of these childhood days, that the young girl from the beginning proposed to write of the legends and tales that immediately surrounded her. She did not have the faintest idea that a book could be made of these adventures

Selma Lagerlöf

which she had heard so often that they seemed to her to be the most commonplace things in the world. When she tried to write she chose materials from her books, and it was with a good heart that she put together stories about the sultans of the Thousand and One Nights, about Walter Scott's knights and the saga kings of Snorre Sturlason.

The young girl composed during these early years in all forms, poetic, dramatic, and narrative by turn; but that which she wrote, she assures us, was "the least original and the most immature that has ever been written." Meantime, however, her irrepressible childhood optimism harbored the happy notion that someone in the guise of Good Fortune would some day come to her, and she would then, without further effort, become a famous author! Her childhood finally gave way to young womanhood, however, without pleasant-faced Good Fortune having made his appearance; and then, because of financial difficulties in her family, she had to leave her quiet, rural Mårbacka for the doubtful advantages of urban Stockholm, there to prepare herself for the teaching profession.

In Stockholm she threw herself into her studies with characteristic fervour, the world of Värmland legends and tales being for the moment almost forgotten. And yet it was here in Stockholm, "among gray streets and houses," in an atmosphere of classroom and text-books and the strain of daily preparation of lessons—all so indefinitely far from Mårbacka, with its warmly picturesque countryside and its easygoing daily routine —that Selma Lagerlöf became vividly conscious of the possibilities of the Värmland tales and legends as materials for a serious literary endeavour. The truth flashed upon her, with the suddenness of inspiration, one strangely thrilling day as she was walking briskly up Malmskillnadsgatan with a packet of books under her arm on the way to her rooms from a lecture. She had been dreaming of Bellman and Runeberg as she swung along—of the matchless poetic materials with which these two poets had to work, the gay world of drinking companions so inimitably caught in the former's songs, the doughty soldiers so humanly portrayed in the latter's verse; when, suddenly, it flashed upon her that the Värmland world of legend and tale in which her childhood fancy had been immersed was equally rich material for poetic romance—if only she could learn how to give it artistic form!

In this way it happened that she first came to see the saga. And at the same moment that she saw it the earth began to rock under her. The whole length of Malmskillnadsgatan from Hamngats-backen all the way up to the fire-station heaved up toward the heavens and sank down again, heaved and sank. She had to stand still for some time, until the street had come to rest; and she looked with wonder at the passers-by, who walked so calmly and had not noticed what had happened.

In this hour the girl resolved that she would write the saga about the Värmland Cavaliers, and she never gave up the thought of it. But many and long years elapsed before the resolution was realized.

Two circumstances now combined to postpone for a full decade the final composition of the saga about the Värmland Cavaliers: first, the young lady who had experienced the start-ling vision on Malmskillnadsgatan, and who had resolved on that occasion to write a saga of some kind drawn from the legends and tales of her native Värmland, had to pour most of her serious energies into the exhausting tasks contingent upon a teaching career; and secondly, when she did put her mind to the task of composing the Värmland tales so familiar to her since childhood she found it unexpectedly difficult to cast these materials into any acceptable literary form.

The experience on Malmskillnadsgatan that revealed to Selma Lagerlöf with such sudden distinctness the literary potentialities of the Värmland tales and legends took place in the late autumn of 1881, when she was twenty-two years of age. *Gösta Berling's Saga* was finally published in the autumn of 1891. Four of the ten years that intervened between the moment she first conceived the possibility of writing about her beloved Cavaliers and that autumn day when *Gösta Berling's Saga* finally appeared in the bookstores of Stockholm were occupied in a strenuous academic preparation for a teaching career. Five years of teaching in a girl's school at Landskrona followed. One year was given over solely to the task of completing the manuscript of her novel.

Despite Miss Lagerlöf's close application to her academic studies, she found time during her years in Stockholm to indulge in an occasional literary exercise; and during these same years, and the Landskrona years which followed, the Värmland saga material came gradually to force its way into the center of her creative efforts. A number of things contributed to this end. She seems, first of all, to have come upon a hero for her saga in the half-legendary person of one Emanuel Branzell, an unfrocked pastor who had lived on in Värmland legend as a marvelously gifted though penniless vagabond who had been befriended by Mamsell Lisa Maja Frychius (the original of the Major's Wife in the *Saga*). Soon afterward her hero received a name—Gösta Berling. How the name came to her she confesses she does not know: "It was as if he had given it to himself." During a Christmas holiday at Mårbacka, the first episode of the saga, the vividly dramatic conception of Christmas Eve in the Smithy at Ekeby, was thought out as Selma sat for several hours bundled up in a sleigh which forced its laborious way slowly along drifted Värmland highways. The episode was composed first in verse, for the original plan was to write a series of tales in imitation of Runeberg's *The Tales of Ensign Stål*; but later it was written in dramatic form, the idea being that it was to comprise the first act in a play; and only finally was it composed in prose—after it had been decided to write the saga in narrative prose form. Meantime a second "chapter" had come into existence—the story of the brilliant ball at Borg and the mad ride of Gösta and Anna Stjärnhök over the snow-packed winter landscape. This tale was not written originally with the idea of its being incorporated in the saga. Rather was it conceived as an entirely independent story, suitable perhaps to be read to occasional "company" in order to provide entertainment on a long winter's evening.

Later, however, it occurred to Selma Lagerlöf that such a tale might well be included in "the saga" in case the individual chapters of the group of tales centering about Gösta Berling were all conceived as individual entities, each of them a complete short story in itself, and all of them woven together only loosely into one broadly unified narrative pattern. Now, at last, she came to see clearly enough the general form of her novel; but much remained to be done—nearly all of the individual tales remained to be written—and actual progress was very slow. Much material was gathered and sifted during these years, but only two stories were actually written.

Was it that her professional duties alone stood in the way? Undoubtedly they had something to do with it; but a stronger power than this was at work constantly interfering with her creative progress. It was the spirit of the age, according to Selma Lagerlöf's own testimony.

All this took place during the '80's, the peak years of the severe realistic literature. She admired the great masters of that day and never thought that she might use another language than that which they employed. For her own part she enjoyed the Romantics more, but Romanticism was dead, and she was not one who thought of taking up anew its form and manner of expression. Even though her brain was overflowing with stories about ghosts and wild love, about wonderfully beautiful ladies and marvelously adventurous cavaliers, she tried to write about them in calm, realistic prose. She was not very clear-sighted. Some one else would have seen immediately that the impossible was impossible.

Finally, however, she came to see how impossible it would be to write about the Värmland Cavaliers in "calm, realistic prose"; and then she wrote—at first, apparently, only for her own amusement—a couple of chapters in a curious rhythmic prose filled with exclamations and apostrophes in an exuberantly Romantic manner. It was, we now know, as a consequence of an accidental reading, in 1884, of Carlyle's *Heroes and Hero Worship* that she discovered a style wherein her Värmland creations might freely move and have their proper being. Two years later, in Landskrona, she devoured with great delight the *French Revolution*; and then she came to see her way more and more clearly. Yet actual composition on her saga still moved at a snail's pace. Even though she was firmly convinced that she *could* write of the Cavaliers in a full-blooded, colorfully rhythmic prose, she still cautiously reminded herself that there could hardly be a public for such prose among Scandinavian readers who had fed for more than a decade upon the sane, balanced, utilitarian realism of the day. She might, it is true, have been somewhat encouraged to break with certain aspects of the prevailing realistic prose by the example afforded in Jens Peter Jacobsen's interesting stylistic experiments in *Marie Grubbe* and *Niels Lyhne*; but the Danish novelist's example, though sufficiently colorful and picturesque to momentarily fascinate her, tended too strongly toward the *précieuse*, lacking completely that crystal-clear simplicity and fresh, rushing vigour of movement which came to be the special mark of Selma Lagerlöf's vivid rhythmical prose in *Gösta Berling's Saga*.

Two outward circumstances, however, finally served to shake Miss Lagerlöf loose from her timidly procrastinating attitude toward working seriously on her Värmland material; and these two circumstances ultimately precipitated the final completed composition of the *Saga*. The first was a poignant personal experience in 1888, when she returned to Mårbacka, presumably for the last time, on the occasion of its sale by auction. Her beloved Mårbacka, together with most of the household effects, had to be sold because of the severely straitened family circumstances following upon the death of her father. Strangers were now to come into possession of that which from childhood she had held most dear. The experience stirred her very deeply—so deeply, she tells us in achingly tender phrases of reminiscence, that she now

resolved . . . in all humility to write the book in her own way and according to her own abilities. It should not be a masterpiece, as she had hoped. It would be a book which people might come to laugh at, but she would write it in any event. Write it for herself, in order to salvage for herself what she could salvage of her home: the dear old stories, the happy peacefulness of light-hearted days and the beautiful provincial countryside with the long, narrow lakes and the bluish horizon of hills.

A couple of weeks later, back again in her quarters at Landskrona, Selma Lagerlöf sat down to write.

She had no particular plan: of only one thing was she sure—she would not be afraid of "strong words, exclamations, rhetorical questions." She proposed, in short, *to give herself completely over to her material*—"with all her childishness and all her dreams." The immediate result was astonishing: details swarmed about in her mind at a dizzy pace; words—exuberantly appropriate words—flew in upon her, coming from she knew not where; things she had never dreamed of poured in upon an excited, seething creative consciousness; and page after page of manuscript seemed to *write itself*—that which she "before needed months, yes, years to work out, was finished now in a couple of hours." In one evening she composed the story about the flood at Ekeby and the adventurous trip of the young Countess across the precarious ice of Lake Löfven.

Chapter followed rapidly upon chapter now, though most of them were not composed at the feverish, breakneck speed of the first. A half year later the young schoolmistress at Landskrona had about a dozen chapters written; at this rate the book might be finished in three or four years. It was at this time, fortunately, that the second outward circumstance which was to hasten the composition of the *Saga* took place: the young author, at the insistence of her sister then resident in Värmland, decided to enter a novella competition which had been announced by the Swedish women's magazine *Idun* in the spring of 1890. Her final decision to compete was not made, however, until eight days before the final day set for the submission of manuscripts; and then she decided to submit five chapters taken from the body of her originally planned novel— five chapters which formed a certain rough unity in themselves. Unfortunately only three of them were already composed, and these were in need of considerable revision. The other two did not even exist in bare outline. By the time she had to submit her manuscript, however, all five chapters were finished—this despite the fact that necessary social duties during these days forced her to do most of the composition after midnight, sometimes until four o'clock in the morning. It was in July that the manuscript was sent off to Stockholm; in November the young author was notified that she had won the competition—at least some of her beloved Cavalier legends were now at last to be "led out into the world."

From this point on things moved rapidly. Through friends in Stockholm who were interested in the novel, Miss Lagerlöf

Selma Lagerlöf 185

was released from her teaching duties for a full year and provided with a quiet residence with a family in Sörmland, where she completed the composition of the *Saga*. Within the year after her successful competition with the five chapters of her saga, the completed *Gösta Berling's Saga* appeared in the bookstores of Stockholm, the city on whose "gray streets" she first became vividly conscious of the fictional possibilities of the Värmland Cavalier legends.

The composition of *Gösta Berling's Saga* has thus a long, at times a tortuous, history. The material for it had been a part of the author's earliest childhood memories. Only at the age of twenty-two, however, did she become conscious of the potential material for a novel hidden away in this incoherent mass of finely imaginative material; after which ten more years passed before the published *Gösta Berling's Saga* announced to the Swedish reading public that a promising new novelist was in their midst.

Not immediately, however, did the critics recognize the greatness of this first novel written by a young schoolmistress from the provinces and based entirely upon local provincial materials; though the general reader was on the whole less reserved in his reception of the novel. *Gösta Berling's Saga* disturbed most of the Swedish critics of the day because it was so *different*. As prose fiction it fell into no easily recognized type. Besides, it was too rich in emotional overtones, and entirely too naïve in its glorification of materials and themes which a decade of "sober reason" had come to look upon with disfavor and identify with a clearly outmoded Romanticism. It would seem, indeed, considering the literary tastes of the day, that a young schoolmistress was risking all opportunities for a literary future by making her début at this time with a novel that defied practically every ideal of literary composition which her generation held dear. In place of the photographic realism characteristic of the fiction of her time, Selma Lagerlöf indulged freely in what seemed to be a whimsical, utterly capricious selection of detail both in her highly lyric descriptive passages and in her loose development of plot. In place of a rigidly objective mea-

suring of cause-and-effect relations in human life, Selma Lagerlöf occupied herself quite frankly with the unbelievable, the
fantastic and miraculous, at times even with miracles. In place
of the hopelessly decadent tone of much of the fiction of her
day, Selma Lagerlöf created a world of romantic adventures,
of heroic action, a world in which the sense of joy in life was
permitted to be unobstructed, abandoned, complete.

Little wonder is it then that the Swedish critics of her time
were ready with judgments which ranged from severe general
condemnation to only lukewarm and qualified praise. Wirsén, one
of the older critics, was pitiless in his judgment, suggesting
that as a motto the novel might well use certain of its own
words: "He who is stupid is to be pitied, whoever he is, but
he is most to be pitied if he lives in Värmland." The younger
critics, bound by the severe code of the current realism, were
either highly critical or curiously uncertain in their judgments.
Levertin, the brilliant academic critic of the time was more
impressed, though still somewhat uncertain. Upon reading the
Saga he wrote to Heidenstam:

. . . this work is really most remarkable—it is the most curious
brew of good and bad that I have ever seen—reminiscences and
phrases from the worst of all literatures, the literature of sensation
à la Herman Bjursten—and pages which are *admirable* in their
fantastic power and life. . . . It is the style of the heroic legend that
is attained here—I, poor fellow, am too blasé, as we all are, too much
occupied with modern life. . . . But there she sits, Fröken Lagerlöf, who is a little school ma'am, a little one, who has never been
outside the boundaries of Sweden, but who has lived alone and
has a whole forgotten and concealed provincial mysticism inside her.

Levertin never uttered publicly his opinion of *Gösta Berling's
Saga,* though he did go so far at one point in the letter from
which we have quoted as to suggest that Selma Lagerlöf's
novel was "the first work in accordance with the Heidenstam-
Levertin aesthetics."

It remained for a great critic outside of Sweden—Georg
Brandes—to speak the deciding, and on the whole definitely
favorable, word on *Gösta Berling's Saga.* His review appeared
rather late, in 1893, on the occasion of a Danish translation of

Selma Lagerlöf's novel; but coming at a time when Swedish literature was at last showing unmistakable signs of a break with the traditional realism of the '80's, it weighed very heavily in Selma Lagerlöf's favor among her hitherto rather hesitant countrymen. That the "little school-ma'am," to use Levertin's somewhat patronizing phrase, had finally triumphed was demonstrated conclusively by the appearance of a second edition of *Gösta Berling's Saga* in 1895. Since that year dozens of editions have been demanded by a constantly more delighted Swedish reading public; and in a recent poll taken by *Svenska Dagbladet*, one of the leading Stockholm newspapers, *Gösta Berling's Saga* stands first in a list of the ten most popular novels in Sweden. But far beyond the confines of Sweden has Selma Lagerlöf's *Saga* penetrated. That it has in the most literal sense been "led out into the world" (and in a measure probably never dreamed of by Selma Lagerlöf herself) is attested by the fact that it has been translated into more than thirty foreign tongues and has brought delight to millions of readers far beyond the boundaries of Sweden, in one of whose provinces the story had its humble origins.

II

The realism of the '80's in Sweden, though not as rich in literary output as the same decade in Norway, had made not inconsiderable contributions to modern Scandinavian literature. With Strindberg as its incomparably most vigorous pen, and otherwise represented by such writers as Ernst Ahlgren and Gustaf af Geijerstam in the genre of realistic fiction and Carl Snoilsky and A. U. Bååth in verse, it had thoroughly accomplished the necessary task of removing from the Swedish literary scene the last vestiges of a faded, decrepit Romanticism which had persisted well past the middle of the century, chiefly in the hands of the so-called *signaturer*, a convenient collective term adopted by a group of nine young poets who in 1863 issued a volume entitled *Sånger och Berättelser af nio signaturer* ("Songs and Tales by Nine Pseudonyms"). The late-born Romanticism of these nine poets is clearly enough evidenced in their poetic origins and in their subject matter: they derived primarily from Heine and Byron, to a lesser extent perhaps from Tegnér; and they wrote for the most part rather insipid idyllic poems about birds and flowers and innocent young love. The only poet among the original *signaturer* who found for his pen more vigorous themes than the outmoded romantic idyllicisms of *Sånger och Berättelser* was Carl Snoilsky, who identified his youthful idealism with the hopeless political causes of Poland in January of 1863 and of Denmark shortly thereafter. And though the political idealism of his youth suffered a severe disillusionment in the fates of Poland and Denmark during these years, Snoilsky finally, in the '80's, found his way back to earlier idealisms by identifying himself very closely in his later poetry with the social problems which at this time had come to be the chief concern of nearly all Swedish authors of importance. The realism of the '80's seems thus to have triumphed all along the line, having even drawn into its fold the only pen among the neo-Romantic *signaturer* which had any creative vitality.

And yet this triumph was not without its sacrifices. Swedish literature had not been alone the gainer because of the triumph of the realistic spirit of the '80's. Lyric poetry did not readily adapt itself—perhaps it could not—to the new point of view. Only Snoilsky and A. U. Bååth produced significant poems in the spirit of the '80's; and even they are not usually counted among the truly great Swedish lyric poets—certainly not with Bellman, Tegnér, Fröding, Heidenstam, and Karlfeldt. And prose fiction can be said perhaps to have suffered only less than lyric poetry in the '80's, though this genre could be more flexibly adapted to the new subject matter and point of view. Considerable as was the output of prose fiction during the '80's in Sweden, it remains a rather sad fact that only in some of Ernst Ahlgren's short stories and in a couple of Strindberg's novels from this period does one find fictional performances of lasting importance. The Swedish realism of the '80's had found novel writing sufficiently to its liking, and yet few important novels resulted. The art of story telling—which, after all, is perhaps the central art of the novel—came to be lost in the realist's consuming passion for objective "photography," in his almost complete immersion in the detail study of milieu, in his constant seeking after cause-and-effect formulae in the portrayal of character, and in his persistent preoccupation with so-called "social problems."

Heidenstam and Levertin vaguely sensed this difficulty, and tried to introduce modified narrative forms based upon an aesthetics in almost diametric opposition to realism and naturalism; but by the early 1890's they had produced nothing in prose fiction which gave any real promise of genuine narrative abilities. It was not until 1897, six years after the appearance of *Gösta Berling's Saga*, that Heidenstam came finally to reveal distinguished narrative gifts. It remained for Selma Lagerlöf, a shrewdly naïve product of the provinces, to rehabilitate the Swedish novel, which had fared so equivocally in the hands of her immediate predecessors.

The central fact about Selma Lagerlöf as a novelist is that she is a born story teller. It can be said without exaggeration, I think, that not since Hans Christian Andersen delighted old and young alike with his fairy tales had a Scandinavian story teller so fascinated his public with pure *narrative* abilities as did Selma Lagerlöf in her tales of the Värmland Cavaliers; and among Scandinavian novelists since the publication of *Gösta Berling's Saga*, only Hamsun, in certain of his more mellow moments (as in those late semi-picaresque novels beginning with *Vagabonds*, 1927), can compare favorably with Selma Lagerlöf as a literary artist whose chief concern seems to be in the conduct of the *story as such*. In the handling of scene the author of *Gösta Berling's Saga* is equalled by many, and distanced by some; in variety and profundity of character analysis she must be said to rank rather low among Scandinavian novelists of first importance; but as a direct, spontaneous, vividly moving teller-of-tales she remains in her fictional achievements all but alone in the long line of Scandinavian novelists down to our day.

The chief secret of her story telling ability in *Gösta Berling's Saga*, as well as in a host of other Värmland tales more or less closely related to the Cavalier legends, lies in the frank and unabashed naïveté of her narrative point of view. Impatiently casting aside the elaborate machinery of fictional techniques that had become characteristic of the novel of her day, she resolved to write spontaneously, without reflection—"with all her childishness and all her dreams." How literally she meant these words is illustrated at a hundred points in the pages of *Gösta Berling's Saga,* nowhere in a more frankly confessional mood than in the paragraphs with which she prefaces the chapter called "Ghost Stories"—

Oh, children of a later day! I have nothing new to tell you; nothing but what is old and almost forgotten. Tales from the nursery, where the children sit on low stools round the white-haired story-teller, tales from the workmen's kitchen, where the farm laborers and crofters gather about the pine-wood fire. From the leather sheaths hanging round their necks they draw their knives and butter themselves thick slices of soft bread, as they sit about and chat, while the steam rises in clouds from their wet clothing. And I have tales from the sitting-room, where old gentlemen sit in their rocking-chairs and, inspired by a glass of steaming toddy, talk of the days that are past and gone.

And listening to these stories, a child, standing at the window on a wintry night, would see, instead of the clouds, cavaliers sweep over the sky in their light shays; to her the stars were waxen lights shining from the old mansion on Borg Point, and the spinning-wheel which hummed in the next room was turned by old Ulrika Dillner, for the child's head was full of these men and women of the olden days, and she lived and dreamed among them.

Selma Lagerlöf resolved to tell these tales as they had been told to her . . . naïvely, with none of the reservations of a sophisticated maturity, and as if by word-of-mouth—only with the addition, and this is important, of what Wordsworth at one time called "a certain coloring of the imagination." It was an artistic accomplishment of no mean order to do this, and do it well, in "the enlightened 1890's"; but she did it so well that even the cosmopolitan, worldly wise tastes of Georg Brandes, whose custom it was to make short shrift with the imaginative vagaries of "Romanticism," was forced to admit her narrative triumph.

We have noted that *Gösta Berling's Saga* is made up of a
succession of more or less closely related tales, each of them
an entity in itself, and the whole held together in a rather loose
narrative pattern. This pattern centres, on the one hand, upon
the adventures of Gösta Berling, the hero of the novel, and, on
the other hand, upon the strange fate of the Major's Wife at
Ekeby, whose strength of character and thoroughly masculine
abilities had made her the most notable person in the whole
province of Värmland. The unity of the novel, such as it is,
cannot alone be maintained, however, by centring our attention
upon the double story of Gösta Berling and the Major's Wife;
for the tales of which the novel are composed are so various in
both content and intent that for scores of pages at a time neither
Gösta Berling nor the Major's Wife actually appear in the action
of the novel. The more constant, immediate unifying elements
of the novel are those of time and place—most of the action
taking place within the limits of exactly a year and a day, and
all of the stories converge intimately upon Lake Löfven, that
long chain of three fairly distinct bodies of water that cut from
the north to the south down through the heart of Värmland.
More particularly it might be said that the action tends to converge upon Ekeby Manor, the then famous residence of the
wealthy Major's Wife. It is at Ekeby Manor that a house (the so
called "Cavalier's Wing") had been set aside for the motley band
of Cavaliers, most of them notable figures in their earlier years,
all of them highly original characters whom it had been one of
the half-whimsical desires of the Major's Wife to befriend. Gösta
Berling, former priest, and most fascinating of all these Cavaliers, had early in the novel become the leading member of this
curious group of vagabonds, the Major's Wife having rescued
him from suicidal intents on the occasion of his having been
unfrocked because of "conduct unbecoming a clergyman."

The novel opens with an episode which treats of Gösta
Berling's last sermon—a sermon which was to have been a personal defense of his rather abortive clerical career, but which
characteristically becomes an eloquent pastoral message, loaded
with sentiment and filled with rhetorical flights, in which Gösta
forgets his own immediate plight, "the brandy and the Bishop"

(the latter was the judge in official attendance), and instead proceeds to "testify to the glory of God." The sermon disarmed criticism, of course, and Gösta's accusers become his champions; but a blunder by a practical joker—one of Gösta's former boon companions, the stupid giant Captain Christian Bergh—results in the final unfrocking of Gösta. It is shortly thereafter that the Major's Wife brings the brilliant but dishonored priest to the Cavalier's Wing at Ekeby.

From this point on tale follows upon tale in rapid succession, each of them more or less related to life at Ekeby, all of them in the high romantic tone of the opening episode—some filled with a pathos just short of the tragic ("Ebba Dohna's Story"), others adventurous in the grand manner ("The Ball at Ekeby" and "The Paths of Life"), some inspired by the half-dismal terrors of native superstition ("Ghost Stories"), and still others packed with a sparkling, rollicking humor ("The Old Carriages" and "Squire Julius").

The plot of the novel—in the sense that there is a discernible plot in this strange congeries of Värmland legends—develops around the conflict between the Major's Wife and the Cavaliers for the possession of Ekeby. Early in the novel the Cavaliers had driven their redoubtable Mistress from Ekeby under the influence of certain fantastically romantic pretensions; and while she roams the highways as a beggar and fugitive, the Cavaliers proceed to ruin Ekeby in accordance with their grotesque agreement with "the Black One," who had resolved to wreck the local power of the Major's Wife.

"But notice," said Gösta, "we take the seven foundries to save our souls—not for the sake of being rich, prosperous people, who count their money and weigh their iron. We refuse to be dried-up parchment or tied-up money pouches; we are, and still remain, cavaliers."

"The very words of wisdom," mumbled the dark gentleman.

"So, if you give us the seven foundries for one year, we will take them; but remember this, if during that time we do anything which is uncavalierlike, anything sensible or useful or effeminate, you can take all the twelve of us, when the year is out, and give the foundries to whom you like."

The wicked one rubbed his hands with glee.

"But if we always behave like true cavaliers," continued Gösta, "you must never again make any contract about Ekeby, and you forfeit your wage for this year, both from us and from the Major's wife."

The parallel of this scene to the Faust legends is apparent; but never, it would seem, has the detail of "the bargain with Hell" been treated by a modern author with a more impishly playful humor. Here, in fact, Selma Lagerlöf identifies her art with a very old form of artistic naïveté: we have to go back, indeed, to the medieval miracle and mystery plays to find a similar spirit of roguishness and sly impertinence in the dramatic handling of "the Black One."

Selma Lagerlöf had, during her childhood, not only heard much local legendary material by word of mouth, she had also roamed rather freely in her early reading in the world of the Icelandic saga; and it is possible that these sagas left traces upon her narrative manner in *Gösta Berling's Saga*. They may well have contributed certain qualities to the narrative method: to its directness; its rapidity of action; its occasional use of saga *motifs* such as the Witch of Dovre, the Lady of the Woods, and the sea-nymph from Löfven; and its employment of certain stylistic tricks such as parallelism and repetition. Besides, Selma Lagerlöf identifies herself with her characters with the same naïve intensity as do many of the writers of the older sagas.

It may have some significance also that, like the heroes of the Icelandic biographical sagas, Gösta Berling is not a successful man as his saga comes to a close. It must be pointed out in this connection, however, that the spirit of Christian resignation with which Gösta takes his exit in the final scene of the novel is hardly the note on which most of the old biographical sagas close. It is rather on a note of genuine tragedy—such as that of *Lear*—that the Icelandic saga usually is brought to an end. It seems, however, that neither the general spirit of the largely carefree Värmland Cavalier legends, nor the essentially sunny temperament of Selma Lagerlöf, could permit a more severe judgment upon Gösta than is implicit in the Christian spirit of resignation.

Gösta Berling's Saga differs in narrative technique from the old sagas, moreover, in the constant intrusion of its author upon the story in the form of those lyric outbursts which so frequently interrupt the smooth flow of the narrative movement—introducing episodes, commenting upon the action, and offering, not infrequently, the author's generalizations, often in a moralizing manner, upon the world in general and upon human fate in particular. This is the note of Carlyle rather than that of a typical saga narrator. At times these extra-narrative intrusions do not unduly disturb the reader's concentration upon the story; at other times they seem somewhat forced and unnecessary, definitely breaking the narrative spell that Selma Lagerlöf has previously cast upon us.

Scene, as we have observed, is one of the elements in the novel which give to it a rather closely knit unity not always apparent in the conduct of the medley of tales in themselves. Very early in her novel Selma Lagerlöf pauses long enough in the progress of her story to give us what might be called a full-length portrait of Lake Löfven, together with the partially cultivated countryside which spreads out above its shores and the deep forests stretching off into the rugged, mountainous blue horizon in the distance. To refer to her description of the valley of the Löfven as "a full-length portrait" is hardly exaggerated, for to her sensitively active imagination Lake Löfven *is a personality*. Like a child she invests with vivid, living, intimately human characteristics this long, narrow body of water which cuts a bold channel for itself through the very heart of an only half-tamed Värmland landscape.

The Löfven has its source far in the north, which is a glorious land for a lake, for the forests and hills gather water for it unceasingly, and streams and brooklets pour into it all the year round. It has fine white sand to recline upon; it has islands and promontories to admire and reflect; water-sprites and nixies make it their playground, and it soon grows strong and beautiful. Up in the north it is friendly and gay. You should see it on an early summer morning, when it lies wide awake under its veil of mist, to understand how happy it can seem.

It seems as if it would coquette with you at first, so gently, so gradually does it creep out of its light covering; and so enchantingly beautiful is it that you hardly recognize it, till suddenly it flings its veil aside and lies there naked and rosy, glittering in the sunshine.

But the Löfven is not content with a life of pleasure alone. It pushes its way through the sand-hills on the south; it contracts to a narrow strait, and seeks a new kingdom for itself. It soon finds one, and here again grows strong and mighty; it falls a bottomless depth, and adorns a cultivated landscape. But now its waters grow darker, its shores are less changeful, the winds are bleak, and the whole character of the lake is more severe; yet it remains ever proud and stately. Numbers of vessels and rafts pass over its surface, and it is late before it can go to its winter rest—not until Christmas. It is often in an angry mood, and, turning white with sudden fury, wrecks the sailing boats, but it can also lie in dreamy quiet and reflect the sky.

Still farther to the south, we are told, the lake submits itself again to the momentarily confining shores of a narrow strait; and then it broadens out again, for the last time—though now with less of "beauty and might."

Its shores are lower and more monotonous, wilder winds blow, the lake goes early to its winter sleep. It is still beautiful, but it has lost the strength of its youth and manhood—it is a lake like any other. It throws out two arms to feel its way to the Vänern, and when it finds it, casts itself in aged weakness down the steep slope, and, after this last thundering exploit, sinks to rest.

Paragraph upon paragraph descriptive of the cultivated valleys, the rugged pine forests, and the wide sweep of granite-crowned hills bordering Lake Löfven follow upon the paragraphs we have quoted; and throughout these paragraphs the same tendency to personify natural scene is dominant. All of nature, even its inanimate forms, take on a pulsing, personal life.

It is only at the end of her description of this landscape that Selma Lagerlöf permits man to come into her portrait of the picturesque and rugged Värmland scene; and then he comes naturally, unobtrusively—merely as *an additional personality* into this world of natural phenomena constantly viewed through a creative imagination in which the technique of personification is central.

For many, many generations the plain has been cultivated, and great things have been done there. Wherever a stream, in its rapid course, has flung itself over the sloping shores, mills and foundries have sprung up. On the light, open places, where the plain comes down to the lake, churches and parsonages have been built; and in the corners of the valleys, half way up the hillsides, on the stony ground where the corn will not grow, stand the peasants' huts and the officers' buildings and here and there a gentleman's mansion.

But it must be remembered that in 1820-30 the land was not nearly so cultivated nor so populated as it now is. Much was forest and lake and marsh which is now reclaimed.

The population was scanty, and the people made their living partly by carting and day work at the many foundries; while many left their homes to find work at a distance, for agriculture alone would not pay them. In those days they dressed in homespun, ate oat cakes, and were content with a daily wage of a krona. The poverty was great, but it was mitigated by an easygoing temperament and an inborn aptitude for handicrafts, which greatly developed when those people had to make their way among strangers.

Selma Lagerlöf's manner of personifying natural phenomena had undoubtedly come to her through her early reading of Swedish Romantic poets, perhaps particularly from Atterbom. She uses it fairly persistently throughout the novel, though never with such sweeping consistency and lyric expansiveness as in her full-length portrait of Lake Löfven and its magnificent environs of forest clad granite hills. Usually the manner is caught up in a mere detail, and often in a playful mood—"The funniest of all were the little crinkled parsley leaves, which lifted a little earth above them and played bopeep with life as yet."

Though such a free imaginative handling of natural scene, with its obvious debt to Romantic poetry, was anathema to the photographic realism of the '80's in Sweden, Selma Lagerlöf insisted upon going her own way, here as in so many other things. And certainly the reader of today must admit that her method in the handling of scene is one happily congruous with the half-legendary narrative material of her *Saga,* even though he might be less ready to admit that she ultimately satisfies the modern reader in the measure that certain of her contemporaries, such as Tolstoy and Hardy, do in their treatment of natural scene. One might observe some slight resemblance between Selma Lagerlöf and Hardy; but they are for the most part world's apart, even in their handling of natural scene. Happy in its way as is Selma Lagerlöf's full-length portrait of the Löfven valley, Hardy's magnificent description of Egdon Heath in *The Return of the Native* would seem vastly more satisfactory to a modern critical judgment. Hardy has learned from naturalism and romanticism alike, winnowing the best features of both through the critical discernment of a mature modern spirit, while Selma Lagerlöf tarried alone with the Romantics, with results that to us may seem only half satisfactory.

And yet her technique is really a happy one in *Gösta Berling's Saga* because it is so eminently congruous with the romantically heroic world in which her characters live and move and have their being. The Major's Wife, Gösta Berling, the "Cavaliers" and the host of other characters which swarm upon Selma Lagerlöf's colorful and diversified scene needed just such a half-fanciful natural background for their action as the author creates in her animated personified description of the beautiful valley of the Löfven.

No mean characters, though often enough wayward, were these Cavaliers and their two darlings, the Major's Wife and Gösta Berling; and so the stage on which they played must needs be as strange as were their own curious origins and their fantastic actions.

Look at them sitting round their punch-bowl! They are twelve— twelve men of might. There is nothing effeminate about them, nor are they dandies, but men whose renown will live long in Värmland —brave and strong men.

They are not dried parchment nor closely tied-up money-bags, but poor and reckless men, cavaliers both day and night. They have not lived a life of ease as sleepy gentlemen on their own estates, but they are wayfarers, happy-go-lucky men, the heroes of a thousand adventures.

The cavaliers' wing has stood empty now for many years, and Ekeby is no longer the chosen refuge of homeless adventurers. Penniless noblemen and pensioned officers no longer traverse Värmland in their one-horse shays: but let the dead live again, let the joyous, careless, ever youthful men rise once again!

They could all play one musical instrument, some of them several. They were all as full of peculiarities and sayings and fancies and songs as an ant-hill is full of ants; but each had his special attribute, his highly prized cavalierly merit, which distinguished him from his companions. First of all I must mention Beerencreutz, the Colonel with the thick white moustache, the famous camphio-player and singer of Bellman's songs, and with him his friend and comrade in the wars, the silent Major Anders Fuchs, the great bear hunter. The third in the company would be little Ruster, the drum-major, who for years had been the Colonel's orderly, but his talent for brewing punch and for singing double-bass had raised him to the rank of cavalier. After him came the old ensign, Rutger von Örneclou, a lady killer, wearing a stock and wig and finely starched frill, and painted like a woman. He was one of the chief cavaliers, and so was Kristian Bergh, the strong captain, who was a doughty hero, but as easily deceived as the giant in the fairy tales. In the company of these two you often saw the little round Squire Julius. He was clever, amusing, and talented; artist, orator, and ballad singer, and a good story teller; and he was ever ready with a joke at the expense of the gouty little ensign or the stupid giant.

There was also the great German, Kevenhüller, the inventor of the self-propelling carriage and the flying machine, he whose name still echoes in those murmuring forests. He was a nobleman by birth and appearance, with high twisted moustache, pointed beard, eagle nose, and small, squinting eyes set in a network of wrinkles. Here sat also the great warrior, Cousin Kristoffer, who never went beyond the walls of the cavaliers' wing, unless a bear hunt or a specially foolhardy adventure was "on the *tapis*"; and near him sat Uncle Eberhard, the philosopher, who had not come to Ekeby to spend his life in amusement, but that, exempt from the necessity of earning his bread, he might devote himself wholly to completing his great work on the Science of Sciences.

Lastly, I name the best of the troop, the gentle Lövenborg, the man too good for this world, and who understood little of its ways;

and Lilliecrona, the great musician, who had a good home of his own, and always longed to be there, but who was forever chained to Ekeby, for his temperament required splendor and change to be able to endure life.

And in this group of gay though graying Cavaliers was to be found one who was much younger than the others, their darling and their leader—

. . . Gösta Berling, the cavalier of cavaliers, who in himself was a greater orator, singer, musician, drinking champion, hunter, and gamester than all the others. He had every cavalierly virtue. What a man the Lady of the manor had made of him!

These gay Cavaliers were preeminently children of instinct; and as such they were symbolic of the Värmland character itself— only in a heightened, a marvelously magnified form. "They were all just like children," Marienne Sinclaire had observed of the individuals who peopled her picturesque native province. "They followed whatever impulses came to them."

Everywhere in *Gösta Berling's Saga* action is directly motivated by an ebulliently spontaneous impulse; never is an action the result of mature, deliberate reflection. The abortive effort on the part of Squire Julius to escape from the carefree Cavaliers' Wing in order to prepare himself more worthily to "meet Death" was motivated by impulse—as was his subsequent, humorously ignominious return to Ekeby. Likewise determined by impulse was Gösta's gallant sacrifice of his love for Anna Stjärnhök, in order that she might make others happy. Equally impulsive were the spirited musical improvisation of the "La Cachucha" and the fantastic agreement between "the dark One" and the Cavaliers which resulted in the banishment of the Major's Wife from Ekeby.

And even at the end of the novel, where impulse might conceivably be expected to submit to some "higher law of being," we find it still the determining power in the final action of Gösta; though at this point Gösta's impulse has undergone a kind of transformation—it is less violent than heretofore, and more socially constructive in its motivation, combining at the last, curiously enough, with a partly chastened spirit of Christian resignation. It is important to note, however, that Gösta has not *changed* essentially when he makes his final decision to live a simple life of humble service among the peasant-folk of his beloved Värmland. "You must believe me, dear lady," he insists in his last conversation with the dying Major's Wife, "I am the same crazy Gösta Berling I have always been. A village fiddler is all I can be, but that is enough. I have many sins to make good, but tears and grieving are not for me. I will give joy to the poor—that shall be my penance." Here he is still the same creature of impulse that we find in the opening scene of the *Saga*: he still enjoys the romantic luxury of the impulsive gesture, though the gesture is less vehement now, less grand in its proportions, less essentially heroic perhaps.

It is important to note, moreover, not only that the characters in *Gösta Berling's Saga* are essentially children of impulse, but also that their impulses, almost without exception, are fundamentally in intent *good*. These characters are scarcely ever motivated by mean or ignoble impulses, though they may often for a moment be weak and childish enough. Even in such characters as Melchior Sinclaire, whose violent brutality toward his beautiful daughter Marianne seems quite indefensible . . . or the Broby clergyman, whose inhuman parsimony has made him all but a pariah in the parish which he officially ministers unto . . . or the Mephistofelean Sintram, the darkly mysterious "villain" of the novel—in all of these characters Selma Lagerlöf manages somehow in the end to find some worthy traits at the core of their natures. Of Melchior Sinclaire we finally hear, "It was impossible to find a more noble and kindly old gentleman"—though the reader still pauses long enough to remember, as he reads this well meant eulogy, that nothing short of a stroke has brought about the final reclamation of Melchior Sinclaire. Of the Broby clergyman we are presently told that his extreme miserliness has its origins in certain immediate personal trials during his early career; and before the novel closes we find that this unworthy clergyman repents of his sins, admitting them publicly from the pulpit in the presence of those whom he had wronged. And as for Sintram, his evil deeds are perhaps never taken too much to heart by the reader. The naïve grotesquerie with which Selma Lagerlöf manages to invest this local "dark One" leaves us so well entertained that we feel it is gratuitous either to reproach or to condemn.

Only in the case of Countess Märta—an accomplished, egotistical woman of the world, who indulges in certain curiously sadistic practices at the expense of the innocent young Countess Ebba Dohna—do we find a thoroughly despicable character. And yet even in her case we are told at one point that she "was not conscious of doing evil. She believed herself to be punishing a frivolous wife, so she lay awake sometimes in the night contriving new tortures."

Little wonder is it, in the light of these facts, that the chief fault which Georg Brandes had to find with *Gösta Berling's Saga* was the over-simplified treatment of character which results inevitably from Selma Lagerlöf's optimistic view of human impulse. The Danish critic objected vigorously to the child-of-impulse psychology that lay at the base of character portrayal in the novel; and by implication he rejected Selma Lagerlöf's easy acceptance of that sentimental view of human nature which found impulse almost invariably good at base. Brandes is ready to applaud without reservations the fresh naïveté of manner which animates Selma Lagerlöf's strictly narrative technique; but he condemns heartily the carrying over of this naïveté into the author's treatment of human character.

There is in the representation a warm, living fancy, like that of a child. Just like that of a child. The whole appears like memories and tales and sagas which the narrator has heard as a child; she appears constantly as one who is re-telling the tales. She is herself amazed and astonished at how remarkable the people were at that time. Their passions and experiences have gone through her imagination before they reach us, and have not thereby become any less wonderful; but she is not always sure in her understanding of them. She is more concerned about presenting their experiences in lifelike form to us than about interpreting their inner lives. The psychology of these tales is the weak side of *Gösta Berling's Saga*.

Selma Lagerlöf is particularly weak, he feels, in the portrayal of love between the sexes. Much talk is there in the novel about love, but one feels throughout that the narrator is an unmarried lady, for whom a great province of life, even of the life in Värmland and in Dreamland, is a closed book, or who at least wishes to and must handle life in such a way. Love plays a very important part in her *Saga*. It is rich in abduction scenes and in kisses, and it contains many an eloquent and fervent hymn to Eros, but the hymns are without a spark and the kisses without fire, and the abductions occur, indeed, at a gallop in a sleigh over the snow at night time, but the embraces are as cold as the snow and the night. All of this is but the old type of abduction scene; we do not feel contemporary with any of it.

Of Gösta Berling himself, Brandes points out, we know only "the outlines of his person," though he is the hero of the *Saga*; and nowhere in the novel, with the single exception of Marienne Sinclaire, do we come upon a character which is even remotely conceived in the penetrating lights and shades of a thoroughly modern view of human psychology.

That there is considerable truth in Brandes's judgment of the limitations in character portrayal in *Gösta Berling's Saga* would seem sufficiently apparent. The childlike naïveté in point of view, so eminently successful in the purely narrative technique of the novel, could hardly be maintained in the processes of character analysis without certain serious consequences. The modern reader—perhaps in some cases against his will—seems forced to conclude that the characters in *Gösta Berling's Saga* tend to be superficially rendered, over-idealized, reduced almost to the psychological level of the nursery tale. It should be recorded, however, that Selma Lagerlöf herself was at least partly conscious of the difficulty. In defense of her own procedures she suggests at one point in the novel that "One must treat old tales with care; they are like faded roses. They easily drop their petals if one comes too near to them." And at another time, when she fears momentarily that the not too credulous reader may wish more detailed evidence on the motivation of Countess Elizabeth Dohna's love for Gösta, she shunts our curiosity off with the following evasively ambiguous paragraphs:

It is easy to believe they loved one another, but who can be sure of it? Only disjointed and stray accounts of the brilliant events of their lives have reached me, and I know nothing—less than nothing, of what passed in their innermost hearts.

What can I tell you of the motives which inspired their actions? I only know that a young and beautiful woman risked her life, her honor, her reputation, and her health, that night, to bring a miserable wretch back into the right path. I only know that Gösta Berling let the honor and glory of beloved Ekeby fall that night to accompany her, who, for his sake, had overcome the fear of death and shame and punishment.

It would seem that the most plausible defense of Selma Lagerlöf's tendency to over-simplify in her character portrayal is one that she herself may be said to suggest only by implication in her novel. It might very well be argued that any other method of character analysis—particularly a thoroughly modern one—would be quite inconsistent with her narrative material, a simple body of local folk legends. It seems, in short, that Selma Lagerlöf may have deliberately chosen to simplify her characters in the interests of artistic congruity. The discriminating reader senses this at many points in her novel, nowhere more consciously, perhaps, than in the paragraphs with which she opens the chapter entitled "The Auction at Björne," which includes a strong, though somewhat veiled, attack upon the modern novelist's critical approach to human psychology— at least as it might affect the handling of character in *Gösta Berling's Saga*. "One of the people of those old days," she admits, with reference to Marienne Sinclaire,

had opened her soul to that spirit [the modern spirit of cold, critical dissection]. He sat there watching at the font of all impulse, sneering both at the good and the evil, understanding all, judging nothing, examining, searching, and plucking to pieces and paralyzing all emotions of the heart and all strength of thought by smiling scornfully at everything.

Marienne Sinclaire bore the spirit of self-analysis within her. She felt his eyes follow every step, every word of hers. Her life had become a play, at which she was the only spectator. She was no longer a human being—she was neither wearied, nor did she rejoice, nor could she love. She played the part of the beautiful

Marienne Sinclaire, and the spirit of self-analysis sat with staring eyes and busy fingers and watched her acting. She felt herself divided into two, and half of her being—pale, unfeeling, and scornful—watched the other half's transactions; and the spirit which thus plucked her asunder had never a word of kindness or sympathy for her.

Here, indeed, is a character sketched in a thoroughly modern spirit. Deliberately introspective, a curiously sterile example of the split-personality, Marienne Sinclaire seems made to order for the sophisticated present-day reader of fiction. But Marienne Sinclaire, it is to be noted, is felt to be exceptional in the world of Värmland folk legends; and her story remains in consequence only a disturbing interlude in Selma Lagerlöf's novel— a fragment sketched only in the barest of outlines. It is obvious that the author had a distinct distaste for such a character— perhaps because she did not understand the type?

Whatever the reason, it is clear that Selma Lagerlöf's best creative powers were active only when she busied herself with such characters as were dominated by impulse alone—Gösta, the Major's Wife, the Cavaliers, and in one way or another nearly all the other individuals who people the pages of her first novel. Each of these characters is interesting enough in himself; and yet each of them is perhaps even more interesting as an individual who personifies, each in his own way, the general folk-character of Värmland. It is a collective, almost racial conception of character which is after all Selma Lagerlöf's primary preoccupation in *Gösta Berling's Saga*.

For this novel is primarily the saga of a province—not a story whose chief concern is with individual characters. The real hero of *Gösta Berling's Saga* is not Gösta Berling but *the collective character of Värmland*. This primary preoccupation of the novelist with a provincial type, rather than with individuals as such, is given its most eloquent direct expression in the address—hyperbolic and fanciful on the surface, and yet instinct with a deeply serious undertone of meaning—which the lovable old Squire Julius improvises on one famous occasion.

"Ah, Värmland, my beautiful, my glorious Värmland! Often, when I have seen thee before me on a map, I have wondered what thou didst represent; but now I know what thou art. Thou art an old, pious hermit that sits motionless and dreams, with legs crossed and hands resting in his lap. Thou hast a pointed cap drawn over thy half-closed eyes; thou art a muser, a holy dreamer, and art very beautiful. Wide forests are thy dress. Long bands of blue waters and chains of blue hills border it. Thou art so simple that the stranger sees not how lovely thou art. Thou art poor, as the devout desire to be. Thou sittest still, while Vänern's waves wash thy feet and thy crossed legs. To the left thou hast thy mines and thy fields of ore; there is thy beating heart. To the north thou hast the dark, lonely regions of wilderness, of mystery, and there rests thy dreaming head.

When I behold thee, majestic, serious, mine eyes fill. Thou art austere in thy beauty; thou art meditation, poverty, resignation. Yet back of thine austerity I see the gentle features of kindness. I see and adore! If I but glance into thy deep forests, if only the hem of thy garment touches me, my spirit is healed. Hour after hour, year after year, I have looked into thy holy countenance. What mysteries art thou hiding under lowered eyelids, thou spirit of resignation? Hast thou solved the enigma of life and death, or art thou still pondering it, holy giant? For me thou art the keeper of great, serious thought. But I see beings creeping about upon thee, creatures who never seem to note the majesty of earnestness on thy brow. They see only the beauty of thy face and limbs, and are so charmed that they perceive naught else.

Woe is me, woe to us all, children of Värmland! Beauty, beauty, and nothing more, we demand of life. We, the children of renunciation, of seriousness, of poverty, raise our hands in one long prayer and ask but for this one good, beauty. May life be like a rosebush, with flowers of love, wine, and pleasure, and may its roses hang within every man's reach; that is our heart's desire, and our land wears the features of sternness and renunciation, but we have no thoughts!"

The exaggerated hyperbole of this passage, with its love of generalization, its sparkling paradoxes, and its constant appeal to purely local sentiments, would hardly be expected to impress the critical spirit of Georg Brandes; and yet had he paused long enough to ponder such paragraphs as these he might have at least partially qualified some of his severe animadversions on Selma Lagerlöf's treatment of character in *Gösta Berling's*

Saga. He might still have insisted that such paragraphs are foreign and distasteful to what is called "the modern spirit"; but he could hardly have denied that they were appropriate to Selma Lagerlöf's immediate purposes and eminently congruous with her general narrative methods. To Brandes's charge that Gösta himself is only revealed to us "in outline," one might at the last counter that this is so because Gösta is to be considered by the reader, not as an individual in the ordinary sense of the word, but rather as the most profound individual representation of the collective character of Värmland. A highly individualized character in keeping with modern psychological demands would seem in this instance to be curiously inappropriate.

It is customary among even sympathetic critics of *Gösta Berling's Saga* to decry the serious moralizing tone with which the novel is brought to a close. Gösta, they reason, should not be reduced at the end to a moral being, sober, reformed, and contrite; for the novel as a whole is one of romantic high adventure in which the world of normal moral values has no real place. Though such a view of the didactic closing scenes of the novel may at first seem reasonable enough, it is in reality based on a very superficial reading of *Gösta Berling's Saga.* The chief contention of these critics—that the moral has been gratuitously "dragged in" near the close—is a fundamentally false one; for in almost every chapter of Selma Lagerlöf's novel the moral emphasis is present, sometimes being given direct expository expression, at other times unmistakably implied in the conduct of narrative episode. It may well be true that a group of rollicking stories of high adventure, even when interspersed with tales of tender sentiment, is not the most appropriate vehicle for ethical utterance; but it is emphatically *not* true that Selma Lagerlöf saves her sermon until the last pages of *Gösta Berling's Saga.* The ethical note is struck definitely already in the closing paragraphs of the opening chapter of her novel—

It [the unfrocking of the hero of the novel] was the first misfortune that befell Gösta Berling; it was not the last.

Young horses who cannot bear the whip or spur find life hard. At every smart they start forward and rush to their destruction, and when the way is stony and difficult, they know no better expedient than to overturn the cart and gallop madly away.

And at scores of points in the succeeding pages this note is struck again, at times with an even more severely didactic tone.

It is true that we are permitted on occasion in *Gösta Berling's Saga* to revel as children in a fictional world of pure high adventure; but never for long in these pages are we allowed to remain forgetful of the sterner demands of an actual world governed by certain severe moral laws. Gösta—whether we like it or not—is conceived by Selma Lagerlöf as one hero of high romance who is simply a young colt which must become accustomed to harness and a load. His actions are at times irresponsible, but never does his conscience cease to operate; and at the last his inner voice, taught by sad experience, comes to chasten, if not subdue, the ebullient, youthful effervescence of his carefree cavalier spirit.

The close student of Selma Lagerlöf's novels is not surprised by this, for everywhere her genius has revealed a thoroughgoing ethical bias. Moreover, it is not to be forgotten in the present instance that the tales of which *Gösta Berling's Saga* are composed find their direct origins in local Swedish folk legend, where moral considerations are found to be not infrequently present. To say that the romantic high adventure of Selma Lagerlöf's *Saga* is inconsistent with a normal world of moral values is to assume that the author in this case derives primarily from the amoral regions of a sophisticated *literary* world of high romance. Nothing is farther from the truth. She had, indeed, as a girl ploughed through her share of artificial, high-flown, fantastic literary romances; but this reading, it is clear now, left upon her mature creative spirit only occasional traces. Her essentially balanced and sane temperament drank much more deeply of the pure, cold springs of Swedish folk legends—local legends which had retained a certain equilibrium even in the midst of a nimble folk fantasy, remaining always of the earth earthy (even while hobnobbing with fantastic primitive superstitions), and seldom failing to harbor sound, healthy moral implications.

In Selma Lagerlöf's general conception of the world the fundamental conflict in life does not lie between good and evil. To her essentially sunny, almost naïvely optimistic temperament evil does exist, to be sure—but only as a shadow that may cast itself temporarily over experience, not as a basic, constantly present determining condition of existence. The human soul is not to her primarily a Manichaean battle-ground between the power of evil and the power of good. She conceives of the world rather as a state of existence fundamentally good in all essential respects—disturbed, perhaps more than occasionally, by evil, but never for long dominated by it. It is therefore that she looks upon the central problem of life as a seeking, on the part of the individual soul, for a proper balance between joy and virtue, gaiety and goodness. It is to be noted that the Cavaliers, including Gösta, must at last depart from Ekeby because their gaiety, though innocent in intent, was often evil in its consequences. The spirit of *joie de vivre* which animated these gay Cavaliers had not been accompanied by a corresponding desire to do good; and the consequence had been that during the fantastic year of Cavalier reign over Ekeby there was a constant wasting away of property values on the estate, suffering was widespread among the people dependent on the Ekeby manor, and decay was everywhere rampant on lands which before had blossomed and borne fruit under the iron will and strong hand of the Major's Wife. Gösta—who had been the gayest of the gay in the heyday of Cavalier power at Ekeby—came to pass the final sober judgment upon his companions and himself at the end of that fateful year:

. . . he talked to them, to those light-hearted men hardened against all chances of fate. Once again he called them gods and knights who had arisen to bring back joy to the ironland in iron times. Still he bewailed that the garden where butterfly-winged joy had abounded should have been filled with destructive caterpillars, and that its fruit was shrivelled. He knew well that joy was a blessing to the children of men, and that it must exist; but like a great mystery the question still hung over the world how a man was both to be joyous and to be good. He said it was both the easiest and the most difficult of things. They had not been able to solve the riddle before, but now he believed they had all learned the lesson. They had all learned it during that year of joy and of want, of happiness and of trouble.

The gay Cavaliers—old men by this time, and most of them homeless—had to depart from Ekeby for the simple *moral* reason that they had not been good husbandmen in the vineyard.

The parallel here to New Testament Christian ethics is obvious. And yet one must not insist upon the parallel too rigidly. Certainly the Pauline dualism, whose fundamental postulate is the ceaseless battle between the flesh and the spirit for the possession of the human soul, does not exist in *Gösta Berling's Saga*. Flesh is no more antipathetic to spirit in the world of Selma Lagerlöf than it is in the world of Robert Browning. Flesh and spirit are viewed by Selma Lagerlöf as possible of combination toward a common noble end. And as there is no basic conflict between the flesh and the spirit, so is there none between the spirit of joy and the spirit of goodness properly understood. Nor is impulse to be stultified—rather is it to be guided carefully into channels of goodness. Resignation, the will to endure, has its place in Selma Lagerlöf's view of life, and likewise penitence of a kind; yet it is to be remembered that Gösta, though resigned at the end of the novel, is not finally penitent, and romantic impulse still stirs deeply in his soul, dictating his last decision in the *Saga*. In the central ethical implication of *Gösta Berling's Saga*—that impulse is fundamentally good—Selma Lagerlöf joins hands with the primitivistic ethics of Rousseau, though she might hesitate to admit the kinship.

Her positive ethics in *Gösta Berling's Saga* reminds one, perhaps, even more definitely, however, of Carlyle, particularly in the late chapters of her novel, where she preaches with an ever increasing emphasis the constructive doctrine of work. The Cavaliers, we remember, had early in the novel signed a curious contract with "the dark One" to take over Ekeby, with the understanding that if they did "anything sensible or useful or effeminate" the devil might take all twelve of them "when the year is out." They proceeded to keep their promise; but goodness being more powerful than evil in the world, the Cavaliers stood ultimately condemned by the law of goodness which dominates life. They were judged unworthy simply *because they sought pleasure rather than work*—"the garden where butterfly-winged joy abounded" had become "filled with destructive caterpillars, and . . . its fruit was shrivelled." These final words of Gösta's, in their condemnation of a gaiety at constant enmity with utility, are thoroughly consistent with Carlyle's doctrine of work as developed in the picturesquely explosive rhetoric of *Sartor Resartus*. "Produce! Produce!" is the vehement Carlylese exhortation of Professor Teufelsdröckh. "Were it but the pitifullest infinitesimal fraction of a Product, produce it, in God's name! 'Tis the utmost thou hast in thee; out with it, then. Up, up! Whatsoever thy hand findeth to do, do it with thy whole might. Work while it is called Today; for the Night cometh, wherein no man can work." It is of course to be admitted that Gösta Berling and Professor Teufelsdröckh arrived at their respective conclusions on the subject of work, and on the related doctrine of resignation, under vastly different circumstances; but the central ethical concepts that finally come to govern the action of each of these characters are strikingly similar in each case. Swedish critics have occupied themselves more frequently with Selma Lagerlöf's stylistic indebtedness to Carlyle in *Gösta Berling's Saga* than with the possible influence of Carlyle's ethics on the novel; and this is perhaps the proper emphasis. It is my feeling, however, that a careful, detailed investigation of Selma Lagerlöf's ethics as related to Carlyle's might prove eminently revealing.

Besides the probable influence of Carlyle on the general ethical concepts and on the stylistic lyricism of *Gösta Berling's Saga,* Selma Lagerlöf may possibly have been indebted in some measure to a few of her immediate Swedish contemporaries who were beginning to deflect in certain new directions the literary currents of the time in Sweden. We have seen in the chapter on Heidenstam that his critical essay "Renascence," from 1889, had advocated a return of literature to a more spontaneous, warmly colorful imaginative response to the phe-

Selma Lagerlöf

211

nomena of existence in direct opposition to what he called "the vogue of the day constantly to present the world in gray weather colorations." Selma Lagerlöf could certainly sympathize with this sentiment in its general drift, and yet it does not seem that she was ready to give more than a broadly inclusive assent to Heidenstam's early aesthetics, chiefly perhaps because the essentially pagan and classical conception of joy in life advocated in Heidenstam's early work may have seemed somewhat too exclusive for her own more broadly humanitarian, democratic, and fundamentally Christian social instincts.

My feeling is that it is with Gustaf Fröding, the poet of Selma Lagerlöf's native Värmland, that the author of *Gösta Berling's Saga* has had the most deep-seated affinities among her immediate Swedish contemporaries. Selma Lagerlöf cannot, of course, be said to command anything like the artistic range or the psychological depth of Fröding. Her artistry is everywhere more limited, less varied, for the most part less subtle; and her understanding of the "dark side" of human destiny is never as poignantly penetrating as is that of Fröding, whose sensitive poetic spirit, constantly hovering over the abyss of insanity, finally crashed into its hideous depths—meantime, however, creating a body of lyric poetry so exquisite in its form and so intense in its achingly tragic intimacies that Fröding is to be ranked perhaps first among lyric poets in a nation whose chief claim to literary fame lies in the field of the lyric. But if an understanding of that night-side of life which finds such powerful expression in Fröding's greatest poetry was denied the basically optimistic genius of Selma Lagerlöf, she shared in her own way with Fröding a deep sympathy toward human suffering and a rich, warm, all embracing humor. Fröding and Selma Lagerlöf, both children of Värmland, had inherited that well-nigh indefinable, richly human bonhomie so characteristic of the natives of Värmland; and much of their most typical work reflects this carefree, lovable, impulsively human spirit of the *Värmländing*.

And yet where there is joy and laughter there is often tears. All deep, abiding humor retains, mayhap unconsciously, behind its gay smile a warm, human pathos which is prepared to call forth on occasion a profoundly moving human sympathy. To the brooding speculative genius of Fröding this close affinity between humor and pathos ultimately resolved itself into a profound theory of art. Humor—Fröding reasons in his essay "On Humor" (1890)—is simply to be looked upon as the great means of artistic reconciliation with an otherwise largely hopeless human existence. To the more purely intuitive and less darkly complex genius of Selma Lagerlöf, such a theoretical justification of humor as the basis of a philosophy of art was hardly necessary. Still the result was not dissimilar in the art of both Selma Lagerlöf and Fröding. Rollicking gaiety and high seriousness exist side by side everywhere in both novelist and poet. Setting out often to seek beauty in innocent gaiety of spirit—as *Värmlänningar* are wont—both novelist and poet frequently find this beauty, paradoxically, in the spirit of resignation, in penitence, in the namelessly poignant reminders of a nobly aching heart. Nothing can be more impertinently impish than Fröding's "Little Karl Johan"; and yet it must not be forgotten that the same poet conceived the humorously sad lines of "The Poet Wennerbom," the harshly tender pathos of "Hunter Malm's Wives," and the delicately poignant mood of "Sigh, sigh, rushes!" Nothing is more rampantly spirited in its realistic description of a peasant dance than Fröding's "They danced by the road-side on Saturday night"; and yet the poem closes on an exquisitely soft idyllic note—dreaming—dreaming with an exquisite musical accompaniment into the lovely mystery of a moon-drenched Värmland landscape of a summer night.

How inevitably one is reminded as one reads Fröding's poem on this roadside dance of the Squire Julius chapter in *Gösta Berling's Saga*! Rollicking are the opening measures in Selma Lagerlöf's chapter, as gay as a summer day along the Löfven . . . and yet to what a quietly solemn close is the episode at last brought—a close solemn in a beauty which has touched the garment of a profoundly moving humor, and by this act has come upon a new, transcendant form of virtue.

Intimate, however, as is Selma Lagerlöf's spiritual kinship to a certain side of Fröding, it seems on the whole very doubtful that she was directly and appreciably influenced by him in *Gösta*

Selma Lagerlöf 213

Berling's Saga; for she was well along toward completion of the manuscript for her novel before Fröding's first volume of poems *Guitarr och dragharmonika* ("Guitar and Concertina") appeared in May of 1891.

I am convinced, indeed, that no merely literary source had the importance in shaping Selma Lagerlöf's general view of life as expressed in *Gösta Berling's Saga* that her parental home had. Any student of the sources of Selma Lagerlöf's characteristic attitude toward life must constantly return to Mårbacka; for here it is that her deepest and strongest roots have sunk. It was not merely a romantic gesture that led her to repurchase Mårbacka years after that sad day when it had gone out of the possession of her family. She bought Mårbacka in 1907 because she realized deeply within her own being that she needed it. She not only bought it, she returned to it, making it finally her permanent home—for only at Mårbacka could she find genuine happiness, complete peace, a sense of that without which life for her would be unnatural, a mere existence without roots or meaning.

It is with characteristically simple, unassuming words of deep affection that she describes the Mårbacka of her childhood in "A Saga about a Saga"—

. . . It was a little estate with low buildings which were overshadowed by great trees. At one time it had been a vicarage, and it seems as if this must have placed a mark upon it which it could never lose. People seemed to have more time for books here than other places, and there always lay a quiet peace over the estate. Nervous hurry with work or fuss with servants was never permitted there. Nor were hate or dissension tolerated there; and he who lived there was not permitted to take life too seriously, but must feel it the most important duty to be carefree and believe that for everyone who lived there *Vår Herre* [poorly translated "Our Lord"] arranged everything for the best.

It was to this home, Selma Lagerlöf goes on to tell us, that the *Saga* came—in bits, only fragmentarily, quite unorganized, in its wandering about among the manors and mine properties, the vicarages and officers' homes "in the beautiful province"; and it was in this home that the *Saga* at last came to find as permanent a home as such a curious medley of tales might ever hope to find. The tales that were to become the *Saga* brought something strange, something marvelous into this quiet home at Mårbacka—fantasy, high adventure, handsome heroes and beautiful heroines, all the world of brilliant and brave romance. But it should be added—even emphasized—that Mårbacka in turn gave something to the *Saga*. It brought to these strangely fanciful and motley tales a certain sense of balance and proportion, an artistic unity of a sort; and above all, perhaps, it brought to them a deeply prevailing sense of moral values not too apparent in the original form of at least some of these tales.

One could play at Mårbacka, but one must also work; both activities were equally welcome, each had its natural and appointed place. It is over against the background of this Mårbacka that we can most readily come to understand the origins of Gösta's final attitude toward life: "that joy was a blessing to the children of men, and that it must exist; but like a great mystery the question still hung over the world how a man was both to be joyous and good." Though perhaps theoretically this problem could never be solved, Gösta came to feel, dimly, and yet strongly, that the "great mystery" might be lifted by means of practical activity—a life of work, of humble service to his fellow men.

Certainly it is fitting that Selma Lagerlöf should find her ethical roots in Mårbacka, even as she had found at Mårbacka her tales, her characters, and many of the details of her fictional method; though some modern readers will doubtless feel a certain limitation in the optimistic ethics of Mårbacka, and in doing so they will perhaps turn with more satisfaction to Sigrid Undset, a woman moralist in the Scandinavian novel of an entirely different order. Selma Lagerlöf never outgrew the simple, optimistic ethics of Mårbacka. This explains why she deals so satisfactorily with legends and with peasant characters in semi-primitive environments; and this explains also why her art is so uncertain when it seeks to come at grips with other, more complicated materials.

Selma Lagerlöf

III

Happy as was Selma Lagerlöf's choice of Värmland folk legends as the material for her first novel, and exquisite as was her artistic handling of this material, she seems to have felt upon the completion of *Gösta Berling's Saga* that she had at least temporarily exhausted the possibilities of such material. It was not until 1908—seventeen years after the publication of *Gösta Berling's Saga*—that she returns definitely to Värmland materials and uses them as the primary basis of her fiction. Meantime, however, she was engaged in a sufficiently prolific literary production, most of it in the form of legends and short stories, though the period also includes the nobly conceived and brilliantly executed novel *Jerusalem* (1901-1902), and *The Wonderful Adventures of Nils,* a children's book which ranks among the most perfect productions of its kind that have ever been written.

"A Christmas Guest," the first Cavalier tale to appear after *Gösta Berling's Saga,* is contained in the miscellaneous collection of tales and legends entitled *Invisible Links* (1894). Otherwise this volume has little to do with Värmland. In *The Miracles of Anti-Christ* (1897) Selma Lagerlöf departs entirely from Värmland. This novel, whose scene is the little town of Diamante in Sicily, is a partially symbolical treatment of a contemporary social and political phenomenon; but the problem itself is handled in a rather unsatisfactory manner, and the chief virtue of the novel lies in its delicate manipulation of Italian folk legends and in its sensitive description of Italian landscape and Italian small village life toward the end of the nineteenth century. Selma Lagerlöf, it must be admitted, had little ability in writing a "problem novel," though *The Miracles of Anti-Christ* must always stand as evidence of her profound sympathy with the condition of the lower classes and her deep interest in modern social problems.

A volume appearing in 1899, entitled *The Queens of Kungahälla, Legends, and Tales,* is as miscellaneous in content as was *Invisible Links.* In it appears only one tale, "The Story of Halstanäs," which belongs to what might be called the Cavalier canon. It deals primarily with an Ensign Vestblad, who is absent from the pages of Selma Lagerlöf's famous *Saga*; and it also touches upon the marvelous weaving abilities of Colonel Beerencreutz, a character made famous by the *Saga*. *The Story of a Country House* (1899), a tender idyll (somewhat reminiscent of Goethe's Mignon motif) of madness conquered by an innocent young girl's love, has its scene interchangeably in Dalarne and Värmland; but it can hardly be said to be a typical tale of Värmland, and it certainly has little in common with *Gösta Berling's Saga*. In *The Christ Legends* and *The Treasure,* both appearing in 1904, the author has again departed entirely from the Värmland scene. The former of these is a delicately sensitive retelling of Eastern legends concerning the Christ child; the latter is a tale of terror, of revenge and penitence, whose action goes back to the sixteenth century and whose sinisterly appropriate background is the severely primitive, rock-bound western coast of Sweden. In *The Wonderful Adventures of Nils* Värmland is touched upon as a matter of course, though no more than the other Swedish provinces which figure in this fascinating children's story whose primary aim is to introduce Swedish geography, its flora and fauna, to Swedish school children.

The novel *Jerusalem*, though its action takes place in Dalarne and in the Holy City, might be said to be more closely related to *Gösta Berling's Saga* than any of the other volumes which came from Selma Lagerlöf's pen between her literary début in 1891 and the publication of *The Wonderful Adventures of Nils* in 1906-1907. On first thought, to be sure, more than the accident of scene seems to separate *Gösta Berling's Saga* and *Jerusalem*. The quietly dignified movement of the sober religious tale which is unrolled for us in *Jerusalem* seems to have none of the characteristics of high romance so typical of the earlier *Saga*—its venturesome action, its rapid, colorful movement, its stylistic vehemences, and its fanciful world of dream and ideal floating almost "beyond the farthest ken of human thought."

And yet the two novels have much in common. *Jerusalem* is hardly less lyric in its basic tone than is *Gösta Berling's Saga*.

Selma Lagerlöf 217

Its lyricism is merely conceived in a different manner: less spontaneous, though no less intense; less ecstatic, yet no less elevating; less brilliant, and yet just therefore, perhaps, more substantial, more profound, more penetratingly sensitive in its seeing and in its feeling. In short, Selma Lagerlöf's lyricism in *Jerusalem* is a more mature lyricism. If *Gösta Berling's Saga* may be said to represent Wordsworth's definition of poetry as "the spontaneous overflow of powerful feelings," the novel *Jerusalem* may be held to typify the more characteristically Wordsworthian definition that "poetry is emotion recollected in tranquillity."

It should be remembered that the story of Gösta Berling and the Cavaliers at Ekeby had gripped Selma Lagerlöf's youthful imagination with a uniquely direct intensity. She did not *choose* to write this story—it demanded to be written, and it therefore wrote itself. Selma Lagerlöf *did choose* the material about which she wrote in *Jerusalem*; but after she had decided to write the strangely moving religious story of the picturesque parish of Nås in Dalarne the subject gripped her no less deeply than had her earlier Värmland materials, and the result, stylistically, was a prose of delicate, restrained, and yet strong lyric power. The very subject matter of *Jerusalem* called, of course, for a sober and restrained stylistic lyricism; and in addition it seems very probable that outward literary influences to an extent determined the prose style of this novel. The prose style of *Jerusalem* seems to reveal even more consistently the imprint of the ancient Scandinavian sagas than does *Gösta Berling's Saga*. It seems apparent also that Bjørnson's early peasant tales, themselves influenced by the sagas, have placed their mark upon *Jerusalem*.

The ethics of *Jerusalem* is that of *Gösta Berling's Saga* except that in the later novel the ethics of the *Saga* is more consistently developed, and it has a much more definitely conceived religious motivation. The story of *Jerusalem* is primarily a religious one. It is concerned with the fortunes of a small group of peasants from Dalarne, who a few years before Selma Lagerlöf's first residence in this province, which lies just north and a bit east of Värmland, had felt "called" to sell their farm holdings in the home parish and emigrate to Jerusalem to await "the imminent coming of the Lord." The purely religious aspects of this little sect received Selma Lagerlöf's sympathetic attention; but she seems on the whole much more concerned with the ethical considerations of her subject, especially as these considerations relate themselves to certain qualities of peasant character as represented in the sturdy *odalbonde* (yeoman farmer) of Dalarne.

The action in the first volume of *Jerusalem*—the volume which by common consent is the more successful of the two—takes place in the little parish of Nås, which for many generations had been dominated by the substantial old yeoman family of Ingmarssons. The volume becomes, in consequence, an impressive study in the stubborn conflict between fanatical, though sincere, religious motives and the more naturally conservative, earth-bound virtues of the ancient peasant stock of a typical Dalarne parish. The Ingmarssons had always been religious—independent, upright, and scrupulously honest in character since days beyond the memory of man. But their religion had been one that identified itself with relatively immediate, palpable values—their love of the soil, their conception of family and race, their practical moral relation to an immediate economic and social community. It was only with difficulty, therefore, that they could come to identify themselves with the mystical sectarian concepts which were introduced into their quietly substantial rural community by a returned Swedish emigrant who had become associated, during a stay in America, with a small group of idealistic religious fanatics which had originated in a small way in Chicago and later had established a small communistic Christian community in Jerusalem. And yet despite the earth-bound religious conservatism of these yeoman farmers, half of the little parish, including some of the Ingmarssons, did "accept the faith" ultimately, and moved on to Jerusalem in obedience to "the call."

It is to be noted, however, that Young Ingmar, the central figure in the present Ingmar generation, never became a member of the sect, though he did spend some years helping the little community in Jerusalem. *He* could not forget the old family traditions, the ancient soil of his ancestors, and the necessity of carrying on the Ingmarsson heritage at home in his native parish; and it is in his character that Selma Lagerlöf has laid down her most loving and brilliant work in the novel. And this is natural, for in Ingmar's steady, deeply instinctive feeling for the soil, in his profound consciousness of the demands of a racial and family heritage, and in his love for the ancient family holdings of the Ingmarssons—in these at one and the same time physical and spiritual bases of value we find an intimate reflection of Selma Lagerlöf's own deep and abiding love for her native Värmland, for her family . . . for, in a word, Mårbacka, home of her childhood experiences and dreams, and the home to which she was to return to spend the late rich decades of her life.

When Selma Lagerlöf describes the deep pangs of Young Ingmar on the occasion of the sale of the family properties before the emigration to Jerusalem, she is but recalling her own poignantly sensitive feelings when her beloved Mårbacka passed out of her family's hands over the auction block. Selma Lagerlöf, like Young Ingmar, had kept the faith with her childhood home during days of trial, ultimately to return to it and live out her years of maturity on the soil that for generations had fed and clothed and given adequate spiritual sustenance to her ancestry. With Young Ingmar the author identified herself in *Jerusalem* . . . and also with Barbro, Young Ingmar's wife, who in the last scene of the novel comes to find a deep-rooted joy and strength, after a period of uncertainty and trial, in the physical *things* that immediately surround her in the great hall of the substantial old peasant home of the Ingmarssons—

. . . But then she looked about her, embraced with her eyes the entire room, the long, low window, the benches along the walls, and the open fire-place, where generation after generation had sat at their tasks in the light of the open fire. All of this enveloped her in a tranquil feeling of security. She felt that it would shelter and protect her.

It was no doubt with similar feelings that Selma Lagerlöf returned to Mårbacka, only six years after she had penned these quietly dignified lines about the family home of the Ingmarssons in Dalarne.

The year 1908 marks both Selma Lagerlöf's actual and her literary return to Värmland. It was in this year that she re-purchased Mårbacka and established her residence there once again—at first only during the summer season, in 1919 as her permanent all-year-round home.

Selma Lagerlöf had wandered far afield in her search for literary materials in the sixteen years since the publication of her great Värmland novel *Gösta Berling's Saga*; but she had never forgotten her first love, as is evidenced by its cropping up incidentally at the most unexpected places in her literary production during these years—and now at last she finds the fascination of Värmland stirring strongly in her again as she comes to make her home in the midst of the places filled with the countless voices of old, still vigorously living memories. The result is a mellow late harvest of new Värmland novels and tales. None of these stories quite approximates the sparkling literary triumph of *Gösta Berling's Saga*; but each of them has an undeniable charm of its own. They are for the most part less spontaneous than the tales included in the *Saga*; and yet in their quietly pulsing, finely mellowed tone and in their subtly modulated humor, they reflect the mature Selma Lagerlöf's ingratiatingly delicate art and her richly warm humanity.

Already in *The Girl from the Marsh Croft*, the volume which came out in the year of Selma Lagerlöf's purchase of Mår-backa, do we see evidences of her desire to return to the Värmland materials. Three of the eight tales included in this volume have Värmland settings and Värmland characters, two of them dealing with the famous Värmland itinerant "fiddler" Jan Öster. The volume also contains, very appropriately, the essay "A Saga about a Saga.' In *Lilliecrona's Home* (1911) Selma Lagerlöf deals directly with a past generation of her own family at Mårbacka. The "Lövdala" of the novel is Mårbacka; the central character, Lilliecrona, is the author's grandfather; and the narrative conflict, particularly that between Maia Lisa and her stepmother, is a free handling of an actual situation in an earlier generation of the Lagerlöf family. In *The Emperor of Portugallia* (1914) we find another example of free handling of an actual Värmland character, a pathetic, harmless old madman, whom Selma Lagerlöf herself had seen occasionally during her childhood at Mårbacka. Difficult as is the subject of this novel, Selma Lagerlöf manages to avoid the dangerously sentimental which is potential in her subject and creates for the reader a character of genuine tragic pathos; and in the early chapters of the novel the author is at her best in humorous characterization, much of the humor being conveyed to the reader (only to the Swedish reader, alas!) by means of skillful use of dialect.

The World War dealt a crushing blow to Selma Lagerlöf's creative energies. The first volume of *Trolls and Men* came from her hand in the second year of the War. It is a curious miscellany of tales, legends, addresses, and essays, very unequal in quality, several of the stories revealing that strange fascination which grim peasant superstitions and the horror theme have on occasion held for Selma Lagerlöf. Only one of her stories from the War years—*The Outcast* (1918)—uses the War as a background; and this tale is not one of the author's best, though some Swedish critics dispose of it somewhat too summarily. A second volume of *Trolls and Men* appeared in 1921, something of an improvement on the earlier miscellany with the same title.

In 1925 something more pretentious in the way of pure fiction came from Selma Lagerlöf's hand. This year saw the appearance of the first two volumes—entitled *The General's Ring* and *Charlotte Löwensköld*—of a rather ambitious trilogy which now goes under the general title *The Ring of the Löwenskölds*. The third volume, *Anna Svärd*, was published in 1928. Though *The Ring of the Löwenskölds* has its setting in Värmland, the province which had most consistently stirred Selma Lagerlöf's best creative efforts, the novel is on the whole very disappointing, except for some inimitably rollicking humorous episodes in which the author's earlier impishness of spirit sparkles again in its most characteristic and irrepressible form. Even the humor, however, is at times forced and flat, never approximating the profoundly sympathetic humor of the early chapters of *The Emperor of Portugallia*; and otherwise the novel has little to recommend it. The first volume is for the most part merely a moderately skillful manipulation of the horror theme in fiction; and the last two volumes are saved from mediocrity only by the characterization of the two heroines whose names provide the titles for these volumes. The minor characters give the impression of having been "worked up"; and the hero of the last two volumes—with whom both Charlotte Löwensköld and Anna Svärd had fallen in love—is a thin-blooded idealist-fanatic in whom the reader loses interest almost immediately despite the author's obvious efforts to save him from fictional oblivion. It is very difficult to see how either Charlotte Löwensköld or Anna Svärd—each an admirable young woman in her way—could have been any more interested in Karl Arthur Ekenstedt than is the reader.

The decade, however, which witnessed the appearance of *The Ring of the Löwenskölds* brought us something much more satisfactory from Selma Lagerlöf's pen—the two volumes of autobiographical reminiscences from her childhood, *Mårbacka* (1922) and *A Child's Memories* (1930). The chief charm of these autobiographical fragments lies in their utter self-forgetfulness. It is doubtful that autobiography has ever been written with a more complete exclusion of self. The two volumes deal with Mårbacka, with Selma Lagerlöf's parents, her brothers and sisters, and the family servants, with the originals of certain characters in *Gösta Berling's Saga*, and with legends and tales current among the country-folk in the neighborhood of Mårbacka; but neither of the two volumes, curiously enough, can be said to deal immediately with *Selma Lagerlöf herself*— except insofar as her childhood character is revealed indirectly through these childhood memories.

This artistic reticence is one of the most ingratiating elements in Selma Lagerlöf's character. It is natural with her. She never takes the reader into her confidence in the manner that has become so popular with authors since the years when the vogue of Romantic egotism first swept the literary world with its confessional strain—a manner which soon came to harden into a confessional pose or degenerate into a confessional hysteria. Selma Lagerlöf's artistic reticence grows naturally out of her essential modesty of person. Always has she been ready to give to others the credit for her own success as a novelist. Never does she take credit to herself. Perhaps the most ingratiating evidence of her literary modesty is to be found in the little address which she delivered before the distinguished audience which had gathered to do her honor in December of 1909 on the occasion of the awarding to her of the Nobel Prize in Literature. The entire address is a simple, unassuming confession of her deep feeling of indebtedness to a host of others who in one way or another had made her work possible: first, to her parents, especially her father, who had read to her as a child from Bellman and Tegnér, Runeberg and Hans Christian Andersen—in whose pages she had first learned "to love the sagas and deeds of heroism and the life of man in all its greatness and all its weakness". . . . then to Värmland, to its many good and simple people who had opened to her the rich store of Värmland's peasant legends . . . also to Dalarne, the province which had brought to her the profoundly gripping story of "the Dalarne peasants who took their way unto the Holy City" . . . then to all that varied host of literary figures "who have cultivated language, who have forged and hammered out the good instruments and taught me to make use of them". . . and finally to her readers and to her critics—"both to those who have praised and to those who have found fault."

It is to her father—whom she whimsically conceives in her address as sitting in heaven witnessing her present triumph—that Selma Lagerlöf recounts her debt to all who have contributed to her successful literary career. How—she breaks out impatiently in this confession of indebtedness—is she to repay the debt that she owes to others? At first her father smiles, reassuringly when she raises the question; but at the last even he finds himself, at least momentarily, almost as puzzled as is his now famous daughter.

Father has lowered his head and does not appear so hopeful as at the beginning. "I believe really that it will not be so easy to find help for you, my little girl," he says. "But now, at least, you must have exhausted the list of your debtors?"

"No, hitherto it has in any case been so that I have been able to bear it," I say. "But now the very worst indebtedness comes. It was therefore that I felt forced to come to you and ask for counsel."

"I cannot understand that you can get into worse debt," says father.

"Oh, yes," I say, and then I tell him about *it*.

"Never can I believe that the Swedish Academy . . . " says father. Yet at the same time he looks at me—and then he understands that *it* is true. And every wrinkle in his old face begins to twitch, and he has tears in his eyes.

"What should I say to those who have decided in this matter, and to those who have recommended me for the Prize?" I say. "For think of this, father: it involves not only glory and money, that which they have given. They have had such a beautiful faith in me that they have dared to distinguish me before the whole world. How shall I cancel that debt of gratitude?"

Father sits and broods a bit, but then he wipes the tears of joy from his eyes, shakes himself, and then strikes the arm of the chair with his fist. "I will not sit here longer and ponder over things about which no one in heaven or on earth can answer," he says. "Is it so that you have received the Nobel Prize, then I shall bother with nothing other than to be happy."

Royal Highnesses! Ladies and gentlemen! Inasmuch as I have not received a better answer to all of my questions, I can only ask you to take part in the *skål* of gratitude which I have the honor to propose to the Swedish Academy.

Never has a more whimsically appropriate address been given by a winner of the Nobel Prize in Literature on the occasion of the public honor extended upon the formal awarding of the Prize. Addresses on such occasions are prone to be reasonably elegant, if not actually serious or academic. The occasion itself is invariably impressive, for the Swede loves solemnity and elegance on such formal occasions. The blood royalty of Sweden is gathered, as well as the royalty of scholarship, of literature, and of the arts. Formal dress is the rule, and many of the guests wear the insignia of illustrious orders. Faces tend to be drawn, dignified, almost preternaturally serious.

But on at least one of these normally solemn occasions—the evening of December 10, 1909, when Selma Lagerlöf received the Nobel award at Stockholm—the impressive solemnity of an attentive audience gradually became transformed into a warm geniality of feeling, bordering, perhaps, on the contagious gaiety of those lovable old Cavaliers at Ekeby whom Selma Lagerlöf had brought to such a vivid, pulsing life in her famous *Saga*. Selma Lagerlöf's whimsicality on this occasion was too infectious, her humor too ingratiating, her modesty too natural and appealing to permit the normal solemnity of the hour to remain unbroken. The audience caught the playfully serious spirit of her words, twitching their lips perhaps cautiously at first (not being sure but that this *was* an hour for unmixed solemnity), but soon breaking into a broad smile, happy as children that the author of *Gösta Berling's Saga* had not lost that strangely simple witchery of words which had long before made her the most beloved among Sweden's living authors. Even to read her words today on the cold opaqueness of the printed page is to enter into the genial spirit which Selma Lagerlöf brought to the occasion on that evening in Stockholm in December of 1909; and the reader today can vision, almost as if he were present on that earlier date, the gayly warm human spirit which played over the faces of those who were privileged to hear Selma Lagerlöf's voice reading, with a quiet, warmly human serenity, those simple, moving words from a manuscript which breathed in its every phrase the note of—humble self-effacing gratitude.

MAN AND THE SOIL
KNUT HAMSUN

IN the early autumn of the year 1888 a young, quite unknown, Norwegian author, just returned to the Scandinavian countries from a stay of two years in the United States, entered the Copenhagen editorial offices of Edvard Brandes, journalist, critic, and brother of the famous Georg Brandes. The young Norwegian was slovenly in dress, his clothes tattered and dirty, and his face, though strong and aristocratic in its outline, was almost grotesquely emaciated, intensely drawn by the severe, nervous lines of hunger. He had brought with him the inevitable bundle of manuscript, and all but begged Brandes to look it over and express a judgment. Brandes, curiously affected by the strange blending of pathos and nobility in the young man's face, hesitatingly agreed to glance over the manuscript as soon as possible, asking for the young man's name and address. The young man was Knut Hamsun; the manuscript was a fragment of his first important novel, *Hunger*.

Axel Lundegård, a contemporaneous Swedish author closely identified with Danish literary circles of the day gives in some reminiscences entitled *Sett och Känt* ("Seen and Felt," 1925) a vivid account, as related to him by Brandes, of this meeting between the Danish editor and Hamsun—together with a note on its immediate consequences.

"Can you imagine," he began—"as I sat in my editorial offices today, a young Norwegian stepped in and wished to talk with me. And quite naturally he had a manuscript in his pocket! But this interested me from the outset less than the man himself. I have seldom seen a man more derelict in appearance. Not only that his clothes were ragged. But that face! I am not sentimental, as you know. But that man's face gripped me.

"I took his bundle of papers. It was a story. Entirely too long for a number of *Politiken*—this I saw immediately—it would have filled half of the paper. And for a serial it was too short. This I said to the author, and wished to return the manuscript. But at

the same time I noticed the expression behind his spectacles . . .
and could not force over my lips a rejection. I promised to read
the bundle—received the author's address. And so he went.

"I put the whole matter aside and sat down again to work. But
I could not rid my mind of him. The expression in his quivering,
pale face haunted me. There was something about him—something
I could not explain.—Now I understand it better.

"I took his story with me when I left the city. And after dinner
I began to read. It gripped me immediately. And the more I read
the more was I gripped. This was not only full of talent, as so
much else. It was more. Here was something that shook one to the
marrow—Here was something of Dostoievski—

"When I had read half of the story it occurred to me that the
author was wandering around there in town and starved. It struck
me as a shame. And I dashed off to the railway station like a silly
girl, sending him ten crowns.

"Then I returned home and sat down to read further. And the
deeper I got into the story the more shame-faced I became. But
when I came to the end I was really sheepish. Listen!"

He took the last page of the manuscript and read aloud.

It dealt with one who was starving and homeless, an author
without a name. How he, in order not to be forced to spend the
night out-of-doors, sneaked on stocking-feet up the stairway to his
pitiful gable-room, where he had recently lived, but where he did
not dare openly return because he could not pay the rent; how he
finds a letter on his table and again sneaks away. The letter was
from an editor of a newspaper to whom he had turned over a
manuscript. He reads by the fluttering glimmer of a street light.
And a stream of light flows through his breast. The manuscript
was accepted, sent immediately to the composing room.

A few insignificant changes . . . corrected a couple of errors
. . . written with talent . . . will be printed tomorrow . . . ten
crowns.

Edvard Brandes smiled again, with that embarrassed smile of
his, as he laid aside the written pages:

"You understand that I felt sheepish about my pitiful ten crown
note?"

"Yes, that I understand."

He looked at me:

"If you had read the whole of the story, you would understand
it even better."

"Is it so excellent?" I asked. "What is it called?"
"Hunger."

In November 1888 the Danish literary journal *Ny Jord* devoted twenty-nine of its pages to the publication of a section of a novel by Hamsun—the fragment of *Hunger*, certain pages of which had gripped Brandes so deeply not many weeks before. A year and a half later the entire novel was published by Philipsen in Copenhagen.

Meantime Hamsun had established something of a reputation for himself, originally, of course, through the fragment of *Hunger*, and later with other things, chiefly critical, among which was the violent attack upon American "culture" as contained in his first published book, *Fra det moderne Amerikas Aandsliv* ("The Cultural Life of Modern America," 1889). This book, it is interesting to note in passing, Hamsun has since forbidden to be republished, on the grounds that it no longer represents his conception of American culture. In an article published in 1908 Hamsun refers to his book on America as a sin of his youth, "terribly poor and childishly written." Thin as the book is, however, it was written with a certain stylistic verve and a fairly telling satiric thrust. Americans of today would find it amusing, perhaps instructive even, despite its tendency toward exaggeration and its only fragmentary knowledge of the subject with which it proposes to deal.

I

Knut Hamsun was a man of thirty when his novel *Hunger* first startled the Scandinavian reading public into the realization that another Norwegian author of significance had appeared, one who might perhaps continue in some sense—though, it seemed apparent even then, in a very different sense—the literary triumphs of the aging Ibsen and Bjørnson. Very hard had been the years of Hamsun's youth and early manhood, particularly the years immediately preceding his first general recognition as an author. In fact even his boyhood had not been without its period of severe hardship, though the earliest of these years were reasonably pleasant and satisfying. He was born in 1859 in Gudbrandsdal, famous agricultural district of central Norway, of poor though respectable and somewhat unusual parents. Scarcely three years of his life had passed, however, before the family emigrated to Hamarøy in the Far North. Here the young boy lived a relatively happy and carefree existence, until circumstances brought him at the tender age of nine under the immediate surveillance of a hard, oftentimes brutal taskmaster, his uncle Hans Olsen, who carried on a variety of occupations at Hamarøy, among others that of village postmaster, and who needed a "secretary" to help expedite his numerous petty affairs. The boy Knut served under this uncle for five years—years full of physical trials, even of hunger at times—not breaking away until he had finished his schooling and went south to Gudbrandsdal in order to be confirmed. Here, in Gudbrandsdal, he worked as a clerk in a general store maintained by a near relative, and at the end of the year he was duly confirmed.

Then followed years of a strenuous wandering existence. Though some critics have referred to this period in Hamsun's life as one of "vagabondage," the word is somewhat misleading; for even though at first thought Hamsun's early foot-looseness, his continual moving on from job to job, and his growing restlessness of spirit seem to suggest something of the carefree existence of the typical vagabond, he never for a single moment during these years lost sight of an intense guiding purpose in his life —a burning desire to write. It is now sufficiently clear that his restlessness during these years was a result primarily of his growing consciousness of the wide disparity between the richly seething creative sources within him and the paltry outward circumstances of a life which forced him to any and all physical labors in order to gain no more than a mere subsistence.

During the years following immediately upon his return to Nordland from the confirmation interlude in Gudbrandsdal, he became in rapid succession: a clerk in a store in the thriving commercial village of Tranøy; an itinerant on-his-own merchant in a small way among the widely scattered villages of Nordland (an experience upon which he draws copiously for the material in one of his late novels, *Vagabonds*, 1927) ; a shoemaker's apprentice in Bodø; sheriff's deputy; school teacher; and finally an author in a small way, publishing in 1877 a little story *Den Gaadefulde: en Kjærlighedshistorie fra Nordland* ("The Mysterious One: a Love Story from Nordland"), and in 1878 a more extended story entitled simply *Bjørger.*

At the age of twenty, after five years of such diversified activities, Hamsun departed from Nordland for the South, settling first at Hardanger and later in Kristiania. Bolstered financially for the time being by a fund of a thousand crowns provided by K. Zahl, one of the most successful merchants of Nordland, the energetic and restless young Hamsun concentrated all his energies on writing, incidentally as a journalist and lecturer on literary subjects, more seriously as a prospective novelist. In journalism he succeeded moderately, though he made little if any money by it; in the more exacting field of serious fiction he failed. Becoming desperately poor during his stay in Kristiania, he turned finally to the hard physical work of a highway laborer in Toten, eastern Norway, in order to earn a living at least— continuing all the while, however, with his literary interests, writing some hours almost daily and reading with a nervous, gnawing intensity whatever books he could lay his hands upon. An amusingly pathetic anecdote from Hamsun's first days on the Toten road project gives us a vivid momentary glimpse into the circumstances of his life at this time. He lived during these days in a little cottage of an old woman called Torger-Maria, who had much to tell among her neighbors about her young lodger. "He is terribly learned and industrious," the good old lady was wont to confide to her neighbors, "but otherwise he was in a sad state when he came to me; five shirts he had, but all of these he was wearing at one time. Now I have managed matters so that he wears only one at a time and changes every Saturday." When one remembers how immaculate Hamsun has always tried to be in his dress, one can imagine something of the state of living to which he must have been reduced in those last hard months in Kristiania. After two years of back-breaking labor on the Toten highway construction, years of rapidly growing disillusionment as to the possibilities of breaking through as a literary man in his own country, Hamsun decided to emigrate to America.

The problem of financing such a venture was a serious one, but a happy juxtaposition of circumstances produced a person who believed in the young Hamsun sufficiently to guarantee the price of passage. He sailed from Hamburg in January 1882; and upon his arrival in the United States set out immediately for the Norwegian settlements in the Middle West. His first stop seems to have been at Madison, Wisconsin, where he presented a letter of introduction from Bjørnson to Professor Rasmus B. Anderson, who occupied the chair of Scandinavian at the State University at the time. Apparently little encouraged by Anderson, Hamsun moved on to Elroy, Wisconsin, where his eldest brother was settled as a tailor, and took up farm labor nearby. A few months later we find him putting his knowledge of general stores to good account by becoming a clerk in a store owned by a certain John Hart of Elroy. Here he remained for a year and a half, studying English during off hours under the tutorship of a local school teacher, whose last name was Johnston, and planning a lecture tour which was never carried into fulfillment among his countrymen in Wisconsin. Later he turns up in Madelia, a town in south-central Minnesota; and it is here that he met, quite by accident, Kristofer Janson, the man who probably did more for Hamsun than anyone else in America. Janson was a Norwegian, of no small literary abilities, who had emigrated to America some years earlier and had finally settled in Minneapolis as a Unitarian minister. Janson describes his first meeting with Hamsun at Madelia thus—

I happened to notice a tall, erect man with gold-rimmed spectacles and an aristocratic, intelligent face who was working in a lumber yard there and who spoke Norwegian. I came to talk with him. It was one Sunday, and he had time to wander about with me in the woods. I asked him if it satisfied him to be here and load and unload planks.

"No, certainly not,—but one must live."

"But he would then prefer intellectual work?"

"Naturally, but where was it to be found?"

I told him then that I needed a secretary, who could help me translate for *Saamanden* ["The Sower," a religious paper which Janson edited] and occasionally give a lecture for me. And I asked him if he had religious interests.

No, this he could not honestly admit. . . .

Janson, however—fascinated by the young Norwegian, and hoping that religious interests might come with time—told him of the liberal tenets characteristic of Unitarianism; and finally it was agreed that Hamsun should try his hand at the miscellany of religious and semi-religious tasks which Janson proposed.

But my hopes that he might develop religious interests were sadly enough disappointed. He became more and more opposed to anything that smelled of theology. . . . But at our intimate church socials he was indispensable. I remember, for example, a talk he gave at a *lutefiskfest* [codfish feast—very famous among Scandinavians during the Christmas season] we held in the basement of our church, and which was very successful. . . .

It was in the winter of 1883-84 that Hamsun came to Minneapolis; and he remained with Janson, serving in various capacities—as translator, as Sunday school teacher (of a sort), as an occasional lecturer, and even filling Janson's pulpit in extreme emergencies—until he became violently ill in the fall of 1884, spitting much blood and losing considerable strength. His illness was diagnosed, inaccurately, by a Norwegian-American physician as galloping tuberculosis; and he was given little more than a month to live. His friends hastily gathered funds to send him back to Norway—and by the time he reached his homeland he was almost entirely recovered! The details of Hamsun's hasty exit from Minneapolis have been related by one of his Norwegian friends there.

One evening, when he was serving strenuously as an auctioneer at a bazaar in Minneapolis he exerted his strong voice with all its power—and he felt that something burst in his chest. He began to spit blood and had to lie abed. . . . He left Minneapolis, even though he certainly did not believe that all was over with him. He has since related that he rode on the locomotive tender during the three day trip to New York and allowed the violent rush of air that the speed of the train generated to flow into his lungs. When he came to New York, he was already half-recovered from his illness. . . .

The latter part of this story is rather fantastic, and if it suggests anything of the exact truth it should merely give support to our suspicion that Hamsun's illness was not anything like as serious as the physician's diagnosis had claimed it to be. Not even a man of Hamsun's superb physique would recover hastily from galloping tuberculosis by the adventurous expedient of riding on an engine tender from Minneapolis to New York in the late fall of the year! Doubtless Hamsun was indulging in some of his grotesquely exaggerated self-irony, not at all unusual with him, when, and if, he ever gave such an account of his method in overcoming this attack of illness.

Upon his return to Norway Hamsun went to Valders for some certainly needed rest and an opportunity to recover fully from his illness. Here he settled down for a full year, earning a meagre living by substituting as local postmaster and by publishing occasional articles and sketches in the newspapers. It was at this time that he published an article on Mark Twain, in whom he had become much interested while in America; and curiously enough it was the accidental occurrence of a printer's error in the spelling of his own name in this article that determined Hamsun to spell his name as the world has come since to know it. His original name was Knut Pedersen Hamsund, the last name being the place-name of his parents' farm on Hamarøy. As a young man Hamsun had signed his name interchangeably Knut Pederson or Knut Hamsund up until the time of the printer's error in the Mark Twain article; and now, with the unpredictable whimsicality typical of many of the central characters in his later novels, Hamsun determines to retain the form of the name accidentally produced by a printer's error.

Though the period of his Valders semi-convalescence was a reasonably happy one for Hamsun, the year which immediately followed was a very severe one for him. "The year 1886," he has written to John Landquist, the eminent Swedish critic who has penned what is probably the most penetrating critical study on Hamsun, "I again tried life in Kristiania; applied for positions; nothing succeeded for me; I was very poor, and received now and then a few crowns for a newspaper article." These few words are in substance a laconically objective statement of the experience which later is to become the basis of the story contained in the novel *Hunger*. Meantime the immediate consequence of these desperate months in Kristiania is that Hamsun has become so discouraged at the slim prospects for an ambitious young literary man in Norway that he returned again to the United States, from whose shores he had sailed so gladly scarcely two years before.

His second stay in America, however, was to be still shorter than his first, which had been scarcely more than two and a half years; but the second stay was probably much more important from the standpoint of his intellectual and literary development. He stopped first this time in Chicago, and for a short time had work as a street-car conductor. These were very hard days for him, however, and when he wished to leave Chicago he had no money for a railway ticket out of town. With characteristically sardonic humor he conceived then the fantastic notion of writing to Armour, the millionaire packer, and asking for twenty-five dollars, probably not expecting anything from this bit of impertinent tomfoolery, except, perhaps, the pleasure of seeing another momentarily nonplussed by his practical joking. Hamsun wrote the letter and delivered it himself, waiting in an outer office for an answer. In a few minutes the attendant returned and shoved the requested sum into the astonished face of the young Norwegian. Hamsun closes his account of the amusing episode in the following words: "It took me a while to gather my wits,—I asked, then, idiotically: 'May I have it?' 'Yes,' smiled the man. 'What did he say?' I asked. He said that 'your letter was worth it'"! Hamsun left immediately for Minneapolis, where he earned a bare living by newspaper work, lecturing, and working as a day laborer during the harvest season in nearby North Dakota. We are not surprised to find that he identified himself at this time with some rather "radical" young Scandinavians, chiefly newspaper men, in Minneapolis. Encouraged by these friends, he arranged a series

of lectures on a medley of literary personages: Ibsen, Bjørnson, Strindberg, Lie, Kielland, Garborg, and according to
some accounts also Zola, Dostoievski, and Tolstoy. Later, in the
spring of 1888—just before Hamsun's final departure from
Minneapolis—he held a rather ambitious farewell address, which
was meant to be a challenge to his time. It was concerned largely
with a violent denunciation of what he considered to be the narrow, brutal, crudely bourgeois cultural ideals of America at this
time. This lecture was doubtless the seed out of which his
notorious book *The Cultural Life of Modern America* ultimately
grew.

Hamsun's second stay in America, however, seems to have
been a comparatively happy one, despite his restlessness and his
growing distaste for American "cultural values" in these years
when Big Business tended more and more to crush the sensitive
individual in its brutally egotistical pride in the ideal of a "rugged American individualism." Particularly did Hamsun's personal contacts with certain young Scandinavians in Minneapolis
tend to restore his own spirits and his confidence in himself,
after those desperate last months in Kristiania. He readily
identified himself with most of their advanced social ideas,
distinctly radical for that day. They were among other things,
however, temperance enthusiasts, strenuous believers in "pro-
hibition," and they agitated for the abolition of the saloon. In
this "advanced ideal" Hamsun could hardly follow them in good
faith. It is recorded, however, that he did yield for the moment
to their efforts to reform him in this matter—and actually
learned to drink buttermilk. His "conversion" to buttermilk,
however, was short-lived. In a review which Hamsun came to
write in Copenhagen shortly after the Minneapolis days, he re-
calls jocularly from these days a certain John Hansen, "an over-
speculative man, who got me into the habit of drinking buttermilk, so that finally I could taste nothing else. Soon after I had
come far out on the Atlantic, I insulted all the stewards on board
by following them about and demanding buttermilk. . ."!

II

Though Hamsun is often popularly identified as "the author of *Hunger*," the appellation is on the whole rather misleading; for his first novel, except in certain stylistic details, differs rather markedly from most of his later work. In its subject matter and in the constantly sustained nervous intensity of its tone it is really in a class by itself among Hamsun's novels, though *Mysteries* does remind one rather strongly of it at times. The chief feature which *Hunger* clearly has in common with many of Hamsun's other novels is that it centers its attention on a highly individualized character, as do most of Hamsun's early novels, notably *Mysteries* (1892) and *Pan* (1894); and this individual —the unnamed hero in *Hunger*, Nagel in *Mysteries*, and Lieutenant Glahn in *Pan*—is highly sensitive, having a delicately balanced nervous equipment, which predicates the most subtle oftentimes unpredictable emotional responses to the most minute, seemingly insignificant phenomena in the character's immediate environment. But here the likeness between *Hunger* and Hamsun's immediately succeeding work ends; for the central character in *Hunger* is abnormal in the most extreme sense of the word—he is a Dostoievskian hero, sick in body and soul, the pangs of a lacerating hunger having forced upon his inner life a series of violently nervous, grotesquely hectic, other-worldly hallucinations. The novel is given over entirely to a delicately sensitive objective study in the nature of nervous hallucinations brought about by a highly abnormal physical condition—that of severe hunger.

Hamsun's production was extremely prolific between the publication of *Hunger* (1890) and *Growth of the Soil* (1918), the novel with which the present essay is primarily concerned. In addition to more than a dozen full-length novels, he published a very long dramatic trilogy, collections of short stories and lyric poetry (such as *Siesta* and *The Wild Chorus*), and innumerable articles and pamphlets. Never did his pen seem at rest. Vast and diversified as this body of material is, one seems to find definite lines of development in it, a certain *direction,* which, I think it can be demonstrated, leads Hamsun's genius logically and inevitably to the view of life that we find represented in the Isak of Sellanraa farm in *Growth of the Soil.*

In the years immediately following upon *Hunger* in 1890, Hamsun's chief concern in his novels seems to be a close psychological analysis of certain "outcasts from society," i.e. certain highly sensitive, often over-cultured men who live pretty much their own lives in complete independence of the ordinary mores of the society about them. Spectators they are for the most part, not active participants in the group activities of life. Their attitude toward society is critical and superior, though they choose to be passive with reference to it.

Hamsun's early predilection for such eccentric psychological types was doubtless a direct outgrowth of his strong reaction against the one-sided insistence in Scandinavian literature during the late decades of the nineteenth century upon "social problems" as the essential material of literature. We have noted in some detail in our Introduction the part that Georg Brandes and Strindberg in Denmark and Sweden respectively had played in the tendency toward making literature a medium for social reform, and we have indicated the extremes to which Bjørnson and Ibsen had forced this development in the Norwegian literature of the '80's. Though Hamsun had always admired his countryman Bjørnson for his rich and warm creative vitality, it seems that he could never work up any enthusiasm for Ibsen; and by the time Hamsun came to write *Hunger* he had developed a theory of literature in strong opposition to the "problem literature" for which Ibsen and Bjørnson had been primarily responsible in Norway. He admits, in a review published in *Samtiden* in 1890, that he wept while reading Bjørnson's *På Guds Veje* ("In the Paths of God," 1889); but still he has certain negative comments on the book—chiefly does he react against its strong moral emphasis. In a lecture tour in Norway during the summer and fall of 1891, Hamsun developed further his opposition to a theory and practice of literature which centred its interest upon "the social problem." He proceeded vigorously to the attack in these lectures, condemning with little qualification Ibsen, Bjørnson, Kielland, and Lie, chief representatives of "the world famous Norwegian literature," because of their insistence upon making literature simply a medium for social or economic or political or religious reform. Hamsun's strictures fell with particular violence upon Ibsen: he had little admiration for Ibsen's art, and he characterized Ibsen as "a dilettante in thought." One wonders what the aged Ibsen himself thought on the occasion, in October 1891, when he occupied a front row seat at one of these lectures in Christiania. Some critics have hazarded the theory (not at all fantastic) that the old master of irony found something not entirely inappropriate in this direct attack upon himself, and *The Master Builder* became in consequence his own final ironic commentary on the subject of his relationship to the "younger generation" represented for the moment in the rather too violent young author of *Hunger.*

On the positive side Hamsun insisted at this time that literature should have a psychological rather than a social emphasis. Literature should seek to reflect the most subtle inner workings of the mind in all of their subconscious and unconscious manifestations. And to the Hamsun who promulgated this doctrine, the unusual, the eccentric, the amoral individual was far more fascinating as the subject matter for literature than "the average man," the citizen of a fixed society in the ordinary bourgeois sense. It is therefore that he has created the so-called "outcast from society" (*en Tilværelsens Udlending* as he called the type in *Mysteries*), a character type central in all of Hamsun's early novels—Nagel in *Mysteries,* Lieutenant Glahn in *Pan,* and so on.

It is obvious, however, that Hamsun could not indefinitely concentrate his attention upon these highly individualized characters alone; for such characters live in a world peopled by other human beings, and they are constantly reacting against this world in one form or another even though they seek isolation from it and express a contempt for it. And so by degrees the incidental critical strictures upon society of Hamsun's early heroes becomes transformed in Hamsun's middle years into the broader, more detailed, and maturer social criticism which appears in such novels as *Children of the Age* (1913) and *The Village of Segelfoss* (1915). In contrast to the point of view in his earlier novels, which concentrated too often on an individual character, or at best on a small group, and which gave only oblique, fragmentary, and totally inadequate glimpses of the society with which such characters were in conflict, Hamsun presently comes to study society more directly *as such*—dozens of characters, entire communities of people, now tumble about on his scene. And with all this comes greater critical maturity. No longer does Hamsun see the problem of humanity as simply as can be postulated in the conflict between a highly eccentric individual and a doggedly narrow bourgeois society—an over-simplification too often insisted upon by many artists, and so impertinently summed up in an epigram attributed to Flaubert: "The beginning of virtue is to hate the bourgeoisie." Society itself? civilization?—what might be *its* values, *its* limitations—considered broadly in terms of some of its most characteristic manifestations in a modern world? It is sufficiently clear that such questions as these seethed continuously in Hamsun's mind long before he dealt directly, at some length, and maturely with certain of the central problems of modern society. And as he grappled with such problems he was inevitably forced to face the most significant fact of modern civilization—the growth of modern industry and its effect upon the life of man.

It is the problem of modern industry and commerce that occupies Hamsun's attention primarily in *The Village of Segelfoss*. This novel is really a sequel to *Children of the Age*, which introduces us to the rapid transformation, within a period of ten or fifteen years, of a famous old estate in Nordland into a thriving industrial village. The *Village of Segelfoss* then continues the story of the transformation, concentrating particularly, now that Segelfoss has become an industrial centre of a sort, upon the numerous social and economic problems which result from such a transformation. Holmengraa, the emigrant boy who returns to his native land after having made a fortune in Mexico, is in *Children of the Age* the successful business man who transforms Segelfoss into an industrial community by gradually gaining control of the holdings of Lieutenant Willatz Holmsen, whose family, in fine old patriarchal dignity, had dominated the district for generations. In *The Village of Segelfoss* we continue to follow the fortunes of Holmengraa, though his day is really done and his doom is sealed; he himself, ironically enough, becomes a victim of the industrial forces that he had set to work here in the Far North.

We follow also in these pages the unfolding of a problem much larger than the tragic fate of any single individual: we witness the gradual disintegration of the whole society of man which makes up the striving, ambitious, forward-looking industrial village of Segelfoss. It is in the person of the merchant Theodor paa Bua that we find the very quintessence of the modern commercial spirit in Segelfoss; and as such he becomes one of the chief immediate instruments toward the moral degradation that gradually penetrates the whole community. He is the "apostle of civilization" in this far northern hinterland of fisher-folk and small farmers. He piles up immense stores of canned preserves and patent leather shoes, which he proceeds to unload on these simple folk of the Far North who had never seen such things before and certainly did not need them . . . he induces the peasants and fisher-folk to substitute Pellerin, a patent oleomargarine, for their home-churned butter—it was easier to buy this from Theodor paa Bua than to churn one's own . . . he builds places of cheap entertainment . . . he is a past-master at cheating these simple folk of the village . . . cheating them, yes—but, more seriously, *debasing* them little by little. Instead of the fine simplicity of taste and the genuine forthrightness and honesty of character typical of the people of these parts before an industrial village pushed its busy way into their midst, the population now turns to cheap imported preserves, patent leather boots, and the most vulgar of modern amusements. The effect on character is what one might expect: instability, restlessness, and futile, loud-mouthed labor agitation . . . a thriving village of misled, child-like fisher-folk and farmers—the pathetic "fruits of civilization"!

Some critics might argue that Hamsun has over-drawn his picture. This is a matter of opinion; and in any case exaggeration has always been considered one of the legitimate methods of the satiric art. Still, one might object, an isolated Arctic village is hardly a representative place in which to study the ultimate results of an industrial revolution. Much more convincing and valid than Hamsun's *The Village of Segelfoss*, some critics might argue, are such fictional studies as Max Kretzer's *Meister Timpe*, dealing with the social, economic, and political consequences of the conflict between hand labor and the factory system in a modern industrialized Berlin; or Zola's *Germinal*, concerned with the conflict between labor and capital in the vast mining regions in the north of France; or Dickens's *Hard Times*, occupied with labor problems in nineteenth century England— because, the argument might run, these novels attack the problem of the social, economic, and political consequences of the industrial revolution in a larger environment and at more crucial and representative points. The question is debatable; for it can hardly be denied that, though Hamsun's scene is admittedly more limited, he does get as definitely at the core of the problem —the ultimate *moral* values involved and the whole question of human happiness—as does either Kretzer or Zola or Dickens; and he completely avoids the pitfall of mere sentimentality which too often motivates the rather muddy critical analysis of Dickens in the genre of the problem novel. It should be noted also that Hamsun has on the whole a far broader perspective in his criticism of a modern industrial civilization than that shown by Kretzer, Zola, or Dickens: instead of dealing in detail with some special problem arising out of the industrial revolution, he boldly questions, in the spirit and something in the manner of Tolstoy, the whole desirability of a modern industrial civilization.

Hamsun had thus in the years around the outbreak of the World War grappled seriously with certain of the basic problems arising in an intricate modern industrial civilization; and he had found such a civilization in many ways ill adapted to the fundamental needs of man.

It is to be observed, in addition, that during the years between *Hunger* and *The Village of Segelfoss* he had come to certain, at least tentative, conclusions as to the essential inadequacy of the passive wanderer type of character which had occupied such a central place in his earliest novels. This eccentric wanderer, though critical toward modern civilization, was in his way equally incapable of being a sound constructive force in life. It is not until late years (in the tetralogy *Vagabonds, August*, and *The Road Leads On*, appearing between 1927 and 1934) that Hamsun has provided us with a careful, full-length study in the essential inadequacy of the "outcast from society." But already well before the publication of *Growth of the Soil* in 1918 Hamsun has subjected the lovable wanderer type of his early fiction to something approaching a final critical appraisal. This is in a series of novels including *Under the Autumn Star* (1907), *A Wanderer Plays on Muted Strings* (1909) and *The Last Joy* (1912). Hamsun does not in these novels attain his end by means of a direct obvious attack on the essentially lovable wanderer type. Rather does he merely imply, with a very subtle, marvelously indirect art, the basic failings of his earlier type of vagabond hero—by means of a partial *transformation* of the type. In these novels the central character, Knut Pedersen, is still a sufficiently ingratiating wanderer—gentle, sensitive, foot-loose, a lover of nature reminiscent of the Lieutenant Glahn in *Pan*. But it is to be noted that Hamsun's new character is foot-loose *with a difference*—the still lovable wanderer is now a man who works with his hands, with his whole body, industriously, seriously, with something even of a purpose. Thus by suggestion, by subtly modulated indirection, does Hamsun at least partially deplore the fluidity, the rootlessness, the instability, the paradoxical inconsequence of his earlier wanderer heroes. And logical enough it is, then, that in *The Village of Segelfoss* Hamsun comes to condemn a modern industrial civilization, which in its vulgar haste and its mechanical ideals, so inevitably in conflict with an organic, deeply rooted culture, instills a similar restlessness and instability in a whole community of people.

Has Hamsun's criticism of life led him down a blind-alley, now that he has judged both the wanderer type and modern civilization, and found them wanting? Has he become a cynic? —one who sees no hope for a humanity sailing forlornly between the Scylla of rootless individualism and the Charybdis of modern industrial civilization? The answer to these questions— at least for the time being—comes just a few years after Hamsun had finished penning the depressing scenes of *The Village of Segelfoss.*

III

In the summer of 1916 Hamsun wrote a note to his publisher, announcing that he was deeply immersed in a new novel but that it could not be finished for the Christmas book season. "I have something good, and it is well begun," he writes, "but it is too big in its plan, and I will certainly not have it finished. . . ." Later, in the fall, while he was much taken up by certain details connected with the proposed sale of his farm at Hamarøy, he admits that he finds it very hard to write, or even to work on the soil, "which was the happiest thing I knew. Sweat now pours off me if only a cow gets loose or the chickens break in upon my neighbor's land. . . . And I, who have a great work under way which should be a challenge to my generation! I know well that the world can do without me, but—"

The work to which Hamsun refers is *Growth of the Soil.* It appeared in the fall of 1917; and its instantaneous success, in Norway, and in translated form in nearly every country in the world, has demonstrated that Hamsun was not wrong when he referred to it, even while it was in the process of becoming, as "something good . . . big in its plan" and "a great work . . . which should be a challenge to my generation." It was all of this, and today by almost unanimous critical consent it is admitted to be the greatest of Hamsun's novels. One is reminded, as one reads Hamsun's words about his great novel, of certain prophetic words written by one of the great masters of English poetry— "One day I shall write a book which the world will not willingly let die." And when one has read the great Norwegian prose epic *Growth of the Soil,* one feels that to link Hamsun thus with Milton is not to do an injustice to the great master of the English poetic epic of more than two centuries and a half ago.

And yet what a difference between *Paradise Lost* and *Growth of the Soil*! . . . Milton, in whose genius is magnificently merged the double artistic tradition of the Middle Ages and the Renaissance, works out a poetic tapestry of rich and intricate pattern—colorful, musical, everywhere instinct with the weight of whole civilizations of culture. Hamsun, the modern child of a more primitive artistic tradition, writes simply, with a strangely effective laconic terseness: his manner bare, firm, almost stolid in its refusal to indulge in rhetorical poetic flights. . . . Milton sings of angels and archangels, of the succession of hierarchies culminating in the Godhead—too often, perhaps, forgetting to keep Adam, and *his* tragedy, at the centre of the poet's picture, too often forsaking the solid things of the earth for the magic music of the spheres. Hamsun, on the other hand, remains ever firmly on earth: mysteries enough his Isak comes upon, but they are not garbed in the imagery of a long ecclesiastical tradition. . . . Milton boldly and solemnly announces his theme in the opening lines of his epic. Hamsun, less bold, less formal, *insinuates* his theme, quietly, simply, usually in a loose, fragmentary form, into the very fabric of his story. . . . Milton approaches his ethical problem largely in terms of a traditional theology. Hamsun, scarcely less interested in the problem of evil, approaches the moral issue free of any traditional preconceptions either as to the nature of evil or the way of salvation.

Everywhere does one find such contrasts as these between *Paradise Lost* and *Growth of the Soil*; and the contrasts, it might be said, represent the difference between a world of form and idea still steeped in a mass of literary and ecclesiastical traditions and a modern world in which the artistic spirit has been permitted to move more easily, more freely, less weighed down by ideas and forms encased in a world of tradition.

It is a simple story that unfolds itself in the pages of *Growth of the Soil*—the simple story of a simple man, Isak by name, who comes at first alone into an uninhabited wilderness, and by hard, persistent labor finally conquers the soil and builds

Sellanraa farm, which ultimately produces for him and the family which comes to him all of the necessaries of life. It is a story of the blessing that human labor can bring to the soil when it works in close collaboration with nature. "The wilderness was inhabited and unrecognizable," we are told, after we have followed the fruitful pioneer work of Isak for some years; "a blessing had come upon it, life had arisen there from a long dream, human creatures lived there, children played about the houses. And the forest stretched away, big and kindly, right up to the blue heights." And yet nature is not always smiling and helpful to these children of "the great Almenning"—droughts come, and lean seasons. Still, on the whole, and in the long run, nature is ready to cooperate with men of simple industry and dogged perseverance. It is civilization, not nature, that gradually comes to bring pestilence into the life of man; and though Isak himself has the solid stability which withstands the canker of civilization, his family is not always as strong as he.

The purely artistic triumph that Hamsun attains in his novel lies largely, perhaps, in his ability to reduce life to its simplest, most elemental forms, disdaining completely certain romantic techniques of story-telling often employed by even the best of novelists. Hardy, for example, in *The Return of the Native* must make central in his story of an otherwise essentially rural Egdon Heath the mysteriously exotic character of Eustacia Vye. With Hamsun in *Growth of the Soil* there is nothing of this kind. His central characters, Isak and Inger, are simple souls, and neither of them, we are assured, is beautiful to look upon. Of Isak—"the man . . . was no way charming or pleasant by his looks, far from it; and when he spoke it was no tenor with eyes to heaven, but a coarse voice, something like a beast's." Of Inger—"a big, brown-eyed girl, full-built and coarse, with good heavy hands, and rough hide brogues on her feet as if she had been a Lapp, and calfskin bag slung from her shoulders. Not altogether young; speaking politely, somewhere nearing thirty." And of the two of them, after their mating—

And now it was another life for the solitary man. True, this wife of his had a curious slovenly way of speech, and always turning her face aside, by reason of a harelip that she had, but that was no matter. Save that her mouth was disfigured, she would hardly have come to him at all; he might well be grateful that she was marked with a harelip. And as to that, he himself was no beauty. Isak with the iron beard and rugged body, a grim and surly figure of a man; ay, as a man seen through a flaw in the window-pane. His look was not a gentle one; as if Barabbas might break loose at any minute. It was a wonder Inger herself did not run away.

The events of the story are as unassuming as the characters—unassuming, and yet basic, for they treat with a direct, laconic simplicity of such natural phenomena as birth and growth and death, of human mating, of man earning his bread by the sweat of his brow. And with an unerring sense of the appropriate, Hamsun no more seeks to surround these fundamental functions of life with the sentimental trumpery of the average novelist than he tries to make Inger beautiful or Isak handsome.

Out of such material as this it is that Hamsun's theme gradually emerges: man has all he needs when he is at work close to the soil—the so-called "values of civilization" being in reality merely will-o'-the-wisps that man pursues always at his own risk. Nowhere in the novel is this theme more suggestively put than in a passage coming close on the heels of the account of the collapse of certain mining operations near Sellanraa. This exigency had violently upset the calculations of one Andresen, a merchant who had established himself in the neighborhood for the purpose of profiting from the industrial development, but it had only momentarily disturbed the equilibrium of most of the peasant settlers in the region.

. . . Folk and things were unaltered; the mining work had turned away to other tracts, but folk in the wilds had not lost their heads over that; they had their land to till, their crops, their cattle. No great wealth in money, true, but in all the necessaries of life, ay, absolutely all. . . .

No, a man of the wilds did not lose his head. The air was not less healthy now than before; there were folk enough to admire new clothes; there was no need of diamonds. Wine was a thing he knew from the feast at Cana. A man of the wild was not put out by the thought of great things he could not get: art, newspapers, luxuries, politics, and suchlike were worth just what folk were willing to pay for them, no more. Growth of the soil was something different, a thing to be procured at any cost; the only source, the origin of all. A dull and desolate existence? Nay, least of all. A man had everything; his powers above, his dreams, his loves, his wealth of superstition. Sivert, walking one evening by the river, stops on a sudden; there on the water are a pair of ducks, male and female. They are aware of man, and afraid; one of them says something, utters a little sound, a melody in three tones, and the other answers with the same. Then they rise, whirl off like two little wheels a stone's-throw up the river, and settle again. Then, as before, one speaks and the other answers; the same speech as at first, but mark a new delight: *it is set two octaves higher*! Sivert stands looking at the birds, looking past them, far into a dream. A sound had floated through him, a sweetness, and left him standing there with a delicate, thin recollection of something wild and splendid, something he had known before, and forgotten again. He walks home in silence, says no word of it, makes no boast of it, 'twas not for worldly speech. And it was but Sivert from Sellanraa, went out one evening, young and ordinary as he was, and met with this.

The wilderness has all, yes—food and clothing and shelter in plenty for those who will work . . . and so much more, even, for those who work and are sometimes fain to dream.

It should be emphasized that Hamsun's conclusions in *Growth of the Soil* on the relation of man to the soil and the deteriorating effects on man of an industrial civilization were not inspired by the naïve creative desire simply to give renewed expression to one of the forms of an old Romantic nostalgia. It should be apparent from our analysis of Hamsun's earlier novels that the story contained in *Growth of the Soil* is rather the inevitable logical result of his artistic and intellectual development in the years before 1917. It should be remembered also that Hamsun himself had turned farmer in 1911, settling down on a farm in Nordland, which he did not abandon until the year that *Growth of the Soil* was published in 1917, and then taking up another rural holding in more southerly regions at Larvik. Though he, of course, had help on the farm in order to have time over for his literary work, he was not merely a "gentleman farmer" in the usual sense of this phrase. During these years he took an active part in the work on his own farm; and his

growing theoretical interest in the problem of man and his
relationship to the soil is amply attested by numerous articles
on the subject which he contributed to newspapers and journals
in the years just before the publication of *Growth of the Soil.*
One is reminded somewhat of Tolstoy and the Yasnaya Polyana
days.

It may be significant, moreover, in considering those forces
which led Hamsun to the conclusions reached in *Growth of the
Soil,* that the pages of this novel were penned in the heart of the
War years. Nowhere in the novel does one come upon any
specific evidences to justify the supposition that Hamsun was
directly reacting against an over-developed civilization which
had made possible the fearful carnage of the World War, and
no other evidence, so far as I know, has been turned up to prove
the point. Still one is prone to suspect that such evidence is to
be found, probably hidden away in some Norwegian provincial
newspaper files from these years. In any event, it seems difficult
to believe that Hamsun was not aware of the arguments against
a modern war implicit in the general thesis of *Growth of the Soil.*
The problem treated in *Growth of the Soil* is a universal problem, everywhere and at all times present; and so Hamsun sees
no necessity of narrowing his argument or its application to
any particular time or place. It is simply a story of *man*—not
a man—at work with nature; it relates the epic struggle between
the eternal processes of nature and an encroaching modern
industrial civilization. The World War—being peculiarly
destructive because modern industry provided the belligerent
nations with weapons never previously known in the history
of warfare—must have seemed peculiarly horrible and futile
to the man who in the healthy rural isolation of Nordland
was composing *Growth of the Soil* in the years 1916 and 1917.

One need not read beyond the first chapter of the novel to see
that Hamsun intended his story to be universal in its appeal
and in its application; and all the succeeding chapters confirm
this first impression, culminating ultimately in the magnificently
conceived simplicity and power of the final paragraphs of the
last chapter—

Isak at his sowing; a stump of a man, a barge of a man to look at, nothing more. Clad in homespun—wool from his own sheep, boots from the hide of his own cows and calves. Sowing—and he walks religiously bareheaded to that work; his head is bald just at the very top, but all the rest of him shamefully hairy; a fan, a wheel of hair and beard, stands out from his face. 'Tis Isak, the Margrave.

'Twas rarely he knew the day of the month—what need had he of that? He had no bills to be met on a certain date; the marks on his almanac were to show the time when each of the cows should bear. But he knew St. Olaf's Day in the autumn, that by then his hay must be in, and he knew Candlemas in spring, and that three weeks after then the bears came out of their winter quarters; all seed must be in the earth by then. He knew what was needful.

A tiller of the soil, body and soul; a worker on the land without respite. A ghost risen out of the past to point the future, a man from the earliest days of cultivation, a settler in the wilds, nine hundred years old, and, withal, a man of the day.

Nay, there was nothing left to him now of the copper mine and its riches—the money had vanished into air. And who had anything left of all that wealth when the working stopped, and the hills lay dead and deserted? But the *Almenning* was there still, and ten new holdings on that land, beckoning a hundred more.

Nothing growing there? All things growing there: men and beasts and fruit of the soil. Isak sowing his corn. The evening sunlight falls on the corn that flashes out in an arc from his hand, and falls like a dropping of gold to the ground. Here comes Sivert to the harrowing; after that the roller, and then the harrow again. Forest and field look on. All is majesty and power—a sequence and purpose of things.

Kling . . . eling . . . say the cow bells far up on the hillside, coming nearer and nearer; the cattle are coming home for the night. Fifteen head of them, and five-and-forty sheep and goats besides; threescore in all. There go the women out with their milk-pails, carried on yokes from the shoulder: Leopoldine, Jensine, and little Rebecca. All three barefooted. The Margravine, Inger herself, is not with them; she is indoors preparing the meal. Tall and stately, as she moves about her house, a Vestal tending the fire of a kitchen stove. Inger has made her stormy voyage, 'tis true, has lived in a city a while, but now she is home; the world is wide, swarming with tiny specks—Inger has been one of them. All but nothing in all humanity, only one speck.

How inevitably the elevated, universal tone of this closing scene turns the reader's memory back to the first scene in the novel —Isak, alone at first, struggling through the wilderness, plodding across the far-stretching, seemingly interminable hills . . . seeking, seeking.

The long, long road over the moors and up into the forest—who trod it into being first of all? Man, a human being, the first that came here. There was no path before he came. Afterward, some beast or other, following the faint tracks over marsh and moorland, wearing them deeper; after these again some Lapp gained scent of the path, and took that way from field to field, looking to his reindeer. Thus was made the road through the great Almenning— the common tracts without an owner; no-man's-land.

The man comes, walking toward the north. He bears a sack, the first sack, carrying food and some few implements. A strong, coarse fellow, with a red iron beard, and little scars on face and hands; sites of old wounds—were they gained in toil or fight? Maybe the man has been in prison, and is looking for a place to hide; or a philosopher, maybe, in search of peace. This or that, he comes; the figure of a man in this great solitude. . . .

The man is a settler; he is intent upon finding a desirable spot in this wilderness—a place where he can till the soil. At last he finds it.

The worst of his task had been to find the place; this no-man's-place, but his. Now there was work to fill his days. He started at once, stripping birch bark in the woods farther off, while the sap was still in the trees. The bark he pressed and dried, and when he had gathered a heavy load, carried it all the miles back to the village, to be sold for building. Then back to the hillside, with new sacks of food and implements; flour and pork, a cooking-pot, a spade— out and back along the way he had come, carrying loads all the time. A born carrier of loads, a lumbering barge of a man in the forest— oh, as if he loved his calling, tramping long roads and carrying heavy burdens; as if life without a load upon one's shoulders were a miserable thing, no life for him.

It is significant that we do not even know his name at first— "The *man* comes walking to the north." A *worker* he is—"a born carrier of loads. . . ." Neither in time nor in space is he localized—merely "a lumbering barge of a man *in the for-*

est. . . ." What matters it where he struggles? or in what period of time? He is the symbol of the Worker, the eternal Sower— in all generations, in all climes,—"a ghost risen out of the past to point the future, a man from the earliest days of cultivation, a settler in the wilds, nine hundred years old and, withal, a man of the day."

A symbol, yes. . . . Yet what a warmly *human* symbol this "barge of a man" is: strong as an ox, stubbornly persistent in his work, nearly always triumphant in his generation-long struggle with nature, almost a superman in a primitive world of heavy daily tasks this Isak is. And still so naïvely human in his innermost self. Hamsun never ceases, in depicting Isak's early years with Inger, to throw a roguish, kindly searchlight upon Isak's little vanities, especially his childish delight at words of praise from Inger when he has performed some particularly praiseworthy task. One day "he brought home a basket of fish that Inger would open her eyes to see!" Another day he was condescendingly mysterious toward Inger when she inquired as to the purpose of certain preliminary building activities which he was attending to on the farm—"Poor Inger, not so eternally wise as he, as Isak, that lord of creation." Still another day he startled Inger into a vast new admiration by returning the long distance from the village

with a cooking stove, a barge of a man surging up through the forest with a whole iron stove on his back. "'Tis more than a man can do," said Inger. "You'll kill yourself that gait." But Isak pulled down the stone hearth, that didn't look so well in the new house, and set up the cooking stove in its place. "'Tisn't every one has a cooking-stove," said Inger. "Of all the wonders, how we're getting on! . . ."

And when Inger one day outdoes Isak at his own game by returning to Sellanraa with a cow, after a visit to her parents' place, Isak has no rest until he produces an even greater wonder here in the wilderness—a horse!

Perhaps the most riotously roguish bit of humor that Hamsun creates at Isak's expense is his description of Isak's demonstration of the new mowing-machine that he had bought secretly down in the village and had quietly transported to the neighbor-hood of Sellanraa.

. . . There it stands, wrapped up in sacking and paper; he uncovers it, and lo, a huge machine. Look! red and blue, wonderful to see, with a heap of teeth and a heap of knives, with joints and arms and screws and wheels—a mowing-machine. . . .

He stands with a marvelously keen expression, going over in his mind from beginning to end the instructions for use that the store-keeper had read out; he sets a spring here, and shifts a bolt there, then he oils every hole and every crevice, then he looks over the whole thing once more. Isak had never known such an hour in his life. To pick up a pen and write one's mark on a paper, a docu-ment—ay, 'twas a perilous great thing that, no doubt. Likewise in the matter of a new harrow he had once brought up—there were many curiously twisted parts in that to be considered. Not to speak of the great circular saw that had to be set in its course to the nicety of a pencil line, never swaying east nor west, lest it should fly asunder. But this—this mowing-machine of his—'twas a crawling nest of steel springs and hooks and apparatus, and hundreds of screws—Inger's sewing-machine was a bookmark compared with this!

Isak is ready now to demonstrate the machine before his admiring housefolk.

Swelling with mystery, full of pride; with a little lift and throw from the knee at every step, so emphatically did he walk. So a brave man might walk to death and destruction, carrying no weapon in his hand.

The boys came up with the horse, saw the machine, and stopped dead. It was the first mowing-machine in the wilds, the first in the village—red and blue, a thing of splendor to man's eyes. And the father, head of them all, called out, oh, in a careless tone, as if it were nothing uncommon: "Harness up to this machine here."

Difficulties arise—the machine does not run immediately, as it was expected to do; but the boys help figure out the mysterious book of directions, and again all is well.

Isak drives and drives, and everything goes well, and Brrr! says the machine. There is a broad track of cut grass in his wake, neatly in line, ready to take up. Now they see him from the house, and all the women folk come out; Inger carries little Rebecca on her

arm, though little Rebecca has learned to walk by herself long
since. But there they come—four womenfolk, big and small—
scurrying with straining eyes down towards the miracle, flocking
down to see. Oh, but now is Isak's hour. Now he is truly proud,
a mighty man, sitting high aloft dressed in holiday clothes, in all
his finery; in jacket and hat, though the sweat is pouring off him.
He swings round in four big angles, goes over a good bit of ground,
swings round, drives, cuts grass, passes along by where the women
are standing; they are dumbfounded, it is all beyond them, Brrr!
says the machine.

Then Isak stops and gets down. Longing, no doubt, to hear what
these folk on earth down there will say; what they will find to say
about it all. He hears smothered cries; they fear to disturb him,
these beings on earth, in his lordly work, but they turn to one
another with awed questionings, and he hears what they say. And
now, that he may be a kind and fatherly lord and ruler to them
all, to encourage them, he says: "There, I'll just do this bit, and you
can spread it tomorrow."

"Haven't you time to come in and have a bite of food?" says
Inger, all overwhelmed.

"Nay, I've other things to do," he answers.

Then he oils the machine again; gives them to understand that
he is occupied with scientific work. Drives off again, cutting more
grass. And, at long last, the womenfolk go back home.

Happy Isak—happy folk at Sellanraa!

Kindly is all of this humor, with no note of satire in it;
for Hamsun loves his Isak and the simple folk at Sellanraa
farm as he has loved none of his other creations. And this
humor of Hamsun's—in the early parts of the novel so banter-
ing, so sly, so robustly roguish—ultimately comes to reveal
another, profounder side, as does all great, abiding humor. When
we get more deeply into the story of Isak and Inger, we find
Hamsun's roguish spirit blending almost imperceptibly into that
phase of all great humor which we call pathos—a profound,
warmly human pathos in Hamsun, capable of a rich, understanding sympathy toward his chief characters in the hour of
their trials.

Much as some critics have made of certain of the undeniably
great passages in *Growth of the Soil,* particularly the opening
and closing passages in the novel, which lend a tone of such

dignified epic elevation to the story of Sellanraa farm, I have never felt that such passages are Hamsun's greatest creative achievement in the novel. More beautiful, I feel, is Hamsun's treatment of a couple of episodes in the novel which center their attention on the relation between man and woman, Isak and Inger, during moments of deep inner strain and violent potential conflict. At no other point in *Growth of the Soil,* or for that matter in none of Hamsun's novels, do we come upon a more mellow, understanding, profoundly sympathetic Hamsun—nor a Hamsun who is a more delicately sensitive *artist.* The first of these episodes brings to us the laconically tender description of Isak's and Inger's instinctive drawing together, like animals who sense danger, during those months when the shadow of prison walls was the immediate prospect for Inger because she had strangled the child born with a harelip—

And their great sorrow and disaster—ay, it was there, the thing was done, and what it brought must come. Good things mostly leave no trace, but something always comes of evil. Isak took the matter sensibly from the first. He made no great words about it, but asked his wife simply: "How did you come to do it?" Inger made no answer to that. And a little after, he spoke again: "Strangled it—was that what you did?"

"Yes," said Inger.

"You shouldn't have done that."

"No," she agreed.

"And I can't make out how you ever could bring yourself to do it."

"She was all the same as myself," said Inger.

"How d'you mean?"

"Her mouth."

Isak thought over that for some time. "Ay, well," said he.

And nothing more was said about it at the time; the days went on, peacefully as ever; there was all the mass of hay to be got in, and a rare heavy crop all round, so that by degrees the thing slipped into the background of their minds. . . .

Isak took the matter sensibly—what else was there to do? He knew now why Inger had always taken care to be left alone at every birth; to be alone with her fears of how the child might be, and face the danger with no one by. Three times she had done the same thing. Isak shook his head, touched with pity for her ill fate—poor Inger. He learned of the coming of the Lapp with the hare, and acquitted her. It lead to a great love between them, a wild love; they drew closer to each other in their peril. Inger was full of a desperate sweetness towards him, and the great heavy fellow, lumbering carrier of burdens, felt a greed and an endless desire for her in himself. . . .

The second episode is a similarly understanding treatment of certain feminine waywardnesses of Inger after her return from prison, where she had learned some of the precarious ways of "civilization." She was momentarily wayward, Hamsun would have us know—but never viciously so. She was, in the final analysis, too much of a sound, healthy child of nature to be vicious. She had to have her sexual "adventures"; but they were normal, natural—scarcely blameworthy in any final sense. And her conscience is not inactive, a conscience which finds expression in various ways—each of them good for her, perhaps. None of them seemed quite as efficacious, however, as a simple confession that she brought one evening to Isak— Isak, her lord, good, simple, understanding man, who in his awkward fumbling with the elusive concepts of good and evil comes, after all, to the heart of the whole matter when he concludes simply, "None of us can be as we ought." The episode should be quoted in its entirety.

. . . One night she lifted up on her elbow and said:
"Isak?"
"What is it?" says Isak.
"Are you awake?"
"Ay."
"Nay, 'twas nothing," says Inger. "But I've not been all as I ought."
"What?" says Isak. Ay, so much he, said, and rose up on his elbow in turn.
They lay there, and went on talking. Inger is a matchless woman, after all; and with a full heart, "I've not been as I ought towards you," she says, "and I'm that sorry about it."
The simple words move him; this barge of a man is touched, ay, he wants to comfort her, knowing nothing of what is the matter, but only that there is none like her. "Naught to cry about, my dear," says Isak. "There's none of us can be as we ought."

"Nay, 'tis true," she answers gratefully. Oh, Isak had a strong, sound way of taking things; straightened them out, he did, when they turned crooked. "None of us can be as we ought." Ay, he was right. The god of the heart—for all that he is a god, he goes a deal of crooked ways, goes out adventuring, the wild thing that he is, and we can see it in his looks. One day rolling in a bed of roses and licking his lips and remembering things; next day with a thorn in his foot, desperately trying to get it out. Die of it? Never a bit, he's as well as ever. A nice lookout it would be if he were to die.

And Inger's trouble passed off too; she got over it, but she keeps on with her hours of devotion, and finds a merciful refuge there. Hard-working and patient and good she is now every day, knowing Isak different from all other men, and wanting none but him. . . .

A mellow, all-embracing human sympathy, ready to forgive and to forget, incapable of bearing a grudge or passing a final judgment—this is the impressive moral stature to which Isak attains in his quiet, simple, lumbering way. There is nothing of false heroics here, nothing of the cheap, or the theatrical— only a man who believes in the existence of right and wrong, but who does not believe that wrong should be long remembered or brooded over, for nature herself will seek a balance between good and evil and provide at the last any judgment upon man or beast which a sin against nature might perchance incur.

And it is in the spirit of Isak's wise and healthy humanity that Hamsun's own final words of judgment fall upon all of the weak and wayward characters in the novel: first, upon the only momentarily wayward Inger; and then upon the others—upon Brede Olson, the misfit settler at Breidablik; upon "the imperishable Oline," sneaking old busybody; and upon Eleseus and Barbro, two of the children of the original settlers who had become contaminated by life "in the town." Despite Oline's genius for making trouble among the country-folk, it is to be remembered that she

. . . was not overblessed with this world's goods. Practised in evil—ay, well used to edging her way by tricks and little meannesses from day to day; strong only as a scandalmonger, as one whose tongue was to be feared; ay so . . . Her powers were not less than those of other politicians; she acted for herself and those belonging to her, set her speech according to the moment, and gained her end, earning a cheese or a handful of wool each time; she also could live and die in commonplace insincerity and readiness of wit.

Barbro, in her way, is scarcely less despicable than Oline; and yet Hamsun's final judgment on her is one tempered by a spirit of large and forgiving humanity—"Now and again she cries, and breaks her heart over this or that in her life—but that is only natural, it goes with the songs she sings, 'tis the poetry and friendly sweetness in her; she has fooled herself and many another with the same. . . ." And for Eleseus, Isak's misfit son, who ultimately emigrates to America and is never heard from afterward, Hamsun has words of unqualified pity—

Poor Eleseus, all set on end and frittered away. Better, maybe, if he'd worked on the land all the time, but now he's a man that has learned to write and use letters; no grip in him, no depth. For all that, no pitch-black devil of a man, not in love, not ambitious, hardly anything at all is Eleseus, not even a bad thing of any great dimensions.

Something unfortunate, ill-fated about this young man, as if something were rotting him from within. That engineer from the town, good man—better perhaps, if he had not discovered the lad in his youth and taken him up to make something out of him; the child had lost his roothold, and suffered thereby. All that he turns to now leads back to something wanting in him, something dark against the light. . . .

There are really only two characters in the novel for whom Hamsun has no sympathy: first, Fru Heyerdahl, the feminist, who busies herself much more with "advanced ideas" than with the obvious and immediate duties of parenthood; and secondly, Andresen, the petty merchant-adventurer, who in his small way gambles in an industrial development and fails miserably. They represent the canker of civilization in its most unhealthy, its least defensible forms; and as such they come in for Hamsun's most withering irony whenever they appear in the pages of the novel.

Some words about Hamsun's style in *Growth of the Soil*. Its mark is a direct, laconic simplicity; its tone is one of simple epic elevation. Hamsun attains here the heroic manner without ever resorting to the traditional literary means. At no point in the novel does he employ any of the rhetorical tricks which usually accompany the "epic manner." His style is short, clipped, markedly epigrammatic, without ever stooping to the merely banal or to the commonplace. It is idiomatic in the best sense of the word—in the sense that Hazlitt defines the idiomatic in his essay "On Familiar Style." Hamsun has on occasion indulged in a brutally exaggerated realism reminiscent of some of the prose of Strindberg—whom, by the way, he admires greatly. But there is none of this in *Growth of the Soil*. Nor is there anything in this novel of the posed, stilted, dress-shirt manner which Scandinavian authors, particularly lyric poets, so frequently affect. And yet Hamsun somehow achieves "the grand manner" in the sum total effect of *Growth of the Soil*. Impossible is it for the reader to forget the subtly dignified tone of epic elevation attained in the opening and closing scenes of *Growth of the Soil*, a tone gained largely by a marvelously appropriate simplicity of phrase; and scores of other passages in the novel are in their way equally effective.

The secret of this stylistic triumph is that Hamsun never loses sight of the particular world in which his story moves. It is a simple, natural, instinctive world—alone by itself, for the most part, in "the great Almenning." The people in this world are not complex, sophisticated, "civilized"; they go about their simple tasks, performing their daily round of duties, untroubled by those introspective moods that eat at the roots of will and character among more cultured classes. They know the phenomena of birth and growth and death as the everyday phenomena that they are—not artificially, as "objects of analysis." Hamsun keeps all of this constantly in mind, and he fits his style to this instinctive, primitive world of Sellanraa farm. The simple, direct, laconic idiom that he adopts as the primary pattern of his style in *Growth of the Soil* is one which exactly duplicates the thought patterns of the simple folk he is depicting; and, unlike other great novelists who have written of the peasant,

Hamsun maintains the idiom with a marvelous consistency throughout his novel. In the straightforward matter-of-factness of this idiom—an idiom that deviates neither into extreme brutality of phrase nor into sentimental idyllicism of word choice—Hamsun has created an appropriateness of style in the so-called "peasant novel" which is perhaps unique in world literature.

That Hamsun's simple, straightforward prose has, however, a poetry of its own should be sufficiently apparent to any discerning reader of *Growth of the Soil*. It falls, of course, into that species of poetry to which Wordsworth has given the name "the poetry of common life." Hamsun, indeed, goes even a step farther at times than did Wordsworth in actual practice; for he insists upon presenting certain imaginative responses of his peasant characters in the half-formed, fragmentary, only partially articulate lyric manner characteristic of actual peasant thought patterns and peasant speech. Sivert's experience by the river's side one evening, as he caught up the notes of the mating ducks, is a case in point—"A sound had floated through him, a sweetness, and kept him standing there with a delicate, thin recollection of something wild and splendid, something he had known before, and forgotten again." Here there is no effort to analyze, to probe, to get beyond the *actual quality* of Sivert's own half-articulate response—"a delicate, thin recollection of *something* wild and splendid, *something* he had known before, and forgotten again." The experience is one for Sivert to wonder at, to be thankful for, not to talk of or to theorize about. And Hamsun, the author, is no more concerned with theorizing about this experience than is Sivert himself. Hamsun simply *records* the experience, as it had formed itself with a fleeting, formless suddenness in Sivert's consciousness during that marvelous evening hour in the woods at the river's side.

Not always, however, is Hamsun's style in *Growth of the Soil* lyric in the delicate, mystery-filled sense that we find it in the passage when Sivert experiences his sudden glimpse of other-worldly loveliness in consequence of his hearing the musical notes of two mating ducks. Isak and Inger and Sivert have only occasional moments of such rare, inexplicable spiritual content. For the most part their feet are planted firmly on the soil, their concerns, physical and mental, are immediate and of the earth earthy. It is therefore the heavy labors of man and the solid produce of the soil that Hamsun comes to sing most frequently in *Growth of the Soil*: Isak at work in the fields; Inger among her pots and pans or busy in the cow-shed; the marvelous growth of corn at Sellanraa farm; and the vegetables, especially the lowly potato—to Hamsun no mean subject for poetry of a kind!

What was that about potatoes? Were they just a thing from foreign parts, like coffee; a luxury, an extra? Oh, the potato is a lordly fruit; drought or downpour, it grows and grows all the same. It laughs at the weather, and will stand anything; only deal kindly with it, and it yields fifteen-fold again. Not the blood of a grape, but the flesh of a chestnut, to be boiled or roasted, used in every way. A man may lack corn to make bread, but give him potatoes and he will not starve. Roast them in the embers, and there is supper; boil them in water, and there's a breakfast ready. As for meat, it's little is needed beside. Potatoes can be served with what you please; a dish of milk, a herring, is enough. The rich eat them with butter; poor folk manage with a tiny pinch of salt. Isak could make a feast of them on Sundays, with a mess of cream from Goldenhorn's milk. Poor despised potato—a blessed thing!

Here is a prose poem on a subject that would have warmed Wordsworth's heart. And yet I am not sure that Wordsworth would have completely approved of the *manner* in which the paragraph is conceived; for its robust aggressiveness of temper, at once roguish and serious, leaves little occasion for casting over the subject that "certain coloring of the imagination" which Wordsworth felt was essential even in poems dealing with lowly, concrete subjects. Hamsun is here, perhaps, more in the tradition of Whitman than of Wordsworth.

The potato, being useful, is a blessing unto man; and therefore it is an appropriate subject for poetry. Likewise is work— the ceaseless labor of man in loving cooperation with a reasonably fertile and kindly nature. Isak, brute of a worker that he is, becomes in consequence the most poetic of all of the conceptions that Hamsun introduces into his novel. Isak is no dreamer, no gambler—merely a man of stubbornly persistent herculean labors, wresting from the soil what the soil is ready to yield to one who instinctively understands her, loves her, works with her. It is Geissler who is the dreamer, his son the gambler; and both of them are failures, Geissler himself admits to Sivert in that significant passage toward the end of the novel which expounds most succinctly the burden of Hamsun's "message" in *Growth of the Soil*.

". . . Look at you folk at Sellanraa, now; looking up at blue peaks every day of your lives; no new-fangled inventions about that, but fjeld and rocky peaks, rooted deep in the past—but you've them for companionship. There you are, living in touch with heaven and earth, one with them, one with all these wide, deep-rooted things. No need of a sword in your hands, you go through life bareheaded, barehanded, in the midst of a great kindliness. Look, Nature's there, for you and yours to have and enjoy. Man and Nature don't bombard each other, but agree; they don't compete, race one against the other, but go together. There's you Sellanraa folk, in all this, living there. Fjeld and forest, moors and meadow, and sky and stars—oh, 'tis not poor and sparingly counted out, but without measure. Listen to me, Sivert: you be content! You've every thing to live on, everything to live for, everything to believe in; being born and bringing forth, you are the needful on the earth. 'Tis not all that are so, needful on earth. 'Tis you that maintain life. Generation to generation, breeding ever anew; and when you die, the new stock goes on. That's the meaning of eternal life. What do you get out of it? An existence innocently and properly set towards all. What do you get out of it? Nothing can put you under orders and lord it over you Sellanraa folk, you've peace and authority and this great kindliness all round. That's what you get for it. You lie at a mother's breast and suck, and play with a mother's warm hand. There's your father now, he's one of the two-and-thirty thousand. What's to be said of many another? I'm something, I'm the fog, as it were, here and there, floating around, sometimes coming like rain on dry ground. But the others? There's my son, the lightning that's nothing in itself, a flash of barrenness; he can act. My son, ay, he's the modern type, a man of our time; he believes honestly enough all the age has taught him, all the Jew and the Yankee have taught him; I shake my head at it all. But there's nothing mythical about me; 'tis only in the family, so to speak, that I'm like a fog. Sit there shaking my head. Tell the truth—I've not the power of doing things and not regretting it. If I had, I could be lightning myself. Now I'm a fog."

Poetry and substance, symbol and critical analysis—all of these fuse beautifully together in these penetrating words of Geissler, the type of the vagabond dreamer who appears in one form or another with such remarkable persistency in nearly all of Hamsun's novels.

Geissler is severe in self-condemnation here; but his judgment falls even more mercilessly on his son, the modern "man of action," typical representative of a too-busy modern industrial civilization. The "fog," symbol of the dreamer, may on occasion water the thirsty surface of the earth sufficiently to provide at least for the moment against barrenness. But the "lightning," symbol of an over-hasty modern industrial activity, is but a "flash of barrenness"—Geissler's son is but the foolhardy gambler who is ultimately crushed by life itself because he "won't keep pace with life," driving on blindly, madly, with a hectic, nervous haste foreign to those quiet processes of nature which provide sound, healthy, proper growth. The modern man of action plays with the dice rather than labor with the plough; and his end is the end of all gamblers. Isak is not so. Isak is "one of the two-and-thirty thousand" who count constructively in the marvelous processes of nature because he takes up life in life's own terms, instinctively divining the pace that nature sets, and adjusts his willing labors to the tempo and scale which a great and kindly nature intimates to him as he works upon her surface. And as he works he transforms some of nature's features, but he never defaces her, never makes her barren, as does the "lightning" at times—for nature is after all the Great Mother, who gives out a rich, abundant life if only man knows how to find his way to her and use her well.

IV

In 1920 Hamsun became the almost inevitable recipient of the Nobel Prize in Literature, primarily because of the magnificent success of *Growth of the Soil*. Everybody was agreed on this occasion that Hamsun's novel was deserving of the distinction which the Swedish Academy accorded it by awarding to Hamsun literature's most distinguished prize. Its high literary quality was incontestable; and its positive, optimistic tone was sufficiently apparent to satisfy the most rigid interpretation of Alfred Nobel's stipulation that the Prize in Literature was to be awarded for such works only as reflected basically idealistic tendencies. It happens to be one of the rare ironies in literary history, however, that in the days just before Hamsun was being honored in Stockholm for a novel of such buoyant, robustly optimistic leanings as *Growth of the Soil,* he had just finished the composition of his most bitter and disillusioning book, *The Women at the Pump.* It would seem that in writing it Hamsun wished to swing to the opposite pole from *Growth of the Soil*—to unload all his pent up gall upon those artificial, non-productive forms of "life" that he had only touched upon in the occasional negative and satiric portions of his great peasant novel of three years earlier.

In *The Women at the Pump* Hamsun returns to a treatment of small harbor town life. The picture that he gives us of this life is uncompromisingly sordid, petty, mean. We learn of the despicable life of this small harbor town from the meanly slanderous lips of a motley group of village gossips who gather at the village pump and talk over the affairs of their neighbors —hence the title. The object of most of this petty gossip is one Oliver Andersen, a former sailor who had lost a leg and suffered emasculation in consequence of an accident at sea. He had returned to his "home town" after the accident and had married his former sweetheart, Petra, who in the course of her married existence with Oliver has children with two of the most prominent men in the town.

Hamsun's study of the parasitic character of Oliver is a gruesomely cynical one. Though we pick up most of our information about Oliver in cheap little driblets from the busy lips of half-informed, greedily scandalous small town gossips, Hamsun himself takes occasion to add directly some laconically cynical observations—as if the picture were not already nauseating enough. At one point, for instance, Hamsun, with a brutally frank irony, assures the reader that Oliver manages to "get ahead" in his little world simply *because* of his ability to capitalize on his own physical disabilities: his very lack of normal masculine qualities is really the basis of his strength, the secret of his ability to endure, in fact to *thrive*, in the narrowly busy environment of his home town. Consul Johnsen, father of some of "Oliver's children," goes under in the day of adversity, as do many others in the village. But Oliver, we are told, "was of tougher fibre, less refined, less sensitive, more careless, and therefore the right human material; he could endure life. Who had been trodden down more deeply by fate than he? But a little luck, a petty theft, a successful piece of trickery, made of him a satisfied man again."

And this Oliver, petty moral degenerate and social parasite that he is, comes to be, we see ultimately, simply the ghastly human symbol of all of the most characteristic phases of life in the village. The only life which can endure here is the life of the human parasite; the strength to live on comes in most cases only if these people can adjust themselves to their environment by means of false humility, toadying, loss of their sense of honor. The grimly ironic manner in which this point is forced upon the reader throughout the novel reminds one somewhat of Swift in his most bitter moods. Perhaps the culmination point of Hamsun's irony is reached in one of those short, utterly cynical characterizations of Oliver which occur with such sardonic regularity throughout the novel. He "does not brood," we are assured. "If anyone should come and offer him death, he would not wish to accept it—by no means. It is not everybody who is as well off as he. A roof over his head, daily bread, a two crown piece in his pocket, wife and children—and what children! He is the enduring type of mankind."

This Oliver, it is clear, is diametrically opposite in character to the Isak of Sellanraa farm—as *The Women at the Pump* is in general a complete contrast to *Growth of the Soil*. In *The Women at the Pump* we come upon no evidences of a healthy, fertile, productive life. Over the whole action of this novel there hovers a subtle stench of decay, of physical disease and spiritual distortion—and this despite the undeniable liveliness of the scene, the crowding upon the novelist's canvas of dozens of clearly delineated and at least physically active characters. The novel is chiefly remarkable, perhaps, because its decadent tone is so subtly *suggested* in the midst of so much outward bustle, so much lively physical activity. This is a kind of (possibly unconscious) narrative irony not infrequent in Hamsun's novels. His essentially buoyant and healthy genius cannot be weighed down even in the midst of a story of such teeming moral decomposition as his fertile imagination calls up for us in *The Women at the Pump.*

This same buoyancy of temper, casting a curiously paradoxical breath of vitality over scenes of apparent outward decay, is also characteristic of Hamsun's next novel, *Chapter the Last* (1923)—a novel which includes, incidentally, as one of its chief objects of satire the character of a certain Rektor Oliver, one of the "official sons" of Oliver Andersen, parasitic hero of *The Women at the Pump.*

Hamsun seems to have intended *Chapter the Last* as a study in the problem of disease and death. Torahus sanatorium, where the action of the novel centres, has been built purely as a commercial venture. Dozens of people, diseased in body or in mind, stream up to this new sanatorium in the mountains; and here they spin out a part of their tawdry, pathetic existences—some to die here, others to return again to the outside world from which they came, none of the really diseased patients ever experiencing improved health as a consequence of their stay at Torahus. If Hamsun, however, has intended *Chapter the Last* to be a serious fictional study of decay and death, the novel is perhaps to be judged a failure. Certainly by comparison with such works as Thomas Mann's *The Magic Mountain* and *Death in Venice* Hamsun's novel seems strangely thin and inconsequential.

The fact is that we are more conscious of life than of death at Torahus, despite the fact that deaths enough occur in this curiously unreal sanatorium on the Norwegian mountainside. Hamsun never really gets seriously at grips with his apparent subject. It is significant that Rektor Oliver, academic representative of human stupidity at whom Hamsun aims his most

violent satiric shafts, is not a sick man at all. Besides, none of
the characters in the novel who ultimately die at Torahus are
developed sufficiently to attract any active interest on the reader's part; and so we are hardly affected by their deaths. The two
inmates of the sanatorium who do interest us definitely, Fröken
Julie d'Espard and "the Suicide," are both physically well; and
the latter of these two, though he is suffering mentally, is somehow capable of maintaining at all times a robust form of response to life in spite of his mysteriously recurrent threats to
take his own life. *Chapter the Last* is thus in reality a novel
in which the *desire to live* takes precedence over the apparent
theme of death. Death plays only a secondary rôle: it flits about
in the background for the most part, taking the lives of only
those people who never come to loom large in the reader's mind.
We retain, in consequence, a vague sense of a kind of curiously
inconsequential *danse macabre*—as if through a screen, and
nearly always at a safe distance. The actual deaths that occur
seem rather unreal, apparently "manufactured" for the purpose
of forcing the otherwise largely neglected theme of death
upon us.

It must be admitted, indeed, that *Chapter the Last* is one of
Hamsun's least important novels. Some readers might assume
that this falling off in Hamsun's creative powers in *Chapter
the Last* is to be explained largely by the author's age—Hamsun
was sixty-four when the novel appeared. This is only a partial
explanation, however, if any at all; for in 1927, at the age of
sixty-eight, Hamsun published a remarkable new novel, *Vagabonds*, which reminds us instantly of the Hamsun of twenty
years and more before. The years have brought a difference, it
is true, but no real falling off in creative fertility, nor in some
senses even of creative power. The real explanation of Hamsun's failure in *Chapter the Last* would seem to be that his essentially robust genius was temperamentally incapable of entering
imaginatively into the valley of the shadow of death and returning with a creative product that would lead the discerning
reader to accept the author's imaginative experience as valid.
Hamsun is preeminently the author of life—a healthy, pulsing,
vigorously active life. It is when he touches unspoiled nature,

and the more primitive forms of human life, that his pen flows most richly, with the most fertile and sustained creative power. Youth—nature budding, flowering, *growing*—inspires his most happy creative powers. It was by no means an accident that as a man of sixty-one, a man full of years and honors, he toasted "youth" in his informal address at the Nobel Prize dinner at the Grand Hotel in Stockholm in 1920. After thanking the Swedish Academy for the honor that had been extended him, and making some other short introductory remarks, Hamsun said of his book *Growth of the Soil*—

That I have written in my own way. I have learned from things written by others, not the least among them Swedish poets and writers of prose. If I were somewhat experienced in literary analysis, I should no doubt be able to indicate points of contact with the kind speech in my honor; but I shall not do so. . . .

No, what I would rather do at this time, in all this brightness and in this brilliant gathering, would be to go about to each and everyone of you with flowers and poetry and gladness—to be young again, to ride on the waves. This I should wish to do for a great reason's sake, for the sake of a last time. But I do not dare this now; I should not be able to save the picture from caricature. I have become sick of honor and riches in Stockholm today—yes, well . . . but I miss the most important thing, the only thing— I miss youth. None of us is so old that he does not remember it. It is fitting that we old ones step back, but we do it with honor.

What I should do now—that I do not know—for I am an ignorant man, but I beg to empty my glass to Sweden's youth, to all youth, to everything in life that is young!

These were not empty words for Hamsun—words cast off cheaply as a mere "sentiment for the occasion." All of his best work, his most characteristic work, is a robust paean to the spirit that is youth—"to everything in life that is young!" Though Hamsun has written on occasion some profoundly disillusioning studies in social disintegration and some less convincing studies in physical decay and the phenomenon of death, it is not "the great Hamsun" whom we come upon in these more satiric and negative phases of a great creative production. *Chapter the Last* is to be considered as perhaps the most striking illustration of Hamsun's inability to rise magnificently to a theme whose implications are largely negative and critical. The best parts of *Chapter the Last* are those which treat of the will to live rather than resignation to death.

Vagabonds is in almost as complete contrast to *Chapter the Last* as *The Women at the Pump* had been to *Growth of the Soil*. As the first novel in a new, very long trilogy, *Vagabonds* reveals how even in old age Hamsun has retained a rich creative vein in which the pulse beat is scarcely less full and strong than it was in his early novels; and in *August* (1931) and *The Road Leads On* (1934), the story which had been begun so auspiciously in *Vagabonds* is maintained with little if any falling off in sheer, almost exuberant narrative fertility. The three parts of the trilogy, each a bulky, leisurely novel in itself, hold together with a vital artistic and intellectual continuity which is nothing short of amazing when one considers that the first of them was composed by a man nearing seventy and the two later parts came after Hamsun had passed his three score years and ten.

It is, of course, too much to expect that we should meet a new Hamsun in these novels. Neither in subject matter nor in form has Hamsun changed in this important trilogy. Our interest attaches to these novels, however, not merely because they reveal that Hamsun at the age of seventy and more retains the amazing fertility of episode and dialogue characteristic of his early novels. This these novels do attest. But they do more. They are perhaps chiefly significant in that they provide us with a final critical appraisal of the old wandering vagabond hero, the so-called "outcast from society" who had figured so prominently in Hamsun's earliest novels and who had reappeared with such steady persistency in one form or another in nearly all of the later novels—even in *Growth of the Soil*.

Geissler—we remember from the speech to Sivert in *Growth of the Soil*—had half condemned himself: "the fog, as it were, here and there, floating around," though "sometimes coming like rain on dry ground." And his son, "the modern type, a man of our time," Geissler judged even more severely—he was but "the lightning that's nothing in itself, a flash of barrenness." Judgments such as these are hardly cryptic, especially when read in the narrative context of the novel; and yet the analysis of the two rootless, negative types in *Growth of the Soil* is left in rather general form, for Hamsun is much more immediately concerned in this novel with Isak, the massive human symbol of all that is stable, deeply rooted, and therefore positive and permanently constructive in life. In the series of novels beginning with *Vagabonds*, on the other hand, Hamsun concentrates directly on the wandering vagabond type, subjecting it to a detailed, almost ruthless critical examination. In these novels, moreover, the vagabond spirit and the modern spirit are *identified* with one another, united indissolubly in one and the same character, August. This August, a one-time sailor, was rootless and unstable, yet lovable and helpful in his way, dreaming dreams and putting many of his dreams into action, sometimes as a blessing to his fellows but more often as a subtly, disintegrating scourge. August has a free, inventive mind, constantly busy with large, ambitious plans; but he is utterly rootless, nervously restive, quite incapable of foreseeing the ultimate consequences of his work. And therefore it is that August's influence is finally negative, his work is barren . . . and he himself, coming at the last to a curiously empty old age, meets an ironically appropriate death on a mountainside when he is forced over a cliff by the dumb, frightened mass movement of a vast herd of sheep—a herd which represents his last half-fantastic commercial venture! The symbolic irony of this closing episode in *The Road Leads On* is peculiarly Hamsunesque in its flavor.

Hamsun, however, is not satisfied merely to indulge in the irony of suggestion or symbolism in the three novels which describe the illusive character and the fantastic career of August: he studies in minute detail the disintegrating influence of August's spirit upon two entire communities of people; he analyzes with a poignantly ruthless objectivity the tragic fate of one Edevart, by nature a sound, primitive Isak type, who had become a restless wanderer under the amiably seductive tutelage of August; and he finally comes to subject August himself to a penetratingly disillusioning analysis, an analysis which reveals that August's apparently carefree spirit is not without its petty cares, its vaguely aching sense of emptiness, of futility . . . he becomes gradually aware that his existence, lacking any centrality, has no positive significance either to itself or for those people with whom he comes in contact.

The latter part of *Vagabonds* and the whole of *August* are given over largely to a study of August's "great plans" for Polden, a little Norwegian fishing village beyond the Polar Circle into which August's adventurous and restless commercial spirit had brought a new form of life. Much wealth is brought to these poverty-stricken people; the fishing industry is greatly enlarged; real estate values boom; business ventures of all sorts shoot up their mushroom growth. Still all is not well in August's Polden—quite the contrary. The volatile genius of August had brought a restive, nervous spirit into this quiet, conservative little village—and with this new spirit had come more bad days than good. At the close of *August* the natives themselves pass their none too charitable judgments upon the lovable vagabond after he had disappeared mysteriously, under circumstances not entirely to his credit.

The whole thing was, according to Joakim, that August had developed Polden both for better and for worse; he had drained the bog, but he had also encouraged speculation. He was a symbol for the modern age, giving with one hand, stealing with the other—where, then, lay the ultimate gain? He had succeeded in changing things over, but in every single instance his good intentions had resulted in evil consequences. Sometimes, during the course of one of his arguments with Paulina, August had replied that very well, this was the price which progress exacted—struggle and competition. But had that been anything of an answer? "He came to us from the world outside," said Joakim, "and he wanted to teach us modern and outlandish things, but why? Oh, simply to follow the world in the ways of struggle and competition! 'But why?' Paulina used to scream at him. Oh, just so we wouldn't have to go on borrowing money from London, for example!"

"Ha, ha, ha!" laughed Ezra sourly, and he could have spat upon such a doctrine as that. "Ay, it's exactly as you say! How did he carry on? He wasted the living soil here by cluttering it up with a town, caring little whether we starved or not! What did his town have to live on? There isn't enough here for even a crow to peck at, just people and houses. He started a number of things here in Polden: a whole lot of houses, a bank, a factory, Christmas trees, all kinds of things like that, but the last thing I heard about him was that he had been growing tobacco—and what nourishment is there in that? No, he said to me, but that was industrial enterprise, something to make money to buy food with! Money? Ay, money, wages, progress and all that sort of thing. No, it's going backward, that's what it is; we eat and we eat and we eat this fine store food of his and all we do is open our mouths for more—and it's all wind in our bellies after all, it doesn't put any meat on our bones. . . ."

Hard enough words these, especially those of Ezra, the land-mad peasant character in Polden. But brother Joakim's final words of judgment are less critical. August had not been vicious, after all; and he had purposely done evil to no man. Besides, August himself was perhaps to be pitied as much as those whom he had left behind in Polden—

"I began to feel sorry for August, too, toward the end. He told me he knew he was working in vain."

"Ay, can you ever understand it! Everything he turned his hand to went to pieces in the end. His bad luck still seems to be following him as he goes on wandering; he could come back now if he wanted to, but he doesn't know it."

"But you needn't think that it makes any particular difference to him, don't you worry about him!" said Joakim, and once again he began to speak a lofty language. "August, he had to go off wandering again, for his time was over here. His course lies wherever the current leads him and his life is a life of unrest. He will turn up again in some other place on this beloved globe of his and there he will once again be an influence for good and evil. For the restless currents of life will carry him far and wide. Don't worry about August; he belongs to our age and he is at home wherever he is."

In *The Road Leads On* August turns up again, years after his mysterious departure from Polden—but now he is at Segelfoss, the scene of Hamsun's earlier novels *Children of the Age* and *The Village of Segelfoss*. Here August (parading under the whimsical, self-applied by-name *alt mulig*—everything possible!) has become the general handy man and foreman of

Gordon Tidemand, who had taken over the major business enterprises of the village after the death of Theodor paa Bua, the successful small merchant who had figured so largely in *The Village of Segelfoss.* Though August, now grown old, cannot throw off completely the old restless commercial spirit of an earlier day, his ventures are now on the whole less fantastic than those which he had carried on in Polden; and so his influence upon the community of Segelfoss is less marked, either for good or for bad. Hamsun, it seems, is concerned primarily in *The Road Leads On* with August himself, far less with the swarming world of people about August. This closing novel in Hamsun's vagabond trilogy becomes thus for the most part a close and detailed critical analysis of the essential spiritual barrenness of the wanderer type—a type for whom Hamsun had seemed to retain a certain sentimental attachment despite a growing tendency in his later novels to pass rather severe judgments on it.

It is significant that in Hamsun's early novels which had centred their attention on the vagabond hero this type had nearly always been of a certain age, just beyond thirty years— an age, it is to be noted, when man has had a fairly mature experience of life and yet an age when neither physical nor spiritual disintegration has begun to leave its mark upon human character. These "outcasts from society" in Hamsun's early novels could therefore efficiently conceal, perhaps even from themselves, that fundamental spiritual emptiness, that barrenness of mind and soul, which seems to be the distinguishing deficiency in a thoroughly rootless, wandering human spirit. Outwardly only might they be impressive, with their irrepressible bravado, their magniloquent dreams, and their devil-may-care contempt for a settled, reasonably stable condition of society. Much of this was obviously a pose, which might be maintained with some degree of success only during those years of vigorous and independent manhood before age began to eat away at the magnificent superstructure of self-assurance which such characters affected.

In *The Road Leads On,* last volume in Hamsun's recent vaga-bond trilogy, August is an old man, not nearly so sure of him-self as he had formerly been, only occasionally revealing that marvelous gusto for life-as-it-came which had enabled him in the past to sail with such impertinent serenity through both calm and heavy seas. He has become even superstitious with age, and his superstition at times takes on certain curious religious forms. From such superstitions he breaks on occasion outwardly; but it is circumstance that always determines these breaks rather than force of character or any basic inner strength. And not infrequently in his late years does he indulge in a strangely weak sort of inner accounting with himself. He discovers, for instance, in one of his moments of pathetically honest self-searching that he is without depth, that he has no genuine, consistent, and permanent feelings for others. When Cornelia, a young lady of the village for whom August had harbored an old man's sentimental infatuation, had died, August could not bring himself to attend the funeral—or even to feel any honest sorrow. Nor had he any genuine feeling for older friends of Polden days.

In the course of . . . two or three days the catastrophe [Cor-nelia's death] had rapidly retreated into the past and August was already able to regard it with complete indifference. Such was his nature. He was no longer in the slightest degree concerned with Polden which had been the field of his intensest activity a genera-tion ago. He but vaguely recalled his young friend and comrade, Edevart Andreasen, a loyal chap who had sacrificed his life for August. He no longer had a single thought for Paulina, the woman who had come with a large amount of money to place in his hands. Everyone else in Segelfoss had been kind to this splendid person and had given her such pleasant memories as would abide with her the rest of her days, but August had not even taken the trouble to see her off on the ship the day she had sailed, had never even mentioned her name again, had completely forgotten her. Was he dry and sterile of soul, then? He was not without human sympathy; he had a warm heart and he was forever ready with a helping hand. But he was without depth. His soul was that of the age he lived in. He was a man of splendid virtues and brazen faults. This single individual had it in his power to corrupt both town and countryside.

And then he rationalizes, with something of the earlier August bravado—

After all, did he have time to follow a corpse? Wasn't he beset by endless weighty problems requiring his immediate attention? The motorship bringing carpenters and building materials to town had already arrived and it was well that cellar and foundation had been prepared. They had begun to put up the house, and it was so snug and small, although long enough and neatly proportioned in accordance with its height. A genuine artist, that Postmaster Hagen!

On another occasion when August finds himself far up on a mountainside above Segelfoss a vaguely disturbing sense of a pathetic inner emptiness sweeps in upon him as memories of the sea and a consciousness of the magnificently varied mountain phenomena about him mix confusedly in his weakly drifting old man's brain—

Actually, he was out of his element up there. Looking about, he found himself in the midst of an utterly foreign world, a world of riotous peaks and rocky crags, a static confusion of monstrous grey mountains. What use did he have for such a world? He was a man of action, a trader. Up here, as there was nothing which moved—neither bush nor straw—there were no sounds to be heard, only dead silence which crushed him with its weight. Here he sits between his ears and all he hears is emptiness. An amusing conception, indeed!

On the sea there were both motion and sound, something for the ear to feed upon, a chorus of waters. Here nothingness meets nothingness and the result is zero, not even a hole. Enough to make one shake one's head, utterly at a loss.

He did not give the matter much thought; the notion had merely occurred to him, but, as he was somewhat fanciful by nature, it was probable that for a moment his imagination had got the better of him. Such might well have been the case. And if this silence had any meaning at all, it was probably this: I am emptiness! Of all things in the world I am emptiness! Known only as that which is contained in something, a power, an impossibility which no one possesses and no one has sent, but a delirium. I am emptiness!

He has toiled no end, expended his energy. Nor has this climb up the mountain been such an easy task for him. He is an old man and he may be tired, perhaps he is dozing. . . .

A puff of wind sweeps over the mountain, something nearby moves; he glances up but immediately lowers his gaze again. He smacks his lips as though tasting of something, and perhaps his thoughts are off at sea again, his proper home. It is the dog watch and he is standing at the wheel. A clear passage and a calm sea, moon and stars . . . ay, and God, it seems, is at home, for all his heavenly lights are blazing. The dog watch? Oh, the angel watch, no less! Simply that the moon is waxing and each night growing more full is joy unbounded for the man there at the wheel. He hums, he is on good terms with himself, he is bound for a distant port where he will go ashore in a red vest. No wonder that the human being is reluctant to die, for the glories of this earth can not be imagined to exist in any other corner of the universe, not even in Heaven itself. . . .

Thus sentimentally inconsequential are August's dreams in the day of his decline—dreams in which he senses vaguely, not without a weak, half-conscious evasiveness, the essentially ugly sterility of his own mind and spirit. Hamsun handles the scene with a kind of fond, half-hesitant delicacy of feeling, for he would love this August if he could in spite of all.

Still the critical implications of the passage are not difficult to fathom: August is a self-admitted failure in life because he has failed to identify himself seriously with those laws which govern normal life and normal growth. In what marked contrast is August in this episode to Isak in the final scene in *Growth of the Soil*—

A tiller of the ground, body and soul; a worker on the land without respite. A ghost risen out of the past to point the future, a man from the earliest days of cultivation, a settler in the wilds, nine hundred years old, and, withal, a man of the day.

Isak is not clever, he has none of the inventive verve of August, none of the lovable vagabond's imaginative exuberance; and yet Isak *counts*, for he does not evade life's fundamental conditions —he works quietly, doggedly, with a certain brutally beautiful persistence on the soil. And Isak is happy in his simple, lumbering way—has he not Inger and the children, sheep and cattle aplenty, open smiling fields inviting him to lifegiving labor, and all around and above him the strangely beautiful mystery of mountainsides and the infinitely blue deeps of the skies? No emptiness here, no futile sterility either physical or spiritual at Sellanraa farm. Isak labors rather than dreams— or, to put it more precisely, he dreams only seldom, and then incidentally *while he works*. There is, in consequence, "a sequence and purpose of things" in what he does. This is the profoundly contented way of life, possible only to a character deeply rooted in life's fundamental realities.

But if August is in marked contrast to Isak, we find in Edevart Andreasen (comrade of August in *Vagabonds* and *August*) a character who reminds one more than a little of the Isak in *Growth of the Soil*. In Edevart, however, unlike in the case of Isak, Hamsun has sketched a character of magnificently tragic proportions. August's final fate, it must be noted, is by comparison with Edevart's something resembling high comedy; for August, after all, never had been deeply rooted in anything or anybody, and he therefore could not feel within himself any very profound inner tragedy however shifting and insubstantial his life might be. August lived on the surface, only vaguely feeling at the end a kind of flabby, final inadequacy in himself. Not so with Edevart. His story came to be the heavy, tragic saga of the rootless immigrant—an immigrant torn loose against his will from the soil of the homeland, and incapable thereafter of finding happiness either in the new land or, upon his return to the homeland, in the country from which he had originally emigrated. Edevart is from the first a man of the soil—a laborer with brutally willing hands. We see him early in *Vagabonds* breaking the soil for Lovisa Margareta at Doppen farm—

In the morning Edevart improvised a crowbar as best he could. He trimmed two poles from stout rowan wood and began to clear the field. One stone after another he dug up and each hole he filled with earth and turf. Sometimes he needed extra weight on his pole and then both the children would climb upon it—ay, in a pinch even Lovisa Margareta herself would—and all bore down with all their weight. It seemed great fun to the four of them, this clearing a field of stones. A family clearing their land.

The robust idyll of heavy productive labor—this seems to be more than a momentary echo from *Growth of the Soil*! Heavy, solidly productive labor . . . and the naïve pleasure that wells up in Edevart, the man, when Lovisa Margareta admires his magnificent brute labor—is this not the story of Isak and Inger once again? Yes,—it might have been. But Edevart, unlike Isak, finally came to be the tragic, rootless victim of an empty, purposeless modern civilization.

Two immediate personal influences operate on Edevart to rob him of the pleasure of simple labor with the soil: first, he meets August, by nature the most unstable and rootless of individuals; and secondly, he becomes infatuated with Lovisa Margareta, who is sound and robustly naïve enough when Edevart first meets her, but who later becomes unabashedly tainted by the restless virus of modern emigration. Edevart himself finally comes to emigrate—follows, not without deep misgivings, Lovisa Margareta to America, only to return to his homeland after a time . . . a broken man, brooding heavily in spirit despite the fact that he is still physically able—can work and earn his bread in a way. But his way, particularly when he worked again on the soil of his homeland, was the new American way—much heroic activity but little real efficiency.

. . . Edevart's work on the land left much to be desired. He hurried through his tasks. Ezra was systematic and thrifty in all that he did, he saved his turf, harrowed carefully, measured the feed he gave to his animals, gathered loose grain from the ground after harvest. . . . Edevart, on the other hand, worked wildly and performed his labour wretchedly indeed—he proceeded American fashion, relied upon sheer strength, went at his work with a rush. Ezra was obliged to call a halt: "Whoa, whoa, Edevart! If you keep on like that, you'll have me out of house and home!"

"How's that?" asked Edevart.

Why, he was tiring out the horse, ruining tools, leaving too much unploughed surface behind him; he had overloaded the fragile wood-sled with cut birch from the woods, had dulled the edge of the axe on stone. . . .

At carpentry work in Polden, however, Edevart was more successful, and he managed to earn more than a mere subsistence. But he was nevertheless a gloomily tragic figure now: something had broken inside him, something precious, which he could not define nicely for himself—something, alas, which he could never recover in the days of his life. Hamsun reveals to us in a dozen different ways the tragic deeps of Edevart's inner life during these last years in Polden—never more poignantly, perhaps, than in an episode occurring on *Bededagen* (Prayer Day), when Paulina, Edevart's sister, had suggested that he attend the church service with her and he had refused, scarcely knowing why.

He stood looking after her. During his long sojourn in a foreign land, during that long series of crises he had passed through with Lovisa Maragreta, he had faithfully pretended to some manner of religious thought, had he not? But now, coming face to face once more with the teachings of his childhood, he found the whole thing strange to him, his faith had deserted him, had faded out of his soul. How colorless and remote those things of which his sister had spoken now sounded in his ears—and how deeply significant they had been to her! In his own mind they made no sense whatever, sheer empty chatter. Oh, how completely disinterested he was in the Hebrew name for God and all the other Shulamites! Papst— here at once was an entirely different matter, a whole sequence of mental images: watches which ran and watches which stopped, the years of his youth, exciting days at the fair, womenfolk and love-making, mad youth on a rampage, skipper days, voyages along the coast, Doppen, three reefs in the wind. . . .

And even this he lived over again in memory with a dull and lifeless emotion. He did not smile, did not enthuse—it had all been so long ago. He had been off to America and had had it all washed from his soul. And he had gained nothing to take its place. . . .

As Edevart stands there with his dreams, dull, weary, achingly hopeless dreams, Joakim, his brother, appears and asks him why he is there—it being *Bededagen,* isn't he "going to brush up a bit"?

No. And, to be exact, just why was he standing here in the middle of the dooryard? Could he possibly explain to his brother that he had been standing here trying to find his heart again and to put it back in its place? "I was just talking with Paulina," he replied.

With slow steps he walked away from the house and away from the village, out past the New Place and into the open country beyond. It was peaceful and still where he walked, only the aspen leaves murmuring and a small bird fluttering from covert to covert. He sat down. Now and then he heard the bells of the flock reaching him from far away, a gentle lovely sound to his ears; it receded and came near again, an undulating psalm which caused him to utter words, "Dear Lord, dear Lord," for no particular reason at all, save to hear himself say them. . . .

His heart back in its place again—what's that? There was nothing extraordinary about this returned American, Edevart Andreasen; he had become what he was, his heart was in its place. Had life dealt harshly with him? Made him into something other than it had intended? Pushed him off the road? By no means. The Edevart of twenty years ago still lay as a foundation beneath his present life; each year that passed had merely laid itself, crust after crust, upon that original foundation—and none of this was to be got rid of now; there he sits with all his years of encrustations within him, a complete and perfectly developed vagabond.

Why worry, then? Why be depressed? The day was fair; more, it was *Bededagen* and a holiday; there were small birds in the bushes, the sound of sheep's bells in the air, wild flowers in the fields and the woods were all sweetness and tranquillity—but, even so, a grey hopelessness seemed to stifle his soul. Had something within him been laid waste, downright ruined? Is that what his life exuded? H'm, there's a hair-splitting point to consider! Certainly no great sorrow had come into his life to crush him: he had broken no bones and he had several hundred *kroner* in his pocket, shoes with thick soles on his feet. What, then, was lacking in his life? Perhaps nothing save this, that in every thing and in every way he was simply a vagabond come home again. He has become a total stranger to himself; he has rejected his birthright: the soil of his fathers. Gone, too—ay, vanished completely—are all those rich superstitions and prejudices which once had been a part of his soul's estate. His spiritual life has withered into nothingness and poor he has become beyond all belief.

Edevart continues in this same vein of heavy brooding; nothing seems to help him, nothing is able to lift the heavy mantle of hopelessness that weighs down his soul. In fact his brooding only intensifies when he a short time later catches sight of brother Joakim, out for a stroll across the fields on this lovely summer day. "A splendid chap, that Joakim—" Edevart half-consciously muses—"firmly treading the soil of home, healthy in mind, satisfied and happy and strong. If only he weren't so devilish sure of himself!"

Edevart somehow struggles on with life, shattered though his soul be, incapable as he is of finding any meaning, any sense of direction in the tragically aching existence which he is so dumbly spinning out in these last empty years. Never again does he find himself. And at the last he comes to give his life for his friend August, vagabond comrade of old who had first led the mind of Edevart into those dubious ways which ultimately came to spell out the dark letters of his tragic inner fate. Marvelously appropriate is the lovingly simple eulogy on "Big Brother" Edevart which Hamsun places on the lips of Paulina and Joakim many days after Edevart had disappeared—disappeared forever in a storm at sea while in search of August.

She talked with Brother Joakim about the two comrades; remarkable how closely they had clung together, though one of them had been wild and the other tame. Just see, Big Brother had loaned his friend a large sum of money—Paulina didn't know exactly how much and therefore she had been unable to figure in this item; however, she had noted it in her account. Big Brother, he had no further need for money now—well, for that matter, he had never really needed money; no, never; not even a lucky pocket-piece. He had merely been a toiler, and oh God, how big and strong he had been. . . .

"Ay," said Joakim. "We were all like little boys compared with him. That time we were trying to get that safe of yours up from the beach, there were seven of us men, to say nothing of two horses, but we couldn't budge it an inch. But when Edevart took hold, we might just as well have unhitched the horses!" Joakim sat with shining eyes and boasted no end about Big Brother.

"And he was so kind to us all when we were little! Do you remember when he came home after being away?"

Joakim cleared his throat loudly and strode over to the window as though something outside had suddenly attracted his attention. Edevart "had merely been a toiler, and oh God, how big and strong he had been." Big and strong, and kindly—these are the attributes of Big Brother's character that remain in the memories of Paulina and Joakim. His fearful inner tragedy they seldom talk of—perhaps they have little understanding of it, being so stable, so deeply rooted themselves.

The tragic story of Edevart is one of genuinely epic proportions, conceived over against a robust and highly diversified background, one of rapidly shifting scenes. One has the feeling that had Hamsun occupied himself somewhat more closely with this story of Edevart, eliminating some of the extraneously picaresque detail in the two novels in which Edevart appears, and paying somewhat less attention to his friend August, the tragic story of Edevart might easily have been at least as great in its final form as the story of Isak in *Growth of the Soil*. As it is, Edevart's story falls perhaps just short of being among Hamsun's very greatest creations. Never, however, has Hamsun conceived a tragic figure with a more potentially universal appeal than Edevart. Had all of the details of fictional execution been commensurate with the broad outlines of the tragic conception, Norwegian fiction might have had in Edevart a tragic character of the proportions of Sigrid Undset's Lavrans Bjørgulfsson in *Kristin Lavransdatter* or Olav Audunsson in *The Master of Hestviken*. It was perhaps Hamsun's own experience as an immigrant that gives to his treatment of Edevart whatever greatness the tragic conception does attain in that series of fascinating novels beginning with *Vagabonds*.

Knut Hamsun is now eighty, and yet he continues to write. In 1937 his last novel to date appeared. It is entitled *The Ring Is Closed,* and in it we find something that reminds us of both *The Women at the Pump* and the vagabond trilogy that tells the tale of August and Edevart. The action takes place in a small harbor town, which has its inevitable small talk and its share of weak and despicable characters; but such material provides only a semblance of a background for the central story. The reader's attention soon becomes concentrated largely on Abel Brodersen, a strangely apathetic returned immigrant, and his curious experiences with three women: Olga, Abel's boyhood flame who still has a certain vaguely defined fascination for him; Lola, who reveals her love for a largely indifferent Abel in various practical ways; and Angèle, Abel's romantic American love, now only a strangely exquisite memory to the hero of the novel. In Abel himself we find a new incarnation of Hamsun's vagabond hero. Unlike August he lacks completely any bustling activity, any nervous inner urge; and he differs from Edevart in that his rootlessness—originating in his immigrant experience—has resulted in no essentially tragic inner reaction. He is, in short, *the pure vagabond type,* divinely indifferent to life and its petty circumstances, quite capable of living not unhappily if he can remain entirely free from obligations of any kind. He is, in consequence, utterly passive with reference to his environment, exerting himself only to avoid starvation, and then only enough to hold his body together. He is entirely amoral, recognizing only the law of his own being, and yet never aggressively flaunting his demands before a society which he is too indifferent about even to despise. In this complete indifference to society he is quite the opposite of Nagel in *Mysteries,* one of the earliest manifestations of Hamsun's vagabond hero.

The quintessential vagabond type which Hamsun has created in the character of Abel strikes the average reader as something strangely unreal, curiously inhuman and he is to be looked upon, indeed, as a creature of pure fantasy. A character quite isolated spiritually—and insofar as possible even physically—from any actual social environment is bound to take on the substance of a shadow. The fantastic unreality of Hamsun's hero in *The Ring Is Closed* does not represent, however, any significant falling off in Hamsun's creative powers, as might at first thought be concluded. In a sense, indeed, it represents an artistic maturity in which Hamsun's characteristic ironic fantasy reaches new heights. It may be said that the character of Abel in *The Ring Is Closed* bears the same relation to the vagabond tradition in Romantic fiction as the character of des Esseintes in Huysman's *A Rebours* bears to the tradition of the decadent hero in modern fiction. Neither character is "real" in the ordinary sense of the term—nor, it would seem, are they intended to be real. They are, rather, the quintessential, the absolute *type,* each of them an invention of pure fantasy and each a creature conceived in a rare, half-playful vein of modern philosophical irony.

Hamsun, it might be said, could have done nothing more appropriate in his last years than thus to allow his mature and mellow fancy to create the marvelous *tour de force* in the portrayal of the vagabond type which we come upon in Abel Brodersen. The tale itself has no moral, no apparent direction. Hamsun is here merely playing with the materials of life and of fancy, weaving them together according to no particular pattern—as Lear proposed that he and Cordelia might do in the days of the mad King's decline.

> We two alone will sing like birds i' the cage:
> When thou dost ask me blessing, I'll kneel down,
> And ask of thee forgiveness: so we'll live,
> And pray, and sing, and tell old tales, and laugh
> At gilded butterfles, and hear poor rogues
> Talk of court news; and we'll talk with them too,
> Who loses and who wins; who's in, who's out;
> And take upon 's the mystery of things,
> As if we were God's spies: and we'll wear out,
> In a wall'd prison, packs and sects of great ones,
> That ebb and flow by the moon.

In the character of Abel in *The Ring Is Closed* we find neither a note of optimism nor of pessimism, no condemnation of society or of civilization, no striving, no belief in some bracing formula of life such as is implicit in *Growth of the Soil.* Hamsun—now an old man, gray, and not too vigorous—is simply sitting in the corner by the fireplace, warming our hearts by spinning out a bit of fantasy . . . a curiously strange and fascinating tale that the sensitive reader is hardly prepared to judge by any ordinary standards of criticism.

For half a century now we have come to expect a novel every few years from Hamsun's pen. And they have always come, sometimes to give us the richest kind of narrative pleasure, sometimes to bring us momentary, for the most part partial disappointment, always to provide us with something which is provocative, stimulating, bracing. It may well be that some readers of Hamsun will conclude, at the last, that as a critic of modern society he is not entirely satisfactory, chiefly perhaps because his satire is too often directed at obvious, and possibly not characteristic targets—at Fru Heyerdahl, the sentimental feminist humanitarian in *Growth of the Soil*, at Rektor Oliver, stupidly academic pedant in *Chapter the Last*, at cheap journalism and democratic bureaucracy and aesthetic parasites in other of his novels. . . . It should be said, however, that such satiric thrusts are not Hamsun at his greatest, nor are they especially typical. They are to be looked upon rather as but the incidental satiric superfluities thrown off by a somewhat over-rich creative fertility. It should be remembered that Fru Heyerdahl is not central in *Growth of the Soil*, a novel primarily concerned with a positive doctrine in which Hamsun seeks to suggest a necessary balance between man and the soil. And it should not be forgotten also that this novel is but the most clear-cut illustration that can be cited to suggest the vein of a positive social doctrine that appears as one of the most constantly recurring themes in Hamsun's novels.

One need not argue Hamsun's final greatness as a novelist, however, in terms of his adequacy as a social critic. The future may well be little concerned about this phase of Hamsun's work. Hamsun's greatness, in the last analysis, is to be found primarily in his more purely literary qualities. His incontestable contribution to world literature is to be found in a succession of magnificently living individual characters, in a narrative fertility such as the world of literature has seldom seen, and perhaps above all in a prose style which in its sensitivity of utterance often comes as close to sheer, pulsing poetry as any prose well can. Hamsun's prose style is in its way as lyric as is that of Selma Lagerlöf; and though it may not be so consistently even in quality, so invariably delicate and controlled in its tone, it embraces a much greater variety of poetic moods and nuances, ranging from grimly sardonic irony to the most delicately pure lyric tones. One fondly wishes to close a chapter on Hamsun by quoting a passage of his most characteristic prose—and possibly point out, by the way, that which seems to give to this prose its peculiar lyric beauty. But I must desist, in due respect to Hamsun's art; for the real flower of Hamsun's prose must remain forever a part of the Norwegian idiom which is its living glory. To quote Hamsun in translation—even in a good translation, such as Wooster's in *Growth of the Soil*—will scarcely serve to suggest with any real finality that subtly nuanced play of poetic tones and undertones which are the final secret of its fascination and its power.

Hamsun's Anglophobia, which very early asserted itself and periodically appears in his work, erupted during the Second World War in its most extreme form. During the Nazi occupation of Norway, he collaborated with the invader, writing articles in which he urged the Norwegian people to cease resisting the Nazis and insisted that the real enemy was England. After the war he spent time under observation in a psychiatric clinic and an old people's home. The psychiatrists consulted by Hamsun's trial court reported that Hamsun suffered from "permanently impaired mental faculties," a conclusion which in all probability was less motivated by scientific judgments than by a desire not to bring Hamsun to trial. Three years later the ninety-year-old Hamsun published another book, his last, entitled *Paa gjengrodde Stier* (*On Overgrown Paths*), a book which strongly reminds one of the early Hamsun, the Hamsun of such works as *Pan* and *Under the Autumn Star*.

Hamsun's tragic stand in the 1940's has appealed to a certain kind of literary investigator, the most fatuous of whom have tried to find in passages torn from context Nazi sympathies in Hamsun's entire authorship. Only after his death in 1952 has this form of anti-Hamsun reaction subsided.

CHRISTIAN ETHICS IN A PAGAN WORLD

SIGRID UNDSET

TO a casual observer a photograph of Sigrid Undset is at first misleading. The face that we behold is heavy, full-formed, almost placid in its lack of striking lines or marked, sculptured features. The mouth is full, with a heavy under-lip; the nose regular, though rather large than small; the eyes far-off, dreaming, meditative, under a somewhat low yet well-formed brow; the hair dark, luxuriant, hanging low and full over roundly slanting temples. In no feature of this face does an off-hand examination catch the steady, penetrating intensity of mind and feeling that is the most characteristic trait of Sigrid Undset's genius. A second, more careful, examination of those features, however, causes one to pause—the eyes, though dreaming, are not soft . . . they have a certain moody, piercing quality, especially suggested by a sharp, very dark iris; and the generous fullness of lip and nose are not without their intimation of a scarcely slumbering sensuousness. It is these qualities of feature—on first glance not particularly arresting—that reveal to the discerning observer the Sigrid Undset that is to be found everywhere in the pages of her novels.

Sigrid Undset is a moralist, first of all, though she is certainly not by temperament an ascetic. She has a profound, brooding awareness of the domination of the flesh in the average human life, the central place of passion in the average human destiny. To Sigrid Undset the immediate, as well as the ultimate, truth about purely human life is the central reality of sex; and in the recognition of this truth she is one with not a few of her contemporaries. Still she does not—as do some modern authors—accept the actual dominance of sex in human life as essentially a blessing, for which man must be grateful, or as a primarily constructive fact of human existence, upon which an adequate positive philosophy of life may be built. Though sex is to her of central importance, the free, natural functioning of sex is not looked upon by her as an unmixed blessing. It is, rather, simply a fundamental condition of human existence which has in it much of evil, simultaneously with some good—and man never attains the complete, the *good life* by means of it alone. Hers is, in the last analysis, a severe, a high morality: between the flesh and the spirit there exists a constant, intensive strife—and the spirit must eventually triumph over the flesh if man is to be good. This is the dominant theme of Sigrid Undset's two greatest works, the historical novels *Kristin Lavransdatter* (1920-1922) and *The Master of Hestviken* (1925-1927), as well as her novels dealing with contemporary life which have appeared after *The Master of Hestviken*; and the theme is more or less explicit in the long series of early stories which came from her pen before the composition of *Kristin Lavransdatter*.

It is perhaps largely in consequence of such a rigid, uncompromising morality that the picture of the world which we come upon in the pages of Sigrid Undset is so heavy, so unyieldingly realistic, so essentially tragic in most of its immediate implications. No Scandinavian author of first importance—with the single exception of Amalie Skram—has given us a more consistently sombre portrait of life than has Sigrid Undset. Strindberg's naturalistic dramas have provided us with more starkly *concentrated* visions of human tragedy than are to be found in Sigrid Undset's novels. But we remember—to mention only two of Strindberg's other works—that he escapes entirely from the note of bitterness and of tragedy in such a fairy-piece as *Swanwhite* (1902) and in the dominantly humorous peasant novel *The People of Hemsö* (1887); and it is not to be forgotten that in general Strindberg's work is reasonably buoyant and elastic in tone despite his temperamental misanthropy and his intermittent flirting with a theoretical pessimism. Ibsen has brought to us sufficiently powerful and disillusioning tragedy in such plays as *Ghosts* and *Rosmersholm*; but his work on the whole certainly does not have that sheer, brutally consistent *accumulation* of tragic detail and tragic theme which we find in Sigrid Undset's novels. Many of Ibsen's plays contain a vein of humor approaching pure comedy, and in nearly all of his important dramas he employs forms of irony which are certainly not to be confused with the tragic muse in its most sombre dramatic manifestations.

If one wishes to find consistent parallels in Northern literature to Sigrid Undset's intently massive gloominess of spirit one must turn to the women novelists of her country. It remains one of the interesting curiosities in Norway's literary history that a small group of women have contributed to Norwegian literature its most dark and sombre, its most uncompromisingly tragic realistic strain. Camilla Collett may be said to have introduced, tentatively, this sombre strain into the Norwegian novel in her *The Governor's Daughters*, as early as 1855; Amalie Skram continued in a similar strain, intensifying it, brutalizing it, and giving to it the most extreme of pessimistic implications, in a series of novels later in the century, the most important of which is her tetralogy *Hellemyrsfolket* ("The People of Hellemyr," 1887-1898); and Sigrid Undset, together with Nini Roll Anker, maintains this sombre tradition in the novel down into our own generation.

Amalie Skram—except for Sigrid Undset the most significant of these women novelists—reveals in her work a genius quite akin to her more famous successor. She sees life with the same heavy, piercingly brooding absorption; she presents individual scenes with the same fierce, immediate intensity; she is just as uncompromising in her insistence upon presenting reality as she sees it—a sad, aching, hopelessly unrelieved reality. She reminds one strongly of Zola at times, except that her vision, less ranging and inclusive, is correspondingly more intense, more essentially heavy and tragic. The fierce and morbid intensity of her vision finally took its toll upon herself: nervous disorders, at times amounting to a condition of insanity, burdened her last years; and in 1905 she died of a heart attack while at work on her last novel. An uncompromising exponent of naturalism, her sensitive feminine genius broke down, perhaps inevitably, under the appalling implications of a rigidly deterministic view of life.

Sigrid Undset's vision is no less intense than was that of Amalie Skram. She might also, in consequence, have been driven to madness or to suicide had a fundamentally idealistic urge in her temperament not early asserted itself and had she not finally identified her idealism with the positive contents of Christian faith as represented in the Catholic Church. The story of her conversion is a long and involved one, her actual entrance into the Church not taking place until 1925. The details of her religious development must be taken up later in this essay, for they are intimately bound up with her literary development. Here we can only pause long enough to offer one central generalization: her ultimate conversion is to be looked upon simply as the final, inevitable step in a severe moral discipline growing naturally and directly out of her realistic view of human life. Sigrid Undset found life too intricate, too complicated, too fundamentally evil in many of its dominant manifestations to be possible of living without a dogmatic religious faith. God—the God of the Catholic church—became to her a necessary postulate of existence. This, as we shall see, was becoming increasingly apparent to her long before 1925. That year simply marks the final, public acceptance of "the Church" as the ultimate source and guide in her religious thought. Her preoccupation with the Middle Ages in her two most important novels, *Kristin Lavransdatter* and *The Master of Hestviken*, no doubt played its part in Sigrid Undset's final "conversion"; and the novels dealing with contemporary life which appear after *The Master of Hestviken* are for the most part thinly veiled propaganda novels, whose primary purpose seems to be "a dissemination of the Faith."

I

Sigrid Undset was born in the charming little Danish town Kallundborg in Sjælland on the 20th of May 1882. Her mother was the daughter of the mayor of Kallundborg; her father was the well-known Norwegian archaeologist Ingvald Undset. The father was born in Trondheim, and he traced his ancestry back to an ancient Norwegian peasant stock from Østerdalen. His early impressions of the famous cathedral at Trondheim determined his life work. Besides his purely technical studies, Ingvald Undset was the author of *Fra Akershus til Akropolis* (1888-1892), a work rather famous in its day and still very readable, in which he revealed descriptive and interpretative talents which resemble similar abilities in the work of his more famous daughter.

During the first two years of Sigrid Undset's life the family remained in Kallundborg, except for the father's occasional trips abroad, especially to Italy, for purposes of archaeological investigation. In 1884, however, the Undset family moved permanently to Norway, establishing themselves in Christiania so that the father could be near museums and libraries in which he might continue his research. These early Christiania years—down through Sigrid's eleventh year—have been brilliantly chronicled for us in the pages of *The Longest Years* (1934), the first installment in Sigrid Undset's autobiography.

At first the family settled on the outskirts of Christiania, where the children lived a reasonably free, natural existence and where little Sigrid in particular, always intensely sensitive to outward impressions, gained her first vivid knowledge of the fascinating physical world about her. Later they moved down into the heart of the city in order that the father, whose health was becoming year by year more precarious, might be nearer to the museums and scientific collections. Here the little daughter gained her earliest direct impressions of urban conditions, particularly those of the lower middle and poor classes. Her first novels are later to deal with these conditions—poverty, struggle, often narrowly commonplace small tragedy, relieved only partially in these novels by the presence of a rather hesitating, somewhat inarticulate idealism.

Though Sigrid Undset revealed certain unmistakable signs of precocity as a child, she was on the whole a sufficiently normal girl; and her experience and upbringing during childhood— except for an unusual early interest in history and archaeology— did not depart radically from that of most of the children of her class in the Norway of the late nineteenth century. In her earliest years her feelings could be aroused to an intensity that suggests reserves of passion characteristic of her mature authorship; but her parents maintained a certain severity in her upbringing, even though in most matters she was permitted entire freedom. Sentimental confidences between child and parent were not expressly forbidden, but the children somehow understood that these were normally taboo. "Confidences were not much in

Anine's [the mother's] line—the children felt something in their
mother's manner which seemed to warn them; if they had something on their minds which they positively must confide to someone, then she was ready to listen. But she liked them better when
they could get on without it."

The result in little Sigrid was a certain independence of spirit,
a strong-willed brooding over matters upon which she came to
make her own decisions or about which she came to draw her
own conclusions. These conclusions were not always solidly
founded ones, for the child's lack of experience with people and
her limited knowledge of the world provided rather insufficient
grounds for many of her conclusions; and yet a certain innate
taste, sharpened by a precocious, only partly conscious intelligence, quite frequently led her to judgments which were unusually telling and mature. As a mere school-girl she despised
the mawkish, sentimental tales provided for girls in the schools
of the day—translations of German stories for "höhere Toch-
ter" and Louisa May Alcott's *Little Women*. Of the former—

During the needlework lessons the mistress read aloud to the
children. When Ingvild [the name Sigrid Undset gives to herself
in the autobiography] entered the school they were engaged on
a book called *Wild Cat*, by Emmy von Rhoden. When they had
come to the end of it in class, the teacher offered to lend Ingvild
the book to take home—she hadn't heard the beginning, and it *was*
so amusing. Now, Ingvild had not been so terribly amused by the
part she had heard—even at the age of eight or nine the facetious-
ness of German stories for "höhere Töchter" struck her as queer
and insipid stuff. . . .

Of the latter—it was "doubly irritating," after listening to
Svend Dyrings Hus, "to have to hear about Louisa Alcott's
Little Women. They were so insufferably mawkish, whether they
were sweet or refractory or skittish"!

Her parents' condemnation of juvenile literature doubtless
shaped to some extent little Sigrid's reaction; but this cannot be
said to have determined the little girl's reading tastes entirely,
for we know that the parental rejection, or bare toleration, of
racier romantic tales—Indian stories, voluptuously morbid tales
of "high adventure," the whole body of cheap, sensational read-

ing matter which found favor among the servant classes—did not lead Sigrid immediately to reject them. She read considerable quantities of such literature surreptitiously, and not without a delight of a sort; but, even as she enjoyed this reading, she did not fail to recognize the basic faults of these tales. Deliciously real is Sigrid Undset's recollections of some of her clandestine childhood reading—

In the maids' room she read romances—*A Falling Star on Ekeberg* and *The Bergen Regicide, or the Bloody Wedding at Nidaros* and *The Cottage Boy from Odalen* or whatever they were called, all the works of Julius and Rollo and John Flatabø, bound volumes which lay concealed beneath Karoline's underclothes in the bottom drawer but one of her chest of drawers, to which Ingvild had free access. Without the exchange of a word they both knew that Ingvild would not have been allowed to read them if she asked her mother. And indeed she read them with something that resembled a bad conscience but was more than that—she was not blind to their poor literary quality, and patted herself on the back for seeing it. But she saw much more—there was something in these romances which made one think of tainted water that has been forgotten in a carafe, of all the foul and unwholesome smells whereby the town became familiar to her senses. And they fascinated her in precisely the same way as this quarter of the town where she now lived fascinated her and gave her fresh interests day by day—so that she no longer knew whether she liked living here or not.

Her taste here is sure, and it is *her own* in that ill-defined but final sense in which unusually sensitive children have taste. She could not say *why* she in the last analysis disliked the stuff of these tales—except that they reminded her somehow of "tainted water" and of "all the foul and unwholesome smells whereby the town became familiar to her senses."

Sometimes her negative judgments were not so sound, and much more poorly defined—merely a precocious child's perversity, a kind of "spirit of opposition" (the phrase is Sigrid Undset's) for its own sake. Long before the age when she might have been expected to form adequate opinions on subjects that required substantial and extensive knowledge she was ready to react against certain current ideas with what was largely a mere childish perversity. Particularly is this true of her unexpressed though deeply felt reaction toward contemporary political questions, which were frequently discussed in little Sigrid's presence by the "grown-ups" in her family circle.

It is not to be thought, however, that Sigrid Undset's girlhood temper was an entirely negative and critical one. She had some very profound positive enthusiasms, the two most important of which were her rich, sensitive, immediate response to nature and her precocious interest in archaeology and history. Already in her very earliest years she responded with unusual intensity to all the forms and moods of nature that came within the scope of her observation. She spent hours watching "Herr Wister," a kindly neighbor, working in his flower garden; and when he talked to her about his flowers, she was enraptured. She responded with an almost premonition-like fullness to the general phenomena of steady growth and gradual decay in a nature moving ceaselessly, mysteriously with the seasons. She early revealed remarkably exact powers of observation toward the minuter aspects of nature—fine color shadings, intricacies of natural form, the constant, infinitesimal daily changes in plant life. Though all of her senses were marvelously alert to physical impressions, particularly prominent already as a child was her sense of smell. "The impressions she gained through scent," we are told in *The Longest Years*, "were in a way more intimate and happier than any others. . . ."

Scores of illustrations of this statement might be cited from the pages of this autobiographical document; and any reader of Sigrid Undset must be impressed by the marvelously acute sense of smell that is everywhere present in her novels. No novelist, with the possible exception of Zola, has had a more remarkably developed olfactory organ; and Sigrid Undset surpasses even Zola in the marvelous variety and range of her olfactory sensations. Note the variety in the following passage, taken at random from *The Longest Years*—

·The air of the old town had a strange smell peculiar to itself—an acrid odour of filth and all the offal incidental to daily life, and a manifold and powerful scent of all the luxuriant growth and flowering in the little yards and gardens, where the mould had been fertilized by many centuries of human occupation. All the slops from the houses lay stagnant and nauseating in open gutters, till an occasional thundershower came and cleaned them up. The bad smell from the outhouses was allayed by the strange, keen fragrance of the vine-leaves, for most people had a trellised vine on their warmest wall, and one of the local excitements was always—will the grapes ripen this year? In nooks and corners the elder-bushes grew high as trees and made it dark and muggy in their shadows; early in the summer all other smells were drowned in the sweet, cool scent of their thousands of pale yellow blossoms; later on they made the air spicy with their peculiarly rank odour which reminds one of the smell of sweat, but is good all the same. But when the limes were in blossom the whole place was wrapped in their breath of honey and the buzz of myriads of bees and wasps and bumble-bees at work on the pale bunches of blossom beneath the roof of leaves.

One seldom, if ever, comes upon in Zola's pages such a subtle, *finely natural* blending of brutal and delicate physical detail. Sigrid Undset's olfactory sensitivity, in contrast to that of Zola, is always natural, concerned alone with the actual experience of sensation, despite its hypersensitiveness to some detail. Zola's use of the sense of smell, on the other hand, can only be described as *phenomenal*; one is more fascinated by its sheer olfactory gymnastics than impressed by its steady, inevitable realism, its honestly observed foundation in the truth of actual experience. His sense of smell reflects few of those delicately varied nuances which one comes upon so frequently in the pages of Sigrid Undset.

As a child Sigrid Undset was interested in all phases of natural phenomena: in the broad sweep of landscape viewed from some jagged outcropping of *fjeld*; in the immediate details of the open fields in which she played near her first home on the outskirts of Christiania; in the gardens of the neighbors; and in those pathetic, half-stunted efforts of vegetation—"black and dirty so long as they were bare"—which she came to observe in the congested heart of the city. Together with her father, especially in the years just before his death, she read regularly the copy of *Naturen* that came to their home; and here her own direct observations of nature were sometimes verified, sometimes enlarged, nearly always rendered more exact by the precise scientific formulae of these columns usually written by careful, trained naturalists. Her actual observations and such reading combined to develop already in her childhood a remarkably sensitive and accurate sensuous apparatus.

Though her parents, particularly her father, encouraged her childhood interest in all the world of nature about her, she would doubtless have pursued her observations of natural phenomena without any parental urging. More purely a direct result of paternal influence was Sigrid Undset's precocious interest in history. She lived, as a child, in an historical environment. Her father was a historian and scholar of the pure stamp. Though he could take a lively momentary interest in details of the present, he *lived* in the past, handling historical documents and archaeological objects—of which the home was full—with a lovingly severe scholarly enthusiasm. At first little Sigrid could not understand much that her father related to her about these things; yet she kept her eyes and ears wide open, and little by little she came to catch something of the historical vision that dominated her father's short but intense experience of life. Not that she did not mix fact with fancy, particularly in her very early years. On one occasion, for instance, she built up vast, fantastically apocryphal associations (about which she told no one) suggested by certain urns which she knew archaeologists had identified with a certain East Prussian family.

. . . She couldn't have explained to herself why she never uttered a word about all the other things she knew about them. Those that had rings of metal wire strung through their ears were captains, because there was a picture hanging in Henriksen's shop of a man smoking a pipe who had rings in his ears, and he was a captain. The East Prussian captain-urns all had pipes, only they hadn't been drawn in the pictures, and they were full of tobacco inside, like the face-urn she had seen on the bureau at the farmer's. And then because that one was full of tobacco it belonged to the East Prussian family, although it was different from all the other urns; its face was colored and it had a blue coat and a yellow waistcoat over its fat stomach. And when she came to another urn, with an indistinct face and two little breasts modelled in its bulging side, and said it came from Peru, and Peru was in America, her father certainly had no idea that she imagined Peru to be a side-street off the Hegdehaug Road, where the urn woman stood behind the counter in a butcher's shop; she chopped up big joints into smaller pieces and weighed out mincemeat and said: Dear? Oh no, madam, it's cheap for such choice beef as this—and she and her children never had anything for dinner but beefsteak and pork chops.

Later Sigrid's knowledge of history became more detailed and solid, less confused by early childhood's fanciful world of associations; but her response to historical material became scarcely less spontaneous and natural in later years despite an historical discipline little calculated to appeal to a normal child of tender years.

As soon as she had mastered the alphabet she was set to the task of ploughing through Siegwart Petersen's *History of Norway*, distinctly heavy going for a young child. During her early school years she set about on her own initiative reading Daae and Drolsum's *History of the World*—in six formidable volumes. Her father had half jokingly promised her two crowns if she would read it *through*! The task took two long years of the child's spare time, but she persisted, and earned the coveted two crowns. "Afterwards"—the pages of *The Longest Years* testify—"she was surprised to find how little she remembered of it apart from the frequent moral indignation of the authors with the historical personages of whom they treated." In spite of their having scandalized "the professors," she thought the various French Louises and their mistresses really looked attractive—"they were handsome in their big curly wigs and the ladies in their low-necked dresses bedecked with pearls"! Her father not only told his daughter tales based upon historical records ancient and modern; he introduced her to the intricacies of historical method, the severe disciplines necessary in an examination of historical documents. Perhaps the little girl did not understand much of this; but she caught the spirit of it at any rate, and her later historical novels provide evidence that her father's severe distinctions between historical fact and historical fancy were seeds not planted in vain in the mind of his precocious little daughter.

When Sigrid had come to the half-way point in her twelfth year her father died. He was only forty when his little daughter saw him for the last time—"the yellowish waxen image of a man," still and cold in death. She remembered in later years, with a strangely affectionate half-detachment, all of the details of the days which followed: the preparations for the funeral, the act of burial itself, the dreary, dismal, empty days which immediately succeeded.

They went to the cemetery every day during this first time. It snowed and the snow thawed again, the paths were muddy and the black trees hung with drops. The flowers on the grave were withered, nasty, and drenched with rain, the ribbons were limp and sodden. The grinning mound of yellow clay showed through more and more.

They went up there with a wreath which had arrived the day after the funeral. It was from Marit's godfather, papa's best friend in Denmark. It was of laurel-leaves without a single flower; that was fine. On the broad red and white ribbon were some runes and underneath in Danish: "Few better will come after."

Ingvild knew very well where that came from—it was the conclusion of the inscription on the Tryggevælde stone, and it was a wife who had raised it to her husband. And suddenly she seemed to see it all—men dying and dying, they had gone on dying through all the thousands of years, and among all the forgotten dead there had always been some whose loss their nearest and dearest thought irreparable and of whom they said: "Few better will come after." And then they went on living.

The passage is typical of Sigrid Undset: descriptive phrases of an almost brutal realism, relieved momentarily by a sparely expressed note of idealism, which in turn becomes largely dissipated by a sombre generalization about human destiny; and the whole brought to an abrupt close with a short, clipped sentence which brings the reader face to face with the commonplace, undemonstrative reality of everyday life—"And then they went on living."

Her father's death had a profound effect upon the girl Sigrid. With a child's natural resiliency of spirit, she scarcely *brooded* long over the fact; rather had she found new, immediate occa-

sions to discover some elements of joy in life. But serious
thoughts did come to her.

. . . It seemed to her that she already knew so much that was evil
in the world and so much that was boundlessly good that it was
all beyond her—there was so much to shudder at and so much to
rejoice in that for a moment she almost felt weary in advance.—
The little mountain outside shining in the sun, the home that had
drawn closer and was beginning to heal after its loss, the freedom
which awaited her out in the fields—she was so happy in it all that
she could hardly bear such happiness—.

The strong undertone of fatalism in this otherwise rather
buoyant and cheerful passage may be partly that of the mature
Sigrid Undset recollecting, with some additions, her earlier
thoughts; yet whatever the relative proportions of child and
woman in the passage, it is certain that these words are in
thorough keeping with all that Sigrid Undset wrote about life
in that series of novels which began with the publication of *Fru
Martha Oulie* in 1907, thirteen years after the death of her
father.

Meantime she completed whatever scant formal schooling her
widowed mother could afford for her, the last part of which
was spent at the commercial college in Christiania; and at the
age of sixteen she took a clerical position in this city. She retained this position for the next ten years, occupying herself
simultaneously, however, with private studies, especially in the
English Middle Ages and the Renaissance, and with literary
exercises in preparation for a literary career. At twenty years
of age she had completed an historical novel, but the publisher
to whom she turned with her manuscript counselled revision.

II

Her formal literary career began in 1907, with the publication of the modern story of marriage entitled *Fru Martha Oulie*.
Thirteen years were to elapse before the appearance of the first
volume of *Kristin Lavransdatter,* another and infinitely greater
story of married life worked out over against a marvelously
rich medieval background. These thirteen years were marked by
a steady, if not prolific, production of novels and stories, a few

essays, and a single volume of not very distinguished verse. This production, though of unequal quality, is of one piece in its substance and in its method; and though on the surface it does not inevitably point to Sigrid Undset's final great triumph in *Kristin Lavransdatter*, it is to be looked upon nevertheless as the material of a severe and ultimately successful apprenticeship— an apprenticeship which upon close examination serves to explain in considerable measure the superb interpretation of medieval Norway which we come upon in her late historical novels.

We find in this body of early work much that is characteristic of Sigrid Undset at her greatest: a drab, severe, uncompromising realism, quite unafraid in its intensely honest depiction of those narrowly limited milieus in which her characters must live and move and have their being; a sombre, probing preoccupation with human character, for whom she reveals deep sympathies, and yet upon whom she does not hesitate to pass severe judgments; and a thoroughly unsentimental moral idealism, transforming itself by degrees—especially in the novels and short stories which come after *Jenny* (1911)—into a morality increasingly affected by a profound religious instinct. All of this, as we shall see, moves again in *Kristin Lavransdatter* and *The Master of Hestviken*. In these two great historical novels, however, all of this is given a more magnificent perspective: it moves more freely, more easily, more naturally, yet without any loss of solidity, of mass, of honest, forthright realism; and it is conceived with a moral grandeur which is the mark of only the highest tragedy. But these are differences largely in degree, not in kind.

Sigrid Undset's ultimate greatness as a novelist could be attained only by a severe early apprenticeship. Hers is a heavy, uneasy creative genius, which *feels* its way along, cumbersomely, at times awkwardly, with none of that facile spontaneity of genius which explains the relatively rapid literary triumph of Selma Lagerlöf. Sigrid Undset has none of Selma Lagerlöf's immediate lyricism; she deals in none of the rhetorical tricks of the author of *Gösta Berling's Saga*; nor can she see life with the naïve optimism which animates most of the pages of Selma Lagerlöf. Hers is, in strong contrast, a broodingly intense spirit, one that matures more slowly but burns with a more glowing, steady passion. It is impossible to conceive of *Kristin Lavransdatter* as *springing* into a splendid, pulsing existence, as did *Gösta Berling's Saga*, once Selma Lagerlöf had overcome her early diffidence with regard to the form that the novel should take. *Kristin Lavransdatter* came into existence much more laboriously: it *grew*, slowly, painfully, by degrees . . . and at first quite unconsciously, perhaps— stirring about obscurely in some far recess of Sigrid Undset's mind during those more than ten years when she was occupying herself almost exclusively with the fictional material of an immediate contemporary life.

Fru Martha Oulie must have struck its Norwegian readers in 1907 as something peculiarly at odds with the literature of its time. Ibsen had died the year before the appearance of *Fru Martha Oulie*, and Bjørnson was to live only three years longer. Neither of them, however, was at the moment a dominating power in the new literary currents of the day in Norway. The two authors who had perhaps most completely caught the ear of the Norwegian reading public at this time were Knut Hamsun, in the novel; and Gunnar Heiberg, in the drama. Both of them had begun their literary careers in the '90's in strong opposition to the social and ethical emphases of Ibsen and Bjørnson, though by the turn of the century the work of Hamsun and Heiberg had become less personal, less negatively combative, more concerned with new, and what seemed to them more sound positive values. Each of them, in his own way, had come to champion the right of the individual as over against an obtuse and levelling democratic society. We have seen in an earlier chapter that Hamsun's individualism came to find its primary artistic expression in an intensive concern with constantly new variations of his "vagabond hero," the type which had first appeared in the character of Johan Nilsen Nagel in *Mysteries* as early as 1892.

Heiberg's individualism found its central literary expression in a somewhat more fundamental and certainly more radical and challenging form than did Hamsun's. He found the basic conflict between society and the individual to be inextricably bound up with the psychology of love. He found an imperious, passionate love to be an end in itself, operating in constant opposition not only to social institutions but to the basic creative instincts of the artist. Two of Heiberg's most powerful tragedies, *The Balcony* (1894) and *The Tragedy of Love* (1904), develop most sharply the fundamental nature of this conflict. Julia, in *The Balcony*, is the personification of passionate eroticism; she will give herself only to the man who wants *her* above everything else, and who can forget all else *because of her*. Love must be absolute, demanding all, consuming all; it is, therefore, fundamentally anti-social in all of its ultimate implications. Although Karen, the central character in *The Tragedy of Love*, differs somewhat from her earlier prototype, Julia, she still represents the feminine insistence upon the absolute validity of individual love in human experience. Unlike Julia, she does not seek erotic *moments* for their own sake, impulsively following whatever man will bow to her imperious eroticism. She strives rather to find a warm, steady sense of completeness in her love; and when she fails to realize this ideal she chooses death.

It is to be noted that Karen identifies her conception of happiness in love neither with domestic joys and duties, nor with the ties of motherhood and a home; and it is herein that we find the fundamental difference between *The Tragedy of Love* and Sigrid Undset's *Fru Martha Oulie*. "What does love have to do with houses, homes, and all that?" Karen queries at one point in *The Tragedy of Love*. And she concludes, characteristically, that love has nothing at all to do with these. It is against this free, liberal, purely individualistic view of love that Sigrid Undset reacts with all her brooding youthful energy in the pages of *Fru Martha Oulie*.

The heroine of Sigrid Undset's first novel does have, at the first, ideas not unrelated to those of Julia and Karen; but she comes to change them with time, and she finally sees that only in subordinating her individual desires to a severe moral conception of the home can she gain anything like happiness in her life. We find her in the opening pages of the novel married to a worthy, hard-working husband, but one whose views are somewhat narrow and who fails entirely to understand her sensitive "romantic" nature. In consequence she later establishes a liaison with a friend of her husband's; but she finally finds only emptiness in her selfish concern with a purely erotic egotism, and simultaneously she comes to discover beauty only in the stern moral laws of life itself. "In the old days," she comes at last to write in her diary, "I always became angry when it was maintained in books that a woman was happy only when she identified herself entirely with another person. Now I say 'yea' and 'amen' to this—as to all the other worn out and distorted truths which I have denied in my youth."

The bare outline of the story and the theme of *Fru Martha Oulie* which we have sketched seems to suggest a very ordinary tale of modern married life enforcing a very trite and commonplace "moral." And when we remember that the author of this first novel was a young woman of only twenty-five years, we tend to smile a bit at the almost pontifical turn of moralizing that the story takes. This début novel of Sigrid Undset's is not, however, quite as naïve in tone or ordinary in its manner of development as our outline of its contents might suggest. It compares in general quite favorably with other Norwegian fiction being turned out in these years, not the worst years in the history of Norwegian fiction; and in one regard—its steady, sober realism, its honest analysis of human passion, never led astray into hysterical sentimentalities or melodramatic poses— this little novel about domestic life has its own genuine fictional distinction. It is to be emphasized, moreover, that Sigrid Undset's "moralizing" in this novel is motivated neither by the repression complex of mere Puritanism nor by a timidly feminine escape psychology.

Neither in *Fru Martha Oulie* nor anywhere else in her work does Sigrid Undset seek to deny the central validity of love—even passionate love—in human life. In this respect, at least, she is sufficiently "modern"; and in this she is at one with her contemporary Gunnar Heiberg, who is to be looked upon as a typical representative of an early nineteenth century decadent liberalism, a liberalism which had broken away en-

tirely from any extra-individual concepts of authority. Passion
—Sigrid Undset insists already in her first novel—must not be
denied; rather must it be subordinated to certain higher laws
of being. These higher laws of being—so runs the reasoning in
Fru Martha Oulie—have found expression in certain human
institutions, particularly in the institution of the home. Later in
Sigrid Undset's work we shall find her conservative moral
instincts finding other than merely human authority for her
conception of the sacred inviolability of the home. For the present she is satisfied with an idealism founded upon purely natural
and human grounds.

The modest success of Sigrid Undset's first novel encouraged
her to go on with her literary efforts, though she continued to
fill her clerical position as before, not daring as yet to venture
everything upon a literary career. In 1908 she published *Den
lykkelige Alder* ("The Happy Age"), a volume taken up almost
entirely by two short stories which are even more characteristic
of Sigrid Undset's early years as an author than is *Fru Martha
Oulie*. In a sense these stories remind one of her earlier novel;
but on the whole they represent a distinct advance in
narrative technique, being more vivid, more alive, and
carrying their moral more naturally, less obtrusively. Both of
these short stories deal with young women, energetic, capable
young working girls of Christiania, a type which Sigrid Undset
knew at first hand because she herself had come to be of this
class. These young women are rather disillusioned in their
attitude toward life, often depressed by the weary monotony
of their immediate circumstances, the drab commonplaceness of
a working girl's round of existence in Christiania; and yet they
have their dreams—dreams that persist, with a kind of stubborn
buoyancy, in spite of the whole dull play of life about them.

The first of these two tales has a rather artificial plot, and
it reflects at times a form of idealism that seems high-flown
and forced; but the tale is saved from being a failure because
of the intimately realistic study in milieu which it contains. The
second—the tale which is concerned with Charlotte Hedel
and Uni Hirsch—bears the stamp of living reality throughout;
it remains to the present day one of Sigrid Undset's most

consistently living fictional performances despite its short, concentrated *novella* form. Into the two young women's characters Sigrid Undset has poured a great deal of herself: she has not only *observed* such young women—in a sense she has *lived their lives*. She pours all of her sound, healthy natural instincts into Uni Hirsch, whose early dreams are not realized but who finally comes to find in her life certain solid human values of which her late adolescent world of romantic yearnings had never dreamed. Charlotte Hedel, on the other hand, is conceived largely in contrast to Uni Hirsch, especially toward the end of the story. She too has her dreams; but when they cannot be realized in the form which they had originally taken in her dreams she becomes a tragic victim of the eternal conflict between dream and reality.

This Charlotte Hedel is the over-sensitive type of young woman—Sigrid Undset's version of what has been so frequently called "the artist-mentality." She wishes to be an author; and her conception of what she hopes to depict in her stories is Sigrid Undset's own fictional program in the struggling years of her early authorship. In a famous passage in the novel Charlotte Hedel sums up her conception of fiction: the characters are to be "respectable drudges . . . office rats," who insist in spite of their limited circumstances upon living deeply, sincerely within their "own 'burning' hearts"; their environment, the grey work-a-day city (obviously Oslo), is to be sketched with a sharp, relentless realism; their very language is to be reproduced as it is spoken, half-formed, crude, alive; and their insignificant, often sordid destinies are to be followed out into their every meagre consequence, never "alleviated" by a false touch of sentimentality, never "relieved" by a note of vapidly inappropriate "optimism."

The program laid down here is drab, dreary, severe, one perhaps little suited to appeal to the popular reader; and yet Sigrid Undset followed out this program, honestly, with a certain rigidly insistent objectivity, never deviating consciously from the severe restrictions upon her art which such a program necessarily entailed. Her early fiction received a reasonably favorable reception with the Norwegian reading public, though none of her earliest volumes attracted any particular general attention. Sigrid Undset came to be looked upon in those early years of her authorship as a solid workman in her fiction, a narrative artist who could always be depended upon to turn out a sound piece of craftsmanship, and who revealed in her attitude toward life a curious combination of youthful disillusion and idealism that was usually rather intriguing in its forthright, sombre manner.

In 1909 her first published effort in historical fiction— *Gunnar's Daughter*—appeared. It was apparently less of a public success than had been her earlier tales. *Ungdom* ("Youth"), a volume of laborious verse which she published in 1910, proved merely that she had no lyric abilities at all.

In 1911, however, she published a full-length novel which created a small sensation and revealed powers that her earlier fiction had only hinted. This was *Jenny*, the tragic story of a young woman artist, whose late-born erotic experience leads her to hopelessness and finally to suicide because it has been born in impulsive weakness rather than in the strength of her severe conscious idealism. *Jenny* is the earliest novel of Sigrid Undset's which has gained the distinction of an English translation, possibly because of the acclaim with which it has been received by Norwegian critics. I cannot say that I share the almost unreserved admiration which Norwegian critics and literary historians have showered upon the book, though it is doubtless to be ranked as the most *considerable* work of Sigrid Undset's before the publication of *Kristin Lavransdatter*. The novel employs somewhat improbable situations in order to prepare the reader for its final tragic action; it is not without episodes in a highly theatrical, even melodramatic manner; and its composition seems at times more wooden, more self-conscious than is usual even in Sigrid Undset's early work. The translation—as translations are wont—more mercilessly betrays these flaws than does the original; but even the Norwegian text of *Jenny* cannot completely conceal certain limitations in Sigrid Undset's art. Despite these faults, however, the novel does somehow affect

one: we do become intensely concerned about the destiny of
Jenny—perhaps so much so that we are to an extent revolted
(and *not* sentimentally) by the severe judgment which Sigrid
Undset comes finally to pass upon her heroine.

The novel commences in a sufficiently happy vein. The opening chapter introduces us quickly into a mildly Bohemian circle
of Scandinavian artists in Rome in the early years of the twentieth century. Youth dominates the scene—a youth carefree
enough on the surface, yet hard-working, serious, and idealistic
in everything that is central, essential, basic. Jenny Winge,
gifted, capable, independent in spirit, seems to be the most
promising individual in this group—a group which includes also
Francesca Jahrman and Gunnar Heggen, both Norwegians, and
Lennart Ahlin, a young Swedish sculptor. Jenny Winge seems
happy, busy in her work, and confident of a successful future as
an artist.

Very soon, however, complications develop. Jenny, despite her
seeming independence of spirit and her apparent absorption in
her work, feels somehow, vaguely yet intensely, that her final
destiny as a woman lies in her complete and full identification
with another. Helge Gram, a sensitive, and enthusiastic young
archaeologist, meets her at this time—in Rome, in the spring-
time. Before Jenny knows it she is engaged to him. Soon, however, she realizes that Helge—though young and enthusiastic and
sensitive—is really not the man of her dreams, the man in whom
she can completely lose herself. She has really been insincere,
quite untrue to her deepest ideals in her momentary feeling for
Helge Gram. In a moment of weakness—driven on by her
vague inner yearnings, tortured by momentary feelings of
futility and emptiness, and influenced by the countless little outward beauties that springtime in Rome brings to the young—she
had yielded to young Gram, making promises which she knows
that she cannot finally fulfill. An oft-told tale, this—and one
that a less serious young woman than Jenny would have lived
through, with time, and gone on, little changed.

But Jenny is not of this kind. She considers herself soiled,
even though she had merely given a promise—nothing else. She

returns to Christiania; broods constantly, hopelessly; breaks
with Helge, only to become involved with Helge's father,
Gert Gram, a weak, though sensitive man of middle-age, whose
own marriage had been a failure, but who preserved, with a certain sentimental persistency, a dream of *the love*. He was gentle
in manner, and sympathetic with Jenny in her trials. He seemed
to understand how to bring comfort to her tortured spirits. In
a moment of weakness, Jenny yields to Gert Gram—this time
physically. At the very moment of yielding, however, she knew
this to be a feeble love, one born of distress, almost of desperation; and yet she yielded—"she clung to him with a poor, begging love; she did not want him to thank her for it, only to be
fond of her and say nothing." As days and weeks went by she
came increasingly to see that this weak love was built upon deception—not a crude, conscious deception, and yet deception.

Jenny dared not think of what his plans for the future might be.
Did he think they would marry?

She could not deny to herself that she had never for a second
thought of binding herself to him for good, and that was why she
felt the bitter, hopeless humiliation and shame at the thought of
him when she was not with him and could hide in his love. She had
deceived him—all the time she had deceived him.

Her torments grow as she broods over her only half-willing
words and acts of love—

. . . she had been faced with the necessity of saying words stronger
and more passionate than her feelings, and he had believed them.
And it happened again and again. When she came to him depressed,
worried, tired of thinking what the end of it all would be, and saw
that he understood, she used again the tender words, feigning more
feeling than she had, and he was deceived at once.

He knew no other love than the love which was happiness in
itself. Unhappiness in love came from outside, from some relentless fate, or from stern justice as a vengeance for old wrongs. She
knew what his fear was—he dreaded that her love would die one
day when she saw that he was too old to be her lover, but he never
had a suspicion that her love was born a weakling and had in it the
germ that would lead to death. It was no good trying to explain
this to Gert; he would not understand. She could not tell him that
she had sought shelter in his arms because he was the only one who

had offered to shelter her when she was weary to death. When he offered her love and warmth she had not the strength to reject, although she knew she ought not to accept it—she was not worthy of it.

At last she acts, departs from Christiania when she is to have a child.

Then Sigrid Undset pursues her heroine relentlessly to the final violently tragic end. Jenny first finds pathetic temporary refuge with "a teacher's widow" in a dreary little village outside Copenhagen. "The widow lived in a tiny yellow, sadly ugly brick cottage outside the village by the main road, which ran dusty and endless between open tilled fields, but Jenny was pleased on the whole." Later, when time was short before the arrival of the child, she moved on to a dismal north German fishing village.

So she moved from one widow to another, and into another small cottage—this time a red one with white-washed window-sills and standing in a little garden with flagged paths and shells around the flower-beds, where the dahlias and chrysanthemums stood black and rotting. Twenty to thirty similar houses stood along a small street leading from the railway station to the fishing harbour, where the waves foamed against the long stone piers. On the beach, a little way from the village, stood a small hotel with the shutters up. Endless roads, with bare, straggling poplars bending in the wind, led out over interminable plains and swamps past small brick farms with a strip of garden front and a couple of haystacks at the back.

The child which ultimately came to Jenny under these forlorn circumstances was undersized at birth and very feeble. Jenny wanted to believe, however, that it was healthy, even potentially vigorous; and so she did believe—futilely. Sigrid Undset devotes a single mercilessly relentless sentence to the child's death: "Then one morning he fell ill, and by midday it was all over." The blow is a terrible one for Jenny; she struggles apathetically through a severe, protracted illness, but ultimately she regains some measure of health, though not any of the old youthful buoyancy of spirit. She goes to Rome again, planning vaguely to take up her work afresh; but she broods constantly, with heavy fatalistic hopelessness, quite unable to throw off a feeling of utter humiliation, of personal degradation; and she dies by

Sigrid Undset 309

her own hand after Helge had violated her, innocent of any knowledge of the relations between her and his father.

It is characteristic of Sigrid Undset that seventy pages (of the three hundred given over to the entire novel) are devoted to a minute, circumstantial depiction of the horrors of the lonely, terror-filled period of advanced pregnancy and childbirth and the violently tragic aftermath in Rome. The novel reminds one of Guy de Maupassant's *Une Vie* in its brutal *lingering* over the sad details of the tragic dénouement. A normally precipitate tragic action is not permitted here. The reader must concentrate, with whatever patience he may have, upon a slow, steady *accumulation* of tragic detail: he must linger, all but sadistically, over the gradual stages in Jenny's final decay; he must finally come to see, always directly, never by subtle narrative implication, the "inevitability" of Jenny's tragic fate in the light of the severe ethical idealism of her earlier years.

Jenny's moral idealism—founded alone upon an inner consciousness of the good and the beautiful, wholly independent of outward, objective forms or institutions—was in the end too weak to cope with her yearnings, her impulses, and the accidents of circumstance with which life had come to surround her. Sigrid Undset's heroines after Jenny, however, are almost without exception not tragic characters in this sense. Most of them ultimately learn to adjust themselves to life, though only after a more or less severe struggle. This is true of Rose Wegner in *Vaaren* ("Springtime," 1914), Sigrid Undset's most important work in the decade between *Jenny* and the publication of *Kristin Lavransdatter*. This is true also of most of the women characters in the two collections of short stories *Splinten av Troldspeilet* ("The Splinter of the Troll Mirror," 1917), and *De kloge Jomfruer* ("The Wise Virgins," 1918). And this is preeminently true of Kristin in *Kristin Lavransdatter* (1920-22).

It is to be noted that the moral emphasis in the stories which succeed *Jenny* becomes more pronounced with each new volume; and we find more and more that the prevailing moral emphasis in these stories becomes gradually invested with an increasingly significant religious element. In *The Wise Virgins* (the title itself is fraught with strong religious associations) the relation between religious faith and morality is clearly implied. The recurrent theme of this collection of stories is the necessity of a profound spiritual experience as the foundation for any sound, lasting love. Other books from these years reveal even more clearly Sigrid Undset's serious preoccupation with religion and with religious thought. In *Fortællinger om Kong Arthur og Ridderne av det runde Bord* ("Stories of King Arthur and the Knights of the Round Table," 1915) she recasts the chivalric material of Mallory, simplifying it considerably and using it as a means of expressing a basically religious view of life.

In a volume entitled *Et Kvindesynspunkt* ("A Woman's Standpoint," 1919) Sigrid Undset published a series of essays, which had appeared at various times in the preceding decade. In these essays she reacts strongly against many of the ideas commonly associated with "the emancipated woman," insisting that woman's place is essentially that of wife and mother, though she need not therefore forego certain of the "rights" which women have obtained in the modern world. These essays are chiefly important, however, as documents for an analysis of Sigrid Undset's more strictly religious development; they reveal very clearly the general lines of development in her religious thinking, from that of a severe ethical idealism to that of a strong positive religious faith. In the essay "Det fjerde Bud" ("The Fourth Commandment," originally published in 1914) she confesses her belief in the idea of God, an idea which to her is of central importance in the history of man's cultural strivings because it is created by his "will to culture" (*kulturvilje*). In "Efterskrift" ("Postscript," 1919), God is no longer interpreted merely as an idea created by man's "will to culture"; in this essay God is conceived as an *objective reality, the fundamental reality of life*—a reality without which man cannot live. And it is in Christianity that she finds the finest, the most complete revelation of this reality. As yet it is Christianity in general, not the Catholic church in particular. *Kristin Lavransdatter* is to be written first.

It is while she is engaged in writing this great historical novel, and perhaps to some extent because of the historical

studies in the Middle Ages necessitated by the composition of
this novel, that she ultimately comes to turn to "the Church" as
the sole authority in what she conceives to be the true Christian
religious experience. That the pages of *Kristin Lavransdatter*
are loaded with Catholic dogma we tend to take for granted,
since the novel deals with an essentially Catholic medieval world.
This, however, is not the only reason. Sigrid Undset is becoming a convert during these very years. In 1925, three years after
the publication of the last volume of *Kristin Lavransdatter*, she
takes the final, official step—becoming one of the most famous
"converts to the Church" in the early twentieth century.

III

Kristin Lavransdatter is certainly to be counted among the
greatest historical novels of all time, and my feeling is that it
ranks first among novels dealing with the Middle Ages. Precisely wherein this work's peculiar distinction lies I shall attempt
to define later; for the moment it would seem desirable to ask
ourselves why the treatment of medievalism in fiction had in
the main failed before Sigrid Undset penned her great trilogy
of *Kristin Lavransdatter*. The question drives us back primarily
to an analysis of the treatment of the Middle Ages in the
Romantic fiction of more than a hundred years ago.

Ever since Romanticism in the late eighteenth and the early
nineteenth centuries succeeded in rescuing the Middle Ages
from the cold critical strictures of a rationalistically informed
literary Neo-Classicism and gave to the Middle Ages "a new
form and substance," it has been a constantly recurring practice
among poets and writers of prose, especially novelists, to go
back to the Middle Ages for their subject matter, to some
extent even for their forms. Much of this "medievalism" which
we have come to associate with Romanticism, however, strikes
the modern mind as only partially satisfactory as the material
of literary art. This is perhaps because today we recognize, more
or less consciously, the inevitable limitations of the Romantic
enthusiasm for the Middle Ages. We recall that the medievalism
characteristic of the Romantic literature of Europe in the late
eighteenth and the early nineteenth centuries tended to take on

either one of two forms. The first form emphasized the pictur-esque, the colorful, for the most part the outward physical aspects of the Middle Ages; and it combined frequently, as might be expected, with the enthusiasm of the Romantic for nature and for landscape poetry. The chief representatives of this emphasis are probably Sir Walter Scott and Victor Hugo. The second form, more psychological in essence, exploited the morbid, the grotesque elements which might be extracted from such materials as were at hand in the Middle Ages. Its charac-teristic literary type was the so-called "Gothic romance" in England and the more extreme *Schauerroman* in Germany. The author who carried this strain to its ultimate limits was E. T. A. Hoffmann, that half-mad German genius—musician, littérateur, extravagant dealer in the occult, and experimenter with obscure and exaggerated sensory experiences. The Gothic romance, it is clear now, was a curious concentrate of medieval-ism and sentimentalism, two of the most characteristic com-ponents of what has been called "the Romantic fever."

Neither the Romantic vogue for the picturesque nor its mor-bid preoccupation with abnormal psychological phenomena has proved to be a phase of Romanticism which interests the dis-criminating general reader today. The former is too superficial, largely physical in its artistic manifestations; the latter is simply unbelievable—it proposes an approach to life that is too eccentric to have any universal powers of appeal. Scott produced mag-nificently in the first of these two strains; but Scott is little read today (perhaps, in one sense, unfortunately), and the reason, no doubt, is that we are suspicious of his constant commerce with the merely picturesque, and his forgetting too often, mean-while, the artistic demands of a profound and convincing psy-chological motivation in his portrayal of character. The Gothic romance was, broadly in contrast to Scott, sufficiently con-cerned with "psychology," but with a fantastic, highly abnor-mal psychology, which has only a limited possible application to life as we know it, and which, even within these limits, was only superficially handled by those third and fourth rate "ro-mancers" who dispensed Gothic "horrors" to the jaded delecta-tion of Romantic appetites. Wordsworth, already in his famous

1800 Preface to the *Lyrical Ballads,* recognized the psychological inadequacies of these "frantic novels, sickly and stupid German tragedies" (late born progeny of the English Gothic romance) ; and he heartily condemns the "degrading thirst after outrageous stimulation" which explains the popularity of such work. Today we all accept his judgment.

Still another difficulty is to be found in Romantic "medievalism": despite its historical pretensions, it was for the most part founded upon a rather superficial historical knowledge. It is to be recognized, of course, that an adequate historical knowledge of the Middle Ages was not available to authors in the late eighteenth and the early nineteenth centuries; but it must be added that in most cases they were not sufficiently concerned about exact historical knowledge to put themselves in possession even of that which was at hand. This may be explained at least partly by the fact that the Romantic's attitude toward the Middle Ages was often a dogmatic, programmatic one: he accepted, with the naïve enthusiasm of a "discoverer," a largely *hypothetical* Middle Ages, which was conceived simply as in diametric opposition to the traditional Neo-Classical distrust of the Middle Ages. To the early Romantic this hypothetical Middle Ages could not be checked over against an actual Middle Ages; the objective historical scholarship of the late nineteenth century was not as yet available.

Perhaps it is not strange then, in the light of the circumstances under which the historical novel came into existence well over a century ago, that no great historical novel dealing with the Middle Ages came to be written at that time. Not even Scott achieved this, despite his brilliant talent in the genre of the historical novel, his rich enthusiasms for historical material, and his not insignificant historical equipment considering the state of historical knowledge on the Middle Ages in his day. A century was to elapse before an entirely satisfactory historical novel dealing with the Middle Ages was to be written. Sigrid Undset achieved it in her *Kristin Lavransdatter.*

Meantime there had been many more or less successful practitioners in the genre of the historical novel in general, most of them merely pale imitators of Scott, almost all of them only partially successful in their work. Even Flaubert—author of *Madame Bovary,* so frequently referred to as "the perfect novel"—failed miserably, though with a certain florid Oriental magnificence, in *Salammbô* (1862). Thackeray, some years earlier, had succeeded admirably in his fictional treatment of the early eighteenth century in *Henry Esmond* (1852). His *Virginians* (1857-59) was less successful. Tolstoy managed a marvelously intricate historical canvas in *War and Peace* (1869), though the historical material of this novel was close enough to the author's own day so that it can be considered an historical novel only in the most liberal sense of the term. No historical novel of the distinction of either *Henry Esmond* or *War and Peace* was written during these years on the subject of the Middle Ages. The novel in the latter half of the nineteenth century occupied itself almost entirely with contemporary life. Even Thackeray and Flaubert are known primarily for novels other than *Henry Esmond* and *Salammbô*; in *Vanity Fair* and *Madame Bovary* they join with Dickens and Hardy, Zola and Guy de Maupassant, Tolstoy and Dostoievski as authors concerned first of all with contemporary society.

Though Sigrid Undset had begun her career in fiction with a realistic portrayal of modern life, her great triumphs came ultimately to be in the historical novel dealing with the Middle Ages. A marvelously happy combination of circumstances account for her magnificent triumph in a field where so many had failed utterly or had been only moderately successful. In the first place, she came to write historical fiction at a time when our knowledge of human psychology had come to be extended far beyond that of the early nineteenth century when Scott first began to write. Again, she came upon the scene at a time when our historical knowledge had become infinitely more extended and precise; and it was her good fortune, already as a child, under the direct tutelage of her father, to come intimately in contact with the traditions and findings of that great group of historical scholars of the late nineteenth century. And finally, her own genius, marvelously sensitive to historical impressions, was capable of combining the sober, intimate realistic detail of a Flaubert and the rich imaginative historical sweep of a Scott. Her early practice in the realistic contemporary novel had taught her the former; her rich native genius, fired by a passionate historical enthusiasm and intensified by a profound moral consciousness, account for the latter. Just how she managed to combine these two techniques into the subtle and complex historical tapestry of *Kristin Lavransdatter* and *The Master of Hestviken* shall perhaps in the last analysis always remain the secret of her genius. And yet the magnificent *fact* of her achievement is undeniable. These two novels—particularly *Kristin Lavransdatter*—rank Sigrid Undset with Tolstoy and Hardy, with Thomas Mann and Marcel Proust as one of the truly great novelists of our time.

It is not one of the simple problems of criticism to indicate with precision just wherein Sigrid Undset's greatness as a novelist lies. And yet, as Walter Pater has so appropriately informed us, it is the duty of the critic, despite his necessary limitations, "to distinguish, to analyze, and separate from its adjuncts, the virtue by which a picture, a landscape, a fair personality in life or in a book produces this special impression of beauty or pleasure, to indicate what the source of that impression is, and under what conditions it is experienced." What, then, is "the virtue by which" Sigrid Undset produces the "special impression of beauty or pleasure" that we experience in reading *Kristin Lavransdatter*? Despite the undeniable power of Sigrid Undset's novel, it is very difficult to define just wherein that power consists, just how it is managed, just why the reader is affected in the way in which he is. Still we must attempt some answers to such questions.

Perhaps the first thing that impresses us in *Kristin Lavransdatter* is the apparent *effortlessness* of the artistic performance, the seeming lack of any conscious narrative devices or tricks, the complete absence of *style* in the narrow literary sense of that word. It has been maintained by some critics, indeed, that Sigrid Undset is not an artist; and insofar as this means merely that she disdains the formal tricks of the conscious literary artist the judgment is true. She never resorts to artistic artifice; she does not pause to form her sentences with sedulous care, nor does she see any virtue in carefully turning her phrases, in searching intently for *le mot juste,* that will-o'-the-wisp of mid-nineteenth century French fiction, practised with all but religious fervor by Flaubert and his immediate French disciples, adopted by such a master of English prose as Pater, and finding its way occasionally (as in Jens Peter Jacobsen) even into the fiction of northern Europe. Sigrid Undset's art—such as it is—simply *grows,* naturally, intensely, sometimes with strangely awkward pregnancy of utterance, out of the plentiful resources of a deeply sensitive, a profoundly serious genius. In consequence it has its faults : there are passages which might profit by greater concentration of phrasing; there are episodes which might move more swiftly, more decisively; there are details which at times might better be omitted. But by these we are only momentarily disturbed, if at all ; for there is so much else in Sigrid Undset's pages to impress the reader—so much more to make him intensely conscious of the existence in *Kristin Lavransdatter* of a kind of truth in art that is more than art alone.

She has no "style," it is true—she merely *writes,* seemingly without especial care, without any particular form, yet under the marvelously sensitive intuitive guidance of an artistic spirit which has been gripped so deeply by her problem that she somehow finds the word that is appropriate, the image that is inevitable, the stylistic tempo and the narrative tone that fits the peculiar burden of her story. The secret of her art in *Kristin Lavransdatter* is to be found in the remarkable intensity, the brooding tenaciousness with which she comes to grips with her subject. Her style is simply a striking individual illustration of what Newman once happily called "a flowing out of thought into language"; it is a style determined in every detail by Sigrid Undset's characteristic habits of mind—the sombre massiveness with which her spirit broods over the essentially sad yet not ignoble materials of human experience.

This lack of stylistic artifice, this wholly natural narrative manner might be illustrated in a great variety of ways from the pages of *Kristin Lavransdatter.* The note is already struck in the forthright directness of the opening paragraphs in the novel; it accounts for much of the medieval idiom (brilliant in the original, not so happy in the English translation) which gives a natural color to the dialogue; it is characteristic of the incidental manner in which both historical background and natural background are employed throughout the novel; it is the secret of the leisurely tempo maintained in the novel's general narrative movement, and explains the apparently sudden intensification of this movement which we come upon in certain crucial scenes; and finally, it is present in Sigrid Undset's deliberately minute analysis of Kristin's character, and in the author's brooding awareness of the ethical values involved in Kristin's struggle with immediate circumstances and with her God. Some critics have insisted that there is nothing really natural in Sigrid Undset's almost morbid preoccupation with the general problem of evil; but this would be to insist upon a very limited conception of what constitutes "the natural." The most superficial analyses of Sigrid Undset's genius must admit that *to her*, at least, *the sombre is the natural*—to brood intently is to live deeply, strongly, completely. Though such a brooding pre-occupation with the problem of evil might tend to lead other novelists to a spirit of complete disillusionment, to a sense of unrelieved, futile tragedy, even to a state of morbidity which would seem to be the opposite of the natural, it leads Sigrid Undset, in fact, to a grandeur of tragic moral conception which we have become accustomed to identify with great tragedy, with the tragic *katharsis* of the Aristotelian aesthetics.

A comparison of the opening scene of Heidenstam's *The Tree of the Folkungs* with the opening paragraphs of *Kristin Lavransdatter* would be sufficient to give one a preliminary awareness of the comparative lack of any conscious "art" in Sigrid Undset's novel. Even though Lavrans Björgulfsön, Kristin's father, is at the outset of Sigrid Undset's novel repre-sented as having descended from the famous Folkung stock of early Swedish kings (a detail that might easily have at-tracted the author's historical imagination, and led her to some either grandiose or mysteriously Romantic assumptions), Sigrid Undset merely mentions the fact in passing as she details in a simple, matter-of-fact way an account of the family histories of Lavrans and his wife Ragnfrid. And much of the bona fide historical materials elsewhere in the novel—events which have at least some actual historical foundation—are introduced just as incidentally as is the purely invented detail of Lavrans's family history. Nowhere in the novel, moreover, are we introduced directly to the color and pageantry of Court life, nor are we permitted to behold, except at a distance, the characteristic manifestations of Court intrigue in medieval Scandinavia. We catch only fragmentary, indistinct glimpses of court intrigues and royal pageantry, and then only as they come to affect directly the immediate conduct of domestic life on the Norwegian countryside which provides the scene and motivates the central action of the novel.

It is perhaps significant that in the historical periods represented in both *Kristin Lavransdatter* and *Olav Audunsson* Sigrid Undset has chosen decades in the medieval history of Norway about which we know very little. The action of *Kristin Lavransdatter* is represented as taking place between the years 1320 and 1350, three decades in Norwegian history that are singularly poor in living historical records. We have a few documents dealing with these years; but they yield merely names, and none of these names represent personalities which have had any living vitality in historical tradition. Knut Porse, Swedish political adventurer, lord of Skåne and ambitious of power in both Denmark and Norway, is the only historical person (aside from Erling Vidkunnsön, Regent of Norway, and certain members of the reigning Norwegian royal family) who plays any really significant part in the novel. And even Knut Porse does not appear actually as a character—we merely hear of him, as men gossip more or less incidentally about political intrigue. Erlend's ill-fated ventures in the second volume of the novel are identified with Knut Porse's intrigues; but at this point in the story Sigrid Undset is much more concerned with Kristin than she is with Erlend, and so we are permitted only stray notes on Erlend's dangerous political activities and his final political and economic degradation.

Sigrid Undset was guided by a marvelous artistic intuition when she placed the action of *Kristin Lavransdatter* in what one Norwegian critic has aptly called "an historical vacuum" (*et historisk tomrum*) ; for our very lack of precise, detailed historical information on the period from 1320 to 1350 permits the imagination of the novelist to range freely, unobstructed by any of the rigidities of actual historical events. She can shape the materials as she wishes to the immediate inner demands of her story, gaining a vivid sense of historical illusion by a multitude of means other than that of the reconstruction of a succession of actual historical episodes. The details of dress; foods and drink, and their preparation; household customs of all kinds; characteristic turns of speech; the manner of thinking and feeling in a still half-primitive Norwegian society;—these are the "historical materials" that are woven into the marvelously detailed and complex pattern of *Kristin Lavransdatter*. It is in this sense, primarily, that the novel is to be considered "historical." The reader is at no time particularly conscious of the actual historical precision with which Sigrid Undset handles her materials; for they are so subtly subordinated to the absorbing central motive of the novel—the story of Kristin—that they never call attention to themselves.

Natural background plays just as important a part in the novel as does historical background; but Sigrid Undset no more permits natural scene to dominate than she does the pageantry and intrigues incidental to historical episode or the numerous paraphernalia of medieval dress and custom and idiom. We are always subtly aware of the magnificent Norwegian landscape which rises in the bleak, imposing fells close about Jörundgaard, Kristin's parental home at Sil in Gudbrandsdal. Equally conscious are we of the impressive sweep of landscape to be seen from Husaby, the ancient manor home to which Erlend brings Kristin as bride and future mistress. Yet natural background, impressive as it is in these regions of Norway, is never described for its own sake; always it is introduced as an integral, and merely supporting, adjunct of the central action in the novel. In *Jenny*, Sigrid Undset's earlier novel, the handling of natural description had been definitely formal by comparison; it often (as in the descriptions of the Campagna) took on the trite, artificial form of the "landscape perspective" so characteristic of Romantic nature poetry, and it lacked for the most part an intimate personal revelation of the immediate detail of nature.

In *Kristin Lavransdatter,* on the other hand, Sigrid Undset's descriptive powers are of an entirely different order. She knew the Norwegian landscape with which she deals here into its minutest details—every flower that spread over its meadows, every plant or shrub that clung precariously to its mountainsides, all the myriad transformations of color and form in the skies and on the earth, the constant stream of change that accompanies the steady revolution of the seasons. Nothing here is hidden, obscure, vague; all is intimate, vivid, intensely alive. Not only does she *see* these details; she *feels* their surfaces, their varied textures, with an acutely delicate and sensitive touch; she *hears* their faintest traces of sound with an ear that is marvelously alert; and, above all, she *smells* every pungent, acrid odor as well as every gentle fragrance given off by nature in her manifold sensory manifestations. And despite the careful, minutely realistic intimacy with which the reader becomes acquainted with the innumerable details of this natural background, Sigrid Undset can on occasion introduce a superb sweep, a magnificently broad perspective to her natural scene. Yet she does this usually in a single paragraph only, sometimes merely in a sentence, always keeping our attention centred primarily on her characters, her vivid central action. Here, for example, is a characteristic paragraph—

And so they rode out of the courtyard in the grey light. The fog lay white as milk upon the parish. But in a while it began to grow thinner and the sunlight sifted through. And, dripping with dew, there shone through the white haze hillsides green with the aftermath, and pale stubble fields, and yellow trees, and rowans bright with red berries. Glimpses of blue mountain-sides seemed rising through the steamy haze—then the mist broke and drove in wreaths across the slopes, and they rode down the Dale in the most glorious sunshine, Kristin in front of the troop at her father's side.

Another typical sweep of landscape, still more concentrated stylistically, and more realistic, is this—

It snowed next morning, but through the day it turned to rain, and soon roads and fields were a sea of grey mud. Wreaths of mist hung and drifted along the lower hillsides; now and then they sank yet lower and gathered into white rollers along the roots of the hills; and then the thick rain-clouds closed in again.

In the passages from which both of these descriptive paragraphs have been drawn, direct, matter-of-fact action immediately precedes and immediately follows; the reader catches merely a glimpse of the landscape in passing—as we usually do in life. This is Sigrid Undset's customary manner.

Occasionally, however, she makes her landscape more essentially *a part* of the action, i.e. she fuses landscape with inner moods of her characters or with the characteristic tone of her action. Perhaps the most magnificent example of this is to be found in the paragraphs given over to Kristin's final departure from Jörundgaard, the "great farm" upon which she had grown up as a child and to which she had returned later as mistress after the loss of Husaby. This passage is long, but it should be quoted entire.

Up on the church-green Kristin turned about and looked down upon her manor—so fair it lay in the dewy, sun-bright morning. The river shone white. The house-folk stood there yet—she could make out Jofrid's light dress and coif, and the child, a patch of red, upon her arm. Gaute saw his mother's face grow pale with the fullness of her heart.

The road bore upwards through the woods under the shadow of Hammer-fell. Kristin walked as lightly as a young maid. She and her son spoke not much together. And when they had walked for two hours, they came where the way bears off over Rostkampen, and the whole Dovre country-side lies spread before one northward. Then Kristin said Gaute must go no farther with her; but she would sit a while and rest before going on.

Down beneath them lay the Dale, with the river's greenish-white riband wandering through it, and the farms like small green patches on the forest-covered slopes. But higher up the upland mosses arched, brownish or yellow with lichen, inward towards the grey screes and the bare heights flecked with snow-drifts. Cloud shadows drifted over the Dale and the uplands, but northward all was clear among the fells; the heaped-up hills had flung off their cloaks of

322 Christian Ethics in a Pagan World

mist, and shone blue, one behind the other. And Kristin's yearning moved with the cloud-flocks northward on the long road that lay before her, hurried over the Dale, in among the great mountains that blocked the way, and along the steep tracks across the uplands. A few days more, and she would be wending her way downward through Trondheim's rich, green dales, following the river's windings towards the great fiord. . . .

But when she looked back over her shoulder, she could still see a little of the home fell below Hövringen. It lay in shadow, but her well-used eye could see where the sæter path went through the woods. She knew the grey mountain-tops that rose above the cloak of forest—they ringed about the Sil dwellers' old sæter fields.

From the hills above came stray notes of a cow horn—a few clear high tones, that died away and came again—it sounded like children practising them in blowing. Far off tinkling of bells—and the muffled roar of the river, and the deep sighs of the forest in the still, warm day. Kristin's heart trembled with unrest in the stillness. She was drawn as with home-sickness onward, as with homesickness backward to the parish and the manor. Visions swarmed before her sight—pictures of daily life: she saw herself running with the goats on the path through the sparse woods south of their sæter—a cow had got mired in the bog—the sun shone brightly; when she stood a moment and listened, she felt her own sweat bite into her skin. She saw the courtyard at home in a flurry of snow— a grey day of storm, darkening into a wild winter night—She was all but blown back into the outer room when she opened the door, the storm took her breath away; but there they loomed up, two shapeless bundles of men in snow-smothered fur coats: Ivar and Skule had come home. Their ski sank deep into the big drift that ever heaped itself together right across the yard when 'twas blowing from the northwest. On such days there were always deep drifts in two places in the courtyard—and all at once 'twas as though she must think with love and longing of these two snowdrifts that she and all folk on the manor had cursed each winter—'twas as if she were doomed never to see them more.

It seemed as if these yearnings burst her heart in sunder—they ran hither and thither like streams of blood, seeking out ways to all places in the wide-stretched lands where she had lived, to all the sons she had wandering in the world, to all her dead beneath the moulds—She wondered—could it be that she was fey? She had never felt the like of this before—

Then she saw that Gaute was sitting staring at her. And she smiled quickly, as if in excuse—'twas time they should say farewell, and she go on her way.

Farewells are finally said, slowly, sorrowfully; and then Gaute turns heavily toward the home over which he now was to be master.

She stood looking after him, till he sank from sight below the brow of the hill. So comely as he was on the big, dark-grey horse.

She felt her mood a strange one—all things without her came so sharply to her sense: the sun-steeped air, the warm breath of the pine wood, the twitter of tiny birds in the grass. Yet at the same time, looking within herself, she saw pictures like the visions that high fever brings—within her was an empty house, wholly soundless, dark and breathing desolation. The vision changed— a strand at ebb, the tide far withdrawn from it; pale, worn stones; heaps of dark, lifeless tangle; all kinds of driftage—

Then she settled her bag more easily on her shoulder, grasped her staff, and set forth on her way down into the Dale.—If 'twere not fated that she should come hither any more, then 'twas God's will—useless to be afraid. And most like 'twas but that she was growing old—She crossed herself and went her way with firmer step—willing all the same to get down to the hill-slopes where the road ran among the farms.

Only from one short stretch on the highway could one see the houses at Haugen, high on the topmost mountain ridge. Her heart set to throbbing at the thought.

The paragraphs seem at first designed primarily to describe the bold sweep of landscape about Jörundgaard; yet the words come alive finally, ebb and flow with deep undertones of meaning, not because of striking landscape detail, but rather because of the poignant flow of human memory which is active here— the thousand intensely intimate fragments of Kristin's past experience that float with a seething, tumultuous, half-tender, half-aching swiftness through a deeply stirred stream of human consciousness. And it is with this stream of consciousness that we become primarily concerned—not with the landscape as such, majestically diversified though it may be as it spreads out below us while we sit intently watchful at Kristin's side.

In its purely narrative movement the novel is slow, leisurely, unhurried, proceeding with a quietly deliberate solemnity, never impatient of detail, ever subtly alert to all those minute forms and phases of outward phenomena which register their impressions upon human character and human destiny. And yet this steady stateliness of general narrative movement gathers itself together at times, leaps into a blazing intensity of feeling or of action in certain individual episodes, only to recede again into its unhurried way—as unhurried as the ceaseless processes of nature and eternity and God. Suffusing it all there is a note of unutterable majesty, even of sublimity—the poignant sublimity with which a story of human fate can become invested when a profoundly unhurried artistry touches it and brings it into the delicately penetrating focus of an intensely serious creative imagination. In Sigrid Undset's work the majesty of nature combines subtly, as at times in life, with the majesty of a severely elevated moral consciousness; and her unhurried narrative movement is but the inevitable technical accompaniment of her sombre moral theme. Any other narrative tempo would be inconceivable in a story such as *Kristin Lavransdatter*.

Unhurried as the general narrative movement is, however, the story is never flat or insipid or tedious. Underneath the quiet exterior of the leisurely narrative manner lies a latent richness of passionate human life, sensitive, alert, ready at the appropriate moment to spring into a fierce blaze of action; and not infrequently in the novel does this potential action become actual, like the tumultuous precipitations of musical scoring in a Beethoven symphony. And Sigrid Undset shows herself master of a wide range of human emotions in her creation of the crucial episodes in her novel: they vary in their central motifs as well as in their use of detail, in their tempo as well as in their moods. If one is looking for the emotional stimuli of vigorous physical action, there is the magnificent episode of the burning of Olav's Church. If one prefers to witness the tender budding of passionate young love in the spring-time, there is the delicately conceived love scene during early morning hours between Kristin and Erlend after the annual Fair of the Farmer's Guild on the day of St. Margaret's Mass. If one's tastes run toward

dramatic scenes—bordering at times on the melodramatic—
there is the half-sordid, half-heroic episode in which Simon
Andressön confronts Kristin and Erlend in the Oslo house of
ill-repute owned by Brynhild Fluga. If one cares rather for
episodes of a more starkly sombre coloring, episodes in which
the deeply inner tragic note is little if at all relieved by any mere
accidents of outward detail, there is the one in which Lavrans un-
dergoes fearful inner conflict on the night of Kristin's wedding
day . . . or that in which Kristin defies the terrors of ancient
superstition in her night-time journey to the church-yard in order
to fetch a bit of soil wherewith to heal Simon Andressön's
son in accordance with an ancient Pagan ritual . . . or the
episode in which Kristin's body rots upon its frame, giving up
life slowly, in excruciating pain, as a victim of the plague, the
Black Death—most horrible, because most mysteriously relentless, of all deaths known to the Middle Ages.

Each of these episodes—and scores of others in *Kristin
Lavransdatter*—bears its own peculiar mark of beauty: vigorous,
or tender, or passionate, or brooding, or sombre, or ghastly, or
several of these in combination, as the case may be; but all of
them are conceived with that marvelous intensity of mood
which is characteristic of Sigrid Undset's art at its best. In most
of these episodes she focuses her creative energies upon her
materials with the fierce intensity, with the massive clairvoyance
of a penetrating, almost unearthly vision; the details stand out
as if etched by a glowing needle-point, and these details are
pointed and massed into a sum total effect which leaves an
ineffaceable mark in the reader's memory. Probably the two most
powerfully conceived episodes in the entire novel are those
dealing with Lavrans's inner struggle on the night of Kristin's
marriage, and Kristin's gruesome, terror-filled church-yard
errand. Both of them, it is to be noted, begin in the deep silent
hours of the night and close in the cold grey light of dawn—
hours which Sigrid Undset's sombre genius seems to find
especially appealing. Both of them concentrate largely on the
fearful inner struggles through which the characters must go;
though in each case, particularly in the church-yard episode,
our consciousness of fear and potential tragedy is deeply accen-

tuated by the author's skillful use of appropriate physical detail.

All of the hidden tragedy of Lavrans's life—only hinted in the earlier chapters—is brought to a relentless, almost terrifyingly intense focus in the episode which brings to a close *The Bridal Wreath,* first of the three volumes of *Kristin Lavransdatter.* Lavrans had at the last given his consent to Kristin's marriage to Erlend Nikulaussön; but he did so only after there seemed no other way out, and even then against his better judgment, moved by a deep intuition of impending tragedy for Kristin in a union with a man of Erlend's reputation. His daughter has finally been married; but despite the outward revelry of the occasion the reader is made aware that this marriage, conceived in Kristin's and Erlend's hidden sin, was to have much of evil in it.

It is upon the father, Lavrans, that the consciousness of impending evil falls most heavily on the wedding night. On this night his suspicion that Kristin and Erlend had come together before marriage had grown into a virtual certainty; and to the terrible shame of this knowledge is added another fearful burden—the confession on this night of Ragnfrid, his own wife, that possibly her first born, a child that had died early, had not been the issue of Lavrans. Never had Lavrans suspected this last; he had always thought that his wife, so often heavy of mood, "had sorrowed for our children—ay, and that" she was "born heavy of mood." Besides—Lavrans had reasoned down through the years of an only partly happy married existence—their marriage had been in a sense half forced upon them by their parents, he being very young for the match; and in consequence in the early years he had half simulated a passion for the somewhat older Ragnfrid which he could not spontaneously feel until years later.

Such are some of the tragic materials which go into the poignant fragments of dialogue between Ragnfrid and Lavrans in the cold, heavy hours before dawn on the night of Kristin's marriage. No analysis of the paragraphs which sketch the episode, so starkly and yet so tenderly conceived, can do justice to the confused, violently conflicting emotions which find an issue here. Still, how overwhelming is the sense of inner tragedy.

Here we have the shock of a terrible disappointment, a feeling of shame pouring over into nameless, brooding fears, a sense of aching inner frustration piled up with a stark and ghastly force. . . . Here we find a strong, profoundly sensitive man brought face to face with certain of the most terrible and intricate ironies of human fate. . . . Violence, agony, fearful aching pain—all is here. . . . And Lavrans seems helpless, stiff with the pain wrought by an overwhelming consciousness of the brutally conflicting emotions which tear away at his breast. Drawn and pale with his gruesome inner struggle through the hours of this tragic night, Lavrans has but strength enough, as the first cold flickers of dawn arrive, to bring whatever comfort he can to a deeply repentant wife who had hid her secret from the man whom she loved until this late and fateful day.

Long they sat there in a deathly stillness. Then the man asked vehemently of a sudden:

"In Jesu name, Ragnfrid—why tell you me all this—now?"

"Oh, I know not!" she wrung her hands till the joints cracked. "That you may avenge you on me—drive me from your house—"

"Think you that would help me—" His voice shook with scorn. "And then there are our daughters," he said quietly. "Kristin—and the little one."

Ragnfrid sat still awhile.

"I mind me how you judged of Erlend Nikulaussön," she said softly. "How judge you of me, then—?"

A long shudder of cold passed over the man's body—yet a little of the stiffness seemed to leave him.

"You have—we have lived together now for seven and twenty years—almost. 'Tis not the same as with a stranger. I see this, too—worse than misery has it been for you."

Ragnfrid sank together sobbing at his words. She plucked up heart to put her hand on one of his. He moved not at all—sat as still as a dead man. Her weeping grew louder and louder—but her husband still sat motionless, looking at the faint grey light creeping in around the door. At last she lay as if all her tears were spent. Then he stroked her arm lightly downward—and she fell to weeping again.

"Mind you," she said through her tears, "that man who came to us one time, when we dwelt at Skog? He that knew all the ancient lays? Mind you the lay of a dead man that was come back from the world of torment, and told his son the story of all that he had seen? There was heard a groaning from hell's deepest ground, the querns of untrue women grinding mould for their husband's meat. Bloody were the stones they dragged at—bloody hung the hearts from out their breasts—"

Lavrans was silent.

"All these years have I thought upon those words," said Ragnfrid. "Every day 'twas as though my heart was bleeding, for every day methought I ground you mould for meat—"

Lavrans knew not himself why he answered as he did. It seemed to him his breast was empty and hollow, like the breast of a man that has had the blood-eagle carven through his back. But he laid his hand heavily and wearily on his wife's head, and spoke:

"Mayhap mould must needs be ground, my Ragnfrid, before the meat can grow."

When she tried to take his hand and kiss it, he snatched it away. But then he looked down at his wife, took one of her hands and laid it on his knee, and bowed his cold, stiffened face down upon it. And so they sat on, motionless, speaking no word more.

It is sufficiently clear from this passage that Ragnfrid's brooding had been fearful beyond words during the long years since her marriage—a brooding brought on, really, through no fault of her own, for she had been taken against her will by a drunken man whom she did not love. Yet down through the years she had hidden this sad matter from Lavrans, her husband, though her secret had left a ghastly, festering wound upon her inner life, boring down into her conscience with a fiercely relentless power, with an almost diseased moral energy that never rested, never spared itself.

It is to be noted that Ragnfrid's morbidly violent brooding over her secret sin—a brooding which amounted to a kind of self-immolation of the spirit—is typical of the central feminine characters almost everywhere in Sigrid Undset's novels. But in *Kristin Lavransdatter* this type of woman is developed with a relentlessly probing minuteness of psychological analysis nowhere else attained in these novels. Kristin herself is Sigrid Undset's greatest creation in this type of woman, though

Kristin has her fictional prototypes in both Jenny Winge and Vigdis Gunnarsdatter (the latter the heroine in the early historical novel *Gunnar's Daughter*, 1909). Each of these women is violently intense in her inner idealisms, never capable of compromise, ever severe in judgment both upon herself and upon others. In *Jenny* this severity of judgment takes its toll primarily upon the heroine herself. In *Gunnar's Daughter* the heroine takes a fierce, thoroughly pagan vengeance upon the man who had wronged her, this despite the fact that she loved him. And in *Kristin Lavransdatter* both Kristin and Erlend must suffer because of Kristin's constant, brooding consciousness of a past sin, and her tendency, in weak moments, to hold Erlend responsible for all that had befallen her. In each case it is the heroine's inability to forget a wrong which accounts for her brooding, and for her distracted efforts to right in some way or other the wrong that had been done.

In *Kristin Lavransdatter* the type is much more convincing than in either of the earlier novels, perhaps largely because of Sigrid Undset's profoundly understanding ability to conceive of her central character over against a magnificently appropriate background—the complicated, restlessly paradoxical milieu of a relatively primitive society undergoing civilizing processes which as yet have only partially conquered the passionate brutality of an age which had but recently passed.

Certainly the world into which Kristin Lavransdatter was born in the first decade of the fourteenth century was in much a very brutal world. Despite the relative political peace in the North during these years, and the steady humanizing work of the Church, violence lurked everywhere, ready to break out at a moment's notice—oftentimes in starkly brutal primitive forms. The Viking Age had not receded far enough into the past to be inoperative in the temper of the present race; and as yet neither the Church nor the Crown could entirely control that sombre undercurrent of an ancient pagan life which lived on, especially among the country-folk. Grisly pagan superstition cropped up everywhere among the common people; drunkenness and violent physical brutality were commonplaces of life in the country-side. Though the upper classes had advanced considerably in the outward ways of medieval *curteisie,* they were still at heart perhaps only slightly more civilized than the simpler folk of the isolated rural areas. Certainly the eagerness of the men among the upper classes to take up combat on small provocation brings to mind salient characteristics of a more violent earlier age. Brutal drunken bouts were not uncommon among them, now that their energies were no longer employed on Viking expeditions of war and plunder; and drunkenness led to filthy talk, to fierce blows—often, indeed, to bloody sword-play, to murder, even to rapine. It is not to be forgotten that Lavrans himself—the most gentle of all the "great farmers" of Gudbrandsdal, and a man who could trace his blood back to royal stock—had his moments of violence fearful to behold.

And even in the Church, the professed enemy of most of the forms of life an earlier paganism had glorified, there was to be found in the Norway of the early fourteenth century more than occasional traces of a brutal primitive strain little in keeping with a message of gentleness and charity and humble service to one's fellows. Neither the priesthood nor the monks of the day were remarkable for either religious asceticism or religious humility. Yet they were, for the most part, men of comparatively severe virtue and of genuine, though crude, Christian piety; and as such they were doubtless a general stabilizing influence in a still largely primitive political society. At times, as was inevitable, however, pagan brutality would break out even in the ranks of the priesthood and the monks; and then it is that the reader of Sigrid Undset's novel becomes most vividly aware of those powerful primitive urges only momentarily kept quiescent under the thin surface of medieval religious and political civilization in the North. Sira Eirik, the parish priest at Sil, is a case in point. He could on occasion both speak and act with a brutality little consistent with his priestly office; and yet he was in his own crude, lumbering way something of "a Holy Man"—a kind of half-pagan Christian saint. Marvelously revealing is the characterization of this worthy priest in the obituary which Sigrid Undset comes to pen in the novel—

. . . Sira Erik was loved and honored by every man and every child in the parishes round about. Folk had often taken it amiss in the old days, when the priest had striven, with unseemly greed, to enrich and make secure the children he had had unlawfully by his serving-wench; and when he first came to dwell in the parish, the people of Sil could ill brook his masterful sternness toward all who transgressed the least of the Church's laws. A warrior had he been before he took the priestly vows, and he had followed the sea-rover earl, Sir Alf of Tornberg, in his youth; 'twas easy to mark it in his ways.

But even then the parish folk had been proud of their priest, for he was far above most priests of the country parishes in learning, wisdom, strength of body, and chieftainly bearing, and he had the noblest singing voice. And with the years, and under the heavy trials that God seemed to have laid upon His servant by reason of his youthful untowardliness, Sira Eirik Kaaressön had so grown in wisdom, piety, and righteousness that his name was now known and honored over the whole bishopric. When he journeyed to the synod at Hamar town, he was honored as a father by all the other priests, and 'twas said that Bishop Halvard would gladly have preferred him to a church which carried with it noble rank and a seat in the cathedral chapter. But 'twas said Sira Eirik had begged he might be left where he was—he had pleaded his age, and that his sight had been dim these many years past.

To an over-nice twentieth century mind this Sira Eirik might seem to be a strange compound of Christian priest and primitive man of flesh and violence; and yet such was the state of society in late medieval Norway that his contemporaries scarcely held his sins against him—at least not for long. In fact he was rather respected, than not, for those bold, vigorous qualities of temper which in other climes and other times might be considered little appropriate to a "man of God." A warrior-priest was hardly an anachronism in the Norwegian Church of the Middle Ages.

It is into such a world that Sigrid Undset introduces her central feminine character in *Kristin Lavransdatter*: a half-primitive world, Christianized perhaps more in theory than in fact; a world of brutal physical actions and hoary ancient superstitions; a world that was, in consequence, bound to conceive Christianity in its own violent severity of temper, its own heavy sombreness of vision—if it was to accept the faith of "the new God, the white Christ" at all. Little wonder is it under the circumstances that Ragnfrid had brooded over her secret sin with such intense absorption, and that Kristin, Ragnfrid's daughter, came to bring to her own religious broodings a quality of feeling that bordered constantly on the violent and the morbid. Full-bodied, intensely passionate, and loving to excess the man whom she had won despite the opposition of her father, Kristin came to taste before her restless days were ended the full cup of bitterness and agony and fear which a sensitive natural moral conscience, accentuated by the rigidities of a severe medieval Church dogma, could visit upon a strong-willed woman of her day. Living in an age when a brutal pagan violence still stirred strongly in the blood, she comes to be the classical type in Sigrid Undset's novels of the fight to the death between the ancient paganism of the North and the new religion from the South.

Some critics have hailed the character of Kristin as Sigrid Undset's great triumph in the creation of the universal woman —a woman who, in her relation to her parents, her husband, and her children, as well as to the whole general world of moral and religious values, gives a profoundly moving expression to the noble urge supposed to exist in some form in all women of all times toward an ideal moral and religious order. In a sense, possibly, such a judgment is sound; and yet it is not the primary truth about Sigrid Undset's creation of Kristin—for Kristin Lavransdatter is, first of all, *a woman of medieval Norway*. Her unique temper, that which most immediately and most consistently attracts the discerning reader, is that she represents in her person a strong-willed, essentially pagan spirit being slowly broken—in a sense, perhaps, transformed—by the severe moral dogma of the medieval Church. In her we come to find perhaps the most profound delineation in world literature of the struggle between a Christian ethics and a pagan world.

It must be emphasized, then, that Sigrid Undset's analysis of Kristin's character is a triumph first of all in *historical* portraiture; only secondarily, if at all, is she to be considered representative of the purely hypothetical "universal woman" of which some critics have made so much. It is only if we look upon Kristin as a woman of medieval Norway that we can explain the fierce intensities of her moral brooding, the massively sombre coloring of her tragic earthly experience. Sigrid Undset's modern women, it is to be noted, do not brood *quite* as does Kristin—not even Jenny Winge, tragic as is her short, fateful career, and moral as is the very core of her being. Kristin Lavransdatter stands alone, even among Sigrid Undset's women, in her fierce struggle with conscience, in her terrible brooding over moral and religious values.

The actual materials of a not yet dead pagan past existed—though often half hidden, darkly mysterious, full of grim suggestion—all about Kristin already in the days of her childhood. Some of these—objects near at hand, a part of her daily life—scarcely entered consciously into her experience; and yet they served, half-consciously, as reminders of a dim past whose sombre mysteries were not to be irreverently approached by living man. Among such objects was the ancient Mound-house on Jörundgaard farm—"folk said it had stood there ever since the old heathen ages." Other details were a part of the general body of local superstitions, of which little Kristin caught up fragments here and there as they fell more or less casually from the lips of her father's work-folk despite Lavrans's insistence that such "dark talk" cease among his serving people. For the most part these ancient superstitions existed only on the fringe of Kristin's girlhood consciousness, giving to it, only by a subtle accumulation of mysterious suggestions, a darker, more sombre coloring than might otherwise have been natural in a healthy young girl born into a family of well-to-do "great farmers." At times, however, these ancient superstitions entered actively into her experience, bringing to it a conscious sense of dread, a darkly mysterious note—almost of the nature of an omen. The story of Kristin's meeting with the elf-maiden during the trip with her father up to the mountain sæter is a striking illustration. The horror that even the grown-ups felt on this occasion is revealed by Lavrans's sternly impatient rejoinder to the impulsive statement of Isrid, wife of one of his tenants:

"Ay, 'twas the elf-maiden sure enough—she would have lured the fair child into the mountain, trust you me."

"Hold your peace!" bade Lavrans sternly. "Never should we have talked of such things here in the woods as we did—one knows not what may lie beneath the rocks and hearken to each word."

He drew the golden chain from out his shirt and hung it and the relic-holding cross about Kristin's neck and thrust them in upon her bare body.

"But see to it, all of you," he said, "that you watch well your mouths, so Ragnfrid may never know the child has been in such peril."

A Christian charm used to protect the child against heathen magic . . . in this act of Lavrans's we find, early in the novel, an appropriate symbol of the conflict between Christianity and paganism which is to become the central moral and religious burden of the story.

The experience with the elf-maiden came to be an unforgettable memory to Kristin. It gave to her that first vivid awareness of those darkling forces on the fringe of life which the medieval mind felt were ever alert to visit evil upon the human race if man did not hold firmly, at every moment to the eternal verities of "the Faith." It is brought to mind in one form or other on certain occasions in Kristin's later life, always when fear and dread have brought deep disturbance to her spirit. But even in her childhood the memory of the mountain dwarfs is so pervasive that it once entered half-consciously into Kristin's imaginative processes—when she was directly occupied with the materials of Christian worship far removed from the isolated mountain dales where "the little folk" were believed to lurk. Kristin, on this occasion, was present at a celebration of the Mass in Hamar church.

Forward, nigh by the altar, the father bent his knee, and Kristin knelt beside him. She began to be able to make things out in the gloom—gold and silver glittered on altars in between the pillars, but upon that before them shone tapers which stood and burned in gilt candle sticks, while the light streamed back from the holy vessels and the big beautiful picture-panel behind. Kristin was brought again to think of the mountain-folks' hall—even so had she dreamed it must be, splendid like this, but maybe with yet more lights. And the dwarf-maid's face came up before her—but then she raised her eyes and spied upon the wall above the altar Christ

Himself, great and stern, lifted high upon the Cross. Fear came upon her—He did not look mild and sorrowful as at home in their own snug timber-brown church, where He hung heavily, with pierced feet and hands, and bowed His blood-besprinkled head beneath the crown of thorns. Here He stood upon a footboard with stiff, outstretched arms and upright head; His gilded hair glittered; He was crowned with a crown of gold, and His face was upturned and harsh.

Then she tried to follow the priest's words as he read and chanted, but his speech was too hurried and unclear. At home she was wont to understand each word, for Sira Eirik had the clearest speech, and had taught her what the holy words betokened in Norse, that she might the better keep her thoughts with God while she was in church.

But she could not do that here, for every moment she grew ware of something new in the darkness. There were windows high up in the walls, and these began to shimmer with the day. And near by where they had knelt there was raised a wondrous scaffolding of timber, but beyond lay blocks of light-coloured stone; and there stood mortar-troughs and tools—and she heard folks coming tip-toeing about in there. But then again her eyes fell upon the stern Lord Christ upon the wall, and she strove to keep her thoughts fixed upon the service. The icy cold from the stone floor stiffened her legs right up to the thighs, and her knees gave her pain. At length everything began to sway about her, so weary was she.

No doubt the cold and the darkness, together with Kristin's physical weariness after a long and severe journey, account largely for the sombre impression of God crucified that Kristin as a child encounters at Hamar church. But it is certainly not without significance that the pagan hall of the mountain-dwarfs comes into Kristin's mind as her tired eyes seek to penetrate the immense gloom enclosed by the vaguely outlined vaulted arches of the Christian church. And this weird world of pagan association serves to provide even more darkly mysterious regions into which her sense of fear wearily sinks as she beholds "Christ Himself, great and stern, lifted high upon the Cross." It was thus as a small child that Kristin had her first vision of the *stern* Christ, a God of severity and of judgment. The impression was never effaced, and in later years it becomes constantly more real to her as she comes to brood darkly, with little buoyancy and hope, over sins and earthly cares.

It is, then, in such a sombre religious milieu, half-pagan and half-Christian, that Kristin grows up as a girl. Meantime she is protected sufficiently from the more directly disturbing world of outward action so that her sense of religious values remains largely emotional and imaginative in content. When she has grown to early young womanhood, however, she takes the fateful outward step, determined by her self-will, in direct opposition to the fondest desires of her father; and then it is that the ethical problem enters directly into her religious experience, intensifying her religious feelings, giving to them an almost material substance, fusing the practical outward problem of conduct with her inner spiritual conception of God. The act which arouses this sense of moral consciousness, and casts its long aching shadow over her entire earthly future, is her marriage with Erlend Nikulaussön.

Kristin and Erlend had met quite by accident at Oslo, where Kristin was in temporary residence at one of the religious houses. A tenderly passionate love between the two followed almost immediately upon their first meeting. Kristin knew that her father would look with the severest disfavor on Erlend as a suitor for her hand, both because of Lavrans's betrothal agreement with Simon and because of Erlend's questionable reputation with women; and yet her passion is so strong that she is ready, though not without qualms, to sacrifice even her father's feelings in order to gain the object of her love. Clandestine meetings between the lovers had to be arranged, deception of various kinds practised; and so already in the first stages of their young love Kristin found reason to sorrow in the very midst of her tenderly passionate joy in Erlend's love. Even in the moment of her first complete physical yielding to Erlend she was not entirely happy.

She sat upright when Erlend lifted his head from her arms. He raised himself suddenly upon his elbow:

"Look not so—Kristin!"

His voice sent a new, wild pang into Kristin's soul—he was not glad—*he* was unhappy too—!

"Kristin, Kristin! Think you I lured you out here to me in the woods meaning this—to make you mine by force—?" he asked in a little.

She stroked his hair and did not look at him.

" 'Twas not force, I trow—you had let me go as I came, had I begged you—" she said, in a low voice.

"I know not," he answered, and hid his face in her lap. . . .

"Think you that I would betray you?" asked he vehemently. "Kristin—I swear to you by my Christian faith—may God forsake me in my last hour, if I keep not faith with you till the day of my death—"

She could say naught, she only stroked his hair again and again.

" 'Tis time I went home, is it not?" she asked at length, and she seemed to wait in deadly terror for his answer.

"Maybe so," he answered dully. He got up quickly, went to the horse, and began to loosen the reins.

Then she too got up. Slowly, wearily, and with crushing pain it came home to her—she knew not what she had hoped he might do—set her upon his horse, maybe, and carry her off with him so she might be spared from going back amongst other people. It was as though her whole body ached with wonder—that this ill thing was what was sung in all the songs. And since Erlend had wrought her this, she felt herself grown so wholly his, she knew not how she should live away from him any more. She was to go from him now, but she could not understand that it should be so.

Though Kristin's and Erlend's love had thus been consummated, there was little joy and no real peace in the consummation. The physical act itself Kristin had not found entirely beautiful; and more—she had already in the moments following immediately upon this act begun to brood over its consequences. What would her father think? . . . how was she now to deal with Simon? Of the latter, it is true, she does not think overmuch; but she broods constantly in the weeks and months that follow on the wrong which she is doing her father in this matter—and by degrees, also, she becomes acutely conscious of the wrong against God that she is committing in her secret sin. The Church had severely condemned love outside of marriage, as being something purely of the flesh, a deadly sin. Kristin was mindful of this; and yet she *desired Erlend*, desired him with a wildly tender physical passion; and so she must have him regardless of the injustice that she is doing to her father, regardless of the grievous sin which she knew she was committing in the eyes of Heaven.

Lavrans, as we have seen, finally came to yield his consent to a marriage between Kristin and Erlend, though only after months of refusal, and then only when Simon Andressön, realizing the hopelessness of his own suit for Kristin's hand, deceived Lavrans by telling him that he no longer desired marriage with Kristin. Meantime, Sigrid Undset provides us with a minute, profoundly probing analysis of Kristin's emotional life during the long period of waiting: her momentary joys, her wild spasms of fear, her wan hopes, the pride and the bitterness which by turn stir violently through her world of fearful inner brooding. When, finally, Kristin's wedding day is at hand, her thoughts are for the most part sorrowful. Her unsettled, weary mind broods heavily over Erlend's past life, his children by another woman, a mistress . . . this woman herself now dead by a deed of accidental violence . . . and as for herself she was filled with vague dreads, a sense of impending tragedy, of the horror that might dwell in an unknown future.

The horror had come upon her last evening, when they sat over the supperboard at Sundbu, and she met Björn Gunnarsön's lightless eyes fixed on her and Erlend—unwinking, unwavering eyes. They had dressed up Sir Björn in knightly raiment—he looked like a dead man brought to life by an evil spell.

At night she had lain with Lady Aashild, the bridegroom's nearest kinswoman in the wedding company.

"What is amiss with you, Kristin?" said Lady Aashild, a little sharply. "Now is the time for you to bear up stiffly to the end—not give way thus."

"I am thinking," said Kristin, cold with dread, "on all them we have brought to sorrow that we might see this day."

" 'Tis not joy alone, I trow, that you two have had," said Lady Aashild. "Not Erlend at the least. And methinks it has been worse still for you."

"I am thinking on his helpless children," said the bride again. "I am wondering if they know their father is drinking to-day at his wedding-feast—"

"Think on your own child," said the lady. "Be glad that you are drinking at your wedding with him who is its father."

Kristin lay awhile, weak and giddy. 'Twas so strange to hear that named that had filled her heart and mind each day for three months and more, and whereof yet she had not dared speak a word to a living soul. It was but for a little, though, that this helped her.

"I am thinking on her who had to pay with her life, because she held Erlend dear," she whispered, shivering.

"Well if you come not to pay with your life yourself, ere you are half a year older," said Lady Aashild harshly. "Be glad while you may—"

"What shall I say to you, Kristin?" said the old woman in a while, despairingly. "Have you clean lost courage this day of all days? Soon enough will it be required of you twain that you shall pay for all you have done amiss—have no fear that it will not be so."

Lady Aashild's harsh prophecy, though thrown out in a moment of impatience, was to be fulfilled in the years which followed; it was Kristin's morbidly brooding spirit, her inability to forget the past, that came to be the most active single agent in the largely tragic experience of Kristin and Erlend in their married life.

On the night of their wedding day, when Kristin and Erlend, as man and wife, were finally alone together

She threw her arms about his shoulders and sobbed aloud—she had a sweet, wild feeling that now the horror, the phantom visions, were fading into air—now, now once again naught was left but he and she. He lifted up her face a moment, looked down into it, and drew his hand down over her face and body, with a strange haste and roughness, as though he tore away a covering.

"Forget," he begged, in a fiery whisper, "forget all, my Kristin— all but this, that you are my own wife, and I am your own husband. . . ."

But Kristin, complete and passionate as was her love for Erlend, could not "forget, forget all." To her had been given a heavy, infinitely careful spirit—one which came with the years to be morbidly conscious of certain moral and religious values. And yet to her had been given also a wildly primitive emotional urge, whose roots lay deeply imbedded in an imperious physical

340 Christian Ethics in a Pagan World

passion. The combination of these two conflicting strains in one person account largely for the tragic ways which her married life came to take.

The bitterness that came over Kristin during the years of her life with Erlend resulted chiefly from her resentment at Erlend's carefree, irresponsible way of life. She who had such a constant, jealous sense of responsibility for the children who came to them, for the family property (first at Husaby, later at Jörundgaard), and for the future of her growing brood . . . this Kristin became increasingly irritated by Erlend's easy ways, his frank willingness to let the morrow care for itself. And her resentment but grew the more—into a harsh, unbending bitterness—because of the passionate love which she always felt for this man who took life so lightly, never brooding over the past nor projecting worry into the future. Erlend combined in his person the outward social graces of an age of chivalry and the adventurous spirit of an earlier, more violent pagan warrior age. Had Kristin been more lenient of his faults, more understanding in her dealings with her husband, Erlend might have become with the years a sufficiently good husbandman, a man of reasonably proper domestic virtues. As it was his wife's brooding ways, her only half-hidden resentments sometimes flaring up into petulant, bitter observations, drove Erlend ultimately to seek some form of peace in a life lived more and more away from Husaby. And though he yearned constantly for Kristin, for his children, and returned to Husaby frequently, he came ultimately to find much satisfaction in a life of adventure, a life robustly reminiscent, to his mind, of an earlier, more primitive age when violent adventure was the order of the day, that by which man lived in spirit and in deed.

That it was the old pagan spirit which stirred restlessly in Erlend is clear from a number of passages in the novel, nowhere more clear than in an episode at the beginning of the second part of *The Mistress of Husaby*, when Sir Erling Vidkunnsön, Lavrans, Erlend, and some others are engaged in discussing certain rather ominous political developments in Norway at the time. Erlend entered enthusiastically into the discussion, prompted by visions of the warrior deeds of an earlier Norway when men were less cautious of life and property, more willing to accept life as a magnificent gamble. Erlend insists that even the traditionally conservative small farmer, "these stubborn Trönders liked us great folk better in the old days when we led their sons to battle and foray, let our blood flow out over the deck-planks mixed with theirs, and hewed rings in sunder and shared the booty with our house-carls." Such convictions as these come to be the positive reason—whereas the brooding ways of Kristin at Husaby is the immediate negative occasion —for Erlend's later dangerous political ventures, which end in his loss of Husaby and all hope for political eminence in the future.

It is to be noted that Kristin "was following the men's talk intently" on the occasion when Erlend gave such vehement expression to his political ideas; but she did not enter into the discussion—Erlend's world seemed so far removed from hers. And into Erlend's later political machinations she never entered: she felt in her heavy, careful way that no good could come of it. Her cares were for her immediate family; all of her feelings and thoughts centred jealously about her growing brood of boys. After the loss of Husaby and the return of Kristin and Erlend to Jörundgaard, the relationship between husband and wife became daily the more strained, until finally certain bitter words of Kristin's led to an estrangement. Erlend went to live alone on the isolated mountain farm Haugen, while Kristin struggled on at Jörundgaard, becoming more and more embittered at Erlend, half-conscious all the time that it was her own harsh words that had driven her husband to the extremity of estrangement from both herself and the sons whom Erlend loved in his way as passionately as did Kristin.

While Erlend lived she yearned intensely for his love; and yet she could not forgive him for this last act, though on one occasion she did visit him at Haugen and their old love flared up again with a wild new tenderness during the days that she remained at the isolated mountain farm. Erlend on this occasion counselled her to remain with him at Haugen, permitting the boys, several of them young men now, to work out their own future at Jörundgaard. Kristin is tempted—her love for Erlend

so fresh and new and passionate again; but finally she returns
to Jörundgaard, incapable of allowing mother-love to be subordinated to her wild reborn passion for Erlend. "As she rode
by the church"—we are told, on her parting from Erlend—"a
little shudder ran through her. 'Twas as though she were coming
home from the Mountain King's Hall, as though Erlend were
the Mountain King himself, and could not pass the church and
the cross on the green." Thus does Sigrid Undset symbolize, in
the form of medieval ballad superstition, the old struggle between the flesh and the spirit, the fundamental conflict between
the ancient pagan world and a new Christian faith.

Kristin had made her choice; and yet upon her return home
she found no real joy in her sacrifice of earthly love. Her
brooding in the months that followed became even more intense
than before, though she was now more quiet outwardly. She
knew she was not Christian in spirit; for she was not willing
to forgive, and physical passion still stirred powerfully within
her. She prayed constantly, tried to repent—

But in the depths of her heart she felt not that she had forgiven
Erlend. She could not, for she would not. She clung to her cup of
love, would not let it go, even now when it held naught but the last
bitter dregs. In the hour when she could forgive Erlend, could
even think of him without this gnawing bitterness—then would
all that had been between them be at an end.

'Twas thus she stood throughout the Mass, knowing that it
profited her nothing. She tried to pray: Holy Olav, help me; work
a miracle in my heart, that I may say my prayer without deceit or
guile—may think of Erlend with god-fearing peace in my soul. But
she knew she wished not herself that this prayer be heard. . . .

Only upon Erlend's deathbed does reconciliation of a kind
take place between husband and wife. Erlend had returned
to Jörundgaard to defend his wife's honor against the gossip
of neighbors, who had linked Kristin with her house-carl Ulf
Haldorssön when Kristin's last child—conceived at Haugen—
had come. Erlend's death wound followed upon his violent
altercation with these neighboring farmers in Jörundgaard
court-yard. As he lies dying he refuses to accept the last sacraments from the hands of Sira Solmund, the new priest who had

gossiped loosely with the parish farmer folk about Kristin and Ulf.

Erlend's eyes had fallen shut again. Kristin sat staring at his white face—she passed her hand over it now and again. She deemed she saw that he began to sink towards death.

"Erlend," she begged, softly. "For Jesus' sake—let us fetch Sira Solmund to you. God is God, whatever priest may bear him to us—"

"No!" The man sat up in bed, so that the coverings slid down from his naked, yellow body. The bandages over his breast and belly were stained anew in bright red patches by the fresh blood that welled forth. "A sinful man I am—God in His mercy grant me what forgiveness He will; but I feel—" He fell back on the pillows —whispered so that he could scarce be heard: "not long enough shall I live to grow—so old—and so meek—that I can suffer—stay quiet in one room with him that lied of you—"

"Erlend, Erlend—think on your soul!"

The man shook his head as it lay on the pillows. His eyelids had drooped close again.

"Erlend!" She clasped her hands; she cried aloud in utmost need. "Erlend—see you not that, so as you had borne you towards me, this *must* needs be said!"

Erlend opened his great eyes. His lips were leaden—but a shadow of his young smile flitted over the sunken face:

"Kiss me, Kristin," he whispered. There was somewhat like a shade of laughter in his voice. "There has been too much else 'twixt you and me, I trow—beside Christendom and wedlock—for us easily—to forgive each other—as Christian man and wife—"

She called and called his name after him; but he lay with shut eyes, his face wan as new-cloven wood under his grey hair. A little blood oozed from the corners of his mouth; she wiped it away, whispering imploring words to him—when she moved she felt her clothing clinging cold and wet from the blood she had got upon her when she led him in and laid him in the bed. Now and again there was a gurgling sound in Erlend's breast, and he seemed to draw breath painfully—but he heard no more, and most like felt nothing, as he sank steadily and surely towards the sleep of death.

Erlend had remained essentially a pagan in spirit into his last hour. He had reverenced the Church in his own way during his days of life, and he had never denied its teachings; but he would not, when his end came, receive the blessing of the Church at the hands of a priest whom he considered unworthy. He died with a satisfied smile on his lips—lips that had received only the blessing of Kristin's achingly sorrowful earthly love. It was the carefree, unworried death of a pagan. Erlend had met death even as he had lived and loved.

After Erlend's death Kristin became only *less* restless in spirit than she had been before. It was only *a kind* of peace that came to her in the sad, empty months of her bereavement. The flesh died very slowly in her: it *burned out,* largely as a natural process, an overwhelming weariness of life, rather than by an act of moral will. Simon Andressön had on an occasion long before spoken certain words: "All fires burn out at last." Kristin recalled that statement now; and it began to take on a new meaning for her. God, she felt now, was beginning to *force* her into His inscrutable ways. Yet she continued to struggle, as had been her wont so long, in the innumerable meshes of earthly cares: now, she reasoned, the struggle could be alone for her children, the future of those to whom her body had given birth with so much agony and fear. Finally, however, she is forced to yield to circumstances even here; and then it is that salvation comes to her—comes, it is to be noted, not because of her own striving but as a pure gift of God. She leaves Jörundgaard, and with it all the earthly cares that had weighed so heavily upon her spirits down through the years, and journeys northward from Jörundgaard across the mountains to Nidaros, there to give herself up wholly to religious observances. Her pilgrimage northward—a pilgrimage when visions of strange unearthly beauty come to her—is described in a marvelously limpid, solemnly moving prose, some of the best which Sigrid Undset has ever written.

At Nidaros she meets Gunnulf Nikulaussön, priest and brother of Erlend; and after her long, quiet conversations with him about the one who had died, Kristin's restive, nervous, earthbound spirit finds at the last a final, perfect peace.

. . . While she was speaking with him who was the last living witness of the interplay 'twixt seed-time and harvest in her life with the dead man, it seemed to her that she had come to look out over her life in a new way: as when a man comes up on a height above his native place where he has never climbed before, and looks down from it into his own dale. He knows each farm and fence, each thicket, the gully of each beck; but he seems to see for the first time how these things all lie on the face of the land. And seeing things in this new way, she had found all at once words that swept away both her bitterness against Erlend and her terrors for his soul, borne off by sudden death. Ill-will he had never borne to any; she saw it now, and God had seen it always.

So at last she was come so far that she deemed she could look on her own life as from the uppermost step of a glen. Now did her road lead down into the darkling valley, but ere she took that road she had been given grace to understand that, in the loneliness of the cloister and at the gates of death, there waited for her one who had ever beheld the life of mankind as men's parishes look, seen from the mountain brow. He had seen the sin and sorrow, the love and hate, in the hearts of men, as one sees the rich manors and the humble cots, the teeming cornfields and the abandoned wastes, all borne on the bosom of the same country-side. And He had descended; His feet had trodden the peopled lands, and stood in palaces and in huts; He had gathered up the sorrows and the sins of rich and poor, and lifted them aloft with him upon a cross. Not my happiness and my pride, but my sin and my sorrow, O my sweet Lord—She looked up where the crucifix stood, uplifted high over the triumphal arch.

Shortly after these thoughts had been borne in upon her with the finality of a triumphant faith Kristin dies, a victim of the plague. Despite rapid physical disintegration and fearful pain in her last hours, her thoughts are with God: "It seemed to her to be a mystery which she could not fathom, but which she knew most surely none the less, that God had held her fast in a covenant made for her without her knowledge by a love poured out upon her richly—and in spite of her self-will, in spite of her heavy, earthbound spirit, somewhat of this love had become a *part* of her, had wrought in her like sunlight in the earth, had brought forth increase which not even the hottest flames of fleshly love nor its wildest bursts of wrath could lay waste wholly. . . ."

Unquiet and restless had been the years of Kristin's life—ineffably peaceful her hour of death. Passionately she had loved,

346   Christian Ethics in a Pagan World

and with an aching tenderness at times; violent had been her resentments, her bitterness, her fears; jealous had she been for the future of her sons; fearfully restless had been her strivings with her God. Peace she came to find only just this side of death, for her body had scarcely permitted her soul to be at rest in life. Her story ran out its passionate, heavily brooding hours in a turbulent, half-primitive age, when flesh strove more violently with the spirit of man than it has perhaps in later ages. Christian she had ever tried to be, and surely was; and yet within her there lurked not a little of the violent and the pagan. Her story finds its chief significance in the magnificence with which it illustrates the working of a Christian ethics in an at least half-pagan medieval world.

The second of Sigrid Undset's great historical novels—the long tetralogy which goes under the English title *The Master of Hestviken* (1925-27)—is even more heavy and sombre in tone and movement than is *Kristin Lavransdatter*. The scene of *The Master of Hestviken* is farther to the south, at the head of the Oslo fjord, where the country is on the whole more open and smiling than in Gudbrandsdalen and northward over the Dovre mountains to Trondheim, the regions which we came to know in *Kristin Lavransdatter*. Still the second of these novels is definitely more unrelieved and dreary in its coloring, more stark in its general narrative outlines, and more relentlessly bleak in its portrayal of the inner moral struggle of its central character.

The action in *The Master of Hestviken* is pushed back into the latter half of the thirteenth century, when Norway was even less Christian than in the days of the life-span of *Kristin Lavransdatter*. Only in the opening chapters is the reader given a glimpse of something fresh, buoyant, hopeful—this in the innocent youthful love of Olav and Ingunn. Brutally tragic forces lurk on every hand, however, and the charming young love idyll of Olav and Ingunn soon becomes a pathetic sacrifice to the darkling forces of violence and hatred which surround them. Before the end of *The Axe*—first volume in Sigrid Undset's gloomy tetralogy—Olav has committed the sin of the flesh with Ingunn and has killed two men by violence; and yet he is a mere youth in these years, and by nature he is one who loves peace rather than violence. It is clear that the world of *The Master of Hestviken* is primarily a man's world, a world in which the moral struggle is bound to be very harsh in its outlines and in its inner complications—bleak and grim and starkly bare as a far northern landscape.

Olav Audunssön experienced few of the normal immediate pleasures of life. His mother had died upon giving him birth, and his father passed away when Olav was still a young boy. He had lived almost entirely with strangers until he came of age and took over Hestviken, the family estate. Difficult as were these circumstances of boyhood and early youth, he was to find his later mature life increasingly weighted with troubles. When he brought his young bride Ingunn Steinfinssdatter to Hestviken, she was semiconvalescent, the victim of a strange disease, apparently of the nervous system; and she bore Olav only still-born babes, or children that lived but a few days—until in her last days, when Cecelia was born. Dearly as Olav loved his wife, he could have but little pleasure of her. He came to look upon her mysterious ailment as a judgment of God upon himself; and he complained not, though his spirit was fearfully heavy with the burden.

Olav Audunssön's struggle with his conscience and with his God came with the years to be severe and tragic even beyond that of Kristin Lavransdatter. Though Kristin's moral struggle was intense enough at times, and even morbidly violent in its inner repercussions, her spirit was on the whole more resilient, more flexible than was Olav's. Besides, her life, by comparison with Olav's, was relatively protected, working itself out largely within the intimate confines of her home. She had a large, growing family to occupy herself with during the years when Erlend drew slowly away from her; and the busy care she had for her healthy brood of boys provided some compensation for the aching emptiness which she only too frequently experienced because of her struggle with her moral problem.

Most critics have placed *The Master of Hestviken* definitely below *Kristin Lavransdatter* as an artistic performance. In many cases these critics have objected to *The Master of Hestviken* chiefly because of its extreme, unrelieved gloom, its relentlessly brutal accumulation of tragic detail. It would seem, however, that such objections are purely a matter of taste. If Hardy is right in his suggestion that "the time seems near, if it has not actually arrived, when the chastened sublimity of a moor, a sea, or a mountain will be all of nature that is absolutely in keeping with the moods of the more thinking among mankind," *The Master of Hestviken* should be peculiarly adapted to modern taste. Besides, it could be argued that the harsh picture of life that we meet in *The Master of Hestviken* is inevitable in an honest historical depiction of Norway in the late thirteenth century. It might be countered, of course, that the hopeless religious brooding so characteristic of this novel is not consistent with the picture reflected in a contemporary medieval ballad literature. The same objection, however, can be made to *Kristin Lavransdatter*; and besides it is certainly not sound to assume that ballad literature alone provides an adequate basis upon which final conclusions about late-medieval psychology can be formulated. That *Kristin Lavransdatter* is in the last analysis a greater novel than *The Master of Hestviken* must certainly be granted; but its relative greatness is hardly to be found in the fact that it is less gloomy, less essentially tragic in its final moral implications than is *The Master of Hestviken.* The latter novel is inferior to *Kristin Lavransdatter* for another reason.

The chief difficulty with *The Master of Hestviken* is that the religious dogma which determines its moralizing is entirely too obtrusive—never sufficiently subordinated to the narrative pattern of the novel. It must be admitted that *Kristin Lavransdatter* is almost equally full of long moralizing passages, which upon even cursory analysis are seen to contain formal Catholic dogma; but in *Kristin Lavransdatter* such dogma is far more capably worked into the normal narrative processes, and so we find ourselves little disturbed by the dogmatic implications of the novel. In *The Master of Hestviken,* on the other hand, the free flow of narration is too often interrupted by the long moral homily, by a forced and definitely obtrusive religious dogma. In fact, Sigrid Undset is so intently concerned with purely dogmatic questions in this novel that she at times apparently introduces episodes

merely for the purpose of providing a background or an occasion
for the expression of a given dogma. It is difficult to explain at
least two episodes in *The Master of Hestviken* in any other way.
I refer to the curiously inconclusive temptation episode which
takes place during Olav's visit to England after the death of
Ingunn, and to the morbidly brutal episode at Hestviken in
which Eirik attacks Bothild with such horrible immediate
results. Seldom, if ever, it seems to me, has Sigrid Undset been
so tasteless in her choice of narrative episode; and it would seem
that she has been so in these cases chiefly because she is too
intent upon her religious dogma at these points to have any very
nice care for the demands of narrative probability. The first of
these episodes, especially, seems unpardonable in an author of
such an otherwise authentic realism as Sigrid Undset. Almost
every detail in the episode is cheaply reminiscent of the worst
tradition in those Romantic "mystery tales" which concern
themselves centrally with sex in terms of a crudely conceived
"temptation scene." An examination of the episode in its context
will reveal to the most superficial reader that it was used simply
as a "build-up" for the moral homily which follows, and a
"build-up" which, certainly in this case, is not at all convincing;
for Olav has revealed no traits of character earlier in the novel
that would make his actions at this point at all natural.

In most respects, however, the story which is unfolded for us
in *The Master of Hestviken* is quite convincing. The historical
background, everywhere founded upon a minute knowledge of
the times, is subordinated to the main narrative pattern with a
rare intuitive power; the characters of Olav and Ingunn are
revealed with that intimacy and penetration which one might
expect from the author of *Kristin Lavransdatter*; the natural
scene is marvelously alive and thoroughly congruous with the
sombre moral theme; and the moral itself, though obtruding too
obviously in certain episodes, is managed on the whole with a
naturalness and power only exceeded by *Kristin Lavransdatter*.
It might be added, in passing, that *The Master of Hestviken* has
in it touches of humor too frequently lacking in *Kristin Lavransdatter,* though the latter novel is not entirely devoid of
humor. The humor of *The Master of Hestviken* is distinctly

broad, sometimes harsh and grim; but it serves admirably the twofold purpose of providing occasional bits of not unwelcome comic relief and of adding to our sense of historical illusion.

The Master of Hestviken reflects the same intimate mastery of historical and archaeological knowledge that we find in *Kristin Lavransdatter*. Sigrid Undset has steeped herself in a first-hand study of all the details of life in the Norway of the late thirteenth century—in its dress and its domestic customs, in its characteristic moods and ideas and its manner of speech, and most important of all perhaps in that peculiar interplay of political and religious institutions which is characteristic of the Middle Ages in the North. As in the case of *Kristin Lavransdatter,* however, actual historical personages and actual historical events are given a very subordinate place in *The Master of Hestviken.* No actual historical characters play a direct part in the action of the novel. Neither Olav Audunssön nor Ingunn Steinfinnsdatter are historical characters, nor for that matter are any of the other persons who play an important part in the novel. Only one event in the novel has any actual historical basis—the invasion of Norway by Duke Eirik (brother of King Birger of Sweden and husband of Princess Ingebjörg, daughter of King Haakon V of Norway), whose ambition it was to control all of the Scandinavian kingdoms.

Though *The Master of Hestviken* almost entirely avoids concerning itself with historical episodes or with actual historical personages, there is one major phase of the general political and religious development in Norway in the last decades of the thirteenth century which comes to occupy a position of prominence in the first volume of the tetralogy. It happened in these years— very unquiet years internally for Norway—that the barons and the bishops were coming into conflict with increasing frequency over a fundamental difference in their respective conceptions of the basic law of the land. The barons, feeling that their old power was slipping because of the growing prominence of both the Crown and the Church, attempted in every possible way to assert their ancient legal prerogatives, especially in matters of local concern. These prerogatives were, of course, pagan in origin, based primarily upon the ancient Scandinavian conception of personal or family honor, in which the instrument of justice was usually an act of vengeance for the wrong committed. It was against this heathen identification of vengeance with justice that the bishops of the Church came to protest. Their theoretical protests became an active principle of practical law enforcement when they at times claimed priority for canon law in a given offense.

Sigrid Undset finds a natural occasion for introducing into the novel this general conflict between the barons and the bishops when Olav and Ingunn appeal to Bishop Torfinn of Hamar on the occasion of the attempt on the part of Ingunn's relatives, the Toressons and the Kolbeinssons, to thwart the proposed marriage of Olav and Ingunn. Taking the case of the two young people under advisement, Bishop Torfinn arouses the anger and enmity of Ingunn's relatives, who looked upon themselves as representatives of the old law of the barons. The Bishop nevertheless announced an "audience," to which the Toressons and Kolbeinssons and a representative of Olav were summoned. Though the relatives of Ingunn appeared, they did so only under protest. They insisted privately "that here in the Upplands it had never been the custom to let the Bishop of Hamar rule like a petty king—'twas easy to see that the man came from Nidaros, for there the priests did as they liked in everything." The case itself seemed to be proceeding satisfactorily enough from the standpoint of Olav and Ingunn, when the whole matter became severely complicated by Olav's slaying of Einar Kolbeinsson, one of Ingunn's relatives who opposed the match of Olav and Ingunn and whose foul words had precipitated the quarrel in which he was slain. The slaying took place in the guest-house of the convent at Hamar church; and the general conflict which followed upon Olav's deed of violence ceased only upon the appearance of a group of monks and the Prior. Upon being questioned by the Prior, Olav admitted that he had slain Einar.

". . . But the peace was but frail in here the whole evening—long before I broke it. At the last Einar used such shameful speech to us that we took to our weapons.—"

" 'Tis true," said the lay brother. He was an old countryman who had entered the convent only lately. "Einar spoke such words that in old days any man would have judged he died an outlaw's death by Olav's hand."

Haftor was standing by his brother; he turned and said with a cold smile: "Ay, so they will judge the murder in this house—and in the Bishop's. Since these two are the Bishop's men, body and soul. But mayhap the nobles of this land will soon be tired of such dishonor—that every priest who thinks he has authority uses it to shelter the worst of brawlers and lawbreakers—"

"That is untrue, Haftor," said the Prior; "we servants of God will not protect any evil-doer farther than he has protection in the law. But we are bound to do our best that law-breaking be punished according to law, and not avenged by fresh unlawfulness which begets fresh vengeance without end."

Haftor smiled scornfully: "I call them dirty laws, these new laws. The old were better suited to men of honor. . . ."

Thus sharply, in a scene of blood and violence and harsh words, is drawn the conflict between the old laws and the new—the law of a pagan past and the new law of the Church.

Nowhere in *Kristin Lavransdatter* is the struggle between paganism and Christianity drawn quite so sharply as it is here in the early pages of *The Master of Hestviken,* for the world into which Kristin was born saw no such frank outward conflict between two fundamentally different conceptions of law and justice. The law of the Church was not challenged so openly in the relatively ordered years of the early fourteenth century in Norway as it was in the turbulent decades just before the turn of the century. The Crown and the Church had triumphed for the most part by the early fourteenth century; and the law of vengeance, based upon a purely pagan conception of honor, had to yield. It did so only stubbornly, however, and not before many another act such as the one in the convent guest-house at Hamar had taken place.

Olav was imprisoned, to await trial, because of his deed of violence. He escaped abroad, however, and became in consequence declared an "outlaw" in the realm. Only years later, when he had paid a fine which satisfied the Toressons and Kolbeinssons, was he permitted to marry Ingunn and bring her to Hestviken. Meantime a second, and far more severe misfortune befell Olav and Ingunn. During Olav's absence, Ingunn had become with child by a certain Teit, a wandering Icelander. Upon hearing of this from Ingunn's own lips on his return, Olav's anger knew no bounds. He killed Teit, secretly—told no man of it. Thus Olav himself had taken recourse to the ancient pagan law of personal vengeance. This becomes his fateful secret sin, a sin which he could not bring himself to confess either to the Church or to society, despite the fact that the burden of his secret violence ultimately became almost too great for him to bear. From the time of this deed of violence Olav knew no real inner peace.

Upon his return to Hestviken with Ingunn, whom he loves in spite of all, he settles down to a life of hard, incessant labor. He cares for his half-convalescent, morbidly brooding wife with a rare understanding and tenderness. He even has Ingunn's child by Teit fetched to Hestviken, when he understands that Ingunn longs for the child. He deals with his neighbors honestly and straightforwardly. He treats his servants as an exemplary master. But he has no real converse with others. He is a lonely, silent man, growing more lonely and silent with the years; for neither his constant labors nor his deeds of goodness provide healing for the cancer which bores ceaselessly, relentlessly into his conscience. On several occasions he is about to confess his secret sin; but each time he cannot—at the last moment.

We see him, finally, in those last harshly sombre chapters of *The Master of Hestviken* tottering onward toward the grave, the broken shell of the man he once had been—skeletal in appearance, partly paralytic, subject to fits and vomitings and childish ways . . . dreaming of Ingunn and their innocent early love, brooding ceaselessly over his sins . . . a pathetic wreck of a man, whose lucid moments serve but to etch into more severely tragic lines those recurrent periods when a weak, drooling madness is his lot. Only one unshriven sin did Olav Audunsson have; but this sin was his fate, for he could never shake it off, never confess it openly before man and God. A sombre story, this—of man's conscience more brutal than man's outward violence. Only public penitence could help this man; and yet he had borne his secret sin so long within him that his soul at the last could *feel* no penitence.

He had heard a thousand times that God's mercy is without bounds, and in secret he had relied on this: what he fled from was always there, waiting for him when he took courage to turn, since it was all that was outside time and change: God's arms spread out on the cross, ready to enfold him, grace streaming from the five wounds, the drooping Head which looked down over all creation, watching and waiting, surrounded by Mary and all the saints with prayers that rose like incense from an unquenchable censer. His servants were ever ready with power to unlock his fetters; the Bread of Life was ever upon the altar. God was without bounds.—

But he himself was not, he saw that now. It was too late after all. The bounds that were in himself had set and hardened into stone—like the stones folk had shown him here and there about the country, which had once been living beasts and men.

Now he *could* no longer repent. There was no longer any love of God within him, nor any longing to find his way back; now he would rather have gone on and on away from God, everlastingly. That was Hell. That was the realm of eternal torment, he knew it, but the home of torment had become his home.

It is on such a note of hopeless weariness of spirit that *The Master of Hestviken* ends. Olav Audunsson found not the final peace of mind that had been given to Kristin Lavransdatter at the very last, though the Church came at the last to provide the final sacraments for his broken body and spirit in the hour of his death.

IV

Upon the completion of *The Master of Hestviken* Sigrid Undset returns again to the contemporary scene in a group of four novels, *The Wild Orchid* (1929) together with its sequel *The Burning Bush* (1930), *Ida Elisabeth* (1932), and *The Faithful Wife* (1936); and she has published during the past year in addition *Madame Dorthea,* an historical novel concerned with eighteenth century Norway. The novels dealing with the present-day scene lack that sense of an immediate, pulsing physical life characteristic of her earlier, less ambitious tales dealing with contemporary life; and they fall far short of *Kristin Lavransdatter* and *The Master of Hestviken* in rich, intimate intensities of character portrayal. They deal, however, with their immediate contemporary problems in the spirit of straightforward, wholly unsentimental honesty that one has come with the years to associate with Sigrid Undset; and with all of their shortcomings as compared with Sigrid Undset's great historical novels, they are among the most important novels that have come out of Norway in the last ten years.

The chief fault of at least the first two of Sigrid Undset's late group of novels dealing with contemporary life is that they are too patently motivated by a particular religious dogma, that of the Roman Catholic Church. In the historical novels the central inclusion of religious dogma seems, on the whole, natural enough, these novels dealing with historical periods when "the Church" was coming increasingly to dominate human thought and human conduct in the North; though, as we have seen, a too intent preoccupation with dogmatic questions in *The Master of Hestviken* leads Sigrid Undset at times into serious artistic difficulties. In the later novels dealing with contemporary life, however, there seems to be far less necessity for a particular kind of religious emphasis; and it is obvious that Sigrid Undset's inclusion in these late novels of the materials of something just short of religious propaganda has resulted in a distinct falling off in the quality of these novels.

It must be said to Sigrid Undset's credit, however, that her propaganda is effective—particularly, perhaps, on the negative side. She aims her critical shafts with very telling effect at many of the more naïve shibboleths of the late nineteenth and the early twentieth centuries—at a half bourgeois "liberalism" and at a merely sentimental humanitarianism, at scientific optimism and at so-called "industrial progress," at religious sectarianism and at certain late forms of Puritanism, and so on. . . . Some of the liveliest satire in *The Wild Orchid* is directed at modern "psychological" studies in the fields of sexual and religious phenomena. She strikes out vigorously against "the kind of would-be profound psychological books which solemnly and laboriously discourse about unapplied eros and unsatisfied maternal feeling and all that." And of such studies in religious experience as William James's once famous *Varieties of Religious Experience* she makes short shrift—perhaps not without much justice. "Well—" she has one of the characters in *The Wild Orchid* say—

"for its day I suppose it was quite an imposing work. But it always made me think of something like an agricultural handbook written by a man who held an important position in a zoological museum and was in correspondence with experts at laboratories and experimental stations. But who had never milked a cow or helped her to calve, or had to drive the milk to the dairy before school-time or helped to dig potatoes in pouring rain—or tried to get within range of the crow—I won't say anything about seeing a bull turn mad and go for one's father in the narrow byre, when there was nobody else there but oneself, a little girl of nine. . . ."

The fact that Sigrid Undset feels herself on the defensive in her championing of Catholicism in a Norway so predominately Lutheran in religion and so essentially "liberal" in its social, economic, and political thinking accounts to some extent, at least, for the almost acrid sharpness of her attack upon certain developments in modern society.

It must be noted, however—and this is of first importance—that she does not narrow her attack upon characteristic trends in modern society to Norway, though the scene of these novels lie almost entirely within the borders of her own country. Her charges against a bourgeois "liberalism" and a sentimental humanitarianism, and her distrust of "modern psychology," are in the last analysis to be considered only as particular phases of an aggressive frontal attack upon the whole structure of post-war materialism, whose characteristic doctrines, she insists, must be replaced by those of a dogmatic authoritarian Church if society is to survive. This becomes apparent in her late contemporary novels to anyone who reads with but ordinary discernment; and it becomes the central thesis of a series of critical essays which she has published in the two decades which followed upon the fearful cataclysm of the World War.

These essays—often penetrating analyses of post-war psychology and post-war politics—were published for the most part originally in Catholic journals, chiefly in Norway, Sweden, and Germany, and have been gathered together later in two volumes, *Stages* (1929) and *Stages: New Series* (1933). They represent, as the titles hint, certain "stages"—or better, perhaps, "halting-places"—in Sigrid Undset's religious and intellectual development; and as such they are of first importance in any careful study of her general development as a thinker and as an artist. Among the central essays in these two volumes is the one entitled "Reply to a Parish Priest," dating from 1930. In it Sigrid Undset develops certain general views on Christianity and European culture, insisting that if Europe should ever come to reject Christianity its whole culture would be destroyed, for all of Europe's sound moral concepts and her vital artistic values are indissolubly bound up with Christianity. In a series of essays published in Germany in 1931 entitled "Begegnungen und Trennungen. Essays über Christentum und Germantum," she expresses the same general conviction on the relationship between Christianity and a specifically German culture. A materialistic *Weltanschauung*, she insists, destroys all fundamental values in life. And in this connection, it is worthy of note, she does not hesitate to condemn certain Nazi ideals. A dictatorship, she argues, will inevitably produce a "slave state," in which the individual values which lie at the core of Christian faith become entirely and irretrievably lost.

In these essays Sigrid Undset seems to have managed to shake off, at least for the moment, the narrower aspects of a purely Catholic dogma in the interests of a more inclusive, universal Christian view. In fact, she goes even farther at times, championing a kind of general religious view of life in broad opposition to certain tendencies in contemporary European national politics. In an article entitled "Fortschritt. Rasse. Religion," inspired by German persecution of the Jews, she maintains that only through Christianity can both solidarity and freedom be realized at one and the same time; and solidarity can be created only through a religion which includes "all of those people who have the courage to give themselves to a faith in the eternal life, and who have sufficient humility to seek fellowship with their Creator, in place of isolation and a fetish worship remaining within the cult of self-created ideas and things."

In the phrase "self-created ideas and things" lies the basic reason for Sigrid Undset's dogmatic rejection of most modern ideas and most present-day institutions—of certain forms of liberalism and humanitarianism, of religious sects and religious institutions outside "the Church," of political communism as well as political Nazi-ism. Her tendency to hold suspect most of what she terms "self-created ideas and things" goes back to a fundamental trait in her nature—her early distrust of the human ego because of its purely selfish subjective nature. We create what *we want*, she observes—and our desires are seldom good ones. This explains our differences in religious beliefs and becomes the purely subjective basis for recurrent division into religious sects. Our religious confusion arises because we have no positive God, no objective God outside ourselves, who has certain attributes quite independent of *man's conception* of these attributes. Already as a young girl Sigrid Undset had thought of this, though the thought, only half-formed, did not at the time lead her to "the one God." In *The Longest Years* she tells us of her early religious confusion.

As yet it was only a multitude of rapid impressions, reflections which arose of themselves, but which she dispatched without thinking them out because they were troublesome. But they left a deposit in her subconsciousness. She had understood that grandfather's God was mighty, hard in His dealings as the blind fate in which folk believed in the saga time; but grandfather saw fate in another light, as the God whose love was incomprehensible to men, because there were no limits to His seeing, and men see nothing but limits on all sides. Grandmother's God was gentle and kind and consoled her continually. Papa's God was invisible Spirit which men felt within and around them, and to the end of the world men would never be able to express clearly what it was of God that they felt. What mamma really thought about God Ingvild did not know. She met people whom the others called "awakened"; they believed that God sat up in heaven keeping an eye on everything people did so as to fling it in their faces on the day of judgment—then He sent everybody to hell except a few who had disarmed Him in time by believing in a particular way. If they were given to scandal or were sordid and unkind to others, that didn't matter if they repented in a particular way and believed that God's Son had paid their fines in advance. The God of the Salvationists was an uproarious God of blood and fire with a predilection for dreadful color-combinations, navy blue and dirty red and dark yellow. But at school she got the impression that they believed God to be a tremendous and almighty Liberal who went in for co-education and the clean flag, and that about hell wasn't true, at any rate it was abolished now, for God was also on the side of freedom and progress and Norway, hurrah!—God Himself marched in the van of Progress, as He had gone before the Israelites in a pillar of cloud.

As yet she did not know what conclusion she had begun unconsciously to draw from the various and always entirely personal conceptions of God she had already come across. Not until she went to an orthodox Lutheran West End clergyman to be prepared for confirmation and was given his version of the orthodox Lutheran God of West Christiania did she grasp clearly that everybody believed God to be as he or she would like Him to be. Everyone else's personal idea of God was equally unacceptable to her. She too had imagined God as she would prefer Him to be. It was not reasonable that her ideas about God should be any more correct than those of all other people, which she was certain were wrong. But in that case she really believed nothing. For those who said there was no God were in the last resort equally devoid of any reason for their belief except that they preferred to have it so. When they saw, for instance, that at any rate the world was not governed as a God after their own idea would govern it, or something similar. But of course it might be true that there was no God, even if the atheists said so. And He might exist even if the Christians said He did. But she believed nothing—.

This childhood confusion in religious matters was only slowly dispelled.

In her novels and essays are to be traced fairly clearly the successive steps in Sigrid Undset's religious growth. At first she developed a kind of moral idealism, which later became identified with a sort of ethical Christianity independent of church institutions or church dogma, and only finally, in the 1920's, took on a positive, specifically Catholic, form. The Roman Catholic Church, she came ultimately to believe, is the only religious institution which successfully avoids all of the pitfalls of mere sectarianism—a sectarianism originating in man's will to create a God in his own image. To Sigrid Undset God is a fundamental positive reality, not merely an idea conceived by man in the course of his cultural development; and this God has *revealed Himself* through the instrumentality of "the Church," rather than being merely a subjective reflection of man's own religious spirit. This is what gives to the Roman Catholic Church its supreme authority in the life of Sigrid Undset.

It is not our concern here to examine into the soundness of the reasoning which led Sigrid Undset finally into the Catholic Church, nor is it our present purpose to pass judgment on the universal validity of the particular form which Sigrid Undset's religious dogma has ultimately come to take. We simply record the facts here—and add, incidentally, the single general observation that one cannot but admire the thoroughgoing consistency with which she develops Catholic dogma in her late novels and essays and the seriousness with which she is prepared to apply a positive dogmatic Christianity to the ills of a confused modern society.

As to the eminence which she has attained as a creative artist in the novel, I have little to add to what already has been said. Certainly Sigrid Undset stands among the great novelists of all time. Among living novelists one is prone to rank her next to Thomas Mann. Among Scandinavian novelists she has no peer. Among women novelists she probably stands alone.

If one were to compare Sigrid Undset with any other woman novelist of the last hundred years, one is apt to think of George Eliot. This English woman novelist of nearly a century ago has the same profound moral bias as Sigrid Undset, the same deep sympathy for a suffering and fallible humanity, a not dissimilar intellectual and moral strength, and something even of Sigrid Undset's historical interests and massive imaginative power. George Eliot's single historical novel, *Romola,* is not, one must admit, her greatest artistic achievement, despite its sound control of historical materials and its profoundly conceived psychological emphasis. She moves much more satisfactorily in her contemporary English Midlands than she does in late medieval Italy. Sigrid Undset's lasting achievements, on the other hand, are certainly in the genre of the historical novel. Here she ranks with Scott. In fact she has certainly improved upon Scott in many respects, particularly in the profoundly modern psychological realism of her character portrayal; and in this respect she meets the challenge of what is perhaps the very *sine qua non* of present-day critical judgment of fiction. She does not have the facility of Scott, but for this the discriminating reader is certainly thankful. Sigrid Undset's genius is more heavy, more cumbersome—more intent upon other tasks than a merely brilliant depiction of landscape or of architectural detail or a skillful handling of rapid and colorful narrative movement. We have seen that she does not, however, neglect natural background or the detail of historical scene: she subordinates these, rather, with an infinitely happy skill to the primary psychological and ethical demands of her story. Nothing could be in more marked contrast to Scott.

Index

INDEX

366   Index

Index   367

Sienkiewicz, Henryk, 4
Skram, Amalie, 287, 288
Snoilsky, Carl, 131, 187, 188
Strindberg, August, 3, 4, 7, 8, 9, 10,
    14, 15, 17, 19, 20, 21, 27, 28, 89,
    123-9, 130, 136, 169, 187, 188, 235,
    237, 258, 287
Sturlason, Snorre, 179
Swift, Jonathan, 264

Taine, Hippolyte, 15, 16, 19, 121
Tegnér, Esaias, 136, 139, 178, 188, 223
Thackeray, William M., 314
Tolstoy, Leo, 3, 4, 7, 197, 235, 241,
    248, 314, 315
Topelius, Z., 130-1
Turgenev, I. S., 4, 72
Twain, Mark, pseud. *See* Samuel
    Clemens

Undset, Ingvald, 289, 297
Undset, Sigrid, 3, 5, 9, 12, 22-3, 24,
    97, 168, 214, 281, *286-361*

Voltaire, 18

Wackenroder, W., 6
Whitman, Walt, 260
Wilberforce, Bishop, 84
Wilde, Oscar, 35
Wirsén, C. D. af, 186
Woolf, Virginia, 112
Wordsworth, William, 9, 190, 217,
    259-60, 312-13

Zahl, K., 230
Zola, Émile, 42, 44, 47, 98, 119, 120,
    121, 126, 129, 235, 241, 288, 293,
    294, 314